SOME STORIES ARE BETTER THAN OTHERS

SOME STORIES ARE BETTER THAN OTHERS

Doing What Works in Brief Therapy and Managed Care

Michael F. Hoyt, Ph.D.

USA	Publishing Office:	BRUNNER/MAZEL *A member of the Taylor & Francis Group* 325 Chestnut Street Philadelphia, PA 19106 Tel: (215) 625-8900 Fax: (215) 625-2940
	Distribution Center:	BRUNNER/MAZEL *A member of the Taylor & Francis Group* 7625 Empire Drive Florence, KY 41042 Tel: 1-800-634-7064 Fax: 1-800-248-4724
UK		BRUNNER/MAZEL *A member of the Taylor & Francis Group* 27 Church Road Hove E. Sussex, BN3 2FA Tel.: +44 (0) 1273 207411 Fax: +44 (0) 1273 205612

SOME STORIES ARE BETTER THAN OTHERS: Doing what works in brief therapy and managed care

The opinions expressed herein are those of the author, and do not necessarily reflect policies of Kaiser Permanente or any other organization.

1 2 3 4 5 6 7 8 9 0

Printed by Edwards Brothers, Lillington, NC, 2000.

A CIP catalog record for this book is available from the British Library.
 ∞ The paper in this publication meets the requirements of the ANSI Standard Z39.48-1984 (Permanence of Paper).

Library of Congress Cataloging-in-Publication Data
Hoyt, Michael F.
    Some Stories are Better Than Others: Doing What Works in Brief Therapy and Managed Care /
Michael F. Hoyt.
        p. cm.
    Includes bibliographic references and index.
    ISBN 1-58391-041-7 (case : alk. paper)
    1. Brief psychotherapy. 2. Managed mental health care. I. Title.

RC480.55.H683 2000
616.89'14—dc21
                                            99-089147

ISBN 1-58391-041-7 (case)

This one's for Bill

(1943–1996)

In his book, *The Star Thrower,* Loren E. Eiseley talks of the day when he was walking along a sandy beach where thousands of starfish had been washed up on the shore. He noticed a boy picking up the starfish one by one and throwing them back into the ocean. Eiseley observed the boy for a few minutes and then asked what he was doing. The boy replied he was returning the starfish to the sea otherwise they would die.

Eiseley then asked how saving a few, when so many were doomed, would make any difference whatsoever? The boy picked up a starfish and as he threw it back said, "It's going to make a lot of difference to this one."

Eiseley left the boy and went home to continue writing, only to find he could not type a single word. He returned to the beach and spent the rest of the day helping the boy throw starfish into the sea.
> —David McNally (1991), *Even Eagles Need a Push*

> Time comes into it.
> Say it. Say it.
>
> The universe is made of stories,
> not of atoms.
> —Muriel Rukeyser (1968), "The Speed of Darkness,"
> in *Out of Silence: Selected Poems*

Likes and dislikes are the lapdogs and guard dogs of the ego, busy all the time, panting and barking at the gates of attachment and aversion and thereby narrowing perception and experience.
> —Lewis Hyde (1998),
> *Trickster Makes this World: Mischief, Myth, and Art*

This was another divinely beautiful day. Each morning the world rediscovers its virginity; it seems to have issued fresh from God's hands at that very instant. It has no memory, after all; that is why its face never develops wrinkles. It neither recalls what it did the day before nor frets about what it will do the day after. It experiences the present moment as an eternity. No other moment exists; before and behind this moment is Nothing.
> —Nikos Kazantzakis (1961), *Report to Greco*

I was on the lip of insanity. I was knocking on the door—from the inside!
> —Jelaluddin Rumi in Barks & Green (1997),
> *The Illuminated Rumi*

The real work is what we really do. And what our lives are. And if we can live the work we have to do, knowing that we are real, and it's real, and that the world is real, then it becomes right. And that's the *real* work: to make the world as real as it is, and to find ourselves as real as we are within it.
> —Gary Snyder (1980),
> *The Real Work: Interviews and Talks 1964–1979*

CONTENTS

PREFACE

Ever run the short way; and the short way
is the way of nature, with perfect soundness
in each word and deed as the goal. Such an
aim will give you freedom from anxiety and
and strife, and from all compromise and
artifice.
　　　—Marcus Aurelius (167 A.D.), *Meditations*

Surely the continued development of our
knowledge will help us find quicker and less
expensive ways of relieving symptoms and
rerouting misdirected travelers.
　　　—Karl Menninger (1958), *Theory and Practice
　　　of Psychoanalytic Technique*

My principle professional interest continues to be *doing what works* to improve the efficacy of mental health services. Toward this goal, since the publication in 1995 of my book, *Brief Therapy and Managed Care: Readings for Contemporary Practices,* my attention has been increasingly focused on various forms of competency-based future-oriented therapeutic approaches—as reflected in the publication of *Constructive Therapies, Volumes 1 and 2* (Hoyt, 1994a) and *The Handbook of Constructive Therapies* (Hoyt, 1998), and the writings contained hereinafter.

How clients "story" their experience does much to determine what they see and what they do—and what they get. "Many roads lead to Rome"; there are also many routes for clients to take (Gillieron, 1981; Kerfoot, 1997). Working with clients to help them construct therapeutic realities that will bring them more of what they want, and studying different ways that we can go about accomplishing this, turns me on. My interest has led me into the world of narrative construction, with special attention to the writings of Steve de Shazer and Insoo Berg, Michael White and David Epston, George Kelly, Bill O'Hanlon, Ken Gergen, Lynn Hoffman, Paul Watzlawick,

Michael Mahoney, Robert Neimeyer, and others. This book reports some of my recent thinking about ways to assist clients in constructing solution narratives and narrative solutions that will help them get to where they want to go.

The essays and interviews that follow are offered to raise and inform issues, not to settle them. In appreciation of the ideas of "many voices" suggested by Salvador Minuchin (1987) and of "soundings" and "polyvocalism" suggested by Kenneth Gergen (1994a), at places I provide extensive quotations from the professional psychotherapy literature so that some of the many contributors that have added to my understanding can be heard directly. Some of the chapters, in modified forms, have appeared previously as book chapters and journal articles; others were written specifically for this volume. While each can stand on its own, the intention is that the selections be read synergistically, the whole being greater than the sum of its parts.

My style of thinking and ways of knowing tend to be divergent and synthesizing, cross-cutting schools, disciplines, and departments in search of sources, connections, and solutions. These tendencies were strongly reinforced some years ago when I had the privilege to sit at the feet of Joseph Campbell on a number of occasions. In addition to his famous call to "Follow your bliss," Campbell both delighted and incited with his extraordinary combination of erudition and felicitious storytelling. The scope of his grasp—which at times seemed almost to give the lie to Hamlet's (Act I, Scene 5) observation that "There are more things in heaven and earth, Horatio, Than are dreamt of in your philosophy"—encouraged reaching for a much wider view (see Larsen & Larsen, 1991). Also resonating with the observation of Rollo May, Ernest Angel, and Henri Ellenberger (1958, p. 8) that "human beings reveal themselves in art and literature and philosophy" and with Camille Paglia's (1992) call for a more widely intergrated scholarship, in what follows I occasionally endeavor to adduce support and to "thicken description" (Geertz, 1973) with references from the broader humanities and popular culture.

In the first two chapters, I attempt to describe transtheoretical factors that make therapy effective, and then draw metaphoric connections between sports and brief therapy. The third chapter, "Some Stories are Better than Others," from which this omnibus takes its name, attempts to extend this effort by using constructivist and social constructionist ideas as a kind of "unified field theory" (Hoyt & Ordover, 1988; Neimeyer & Freixas, 1990) to integrate various therapeutic ideas taken especially from so-called "brief" and "postmodern" approaches that emphasize the use of "story" or "narrative."

The next four chapters (one written with Steven Friedman) address some of the theoretical, practical, and ethical challenges engendered by the evolution of managed care, which has continued to develop in ways both encouraging and problematical. In the two interviews (one with Matt Carlson), I also provide some personal reflections on recent professional experiences. "To situate my practice," as they say in narrative therapy argot, it is especially important here to recognize that while I read and consult widely, my perspective is influenced by my longtime work in a leading staff-model HMO—colleagues working in other places sometimes tell me I am too optimistic.

Chapter 8 (written with Insoo Kim Berg) details a session of couple therapy, Chapter 9 offers some solution-focused haiku, Chapter 10 revisits a previously published case of single-session therapy with some expanded understandings. In Chapter 11, we see what can be learned from a review of the cases in which the therapeutic genius Milton Erickson did not succeed.

An exercise is provided in Chapter 12 (written with David Nylund), based on ideas drawn from both social constructionist theory and redecision therapy, for learning from our internalized clients. Chapter 13 recounts the proceedings of an in-house conference attended by a number of the leaders of the brief therapy field.

The last two chapters particularly address issues concerning different phases of brief therapy. Chapter 14 (written with Scott Miller) focuses on different strategies that may be applied depending on the client's stage of readiness and the temporal structure and sequencing of treatment. The last chapter fittingly provides an extensive consideration of how and why to end therapy. Notes are collected at the end of each chapter, and all citations in the book are collected in the References section at the end of the book.

Theories are stories. They are useful; indeed, essential. It was Gregory Bateson (1972a) who reminded us that you cannot *not* have an epistemology, even if you are unaware of what it may be; and it was Kurt Lewin (Marrow, 1977) who often remarked that "there is nothing as practical as a good theory." Some theories—like some stories—are more helpful than others. The skillful practice of therapy may be craft-like in its application, but we all need some framework to orient our intention and response. The need to make sense of what we see and do requires *disciplined observation* and *disciplined creation* (see Ellis, Fisch, Hoyt, & Lankton, 1998; Held, 1995).

Conceptual tools are needed to *do what works*. As we move toward a "postmodern" realization that there are many "valid" or "legitimate" ways to look at a situation and meanings to be made (created, not just discovered), the quest becomes one of pragmatism (Amundson, 1996), a utilitarian choice between "truth or consequences" (Neimeyer, 1993c, p. 221). Gale Miller and Steve de Shazer (1998) note Glaserfeld's (1984) distinction between "fit" and "match," and go on (p. 365) to quote from W. T. Anderson (1990, p. 70):

The quest for truth has been dominated by an idea of a perfect "match" between cosmic reality and human understanding of it. The idea of a fit leads to a more pragmatic way of looking at things. A philosophical system, a scientific theory, a religion, or even a personal identity does not have to be a precise mirror of ultimate reality as long as it works more or less well in its context.

David Bohm (1980, p. 17) notes that "our theories are not 'descriptions of reality as it is' but, rather, ever-changing forms of insight." In this regard, I am grateful to my colleague Chris Iveson (1990, pp. 13–14) for using the image of a ladder to call attention to both the value and limitation of theory and working assumptions. He quotes from Umberto Eco's novel, *The Name of the Rose*, in which the character of the medieval philosopher, William of Baskerville, says:

> The order that our mind imagines is like a net, or like a ladder, built to attain something. But afterwards you must throw the ladder away, because you discover that, even if it was useful, it was meaningless. . . . The only truths that are useful are instruments to be thrown away.

Iveson (p. 14) explicates the metaphor:

> This does not mean that a theory is "right"; it is simply a means of making sense to myself of my actions so that I can keep those which work and jettison those which don't. . . . Like [the character] William's ladders, the "truths" or theories have provided a route to where I was aiming to go. . . . If a theory is represented by an extending ladder, then a working assumption is rather like a step ladder—it is unable to reach the dizzy heights but is good enough for most jobs.

To listen to people talk nowadays, it is clear that we have become very much a "psychological society," one that looks for purposes and meanings. In many ways, this seems human and humane. It is desirable—or at least fits with my values—that we strive to appreciate the "inner (and inter) life." I share with numerous colleagues, however, the worry that the so-called therapeutic professions have inundated our day-to-day discourse with psychological terms of pathology and deficit, and that these terms often may do more to shut doors than to open them. In practice, many diagnoses and clinical labels (*co-dependent? borderline? schizophrenic?*) function more like verdicts or sentences than like points of departure for change based on respectful collaboration and client empowerment. If language can function "like a virus," as Bill O'Hanlon (Bertolino & O'Hanlon, 1999, p. 17–45) has suggested, we need to prevent terminology from becoming terminal.

While sharing concern about the possible reification and subsequent "self-*un*fulfilling prophecy" of a disease orientation, I am unlike some of my respected colleagues in that I am not ready to throw over all diagnostic categories. They can provide some useful orientation. If we are going to use such nosologies, however, we need to keep an eye on the individual person. "Seeing is forgetting the name of the thing one sees," said the French poet and philosopher, Paul Valéry (1958). We need to carefully deconstruct any "shorthand" labels to see (and say) what we and the client really mean: the client called *depressed* has little hope or energy and acts accordingly, the client called *borderline* gets very upset and sees the world as all good or all bad, the client called *patient* has many experiences and submerged resources that might be useful in the therapeutic situation, and so forth. Medication might even play a role, too, so long as it is used to help restore and support people's capacities to continue their storying (including making desired behavior changes) rather than usurping or replacing their autonomy (response-ability) with that of the pharmacologist.

Another part of the discourse conundrum has to do with what is meant by the very term *therapy*. Are we talking about an approach to ameliorate or relieve a particular set of symptoms (e.g., panic attacks)? to help ease a difficult life transition (e.g., divorce, bereavement)? to maintain a tenuous psychosocial adjustment (e.g., schizophrenia)? to promote growth and an evolved sense of self-and-others (e.g., midlife crises, relationship enhancement)? (See Whitaker, 1976, 1982; Zeig & Munion, 1990.) Some issues may lend themselves to a more standardized approach, while others, by purpose and definition, may involve greater individualization. (As Lynn Hoffman, 1997, notes, the term "*psycho*therapy" ambitiously suggests that we will somehow help re-make the person's psyche.) What are the often-taken-for-granted implications of a clinical language that speaks of *patients, cases, treatments, cures*, and the like? What are the alternatives? *Problems in living? Art* or *science*? Perhaps *drama? Conversation?* Maybe just *therapy?*

I see validity in each of the following statements:

> I think the development of psychiatric skill consists in very considerable measure of doing a lot with very little—making a rather precise move which has a high probability of achieving what you're attempting to achieve, with a minimum of time and words.
>
> —Harry Stack Sullivan (1954)

> Many of the uniquely appropriate therapeutic gambits arranged by therapists seem to be intuitive. We share the goal of most psychotherapists who strive toward the day when such strokes of genius will be well enough understood to be systematic and commonplace.
>
> — Gregory Bateson, Don Jackson, Jay Haley, & John Weakland (1956)

> And I do wish all that Rogerian therapists, Gestalt therapists, transactional therapists, group analysts, and all the other offspring of various theories

would recognize that not one of them really recognizes that psychotherapy for person #1 is not psychotherapy for person #2.
                                              —Milton H. Erickson (quoted in Zeig, 1980)

Keep it simple.
  —Steve de Shazer (1988)

It's more complicated than that.
  —Salvador Minuchin (quoted in Simon, 1996)

In the spirit that Milton Erickson (Erickson & Rossi, 1979, p. 276) expressed when he said, "You cannot imitate somebody else, but you have to do it in your own way," I hope that readers will find something here that they can use in their own ways.

Michael F. Hoyt, Ph.D.
Mill Valley, California
Christmas Day, 1999

ACKNOWLEDGMENTS

I am grateful to the many people who have contributed to this effort—including my coauthors (Insoo Kim Berg, Jon Matthew Carlson, Steven Friedman, Scott Miller, and David Nylund) on several chapters; other writers, readers, editors, teachers, and students who have offered me so much; clients and patients who have been so instructive; and the various authors and publishers who kindly permitted quotation from their works. It has been my good fortune to have opportunities for interaction with many wonderful colleagues, both here and abroad. I would be particularly remiss if I did not explicitly thank Anthony "Toby" Wahl, Bernadette Capelle, Erin Seifert, and Erica Roache at Brunner/Mazel for their editorial assistance, the Mill Valley Public Library, Kaiser Permanente Health Plan (including medical librarian Cynthia Seay) for its long-term support, and my family for the ground and the sky. For my beloved Jennifer and dear Alex, I borrow from the Bard (Shakespeare, Sonnet 116):

> Love's not Time's Fool, though rosy lips and cheeks
> Within his bending sickle's compass come,
> Love alters not with his brief hours and weeks,
> But bears it out even to the edge of doom.
> If this be error and upon me proved,
> I never writ, nor no man ever loved.

CHAPTER

It's Not My Therapy—
It's the Client's Therapy

> *Macbeth:* Canst thou not minister to a mind diseased,
> Pluck from the memory a rooted sorrow,
> Raze out the written troubles of the brain,
> And with some sweet oblivious antidote
> Cleanse the stuffed bosom of that perilous stuff
> Which weighs upon the heart?
>
> *Doctor:* Therein the patient
> Must minister to himself.
> —William Shakespeare, *Macbeth*[1]
> (Act V, Scene 3, lines 40–46)

When I was a graduate student at Yale writing my doctoral dissertation in the mid-1970s, there was a large sign hanging in the medical library that read: "God Heals the Patient and the Doctor Takes the Fee." (This was before managed care took the doctor's fee—a recent phone call determined that the sign has since disappeared.) I spent a lot of time looking at those words. While not a theist nor particularly humble, I have come to appreciate more and more that, while a clinician can bring certain skills

---

This chapter originally was presented at a symposium (chaired by John C. Norcross), *Three Things that Make My Psychotherapy Effective*, at the American Psychological Association annual convention in San Francisco, August 1998. The other panelists were Laura S. Brown, Albert Ellis, Florence W. Kaslow, Alvin R. Mahrer, and Hans H. Strupp.

to bear, the power is in the patient—the client holds the keys. Hence, the title of this chapter, "It's Not My Therapy—It's the Client's Therapy." As therapists, our primary job is to help clients better help themselves. Our basic strategy should be to ignite their initiative; our basic responsibility is to get them to see and better use their "response-ability." I like to help people see how they're putting their story together and how they might do it in a way that gets them more of what they want.

My own development has taken me through many of the major systems of psychotherapy, and I keep going forward and recycling to new things. My current psychotherapy orientation (which continues to evolve) falls under the general theoretical rubrics of *brief* and *narrative constructivist*. These terms orient toward the explicit intention to be effective and efficient ("not one more session than necessary"), and toward the recognition that humans are meaning-makers who construct, not simply uncover, their psychological realities. My approach is based on the construction that we are constructive, on an "emergent" clinical epistemology that we are actively building a worldview (a story or narrative) that recursively influences our actions; that is, how we look determines what we see and what we see determines what we do, around and around.

My approach is technically eclectic and pragmatic. As described at length in *The Handbook of Constructive Therapies* (Hoyt, 1998) and its predecessors, *Constructive Therapies, Volumes 1 and 2* (Hoyt, 1994a, 1996b; see also Budman, Hoyt, & Friedman, 1992; Hoyt, 1995a), therapists who draw from some of the specific theoretical models that can be gathered under the *constructive therapies* umbrella (such as solution-focused, narrative, Ericksonian, some forms of cognitive-behavioral and strategic-interactional, personal construct, even some psychodynamic aspects) especially appreciate the therapeutic possibilities that open when there is an emphasis on the enhancement of choice and the fuller utilization of clients' competencies and resources.

The goal of constructive therapies is to bring about positive consequences in clients' lives via attention to the social construction of preferred realities. We help them build—and live—better stories, ones that bring them more of what they prefer. The constructive therapist recognizes that we are looking through "lenses," that we are "making history" and not just "taking history," that it is hermeneutics more than engineering and poetics more than physics that are the fields of study which examine the warp and weft of human life. While not ignoring the painfulness of some situations, there is a shift away from pathologizing and toward a more optimistic view of people as unique and resourceful creators—for better or worse—of their own psychological realities.

I should make clear—and I hope help put a tiresome argument to rest—that constructivist approaches, as I understand and practice them, are not license for what Ken Wilbur (1998; see also 1996, pp. 57–68) has called the "postmodern excesses" of "nihilism and narcissism." While constructivist approaches strongly emphasize the role of language and the idea that "reality" is mediated through awareness ("no knowing without a knower"), such approaches recognize that there is a *there* there. It is not "anything goes" or "everything is just an opinion." All the constructivist talk about *therapeutic conversations, cocreation, possibilities, belief systems, second-order change, reframing, deconstruction, externalization, preferred views,* and the like does not obviate the vital truth that there are a physical universe and a world of social forces, some quite pernicious, that are more than "theoretical constructs" in their impact. Do not confuse social constructionism with hard realities.

The chairman of the symposium where this chapter was first presented asked my fellow panelists and me to limit ourselves to three (and only three) factors that enhance our therapeutic effectiveness. Wow! I thought of moments when I have been at my best with clients, when something particularly "good" happened; I thought of watching my mentors and some of my especially brilliant colleagues; I reviewed some of the literature on "common factors" and "unifying language"; I read and reread some of my copanelists' excellent writings. I saw the importance of hope and creativity and honesty and empathy and good listening and clear thinking and skillful facilitation. With all this in mind, I call attention to the continuous and more-or-less simultaneous client-therapist cocreation of (1) *alliance,* (2) *evocation of resourcefulness,* and (3) *achievable therapeutic goals.*

The first, *alliance,* is the soil in which all else may take root. Constructive therapists attend assiduously to forming and maintaining a working relationship, gauging and attempting to match methods with client motivation and readiness (see Horvoth & Greenberg, 1994; Safran & Muran, 1998; Sexton & Whiston, 1994). While we know that we are helpers (or, at least, think that we are), clients may not. Imposition tends to generate opposition. I find such concepts as *customer/complaint/visitor* and *precontemplation/contemplation/planning/action/maintenance* useful (de Shazer, 1988; Norcross & Beutler, 1997; see also Chapter 14, this volume). My style tends to be personal and interactive, and somewhat directive and fairly provocative (read: symbolic-experiential). I try to maintain an awareness of the power dynamic and, at times, minimize hierarchy through practices of transparency and self-disclosure. Respectful collaboration is paramount and, when I am being effective, I think my clients have the clear sense that I am working *with* them.

The second point, *evocation of resourcefulness,* is closely related. While the therapist may have a lot to say, the client's voice is genuinely respected. The client is the senior author. I am in search of *their* solutions, sparkling moments, exceptions, strengths, acquisitional learnings, and the cross-context transfer of their competencies. While not always, I generally have found that the harder I listen, the smarter the client gets. At the same time, it helps to keep a twinkle in one's eye and to allow my own creativity to bubble.

Which brings me to the third feature, the *cocreation of achievable therapeutic goals*. What are their preferences? Their intentions? What would tell them that our work is done—and done well? Whose therapy is it, anyway? Negotiating (and, at times, renegotiating) achievable goals is empowering. Emphasizing choice actively involves the client from the beginning: It excites expectations, calls upon the client's skills, highlights personal autonomy, and sets a template for our continuing client-therapist alliance.

It's really *our* therapy. It's about what can happen when there is connection—when client and therapist step up and are present. Beyond our constructions of three factors, three active ingredients, or three whatchamacallits, we are all in the wonderful business of going into small rooms with unhappy people and trying to talk them out of it. We need to stay in touch with and honor the ideals and purposes that led us into this crazy business: love, passion, compassion, reverence, heart, soul, service, caring, commitment, and so forth. We need to "re-member" (White, 1997) what invigorates us. For me, the magic is in the moment.

☐ Note

[1]All Shakespeare quotations throughout this volume are drawn from *The Riverside Shakespeare* (Evans, 1974).

CHAPTER

A Golfer's Guide to Brief Therapy (With Footnotes for Baseball Fans)

> It's not what the teacher says, but what
> the student hears that matters.
> —Harvey Penick (1993), *And If You Play Golf,*
> *You're My Friend: Further Reflections*
> *of a Grown Caddie*

> In the name of Jack, Arnie, and the Australian
> Shark. Amen.
> —*Frank & Mike in the Morning* (1995),
> KNBR AM-Radio, San Francisco

While Aristotle said, "The greatest thing by far is to have command of metaphor," Korzybski (1933) also cautioned that "The map is not the territory." I recognize that psychotherapy (or life) may not be an adequate symbol to capture the richness of golf (or baseball), but I hope that this chapter will suggest at least a few helpful resemblances. As golfers and ballplayers know, many a useful principle has been revealed on various fields of dreams.

Part of the material in this chapter was presented at the Sixth International Congress on Ericksonian Approaches to Psychotherapy and Hypnosis in Los Angeles, December 1994, and at the First Pan-Pacific Brief Therapy Conference in Fukuoka, Japan, July 1995.

☐ The Front Nine

1. When I was a teenager back in the early 1960s, I attended the Los Angeles Open. I followed Arnold Palmer around the course, and actually got to talk with him a number of times. On one hole, he drove deep into the rough. As he surveyed his next shot, there was a big tree and a long way between his ball and the hole. He walked down the fairway to check the location of the distant flag, and then came back. Standing about 10 feet from him, I asked, "Mr. Palmer, where are you going to hit it?" He looked back and forth several times, and then replied, "In the hole." The ball did not go in on that shot, but it did wind up on the green, and I learned a useful lesson: *It's a long day on the course if you don't know where the hole is. Have a specific goal and be purposeful on every stroke.*

2. "Play it where it lies" is a basic rule (Watson, 1984). This is it, and the craft and art come when one appreciates the wind, the downhill lie, and the bunkers. "Setting up is 90% of shotmaking," says Jack Nicklaus in *Golf My Way* (Nicklaus, 1974). He also advises a high tee, since the sky offers less resistance than the ground. The grip is where inner meets outer— where we and the world connect (Pressfield, 1995). This gets at the importance of *alliance and utilization,* with the key being to meet the client in his or her world and to use whatever is available to achieve therapeutic purpose. Blaming "resistance" is like cursing the ball or throwing your clubs.

3. Another basic rule is to take as few shots as necessary, since the winner is the one who plays the stipulated round (or hole) in the fewest strokes. This requires that we keep score to learn what works, lest the game devolve, as Mark Twain (quoted in Feinstein, 1995) rued, into "a good walk spoiled." Fortunately, successful single-session therapy (Hoyt, 1995k; Talmon, 1990) is not as uncommon as a hole in one. *Making the most of each session—efficiency—defines brief therapy.*

4. A related point is to play in a timely manner. Being ready and being decisive are important, since slow play breaks tempo and results in frustrating delays for others who are ready to go forward.[1] Although the old joke has it that players who dawdle and take innumerable strokes are "getting their money's worth," the truth is that courses with long backups and clinics with long waiting lists are not serving their members well.[2] *Don't rush, but don't tarry, either.*

5. The venerable golf instructor Harvey Penick (1993) suggested that one can build a fair game around two or three clubs; and Lee Trevino once counseled the great woman golfer, Nancy Lopez (1979, p. 24), "You can't argue with success. If you swing badly but still score well and win, don't change a thing." Bobby Jones (1960, p. 17) advised, "Learn by playing," and said that his favorite swing key was "whatever worked best,

last" (quoted in Snead, 1989, p. 34). These solution-oriented ideas appreciate existing abilities.[3] One should also study and expand skills, of course, instead of simply relying on early training or natural talent. Both passion and discipline are required (Wallach, 1995). As Ben Hogan (quoted in Davis, 1994, p. 68) said, when asked about the role of luck, "The more I practice, the luckier I get." *Brief therapists use strengths and hone skills.*

6. "Play the game one shot at a time" is basic advice. As Nancy Lopez (1979, p. 127) said, "If a wasted shot or a poor round keeps gnawing away at your mind and spirit, it's going to affect your next shot or your next round. If you don't let it, it won't." Sam Snead (Snead, 1989, p. 77) similarly recommended: "The key to concentrating properly is to play in the present tense. Don't spend all your energies on something that just happened—either good or bad—and avoid thinking about what lies ahead. . . . I've always told people, you can't do anything about the past, and you've got to play your way into the future."[4] The songwriter and ardent amateur golfer Willie Nelson (1998, p. 110) also counsels: "It's a difficult game to learn. You can't care too much. If you try too hard, you blow it. There's too much and too little. That's a good metaphor for a lot of things." It is interesting to note that Bernard Darwin, the famous golf writer and grandson of evolutionist Charles Darwin, wrote an article in 1925 entitled "To Think or Not to Think: Speculation on Just How Much Mental Activity Is Good for a Golf Shot" (discussed in Rubinstein, 1991, p. 41). Watching Jack Nicklaus or Ben Hogan set up over a shot is a lesson in single-pointed concentration. There is no time but the present and, recognizing this, *brief therapy usually has a here-and-now orientation.*

7. *Keep it in the fairway and seek progress, not perfection.* As another golf adage has put it, "It's not how well you hit it; it's how well you mis-hit it" (see Lardner, 1960).[5] More advanced and strategic players sometimes try to "play the course backward"; that is, they plot backward from where they want to wind up, calculating the best way to get there—sort of like de Shazer's (1988) "Miracle Question" and its progenitor, Erickson's (1954) "Crystal Ball Technique." In *Harvey Penick's Little Red Book,* Penick reminded us that "a good follow-through position. . . is important because [it] is a reflection of what has gone on before it" (Penick, 1992, p. 156).

8. Tom Watson (Watson, 1984), in *The New Rules of Golf,* reminds us that golf may be the only game in which the playing arena must be maintained, in part, by the players. In *Golf in the Kingdom,* Michael Murphy (1972) tells us that you can tell a lot about people by whether they replace their divots. Mark McCormick (1984), the chief executive officer of a major sports management group, recounted receiving in the mail an unexpected envelope containing some cash from golf pro Doug Sanders (who had made a promise that could easily have been overlooked) to illustrate the importance of honesty and building trusting relationships.

Players like Bobby Jones (who once called a penalty on himself that cost him a tournament) and Tom Watson are known for the elegance of their ethics and etiquette as well as for their scores.[6] Among the lessons here are these: *Be respectful, keep your agreements, pass through lightly, and avoid doing harm.*

9. There are these old guys at my home course in Mill Valley, California, who don't hit the ball very hard but always seem to know which side of the fairway gets more roll and which side of the green will trickle down to the hole. The message I get is *use local knowledge* (a term that refers to the wisdom of exploiting vernacular circumstances).[7] There is the "psychotherapy of everyday life" (Bergin & Strupp, 1970) as well as the "rub of the green" (Hallberg, 1988) (that is, appreciating and taking advantage of fortuitous events) and it is wise to look for natural helpers, ethnic angles, and family resources. It may be helpful for therapists to have a few organizing "swing keys." Collaborative, competency-based therapists may like the thought: "I'm the caddy, not the player—my job is often to hand them one of *their* clubs, offer encouragement, and maybe give some advice about traps and strange winds."

☐ Making the Turn

The Basic Rule of Golf, Number 1:1 (Watson, 1984), states that "The Game of Golf consists in playing a ball from the teeing ground into the hole by a stroke or successive strokes in accordance with the Rules." Or, as John Weakland (quoted in Hoyt, 1994b, p. 25) was wont to say, "It's one damn thing after another."

☐ The Back Nine

10. In his humorous collection of golf stories, *Fore! The Best of Wodehouse on Golf* (Bensen, 1983), P. G. Wodehouse told of a fellow who, before he knew otherwise, always shot par because he thought that was all the strokes one was allowed![8] An article in *Sports Illustrated* (Horn, 1994) reported that a 420-year-old Zen temple in Annaka, Japan, now has a special shrine replete with a statue of the Buddhist goddess of mercy, Kannon, holding a putter and surrounded by 13 drivers displayed in the traditional lotus fan shape. (Fourteen is the maximum number of clubs the rules allow.) Above these, in Japanese, are the words "Hole in One." Given the power of self-fulfilling prophecies,[9] brief therapists know that they should *foster hope and expect change.*

11. Although I am normally a "bogey" golfer (i.e., one who typically

shoots around 90), I have had a few (alas, brief) visits to what is sometimes called "The Zone," that space or place where everything "clicks" and one can do no wrong: a few 5-woods here and there, that iron from the rough that hit the flag at St. Andrews, a several-hour taste of Nirvana early one morning on a course near Lake Tahoe. Remarkably, shortly after studying *The Inner Game of Golf* (Gallway, 1981), I scattered balls on a green at the little course in San Francisco's Golden Gate Park and, barely hesitating to line up the putts, made eight of nine varying from 10 to 30 feet! (Since then, I have missed many long and short ones on the same hole.) Another time (at the Banff Springs Course in Alberta, Canada), I just knew I was going to make a monster 60-footer . . . and did! Another time, having to get down in two, on the 18th at Dartmouth I somehow "zoned in" on a 50- or 60-footer with multiple breaks; the ball miraculously followed the exact line I had envisioned, stopping one-half turn from falling into the cup—a putt that allowed me to halve the round and thus avoid being the sole purchaser of the beverages our group was soon to enjoy.

How does one find "The Zone"? We all have been there—that sense of being especially "on," seemingly able to do magic and make anything happen. (Sometimes the opposite is true, too, and we are "off" and nothing seems to work.) Golf writer Lorne Rubenstein (1991, p. 59) quotes philosopher and psychologist William James: "An athlete sometimes wakens suddenly to an understanding of the fine points of the game and to a real enjoyment of it. . . . If he keeps on engaging in the sport, there may come a day when all at once the game plays itself through him—when he loses himself in some great contest." Fred Shoemaker (1996, p. 181) elaborates: "At this point golf changes from a noun to a verb; action, rather than thoughts about action, controls the situation. Golf is not a thing that you enter, golf is *when* you enter." In the wonderful tale *Golf in the Kingdom* (M. Murphy, 1972, p. 64; see also M. Murphy, 1997; M. Murphy & White, 1978), Scottish golf pro Shivas Irons (a kindred spirit of Castenada's Don Juan) advises, "Ye'll come away from the links with a new hold on life, that is certain if ye play the game with all your heart." He then takes author Michael Murphy out for a midnight round (employing whiskey and wielding an old shillelagh as culturally appropriate teaching tools) and instructs him in such vital esotic mysteries as "True Gravity."[10] Brief therapists may find that *staying loose, tuning in, trusting the unconscious* ("no mind"), and *recalling and modeling earlier successes*—the concepts underlying solution-focused (de Shazer, 1985) and solution-oriented (O'Hanlon & Weiner-Davis, 1989) therapy and neurolinguistic programming (Mackenzie, 1990)—may help jiggle the keys to the kingdom within. How much sweeter could it be than the story about Ben Crenshaw winning the 1995 Masters Golf Tournament? Only a few days earlier, Crenshaw had been a pallbearer at the funeral of his long-time teacher, Harvey Penick. As a last lesson, on his deathbed Penick "checked Crenshaw's grip the same way he had been checking it since Ben was a child. Then he said, 'Just trust yourself'" (Reilly, 1995, p. 18).

12. *Individualize treatment to suit the particular person.* As golfer and clinical psychologist, Harry (Bud) Gunn, said in his multileveled book, *How to Play Golf with Your Wife—and Survive* (1976, p. 32), "It is also an axiom that what works for Jack Nicklaus or Arnold Palmer may not work for you or your wife. I don't know about your wife, but mine is not built anything like either of these two gentlemen." This is what Milton Erickson also seemed to be saying in his oft-quoted statement: "Each person is a unique individual. Hence, psychotherapy should be formulated to meet the uniqueness of the individual's needs, rather than tailoring the person to fit the Procrustean bed of a hypothetical theory of human behavior" (quoted in Zeig & Gilligan, 1990, frontispiece).[11] Gunn (1976) also displayed a systemic-strategic therapist's eye when he reported the case of a couple who

> had complaints about their love life, which the wife said was too frequent and the husband said was too sparse. Seeing the enjoyment that I derived from golf, they decided to try it themselves. I cautioned them repeatedly about the dangers, but they went right ahead. To my surprise, they claimed a few months later that golf and not my counseling had provided the answer. It was not so much that my wallet hurt when they informed me they were discontinuing marital counseling, but my curiosity was aroused. With a certain tone of doubt I asked, "You mean that golf has improved your love life?" "Oh, yes," the husband replied, "now I find that while the frequency of love making has dropped I don't complain because I am too tired to care. I get angry just as often, but it's at my golf game and not my wife." (pp. 16–17)

13. Sounding like a narrative constructivist, Rubenstein (1991, p. xiv) said: "To be part of golf is to come upon stories, to become a story, to tell stories." As effective therapists know, *it is important to speak the client's language.* For many people, golf and baseball evoke rich memories, oftentimes rooted in childhood experiences.[12] Sports language has come into common parlance, as we hear someone say about a success that they "hit a home run" or "got a hole in one" and describe something untoward as "striking out" or being "subpar." (This use of "below par" to signify something bad is actually a reversal of the golf meaning, where a low score is good; this appropriation is an example of languages crossing groups and distinguishing different communities—see Rubinstein, 1991, pp. 152–153).

A husband I knew was spending a great deal of time playing golf. He complained of his wife's social and emotional distance but made only weak efforts to engage her more until, after a particularly feeble overture during a counseling session, I dryly commented, "You're still away." (The uninitiated may not have heard the golfer's postflub refrain: "The saddest words they'll ever say, hit again, you're still away.") A colleague (Jeff Goldman, personal communication, 1995) told me about a brief therapy success with an avid golfer who sought treatment because of erectile dysfunction. The client may have been learning something he already knew as he described the details of successful putting: the importance of being simultaneously keenly alert and totally relaxed, "visualizing the ball rolling toward the hole." At the third session, he reported that he was back to "enjoying the game, the walk in the early morning," and "letting the score take care of itself."

14. In *Mind Over Golf*, R. H. Coop (Coop, 1993) discusses the importance of timing in teaching golf to children—matters that could also be applied by therapists who want to work briefly and avoid unnecessary "resistance." He says (p. 150): "The concept of readiness to learn must be understood. One time I asked Jack Nicklaus, the father of five children, how soon kids should be encouraged to play golf. His answer: 'You should start them as soon as they are as interested in golf as they are in chasing bullfrogs.'" (At the time, Nicklaus's youngest son would join the family for a round of golf, hit a few shots, then turn his attention to a pond where a number of frogs made their home.) In addition to *the importance of knowing when,* Coop goes on to suggest a number of useful teaching and therapy pointers: creating positive experiences and associations, stopping a practice session at a good point that will leave the learner wanting more, and starting with high-success experiences.

15. Once I joined some fellows and was hacking my way around the Prince Course on Kauai, Hawaii. On one hole on the back nine, architect Robert Trent Jones, Jr., has laid out a particularly formidable arrangement: A large tree guards the right side and awaited our drives. One of my foursome looked at the tree and laughed with a tickle. "My wife hit six shots into that tree. Damn, that woman could swear!" He looked down the fairway and laughed again. "Are you still married to her?" I asked, noticing something about the "could" in his sentence. "No, she's passed away," he said, pausing—and then looked at the tree and the spot before it and laughed joyously again. Brief therapy involves choosing a "viewing and doing" (Dodson, 1996; O'Hanlon & Weiner-Davis, 1989; Shoemaker, 1996), *constructing a story that provides a useful meaning.*[13]

16. When I am feeling frazzled or overwhelmed, and ready to start calling the patient names like "borderline" or "resistant" (see Vaillant, 1992), I try not to lose my grip or throw my clubs. In what some people call the greatest golf match in history, the 1977 British Open at Turnberry, Tom Watson and Jack Nicklaus played the last two rounds in 65–65 and 65–66, respectively. Their shots were extraordinary, and repeatedly and

reciprocatedly heroic. Even when Watson had all but cinched the match with a great shot dead to the pin on the eighteenth hole—after making a 60-foot putt a couple of holes earlier to pull even—Nicklaus answered by draining a 40-footer on the 18th green. As Nicklaus (Nicklaus & Palmer, 1994, p. 62; see also Wind, 1985) told it: "On the 14th tee that last day, Tom's eye caught mine and he said, 'This is what it's all about, isn't it, Jack?' I agreed with him then, and still do even though I lost." It sometimes helps to remember that *the challenge of tough cases can make us reach in for something extra.*

17. In 1895, Lord Wellwood (quoted in Morrison, 1994, p. 39) noted: "The game is not as easy as it seems. In the first place, the terrible inertia of the ball must be overcome." The seeming paradox is that the strategic therapist (Haley, 1977) *assumes responsibility for making something happen.* We cannot *not* influence, of course; although it requires art and craft, great power and a deft touch, to achieve good results consistently.

18. Getting the job done, finishing successfully, is what counts. In golf, they say, "You drive for show, but you putt for dough" (see Palmer & Dobereiner, 1986; Updike, 1995/1996). In therapy, we call it "termination": knowing how and why to say "when" (see Chapter 15, this volume). To make treatment no longer than necessary, we have to *pay attention to ending.*

☐ Back at the Clubhouse

After a round, golfers may repair to the lounge, often called "The 19th Hole," to seek refreshments, improve their lies, and enjoy fellowship and support. As the famous sportswriter, Grantland Rice (quoted in K. Nelson, 1992, p. 27), observed, "Golf is 20% mechanics and technique. The other 80% is philosophy, humor, tragedy, romance, melodrama, companionship, camaraderie, cussedness, and conversation." We therapists are in the strange but wonderful business of going into small rooms with unhappy people and trying to talk them out of it.[14] *To prevent isolation and burnout, enjoy the 19th hole!*

☐ Notes

[1]This raises the issue of cultural factors, such as the role of authority, the value of emotional expression, various senses of self, time construction, and so forth. Yapko (1990) notes three factors that determine whether a patient will benefit from brief therapy interventions: (1) the person's primary temporal orientation (toward past, present, or future); (2) the general value given to "change"—whether he or she is more invested in maintaining tradition or seeking change; and (3) the patient's belief system about what constitutes

a complete therapeutic experience. In his fascinating account of Japanese baseball, *You Gotta Have Wa*, Whiting (1990, p. 50) notes:

> Perhaps another reason for baseball's attraction for the Japanese is its relatively slow pace. As any Western businessman familiar with Japan will agree, the Japanese are extemely careful. They like to fully discuss and analyze a problem before reaching a decision. On a baseball field the natural break between pitches and innings allows ample time for verbose and dilatory strategy sessions, since the game is never over until the last man is out. Japanese pro games—like Japanese business meetings—can seen interminable. . . . Most games last well over three hours.

[2]The design of certain mental health delivery systems may include incentives to keep patients in treatment as long as possible. As Haley (1990, pp. 14–15) has noted: "When we look at the history of therapy, the most important decision ever made was to charge for therapy by the hour. Historians will someday reveal who thought of this idea. The ideology and practice of therapy was largely determined when therapists chose to sit with a client and be paid for durations of time rather than by results." Those of us who suffered through the U.S. baseball strike of 1994–1995 know the impact money can have on the game. That economics can have a pernicious influence is not new, of course. As the great Buck O'Neil, whose playing was restricted to the old Negro Leagues because of racial segregation, said about Jackie Robinson's integration of the major leagues: "For Jackie to play in the major leagues, that meant that one white boy wasn't going to play. We had played against these fellas and they knew we could play. And they knew if we were *allowed* to play, a lot of them wouldn't play. See?" (quoted in Ward & Burns, 1994, p. 230). Whom do our policies include and exclude?

[3]The value of focusing on what works instead of what does not work was illustrated when the great Henry Aaron went into a rare slump. One day, the story has it, his manager found Aaron reviewing tapes of himself smashing line drives and hitting home runs. "Why aren't you watching tapes of strike-outs and pop-ups, to see what you're doing wrong?" he asked. Aaron replied, "Why would I do that? It wouldn't show me what I need to do!" This also suggests the therapeutic usefulness of *solution-focused body awareness*, having clients recall times when they were in a desired state (e.g., strong and competent) and having them increase verbal/nonverbal congruence by evoking the posture and intonation of these preferred times.

[4]Beware "analysis paralysis." One can prepare but, in the moment, the enactment is mostly spontaneous. The story has it that when Yogi Berra was asked what he thought about while batting, he replied, "I'm not thinking. I'm batting!" Everyone has favorite Yogi-isms, including "When you come to a fork in the road, take it!", "It ain't over 'til it's over," "It's *deja vu* all over again!", and "Ninety percent of the game is half mental!" Once, when asked for the correct time, Yogi replied, "Do you mean now?" It also should be noted that, when asked about the veracity of statements attributed to him, he responded, "I really didn't say everything I said" (Pepe, 1988; Ward & Burns, 1994).

[5]The importance of keeping it in the fairway, of avoiding iatrogenesis by not unnecessarily aggravating a bad situation, was nicely underscored by Sam Snead (Snead, 1989, p. 3):

> By now, I expect most people have heard the story about my debate with Ted Williams, the Red Sox Hall of Famer who was the last major leaguer to hit over 400 for a season. . . . One day we got talking about whether it was harder to hit a baseball or a golf ball. Ted said that hitting a baseball was the toughest act in sports because you were trying to hit a round ball with a round bat and the ball

was traveling around 90 miles an hour. "That may be true, Ted," I told him. "But in golf we have to play our foul balls."

⁶Joltin' Joe, the Yankee Clipper—the epitome of talent, grace, and discipline—also had something to say about impeccability. As George Will told it in *Men at Work* (1990, p. 325): "When DiMaggio was asked why he placed such a high value on excellence he said, 'There is always some kid who may be seeing me for the first or last time. I owe him my best.'"

⁷Golfers used the term *local knowledge* long before Geertz (1983) applied it in anthropology and therapists like H. Anderson and Goolishian (1992), White and Epston (1990), and others took it to mean respecting clients' own expertise. Geertz (1983, p. 69) uses a baseball analogy to illustrate the contextual importance of prior knowledge: "In order to follow a baseball game one must understand what a bat, a hit, an inning, a left fielder, a squeeze play, a hanging curve, and a tightening infield are, and what the game in which these 'things' are elements is all about." de Shazer (1993b, pp. 114–115) extends the baseball analogy to practice as a psychotherapist:

> As we watch a performer, whether it is a sax player or a center fielder, we are watching the culmination of a long practice. That is, in order for a performer to perform, she must master the basic techniques and have absolute control over her horn. This is true in the classical music world and, perhaps more so, in the jazz world and it is certainly true in center field. Without a mastery of the basic skills, the "how" of performance is a mystery. To some extent, the doing of therapy, and the doing of jazz and baseball are very similar. At each point along the way, the performer (therapist and/or the musician and/or center fielder) "spontaneously" decides which of his skills are germane within the context of the endeavor.

Perhaps some of Milton Erickson's long and legendary success was based on the complexity and power of his knowledge; like an old baseball player who has lost a step or two, Erickson knew where to "stand" and used more subtle language to achieve his results.

⁸We sometimes have to stretch our thinking or break out of our "frame" or expectation, as I did when I was listening a few years ago to a radio interview with the great Mickey Mantle. He was asked, "How much do you think you'd make playing nowadays?" and answered, "Oh, maybe $700,000 a year." The interviewer was incredulous: "How could that be, with your stats?" Mickey replied: "Well, you've got to remember, I'm 60 years old!" Milton Erickson, as told to me by Jeffrey Zeig (1994, personal communication), used to provide students with a learning experience in the form of a quiz, asking how many ways could they get into the rooms of a house that he would describe. After the students would exhaust the conventional, pedestrian ways, he would point out options such as driving to the airport, taking a plane to another city, returning via a different route, and then entering through various windows. Baseball fans may enjoy answering the following: What are five ways to get to first base without hitting the ball?

⁹A number of wonderful baseball movies illustrate, in different ways, the power of faith: *Damn Yankees, Field of Dreams, Angels in the Outfield.* In *Bull Durham,* Susan Sarandon's character, Annie Savoy, decided to give baseball a chance after discovering that there are 108 beads in a rosary and 108 stitches on a baseball (Ward & Burns, 1994, p. 101). My favorite remains the elegiac *Bang the Drum Slowly* (with Robert DeNiro in his first major screen role), in which lessons in T.E.G.W.A.R. (The Exciting Game Without Any Rules) teach friendship and creative living.

¹⁰Perhaps this is part of the magic behind Satchel Paige's (1962) sage and natural, "Stay loose," as well as Bernard Malamud's (1952/1993) *The Natural.* Similarly, the Japanese

slugger, Sadaharu Oh (1985/1994, p. 108), who intensely studied aikido to improve his hitting, advised: "If your body is not at one with your mind, you are lost."

[11]Generalities have their limits; the "action" is in the details. As Keith Hernandez (1994, p. viii) commented in *Pure Baseball: Pitch by Pitch for the Advanced Fan*: "When we go to the park or turn on the local television or radio broadcast, we don't watch generic 'pitching,' 'hitting,' and 'fielding.' We watch this pitcher throw to this batter with this glove work and this base running as a result. I can't think about baseball other than in such specifics." He also went on to say: "My motto: Pay attention." (For ways to sharpen attention, see Dorfman & Kuehl, 1989.) The importance of case study also was emphasized by Gustafson (1992, p. viii): "What is very distressing to me is the disappearance of individual patients. Presenters tag one big noun to another like 'resistance' and 'therapeutic alliance' and never tell you about the actual work with a person, or they tell you a success in which the person is a typical case of 'passivity' or whatever. No individual beings loom before us at all."

[12]Childhood sports heroes may model "exceptions" and "sparkling moments" with far-reaching consequences. Consider Archbishop Desmond Tutu's report:

> I must have been nine years of age, and I was in one of our ghetto townships. . . in South Africa. It must have been in winter but I still don't know who bought the tattered copy of *Ebony* magazine that I was paging through. It was the issue describing how Jackie Robinson broke into Major League Baseball. He was going to play for a team called the Brooklyn Dodgers, and what was important to me, I still recall, is how I shot up in stature because although I didn't know what baseball was, what was significant for me was that here was a Black guy, admittedly several thousand miles away, but he was Black and even in that stage of my life I knew we had a commonality and solidarity in our Blackness and that his achievement was somehow my achievement. These guys had been telling us there was a ceiling beyond which we couldn't go, and here was a guy who had broken through that ceiling, overcome obstacles, and therefore, he did something for me—and I think it must have been the case that it would have affected other people—but for me it was an incredible sort of fresh air, a breaking of at least one of the shackles that racism had bound us with (1995, p. 35).

[13]Many therapists are now situating their practice under the theoretical rubric of narrative constructivism, the essence of which may be captured in the story about the three baseball umpires disputing their acumen. The first one, who prides himself on ethicality, saying, "I call 'em as I see 'em." The second ump, who believes in objective accuracy, says, "Not bad, but I call 'em the way they are." Finally, the third ump speaks: "They ain't nothing until I call 'em!" He's the narrative constructivist. (Lincoln & Guba, 1985, p. 70, attribute this statement to the National League umpire, Jocko Conlan.)

[14]I love the story my father told me (recounted in Hoyt, 1995a, pp. 331–332) about the time he was at a baseball game at Wrigley Field in Chicago, and a drunken and belligerent fan in the bleachers was verbally abusing one of the ballplayers. The man let it be known that he was packing a gun, and it became alarmingly possible that he might use it. My father—who was a salesman by trade and something of a strategic therapist by nature—got involved. Dad also was a gun fancier; and he got the irate fan engaged in a discussion about the type of gun, showed some interest, and wound up bargaining for and buying the gun on the spot. (The police never came.) When I asked my father what he had done with the weapon, he said he had taken it to a shop the next day and sold it, for a profit. When I asked why he had done that, he replied, "Hey, you've got to get paid for this kind of work!"

CHAPTER

Some Stories Are Better Than Others: A Postmodern Pastiche

> Haroun lost his temper and shouted. "What's the
> use of stories that aren't even true?"
> —Salman Rushdie (1990), *Haroun and the Sea of Stories*

> "Remember only this one thing," said Badger.
> "The stories people tell have a way of taking
> care of them. If stories come to you, care for
> them. And learn to give them away where they
> are needed. Sometimes a person needs a story
> more than food to stay alive. That is why we
> put these stories in each other's memory. This is
> how people care for themselves."
> —Barry Lopez (1990), *Crow and Weasel*

The doors of therapeutic perception and possibility have been opened wide by the recognition that we are actively constructing our mental realities rather than simply uncovering or coping with an objective "truth." What makes us most human is not our opposable thumbs nor our use of tools but, rather, our capacity to conceive a future, recall a past, construct meaning, and make choices. How we choose to conceive and pattern the present, the past, and the future—the stories we tell ourselves—profoundly influences our course.

We conceive our "reality," creating "his-story" and "her-story" and "our-story" and "your-story," which, in turn, helps to create us, round and round.[1] We can speculate regarding the origins of this narrative function, as does the novelist, John Barth (1995, p. 96):

> [One can] wonder whether people reflexively think of their lives as stories because from birth to death they are exposed to so many narratives of every sort, or whether, contrariwise, our notion of what a "story" is, in every age and culture, reflects an innately dramatistic sense of life: a feature of the biological evolution of the human brain and of human consciousness, which appears to be essentially of a scenario-making character.

Whatever the source, organizing our world through the telling of stories is fundamental (Bruner, 1986, 1987; Hillman, 1983; G. S. Howard, 1991; Kotre, 1996; McAdams, 1993; Omer & Stregner, 1992; Parry, 1991; Polkinghorne, 1988; Sanders, 1997; Sarbin, 1986). As Engel (1995, p. 14; see also Singer & Salovey, 1993) described it:

> Whether a particular story is remembered or not, the act of telling a story is always important to the developing child, because in the telling the child is both practicing telling stories and building up an inventory of stories that contribute to a life story and a self-representation. Who knows how she will use, save, savor, and blend these stories in the future. What does that matter? Because to a great extent we are the stories we tell, and our memories of personal experiences are what give us a history and a sense of who we are—past, present, and future.

How stories bond us is further described by Clarissa Pinkola Estes in *The Gift of Story* (1993, p. 29):

> The tales people tell one another weave a strong fabric that can warm the coldest emotional or spiritual nights. The stories that rise up out of a group become, over time, both extremely personal and quite eternal, for they take on a life of their own when told over and over again. . . . Whether you are an old family, a new family or a family in the making, whether you be lover or friend, it is the experiences you share with others and the stories that you tell about those experiences afterward, and the tales you bring from the past and future that create the ultimate bond.

Mary Catherine Bateson (1994, p. 11) elaborates, highlighting the meanings that a story can carry and convey:

> Wherever a story comes from, whether it is a familiar myth or a private memory, the retelling exemplifies the making of a connection from one pattern to another: a potential translation in which narrative becomes par-

able and the once upon a time comes to stand for some renascent truth. . . .
Our species thinks in metaphors and learns through stories.

Many tales have more than one meaning. It is important not to reduce
understanding to some narrow focus, sacrificing multiplicity to what might
be called the rhetoric of merely: merely a dead sheep, only an atavistic
ritual, nothing but a metaphor. Openness to peripheral vision depends on
rejecting such reductionism and rejecting with it the belief that questions
of meaning have unitary answers.

☐ A Better Story Makes A Difference

> All the world's a stage,
> And all the men and women merely players;
> They have their exits and their entrances,
> And one man in his time plays many parts,
> His acts being seven ages.
> —William Shakespeare, *As You Like It*
> (Act II, Scene 7, lines 139–143)

What makes some stories better than others? Ultimately, of course, the
answer must come from each individual freely, lest we impose our own
values or beliefs. In general terms, stories involve a plot in which characters have experiences and employ imagination to resolve problems over
time (Berg, 1995; see also Bruner, 1986; Gergen & Gergen, 1986; Held,
1995, pp. 202–206; Yeung, 1995).

> Time comes into it.
> Say it. Say it.
> The universe is made of stories,
> not of atoms.
> —Muriel Rukeyser, (1968/1992, p. 135)

Narrative therapist Michael White (1992b, pp. 80–81) elaborates:

> A story can be defined as a unit of meaning that provides a frame for lived
> experience. It is through these stories that lived experience is interpreted.
> We enter into stories, we are entered into stories by others, and we live our
> lives through these stories.
>
> Stories enable persons to link aspects of their experience through the
> dimension of time. There does not appear to be any other mechanism for
> the structuring of experience that so captures the sense of lived time. . . . It
> is through stories that we obtain a sense of our lives changing. It is through
> stories that we are able to gain a sense of the unfolding of the events of our
> lives through recent history, and it appears that this sense is vital to the
> perception of a "future" that is in any way different from a "present." Sto-
> ries construct beginnings and endings; they impose beginnings and end-
> ings on the flow of experience. . . .

This is not to propose that life is synonymous with text. It is not enough for a person to tell a new story about oneself, or to assert claims about oneself. Instead, the proposition carried by these assertions about the world of experience and narrative is that life is the performance of texts. And it is the performance of these texts that is transformative of persons' lives.

The theologian John Dunne (1975, pp. 1–2) paints the "big picture":

> If we are in the story of an adventure, a journey, a voyage of discovery, we are in a story where time is all important. Our journey may in fact be a quest of life like that of Gilgamesh, carrying us to the boundaries of life in an effort to conquer death. Or it may be a return from the boundaries, a journey like that of Odysseus, carrying us from the wonderland of death back into the life that can be lived within the boundaries set for us by time. It may be like a journey through the otherworld, through the land that lies on the other side of death, carrying us like Dante from a hell through a purgatory to a paradise. . . . Within the story of death there is a story of love like that of Odysseus and Penelope or that of Dante and Beatrice, and within the story of love and death, or containing them, there is a story of the world. We enter the story of the world in childhood, that of love in youth, and that of death in manhood.

Similarly, in *The Hero with a Thousand Faces*, mythologist Joseph Campbell (1968, p. 30) describes the central features writ large:

> A hero ventures forth from the world of common day into a region of supernatural wonder; fabulous forces are there encountered, and a decisive victory is won; the hero comes back from this mysterious adventure with the power to bestow boons on his fellow man.[2]

Our focus here is on the therapeutic, making a difference, and the sine qua non must be the ultimate effect or change in the patient's or client's life. "Does the person come away from our conversation feeling bigger (or smaller)?" as I heard David Epston (1995) ask. Thus, Erich Fromm remarked (quoted in Akeret, 1995, p. 234), "I see each patient as the hero of an epic poem"; and Erving Polster (1987) entitled one of his books, *Every Person's Life Is Worth a Novel*. Most of us would prefer images of "self" and "other" organized into a narrative that promotes a sense of autonomy, that "empowers" and allows a reasonably successful pursuit of health and happiness—in whatever way one understands such concepts. Most people who become psychotherapy patients or clients are construing a different kind of story,[3] however, and getting a different result:

> Our many life stories are both our creations and our creators. They are the principal way that each of us participates with others in the making and remaking of ourselves as social beings. When the relationships we count on to sustain and invigorate us are in trouble, however, we often feel ourselves to be less agents in creating our own stories than actors playing roles shaped, if not scripted, by others, in dramas that consign us to unsatisfying

repetitions or direct us toward some painful end. (Roth & Chasin, 1994, p. 187; see also Atwood, 1993)

Within this framework, the therapeutic endeavor can be understood as an attempt to construct and live within a more salutary reality. As H. Anderson and Goolishian (1988, p. 372; see also H. Anderson, 1997) put it:

> Meaning and understanding are socially and intersubjectively constructed. By intersubjective, we refer to an evolving state of affairs in which two or more people agree (understand) that they are experiencing the same event in the same way. . . . Therapy is a linguistic event that takes place in what we call a therapeutic conversation. The therapeutic conversation is a mutual search and exploration through dialogue, a two-way exchange, a criss-crossing of ideas in which new meanings are continually evolving toward the "dis-solving" of problems and, thus, the dissolving of the therapy system and, hence, the *problem-organizing, problem-dis-solving system. Change is the evolution of new meaning through dialogue.*

Similarly, Gale Miller (1997, pp. 213–214; see also G. Miller & de Shazer, 1998) writes in his book *Becoming Miracle Workers: Language and Meaning in Brief Therapy*:

> The facts of life change when we construct new life stories that recast what once was taken as immutable truth and objective reality. Put differently, the stories we tell about our lives, and the meanings that we draw from the stories, often operate as self-fulfilling prophecies. [Or self-*un*fulfilling prophecies—see Hoyt 1994b/1995j.] We use stories to teach ourselves lessons that we already know. Brief therapists use their clients' skills in and proclivity for developing self-fulfilling prophecies by encouraging the clients to construct new stories about themselves and their lives.

While Lax (1992, p. 69) has noted, "Psychotherapy is the process of shifting the client's 'problematic' discourse to another discourse that is more fluid and allows for a broader range of possible interactions," it is important that some of the "possible interactions" be realized. Cade (1986, p. 55) emphasizes the usefulness of a good story:

> I would argue that the realities we construct that help us devise helpful interventions do so because of a *sufficient* fit with significant (to them) facets of family members' *constructed realities*, their ways of thinking about themselves. A family's "reality" will be but one way of making sense of the things and events they experience (real, to them) among the countless available. The therapist's skill lies in finding a way of viewing a family's reality that is near enough to its views to engage it, albeit briefly, in a "shared reality," yet with sufficient different perspectives to help bring about changes in meanings and thus in experience and response.

From this perspective, therapy can be understood as the purposeful development of a more functional story; "better" stories are those that bring more of what is desired and less of what is not desired. Sluzki (1998, p. 163) describes "better-formed stories" as containing scripts that

- appeal to (resonate with, attract) those who consult us
- are richer in connections between individuals and contexts
- do not require the presence of stereotyping and self-perpetuating diagnostic labels
- contain assumptions about evolution and change, progress and hope
- define the participants as active, competent, responsible, and reflexive
- presuppose that the participants follow ethical and moral principles such as good intent, self-respect and respect for the other, avoidance of suffering, promotion of evolution and change, and sense of collective responsibility.

Aesthetics, effects, and ethics all are important. We like stories that are well told; that are vivid and eloquent; that involve the generation and resolution of some tension; that see the protagonist emerge successfully, perhaps even triumphantly. A "good" story does more than merely relate "facts"; a "good" story invigorates:

> There are good stories and mediocre stories and downright bad stories. How are they to be judged? If they do not aim at a static or "literal" reality, how can we discern whether one telling of events is any better or more worthy than another? The answer is this: a story must be judged according to whether it *makes sense*. And "making sense" must here be understood in its most direct meaning: to make sense is *to enliven the senses*. A story that makes sense is one that stirs the senses from their slumber, one that opens the eyes and the ears to their real surroundings, tuning the tongue to the actual tastes in the air and sending chills of recognition along the surface of the skin. To *make sense* is to release the body from the constraints imposed by outworn ways of speaking, and hence to renew and rejuvenate one's felt awareness of the world. (Abram, 1996, p. 265)

☐ Intra/Inter

> It takes two to speak the truth—one to speak and another to hear.
> — Henry David Thoreau, (1854/1975)

Life is not just lived "in the head," of course, so intrapsychic modification is seldom sufficient. "When we talk about life, we're really talking about relationships. We don't exist in isolation. Emotional living is always 'other' involved." (Whitaker & Bumberry, 1988, p. 10). The one is constituted in relation to the many and can show stasis or change only when situated socially. Lacan (1977, p. 49) recognizes the essential "transindividual"; Bakhtin (1981) describes imagination as "dialogic"; Gergen (1994a) sees reality as "relational"; L. Hoffman (1993b) refers to "collaborative knowing"; de Shazer (1991a, p. 50) succinctly says, "Between, not inside."[4]

Inner and outer "interpenetrate" (Cade, 1986). "Any act of epistemology affects how you act as well as perceive—the two are linked as a recursive process" (Keeney, 1983, p. 98).

> In interpreting social behavior we are confronted with a spiraliform model. James anticipates what John will do. James also anticipates what John thinks he, James, will do. James further anticipates what John thinks he expects John will do. In addition, James anticipates what John thinks James expects John to predict that James will do. And so on! We are reminded of the famous illustration of the cat looking in the mirror. In complicated social situations, as in psychotherapy, for example, one may find himself looking at another person through such an infinite series of reflections. (G. A. Kelly, 1955, p. 94)

I also like the way David Abram (1996, p. 53–54) explains it in *Spell of the Sensuous: Perception and Language in a More-than-Human World:*

> Where does perception originate? I cannot say truthfully that my perception of a particular wildflower, with its color and its fragrance, is determined or "caused" entirely by the flower—since other persons may experience a somewhat different fragrance, as even I, in a different moment or mood, may see the color differently, and indeed since any bumblebee that alights on that blossom will surely have a very different perception of it than I do. But neither can I say truthfully that my perception is "caused" solely by myself—by my physiological or neural organization—or that it exists entirely "in my head." For without the actual existence of this other entity, of this flower rooted not in my brain but in the soil of the earth, there would be no fragrant and colorful perception at all, neither for myself nor for any others, whether human or insect. . . . Neither the perceiver nor the perceived, then, is wholly passive in the event of perception. . . . In the act of perception, in other words, I enter into a sympathetic relation with the perceived, which is possible only because neither my body nor the sensible exists outside the flux of time, and so each has its own dynamism, its own pulsation and style. Perception, in this sense, is an attunement or synchronization between my own rhythms and the rhythms of the things themselves, their own tones and textures.

A constructivist position may hold that we always are part of the equation, that there is no knowing without the knower; but there are other, extralinguistic forces to be reckoned with. One who ignores context, circumstances, consequences, events, objects, and various social structures and systems risks ignoring a lot (see Coyne, 1985; Fish, 1993; Held, 1995; Speed, 1984, 1991; White, Hoyt, & Zimmerman, 2000). Someone unmindful of traffic can still be run over—as Bill O'Hanlon and I quipped in a published conversation (Hoyt, 1996e, p. 106), "My karma just ran over your dogma!" We may be meaning-makers only able to know approximately what's "out there" (we always more or less "misread," to use Steve de Shazer's, 1993a; de Shazer & Berg, 1992, term), but there is a *there*.[5]

Stories get created, for better or worse, in the world of human interaction—often in what Whitaker and Napier (1978) called "the family crucible."

> More than a century ago, Sigmund Freud shocked the medical establishment of his day by suggesting that mental illness was caused by childhood physical and sexual abuse. . . . Six years after his professional colleagues blasted his paper on the long-term psychological damage stemming from real injuries inflicted by parents on their own children, Freud recanted. He proposed, instead, that the source of hysteria and other mental problems emerged from children's own unresolved inner *fantasies* about what they *imagined* their parents had done to them. For the next half-century, psychotherapy would essentially ignore actual interactions between family members and concentrate almost exclusively on the private, inner world of the individual. Not until the 1950s did the family therapy movement once again insist that personal relationships—between parents and children, wives and husbands, friends and coworkers—were the key to understanding human emotional life. (Madanes, 1999, pp. 44–46)

"Reality" may be a socially mediated construction but, as Harlene Anderson and Harry Goolishian (1988, p. 377) said, "*We live and take action* [italics added] in a world that we define through our descriptive language in social intercourse with others." We "perform" (Omer, 1993) or "enact" (Sluzki, 1992) our narratives in the world.

> Accordingly, the change in the client's life produced by therapy really exists in an independent, extratheoretic reality—a reality external to the theory in use, including the linguistic constructions the theory comprises. On the basis of this realist position, we may rightly claim that family therapy can change patterns of interaction within a family as those patterns really exist apart from, or in addition to, the theoretical formulations about the family that the therapist adopts. We may also rightly claim that cognitive therapy changes the actual irrational thoughts a client may hold (e.g., that she is an incompetent person in all respects); that change, therefore, also occurs apart from the therapist's theory about those thoughts. Put differently, therapy helps clients solve their problems by changing something *more* than the stories or theories therapists and clients construct about those problems. (Held, 1995, p. 36)

The narrative metaphor entails a shift in interactional viewing:

> A focus on interactional pattern continues to be an essential aspect of a narrative approach although it is understood quite differently than other interactional models of therapy (e.g., Watzlawick, Weakland, & Fisch, 1974). . . . [W]ithin narrative therapy "interactional patterns" can be thought of as the specific contexts in which stories evolve across time and in which the experience of the interaction provides the "stuff" that constitutes stories (Zimmerman & Dickerson, 1994). This represents a change from cybernetic metaphors. A person creates an account to make sense of

their experience that emerges in the context of specific interactions; it is an *effect* of the experience of interactional pattern. . . . Stories also can be experienced as reciprocally influencing each other within the context of a relationship. Thus, the reciprocal quality of an interactional perspective remains while a richness is gained through metaphors that capture a sense of experience over time. (Neal, 1996, p. 75)

For the clinical endeavor to be therapeutic, change must become manifest in the world. Hence, we ask: What (where, who, when) difference will therapy make, and how will we know it?

☐ A Paradigmatic Shift in the Story Psychotherapy Tells

What light through yonder window breaks?
—William Shakespeare, *Romeo and Juliet* (Act II, Scene 2, line 2)

In recent years there has been a psychotherapy movement toward a "new direction" (O'Hanlon, 1994; O'Hanlon & Weiner-Davis, 1989), a "formidable change of seas" (Gergen, 1993, p. ix) that invites fuller appreciation of human agency and potential. As popular response to different publications, workshops, and conferences attests, there is a burgeoning interest in different models of therapy that offer a more optimistic and "user friendly" approach toward helping those that seek mental health services. This movement has been fueled by some combination of desire for more humanistic ways of thinking about human change processes, various theoretical and clinical developments paralleling broader social forces (e.g., computers and the information-processing explosion, ecosystemic environmental awareness, greater recognition of cultural diversity), and—to some extent—the cost-effectiveness pressures of managed care to think about new ways to deliver services (rather than simply doing less of the same). While these "brief therapy" developments may be attractive to those interested in efficacy and efficiency, it should be recognized that such approaches long antedated the drive for cost containment that is now dominating so much of therapeutic practice (see Chapter 4 this volume).

This "new direction" focuses more on the strengths and resources that patients/clients bring to the enterprise than on their weaknesses or limitations. Similarly, more emphasis is put on where people want to go than on where they have been. While not ignoring the painfulness and seriousness of some situations, the shift has been away from conventional psychiatric pathologizing and toward a more optimistic view of people as unique and resourceful creators of their own realities (for better or worse). Fuller recognition is given to the powers of language and imagination plus the principles of collaboration and respect for clients' competencies.

Different paradigms or reality constructions carry with them different "analogies" (White & Epston, 1990) or "observing positions" (Gustafson, 1986) through which we order and attempt to influence experience. As Barbara Held (in Hoyt, Miller, Held, & Matthews, in press; see also Held, 1995) has noted:

> It's very hard to have a method of therapy that doesn't have at least implicit within it some predetermined idea of what the problem is and what are the causes, because even to say "the method is deconstruct the patient's text or give them a new narrative" implies that you think the problem is in the way they're linguistically constructing their experience. It's a very general implicit notion, so there's lots of wiggle room for the particularities compared to traditional, conventional, complete systems of therapy.

As seen in Table 3.1, moving from an understanding based in the physical and biological sciences to one based on social science leads us into radically different ways of construing problems and solutions, of helping people change how they perceive their worlds and conduct themselves.

Underlying these different constructions is the construction that we are constructive, that we are actively engaged in building a worldview that influences our actions—whether we know it or not. "Patients have problems," as Milton Erickson said, "because their conscious programming has too severely limited their capacities. The solution is to help them break through the limitations of their conscious attitudes to free their unconscious potential for problem solving" (Erickson, Rossi, & Rossi, 1976, p. 18). Following Erickson, the essential paradigmatic shift is from deficits to strengths, from problems to solutions, from past to future (Fisch, 1990; Hoyt, 1995a), utilizing whatever the client brings in the service of healthful change (de Shazer, 1988). This change in orientation results in the therapist truly functioning as a mental health (not mental illness) professional.[6]

A variety of terms—such as *solution-focused, solution-oriented, possibility, narrative, postmodern, poststructural, cooperative, collaborative, competency-based, interactional, intersubjective, conversational, dialogic, reflective, Ericksonian, constructionist, constructivist*—can be found on signposts marking this territory. This list is not exhaustive, of course. As will be seen in the discussion that follows, other theoretical schools—including those that go under such rubrics as strategic, cognitive-behavioral, humanistic-existential, personal construct, transactional analytic, Gestalt, Adlerian, Jungian, and some of the newer developments in the psychoanalytic realm—also are more actively recognizing the constructive nature of psychotherapeutic work. As Carlos Sluzki (1988, pp. 80–81) has noted:

> Constructivism is a way of *talking about* therapy, rather than of *doing it*. Being a theory of knowledge rather than a set of techniques, constructivism offers us not a particular way of helping clients, but a way of understand-

TABLE 3.1. Table of analogies

Analogies drawn from	Social organization constructed as	Problems constructed as	Solution constructed in terms of
1. Positivist physical sciences	Elaborate machine, constituted by mechanics and hydraulics	Breakdown, reversal, insufficiency, damage	Isolating cause, precise analysis repair, reconstruct, correct
2. Biological sciences	Quasi-organism	Symptomatic of underlying problem, serving a function, having utility	Identifying pathology, correct diagnosis, operating and excising pathology
3. Social sciences			
a. Game theory	Serious game	Strategies, moves	Contest, countermoves, strategizing
b. Drama	Living-room drama	Roles, scripts, performances	Revising roles, selecting alternative dramatic form
c. Ritual process	Rite of passage	Transition—separation, betwixt and between, reincorporation	Mapping, drawing distinctions around status 1 and status 2
d. Text	Behavioral text	Performance of oppressive, dominant story or knowledge	Opening space for the authoring of alternative stories

Note. From M. White and D. Epston (1990 *Narrative Means to Therapeutic Ends*), p. 6. Copyright 1990 by W. W. Norton and Company, New York. Reprinted with permission of the publisher.

ing how we use our clinical tools and the interplay between practitioners' beliefs and their practice.

They have their differences (see Beyebach & Morejon, 1999; Levine & Stone Fish, 1999; Neimeyer, 1993a, 1993b, 1993c, 1998a), to be sure; although, in clinical practice, they tend to have certain common characteristics: a respectful collaboration between therapists and clients, a fuller utilization of clients' competencies and resources,[7] an emphasis on the enhancement of choice and an appreciation that there is more than one valid way to look at and respond to a situation, and a caring and hopeful eye toward the future (see Table 3.2).

Table 3.2. The process of collaborative helping

Joining →	Stuckness to goals →	Eliciting competencies, perspectives & resources →	Strategizing together →	Recognizing & amplifying change →	Celebrating change
How can client have a *different* conversation?	Ask what client wants to result from your work together	"When does the problem not happen & what is going on then that could be regarded as competent or nonproblematic?"	"Do more of what works for you"	Ask "What is different?" and expect to hear something	Affidavits of change, certificates, etc.
Verbal "ports of entry" (key client words)	*Contract* around goal		Identify the first and smallest necessary step to solution	Implicate agency in any changes—Ask "How did you do that?"	Completion/closure rituals
Map problem's effects on client	Listening for "stuckpoints" & "flipping" them by asking what is wanted instead	Are there problematic patterns that sustain the problem that could be "used" differently?	If others are needed in the solution, ask helpee to elicit their cooperation or convene	Are we "on track"?	Client as consultant to others
Create reflective context for "safe curiosity"	Negotiating a solvable problem in client's language	Questions to mobilize stand against externalized problem	problem-organized system (family, helpers, friends, etc.)	Relapse is part of cure	Symbols of identity transformation
					Self or other rewards
Who else is *organized* by the problem?	"Miracle questioning" to find out significant elements of a satisfactory solution—	Authenticate "small acts" of resistance to problems/ oppression	Identify criteria for minimal success clearly	To challenge identity inquire about what the change says about them and their resourcefulness	"What does this (achieving goal) say about you as a person?"
Resistance = helper inflexibility	"What will you be doing when you have	Benevolent challenges to identities of incompetence			Document "rules" for problem resumption

(continued on next page)

Join them in their struggle	overcome your problem?	Meaning negotiation by working within & expanding on the helpee's language (reframing)	Get specific as to when, how, what, etc.	Recruit audiences for the performance of new competencies by question: "How will others who are important see you then?" or by action before an anticipated audience	Resource "transfer" to other problem contexts
Mirroring & pacing client	Externalizing the problem à la Michael White	Promote reflexive thinking (action/reaction of others loop)	If using/jamming a present problematic pattern, have a rationale consistent with helpee's views of self & problem	Competence-focused letters	Political activism (Examples: Anti-Anorexia/ Bulimia League, accountability structures)
Reflect the emotional essence of what is heard	together to separate person from problem	Scale problems/solutions	Meaningful rituals of change	Ask if changes fit preferred view of self	Reincorporation activities in the manner of rites of passage with members of "problem-organized system" so as to be a witness to new behaviors and problem-liberated identities
	Listen for identity stories & "certainties" of incompetence	Develop sense of audience for performance of change	Tailor-make home-work assignments together	Attention to micro-details of change/ resourcefulness	
	Seek a description of the problematic "solution"	Query competencies shown but not shown in problem area	"Contract home-work"		
	Could exceptions be developed into solutions?				
	One solvable goal at a time in mini-steps (contracted)				

Ongoing: relationship flexibility, contacting/consent, fluency in client's language, the problem (not the person) is the problem, elicit resourcefulness, ambiguities can be tolerable, empathetic reflection, meaning negotiation, maintaining resourceful view of client, involving others who are part of the problem where necessary, eyes on the goalpost.

From Can You Get It Down to One Page? by T. Strong, 1997, *Journal of Systemic Therapies*, 16, pp. 69–72. Copyright 1997 by Guilford Publications. Reprinted with permission of the publisher.

As Bruce Ecker and Laura Hulley (1996, pp. 6–7) put it in their book, *Depth-Oriented Brief Therapy*:

> A constructivist therapist assumes there are any number of viable ways the client's view of reality could change that would dispel the presenting problem, and in a spirit of collaboration, the therapist and client consider and try out such possibilities. The differences among constructivist therapies are differences in how they select an alternative, symptom-free view of reality for the client to experimentally inhabit, and in how they invite and assist the client to do so. Their common ground is this: The therapist does not take the objectivist position of being a diagnostic authority on the "correct" view of reality, but rather offers expert skill in modifying realities so as to eliminate their unwanted consequences. . . . This epistemological position has sweeping implications for conducting psychotherapy. In contrast to (1) the traditional objectivist view of treatment as requiring discovery of factual, causal conditions in childhood and (2) the behaviorist-interactional view of the individual as controlled by the social environment, the constructivist view is that problems are generated entirely by the individual's cognitions and emotions comprising his or her present construction of reality. These present-time elements can, of course, include representations of past experiences, but these representations exist in the subjective present and should not be confused with an objective past.

Each, in its own way, is *constructive therapy*, the building, constructing, or "re-storying" of "solution narratives" or "narrative solutions" (Eron & Lund, 1996; White & de Shazer, 1996), with language or "conversation" (H. Anderson, 1997; de Shazer, 1991a, 1994; Friedman, 1993; Gilligan & Price, 1993) being the map if not the territory.

☐ Really . . . I Mean, Really

> What you've got here, really, are *two* realities, one of immediate artistic appearance and one of underlying scientific explanation, and they don't match and they don't fit and they don't really have much of anything to do with one another. That's quite a situation. You might say there's a little problem here.
> —Robert M. Pirsig (1974, p. 63), *Zen and the Art of Motorcycle Maintenance: An Inquiry Into Values*

In *The Psychology of Personal Constructs*, George Kelly (1955, pp. 6–8) wrote:

> We presume that the universe is really existing and that man is gradually coming to understand it. By taking this position we attempt to make clear from the outset that it is a real world we shall be talking about, not a world composed solely of the flitting shadows of people's thoughts. But we should like, furthermore, to make clear our conviction that people's thoughts also really exist, though the correspondence between what people really think exists and what really does exist is a continually changing one. . . . Some-

times scientists, particularly those who are engrossed in the study of physical systems, take the stand that psychological events are not true phenomena but are rather epiphenomena, or merely the unreliable shadows of real events. This position is not ours. A person may misrepresent a real phenomenon, such as his income or his ills, and yet his misrepresentation will itself be entirely real. This applies even to the badly deluded patient: what he perceives may not exist, but his perception does. Moreover, his fictitious perception will often turn out to be a grossly distorted construction of something which actually does exist. Any living creature, together with his perceptions, is a part of the real world; he is not merely a near-sighted bystander to the goings-on of the real world.

As will be discussed at length below, we make sense of the world—or, some (e.g., Gergen, 1994a; Wittgenstein, 1968) would argue, make the world—through language. So-called "radical constructivists" (such as von Foerster, 1984; von Glaserfeld, 1984; Segal, 1986) have argued that all knowledge is bound by the perceiver. As Paul Watzlawick (1984, p. 9) put it:

> *How do we know what we believe we know?* . . . *What* we know is generally considered to be the result of our exploration and understanding of the real world, of the way things *really* are. . . . *How* we know is a far more vexing problem. To solve it, the mind needs to step outside itself, so to speak, and observe itself at work; for at this point we are no longer faced with facts that apparently exist independently of us in the outside world, but with mental processes whose nature is not at all self-evident. In this respect the title of this book [*The Invented Reality*] is somewhat less nonsensical, for if *what* we know depends on *how* we came to know it, then our view of reality is no longer a true image of what is the case outside ourselves, but is inevitably determined also by the processes through which we arrived at this view.

Along related lines, Lois Shawver (1996, p. 379) quotes French linguistic philosopher, Jacques Derrida:

> And Derrida chafes at interpretations of his work that make him sound as though he does not believe in the world beyond words. . . . He says that his well-known phrase that there is 'nothing outside the text' merely means "that one cannot refer to this 'real' except in an interpretive experience" (Derrida, 1972, p. 148). [Shawver (1996, p. 379) explains:] [P]ostmoderns are most likely to sound as if they are saying that we have only words and nothing else, when they are trying to talk about the way language works to affect how we notice and perceive that which lies beyond our words. . . . language creates categories that structure our understanding. Heidegger [1971, p. 62] says, "The word alone gives being to the thing."

Bill O'Hanlon (in S. O'Hanlon & Bertolino, 1999, pp. 145–146) expounds:

> Radical constructivists and quantum physicists suggest that what we call reality is constructed—fabricated by our beliefs and our neurology. There

is no such thing as reality (or truth, either, which is another matter altogether and a compelling reason not to hire a radical constructivist to handle your cash).

Social/interactional constructionists take a different stance. They (or I should say, "we," since I count myself in their numbers), hold that there is a physical reality out there but that our social reality, being influenced by language and interaction, is negotiable. This social reality can influence and be influenced by physical reality. . . . This social reality is mutable, but within some limits—the constraints seem to be physical, environmental, and traditions/habits. . . . The social reality created in therapy interviews is just that—social. It is cocreated by the therapist and clients, as well as by the culture and social system traditions that influence them. This stance is called social or interactional constructionism.

In her studious book, *Back to Reality: A Critique of Postmodern Theory in Psychotherapy*, Barbara Held (1995, p. 173) writes:

> All theories are constructions. Put differently, constructing theories is the business of science, of all science, including the science of narrative therapy, however antisystematic that science may strive to be. But that fact does not, contrary to postmodern opinion, automatically make all scientists antirealists. . . . Thus, to say that knowledge of (some aspects of) reality involves social/linguistic construction because it involves the use of constructed theories is like making the discovery that we speak prose. Scientists have known the former, and most of us the latter, all along. But then to say, as social constructionists/postmodernists say, that those constructed theories are the *only* reality we have—that is, the reality itself, or knowable reality itself, is *only* a "social construction" (because we supposedly have no direct, theoretically unmediated access or even an indirect, theoretically mediated access to any reality that is independent of the knower/knower's theory)—is to confuse two things: (a) the linguistic status of the theory itself with (b) the (extralinguistic or extratheoretic) reality that that theory is attempting to approximate indirectly.

My own view is that (of course) there is a world outside of language—"a wordless truth, one that came before language, a being, not a becoming," as novelist Salman Rushdie (1999, p. 238) said in *The Ground Beneath Her Feet*. There is a *there* there—but, if you get my meaning, I can refer to it only through language. I interpret my social constructionist position as consistent with what Held (1995) calls a "modest realism," a recognition in postmodern-narrative therapies of both linguistic and extralinguistic realities:

> I want to be very clear about the fact that the postmodern narrative therapy movement . . . already involves a modest, or limited, realism. That realism is found (a) with respect to secondary rational awareness both of theories about narrative and of narratives themselves, and (b) with respect to the implicit reliance on primary rational awareness to make such general claims as the fundamental ones within narrative therapy, namely, that the way

one narrates one's life affects the perception of options in life, and that this perception in turn affects the way life actually gets lived. These claims bring with them the realist imperative that we understand how language or narrative, as a *system*, itself works to produce maximum impact on clients' understanding and behavior. (Held, 1995, p. 192)[8]

Whatever position is ascribed to, language provides the space, the "playground" (Freeman, Epston, & Lobovits, 1997; Gustafson, 1992; G. Miller & de Shazer, 1998; Vaihinger, 1924; Winnicott, 1971) for experimenting with possibilities. Language opens doors into the "Fifth Province" (McCarthy & Byrne, 1988, 1995), into the betwixt-and-between realm of "experience, contradiction, narrative and imagination" (Epston & White, 1990/1992b). Language provides "narrative means to therapeutic ends" (White & Epston, 1990).

> With language and relationships thus foregrounded, two major suspicions are generated. The first is the suspicion of all reality posits. The various accounts brought to therapy by the client—tales of misery, oppression, failures, and the like—serve not as approximations to the truth. . . . but as life constructions, made up of narratives, metaphors, cultural logics, and the like. . . . And their major significance lies not in their relative validity, but in their social utility. In this context the aim of therapy becomes one of freeing the client from a particular kind of account and opening the way to alternatives of greater promise. . . . In each case the attempt is to shake loose the taken-for-granted world and to open new linguistic spaces. These spaces offer new options for action. (Gergen, 1993, p. x)

Constructive therapists know that *ultimately what counts are the real effects* of how people construe their "reality," the goal being to bring about positive consequences in clients' lives via attention to the social construction of preferred ("clinical" or "therapeutic") realities (see Freedman & Combs, 1996; Neimeyer, 1993a; Watzlawick, 1976, 1984, 1992). To use the phrase coined by William James and popularized by Gregory Bateson (Luepnitz, 1988, p. 73), we attend to language to "make the difference that makes a difference" (Bateson, 1972a, 1980; de Shazer, 1991a). As discussed with Michael White (Hoyt & Combs, 1996, p. 34), this is "taking steps on the path" and the "little sacraments of daily existence," with the recognition that alternative discourses "will have different real effects on the shape of the therapeutic interaction, different real effects on the lives of the people who consult us, and different real effects on our lives as well." Thus, Shawver (1996, p. 390) writes:

> In fact, postmodernism might be summarized like this: Language matters, and it matters far more than people have imagined. It does not simply label reality in an accurate or inaccurate way. It creates metaphorical images of reality that take us into different kinds of experience. Having different experiences causes us to do things differently, to create different kinds of institutions and cultures, and lead different kinds of lives.

☐ What Are the Key Elements or Distinguishing Characteristics of Constructive Therapies?

> But we are spirits of another sort.
> I with the morning's love have oft made sport,
> And like a forester the groves may tread
> Even till the eastern gate, all fiery-red,
> Opening on Neptune with fair blessed beams,
> Turns into yellow gold his salt green streams.
> —William Shakespeare, *A Midsummer Night's Dream* (Act III, Scene 2, lines 388–393)

While the therapist is still recognized as bringing certain skills and expertise to the clinical moment—including new information and alternative perspectives—there is a profound shift away from the objectivist notion that it is the therapist who knows what is "right" and thus will "intervene" or "treat" the "patient" (or "client"[9]) to bring about what is "best" (and thus "fix" the "problem"). Rather, the therapist and client are seen as coparticipants in a meaning-generating process that constructs a more hopeful, empowering, and, ultimately, more salutary sense of self-in-the-world. As Lynn Hoffman (1997, p. 337) explains:

> As a result, the field is on the cusp of a philosophical divide. On the one hand you have the traditional or "modern" stance, which is based on the claims to objectivity of modern science. On the other, you have a "postmodern" stance, which is that reality in any complex human sense is never immutably out there, independent of our languaged ways of knowing it.[10]

It is ironic, as Robert Pirsig (1974, p. 119; also see Campbell, 1972, pp. 16–18) noted, that it is science that brought us to this state:

> The purpose of scientific method is to select a single truth from among many hypothetical truths. That, more than anything else, is what science is all about. But historically science has done exactly the opposite. Through multiplication upon multiplication of facts, information, theories and hypotheses, it is science itself that is leading mankind from single absolute truths to multiple, indeterminate, relative ones. The major producer of the social chaos, the indeterminancy of thought and values that rational knowledge is supposed to eliminate, is none other than science itself.

This shift is part of the social constructionist movement in psychology (Gergen, 1985). The constructive therapist recognizes that we are looking through "lenses" (L. Hoffman, 1990/1993c; Keeney, 1982; Zeig & Munion, 1990) or "spectacles" (May, Angel, & Ellenberger, 1958) into a "mirrored room" (Hare-Mustin, 1992, 1994; Rorty, 1979); that knowledge is "perspectival" (C. Smith, 1997); that "how we look determines what we see, and what we see determines what we do" (Hoyt & Berg, 1998/1998); that we are (wittingly or not) engaged in self-recursive autopoiesis (Maturana & Varela, 1980); that we are "making history," not just "taking history" (Hoyt, 1996b; White, 1993a). The constructive therapist gives up "temptations of power and certainty" (Amundson, Stewart, & Valentine, 1993), maintains "curiosity" (Cecchin, 1987) and a "healthy irreverence" (Cecchin, Lane & Ray, 1992; Keeney, 1991), and is "inspired by incompleteness" (Gergen, 1998) and is "suspicious of great subjects and all encompassing theories . . . because no social theory can make claims to validity outside a particular context and value system" (Doherty, 1991, p. 40). The constructive therapist recognizes that psychotherapy is "a process of semiosis" (Gergen & Kaye, 1992, p. 182), an exercise in "aesthetics" (Gilligan, 1996; Keeney, 1983) and "clinical epistemology" (Keeney, 1982; Lankton & Lankton, 1998; Matthews, 1990, 1997; O'Hanlon & Wilk, 1987; Rabkin, 1977; von Foerster, 1984, 1985; Watzlawick, 1984); that it is hermeneutics rather than engineering, and poetics rather than physics, that are the fields of study that examine the warp and weft of human life (Fine & Turner, 1995; Frank, 1981, 1987; Hoyt, 1996b)[11] The constructive therapist forgoes the dryness of the positivist shore, joining the collaborative flow of "the third wave" (O'Hanlon, 1994) as an intersubjective "co-participant" or "co-author." As Brad Keeney (1982, p. 166) explains:

> When you understand that you are an active epistemological operator, you realize that you are always participating in the construction of a world of experience. . . . In other words, you are responsible for contributing to the construction of therapeutic realities. There is no such thing as an observer-free description of a situation that can be objectively assessed and evaluated. What one experiences is constructed. In that recursive process, what one knows leads to a construction and what one constructs leads to knowing. One's knowing is recycled in the constant (re)construction of a world.

The constructive therapist recognizes, as Gergen (1985, p. 267; see also Kenneth Gergen, 1994a; Gergen, in Hoyt, 1996c) has put it, that

> the terms in which the world is understood are social artifacts, products of historically situated interchanges among people. From the constructionist position the process of understanding is not automatically driven by the forces of nature, but is the result of an active, cooperative enterprise of persons, in relationship.

Similarly, Lynn Hoffman (1990/1993c, pp. 89–90) echoes and expands:

> In contrast, social construction theory posits an evolving set of meanings that emerge unendingly from the interactions between people. These meanings are not skull-bound and may not exist inside what we think of as individual "mind." They are part of a general flow of constantly changing narratives. Thus, the theory bypasses the fixity of the model of biologically based cognition, claiming instead that the development of concepts is a fluid process, socially derived. It is particularly helpful for the therapist to

think of problems as stories that people have agreed to tell themselves. . . . Many styles of doing therapy that would otherwise compete can crowd together under its broad rim, as long as their practitioners agree that all therapy takes the form of conversations between people and that the findings of these conversations have no other "reality" than that bestowed by mutual consent.

She goes on to say:

I rely on three powerful new lenses. One is social construction theory. The next is what I call a second-order view. The third is gender. Social construction theory is really a lens about lenses. The other two are only handmaidens in that they dramatize and shake up world views in their respective areas. All three can be metaphorically applied to psychotherapy. All three represent sets of lenses that enforce an awareness that what you thought looked one way, immutably and forever, can be seen in another way. You don't realize that a "fact" is merely an "opinion" until you are shocked by the discovery of another "fact," equally persuasive and exactly contradictory to the first one. The pair of facts then presents you with a larger frame that allows you to alternate or choose. At the cost of giving up moral and scientific absolutes, your social constructionist does get an enlarged sense of choice. (Hoffman, 1990/1993c, pp. 90–91)[12]

Hence, as Steven Friedman (1996, pp. 450–451) has described it, the constructive therapist

- believes in a socially constructed reality.
- emphasizes the reflexive nature of therapeutic relationships in which client and therapist co-construct meanings in dialogue or conversation.
- moves away from hierarchical distinctions toward a more egalitarian offering of ideas and respect for differences.
- maintains empathy and respect for the client's predicament and a belief in the power of the therapeutic conversation to liberate suppressed, ignored, or previously unacknowledged voices or stories.
- co-constructs goals and negotiates direction in therapy, placing the client back in the driver's seat, as an expert on his or her own predicaments and dilemmas.
- searches for and amplifies client competencies, strengths, and resources and avoids being a detective of pathology or reifying rigid diagnostic distinctions.
- avoids a vocabulary of deficit and dysfunction, replacing the jargon of pathology (and distance) with the language of the everyday.[13]
- is oriented toward the future and optimistic about change.
- is sensitive to the methods and processes used in the therapeutic conversation.

Many of the themes to be explored herein are adumbrated by Hugh Rosen (1999, p. 71; see also Hays, 1999; Lipchik, 1999; Mahoney, 1999) in his review of *The Handbook of Constructive Therapies*:

Constructivism is identified as a meaning-making epistemological view in which human agency is the generative motor that shapes our environment and social lives. The social constructionist paradigm emphasizes interpersonal relatedness and the dialogical process through which we construct our visions and versions of reality within a social matrix. The self is, itself, construed as social and communal. Embracing the postmodern motif leads to an emphasis on local knowledge, giving voice to otherwise marginalized groups, celebrating diversity, deconstructing sacred assumptions, and the formation of egalitarian, nonhierarchical therapeutic relationships. The key focus with clients is on their strengths and resources, with a deemphasis on diagnosis and pathologizing. . . . [There are] definite political and ideological implications by striking a blow against society's silencing of marginalized groups and adopting an advocacy stance on behalf of oppressed minorities. The therapist's role . . . is divested of power, but not potency, and a multiperspectivial view of persons and cultures is encouraged.

☐ N = 1: Every Story Is Special

> To restore the human subject as the center—the
> suffering, afflicted, fighting human subject—we
> must deepen a case history to a narrative or tale;
> only then do we have a "who" as well as a "what,"
> a real person.
> —Oliver Sacks (1987, p. viii)

> It's in the telling of the story.
> —Milton H. Erickson,
> (quoted in Haley & Richeport, 1993)

While all therapists get involved with the tension between the uniqueness of the individual and the search for repeatable patterns—which Barbara Held (1995, 1999; see also Hoyt, Miller, Held, & Mathews, in press) nicely describes as the move from *particularities* to *generalities*)—those who ascribe to a postmodern or constructivist orientation especially attend to each client's "local knowledge" (Geertz, 1983), the particular value of each person's story. Thus, Milton Erickson said (quoted in Zeig & Gilligan, 1990, frontispiece):

> Each person is a unique individual. Hence, psychotherapy should be formulated to meet the uniqueness of the individual's needs, rather than tailoring the person to fit the Procrustean bed of a hypothetical theory of human behavior.

When one surrenders certainty and strives to elevate the primacy of the client's construction, extra careful recognition has to be accorded to how the client construes his or her experience.

> If I accept the patient's problem not as pathology, not even as fact, but as simply her story, I can both react to the story—share its sadness or its frustration—and engage, in concert with her, toward the purpose of helping rewrite the story, change its direction, create a new narrative. (Siegel, 1992, p. xxvi)

While general principles and models can be developed, in keeping with the idea that each person creates his or her own meanings, constructive therapists approach each person as an individual (see G. Miller & de Shazer, 1998). We may theorize globally, but we act locally. Thus, while Steve de Shazer and Insoo Berg (1997, p. 123) outlined the general characteristics of solution-focused brief therapy (SFBT),

> Characteristic features of SFBT include:
> (1) At some point in the first interview, the therapist will ask the "Miracle Question."
> (2) At least once during the first interview and at subsequent ones, the client will be asked to rate something on a scale of "0 > 10" or "1 > 10."
> (3) At some point during the interview, the therapist will take a break.
> (4) After this intermission, the therapist will give the client some compliments which will sometimes (frequently) be followed by a suggestion or homework task (frequently called an "experiment").

de Shazer (quoted in Hoyt, 1994b, pp. 37–39) also made clear the importance of taking each client *seriously*:

> Don't let the theory get in the way. Theories will blind you. . . . I know what I don't want, and that's for anybody to develop some sort of rigid orthodoxies. I'm afraid of that. I'm always afraid of that. For me, it's a big point of concern. That there's a right way to do this and that. And to see my descriptions—and they've done this to me; I've probably done this to myself—to see my descriptions as prescriptions.

Along related lines, Hoyt and Berg (1998/1998, p. 335; see Chapter 8, this volume) highlight the importance of working *with* (not *on*) the client:

> By working within the goals, ideas, values, and worldview that clients present, solution-focused therapy is sensitive to the cultures that clients bring to the consulting room. It should be *their* therapy, not the therapist's. The solution must fit their frame of reference, not that of the therapist. Moreover, the therapeutic alliance is foremost, and is based on a high regard and respect for what makes sense to the client, not to the therapist. This means that as therapists, we have to have skills [as well as desire] to join and work with folks of varying ethnicities, and we also have to be clear about what our values (tacit as well as explicit) may be so that we do not impose them.

Similarly, writing within the context of working with clients suffering the effects of trauma, Meichenbaum and Fitzpatrick (1993, p. 698) advise:

There are two important features to recognize about this reconceptualization or new narrative reconstruction process. First, the scientific validity of the specific healing theory that is developed is less important than its plausibility or credibility to the client. Secondly, this entire "narrative repair" effort is conducted in a collaborative inductive fashion and not imposed upon, nor didactically taught, to distressed individuals. The distressed client must come to develop and accept a reconceptualization of the distress that he or she has helped cocreate.

☐ Language and Languaging

> If this be error and upon me proved,
> I never writ, nor no man ever loved.
> —William Shakespeare (Sonnet 116, lines 13–14)

> The rest is silence.
> —William Shakespeare, *Hamlet* (Act V, Scene 2, line 358)

Recognition of the power of language is not new in the psychotherapy field. Thus, de Shazer (1994) borrowed a phrase from Sigmund Freud for the title of his book, *Words Were Originally Magic*. Freud's words (1915/1961a, p. 17):

> Nothing takes place in a psycho-analytic treatment but an exchange of words . . . the patient talks . . . the doctor listens. . . . Words were originally magic and to this day words have retained much of their ancient magical power. By words one person can make another blissfully happy or drive him to despair. . . . Words provoke affects and are in general the means of mutual influence among men.

We "know" and "understand" through our linguistic systems (H. Anderson, 1997; de Shazer, 1991a, 1994; Efran, Lukens, & Lukens, 1990; Furman & Ahola, 1992b; Gilligan & Price, 1993; Lakoff & Johnson, 1980; G. Miller, 1997; G. Miller & de Shazer, 1998; Postman, 1976; Watzlawick, 1978; Watzlawick, Beavin, & Jackson, 1967). *Language and languaging*[14] are the ways we make meaning and exchange information. Language is inherently and intrinsically interpersonal. Subject and context are connected, yin and yang, ocean and shore. "Reality," therapeutic or not, is cocreated in relationships, a social weaving of meaning (Bateson, 1972a, 1980; Gergen, 1994a; Watzlawick, 1976, 1984, 1992; Wittgenstein, 1968, 1980).

Language is a medium, and more. "We see and hear and otherwise experience very largely as we do because the language habits of our community predispose certain choices of interpretation" (Sapir, 1949, p. 162). How we "punctuate" organizes us, formatting our consciousness and structuring our "reality."

The Greek word for "idea,"*eidos*, comes from *idein*, "to see," and is related to the noun, which means two things: (a) something seen like a form and (b) a way of seeing like a perspective. We both see ideas and see by means of them. They are both the forms our minds take and what allows our minds to form events into shaped experiences. (Hillman, 1995, p. 20)

Language is not just a "conduit" (Andersen, 1996; Lakoff, 1995; Reddy, 1993).

> Language molds our thoughts; it gives color and shape to our desires; it limits or extends our sympathies; it gives continuity to our individual self along one line or another. These effects occur whether we are conscious of them or not. (Barzun, 1986)

Highlighting the verbal channel, Rybczynski (1986, pp. 20–21) observes:

> Words are important. Language is not just a medium, like a water pipe, it is a reflection of how we think. We use words not only to describe objects but also to express ideas, and the introduction of words into the language marks the simultaneous introduction of ideas into the consciousness. As Jean-Paul Sartre wrote, "Giving names to objects consists in moving immediate, unreflected, perhaps ignored events on to the plane of reflection and of the objective mind."[15]

Constructive therapists focus on how language builds our worldview and the practical consequences (utility) of these constructions. Watzlawick, Weakland, and Fisch (1974, p. 86) made this clear in their seminal work, *Change: Principles of Problem Formation and Problem Resolution*:

> But since past events are obviously unchangeable, either we are forced to abandon all hope that change is possible, or we must assume that—at least in some significant respects—the past has influence over the present only by way of a person's *present* interpretation of *past* experience. If so, then the significance of the past becomes a matter not of "truth" and "reality," but of looking at it here and now in one way rather than another. Consequently, there is no compelling reason to assign to the past primacy or causality in relation to the present, and this means that the re-interpretation of the past is simply one of many ways of possibly influencing present behavior. In this case, then, we are back at the only meaningful question, i.e., the pragmatic one: How can desirable change of present behavior be produced most efficiently?[16]

In *Shifting Contexts: The Generation of Effective Psychotherapy*, O'Hanlon and Wilk (1987, p. 44) also emphasize the constructive role of "talking therapy":

> Psychotherapy, as we see it, is essentially a problem-solving process consisting of verbal negotiation between client and therapist. The two most fundamental items on the table for negotiation are (1) whether there even is a "problem" as such to solve, and (2) how that problem is to be defined. Whatever the client's presenting complaint and whatever the psychothera-

pist's orientation or approach to conducting the therapeutic interview, the therapist cannot avoid playing a decisive role in determining the outcome of the implicit negotiation of these two issues. The outcome of that negotiation will in turn influence the nature of the ensuing course of therapy, and, ultimately, its outcome.

Within this view, *therapy* is seen therefore as a special kind of *conversation*. H. Anderson and Goolishian (1988, pp. 382–383) highlight some of the therapist's choices in cocreating (or "hosting" to use Furman and Ahola's [1992b] term) such a "therapeutic conversation":

- the therapist keeps inquiry within the parameters of the problem as described by the clients.
- the therapist entertains multiple and contradictory ideas simultaneously.
- the therapist chooses cooperative rather than uncooperative language.
- the therapist learns, understands, and converses in the client's language.
- the therapist is a respectful listener who does not understand too quickly (if ever).
- the therapist asks questions, the answers to which require new questions.
- the therapist takes the responsibility for the creation of a conversational context that allows for mutual collaboration in the problem-defining process.
- the therapist maintains a dialogical conversation with himself or herself.

It is important to keep in mind that *language* and *languaging* need to be conceived more broadly than mere *talk* and *talking*. Terms like *conversation* and *dialogue* seem to focus on the exchange of words and may gloss over various social complexities. Wick (1996, p. 74) comments that "Constructionists have a language myopia." Coale (1992) observes that there is much that goes on in therapy that is not verbal, per se, and notes that "talking about it" may not fit for some clients and may be used as an excuse for not doing anything to change. As they say, "Actions sometimes speak louder than words" and "You've got to walk the walk, not just talk the talk." Goldner (1993, pp. 159–160) explains her preference for the term *discourse*:

> I think "discourse" is our best description of therapeutic dialogue because, as [Michel] Foucault has demonstrated, discourse brings together language, meaning, knowledge, and power. It insists that we see psychotherapy as a social practice shaped by, and embedded in, an elaborate professional culture that inevitably constrains what can be seen and named, and that, like any "knowledge/power discourse," necessarily elevates those who produce and manage it over those for whom it is intended.

Ecker and Hulley (1996, p. 3) call for "active engagement with *full* phenomenology—emotional, cognitive, somatic (kinesthetic and somesthetic), and behavioral, conscious and unconscious." Along similar lines, Strupp and Binder (1984, p. 69) comment:

Narration is thus a process of discovery, a kind of investigation. Retelling or renarrating refer to the concomitant process of change through creating alternative (therapeutic) understandings of a life story. Although the terms *narration* and *renarration* have a certain cognitive quality, the processes themselves should not be intellectualized and to be therapeutically useful must be sustained by vividly experienced emotions.

Tom Andersen (1992, p. 64–65; see also Eron & Lund, 1996) also emphasizes the constructive use of "therapeutic talk" in the development of a new story or "narrative":

> Talking with oneself and/or others is a way of defining oneself. In this sense the language we use makes us who we are in the moment we use it. . . . One might say that the search for new meanings, which often compromises searching for new language, is a search for us to be the selves with which we feel most comfortable. So-called "therapeutic" talk might be regarded as a form of search; a search for new descriptions, new understandings, new meanings, new nuances of the words, and ultimately for new definitions of oneself.

This is part of "retelling a life" (Schafer, 1992), moving from "historical truth to narrative truth" (Spence, 1982), shifting "from trauma to drama" (Hoyt, 1977), becoming "more literate . . . less literal" (Hillman, 1983, p. 28), continuing "the rest of the story" (Meichenbaum, in Hoyt, 1996d), developing a "helpful conversation" (Eron & Lund, 1996), doing the job of helping the client better play "language games" (G. Miller & de Shazer, 1998). How we make sense of our worlds—the stories we tell ourselves and each other—does much to determine what we experience, our actions, and our destinies. When clients need a better story, they often come to therapy.

☐ Taking/Making History

> But how is it
> That this lives in thy mind? What seest thou else
> In the dark backward and abysm of time?
> —William Shakespeare, *The Tempest* (Act I, Scene 2)

All questions are leading questions (Epston, 1995; Freedman & Combs, 1993; Madigan, 1993; Tomm, 1988; White & Epston, 1990), inviting us to focus our attention and consciousness here rather than there, suggesting or giving "privilege" to certain "knowledges" (patternings of awareness and conduct) rather than others. Remembering involves living (re)production (Bartlett, 1932; Neimeyer, 1995), a process more akin to a play or a painting than a videotape or a photograph. Consider the observation of Saint Augustine in his *Confessions* (quoted in Boscolo & Bertrando, 1993, p. 34):

What is by now evident and clear is that neither future nor past exists, and it is inexact language to speak of three times—past, present, and future. Perhaps it would be exact to say: there are three times, a present of things past, a present of things present, a present of things to come. In the soul there are these three aspects of time, and I do not see them anywhere else. The present considering the past is the memory, the present considering the future is expectation.

Memory is active and (re)constructive. As autobiographer Mary Helen Ponce (1993, p. ix) wrote: "The memory is a mysterious—and power-ful—thing. It forgets what we want most to remember, and retains what we often wish to forget. We take from it what we need." Rich Cohen (1998, p. 20) notes: "The story I am left with is therefore not so much one of facts as the noise those facts make passing through time. It is a story of shifting perspective . . . like layering colored glass over colored glass." Henry Miller (quoted in Brassai, 1995, p. 144) avers: "Autobiography is the pur-est romance. . . . What can possibly be more fictive than the story of one's life?" T. S. Eliot (1943b, p. 36) wrote:

> This is the use of memory:
> For liberation—not less of love but expanding
> Of love beyond desire, and so liberation
> From the future as well as the past
>
> . . . .
> History may be servitude,
> History may be freedom. See, now they vanish,
> The faces and places, with the self which, as it could, loved them,
> To become renewed, transfigured, in another pattern.

In *Palimpsest: A Memoir*, Gore Vidal (1995, p. 6; see also Zinsser, 1995) says: "This is pretty much what my kind of writer does anyway. Starts with life; makes a text; then a *re*-vision—literally, a second seeing, an afterthought, erasing some but not all of the original while writing some-thing new over the first layer of text." Novelist Vladimir Nabokov (quoted in McGoldrick, 1995, p. 58) also reminds us that the stories we hear are subject to various influences: "Remember, what you are told is really three-fold: Shaped by the teller, reshaped by the listener, and concealed from them both by the deadman of the tale." Aesop's fable of the three blind men examining the elephant, William Faulkner's (1956) *The Sound and the Fury*, Robert Browning's (1868/1989) *The Ring and the Book*, the recent film *Being John Malkovich* and the Japanese classic film *Rashomon* all illus-trate the profound influence of perspective.[17]

Milton Erickson (1980a, p. 27) spoke of the "unconscious" as a "store-house" and a "reservoir of learning," and commented "any knowledge acquired by your unconscious mind is knowledge that you can use at any appropriate time. But you need not necessarily be aware that you have that knowledge until the moment comes to use it" (quoted in R. A. Havens, 1989, p. 69). The past inhabits us. Mary Catherine Bateson (1994) referred to "peripheral visions: learning along the way." Carol Lee Flinders (1998, p. 158) agrees:

> At some point during the construction of a useable past, one finds herself drawing not merely on collective history or even imagined reconstruction of that history, but on personal history as well, and these bright bits of one's remembered experiences as girlchild or woman complete the work.

With this awareness, one can assist a client in "looking back" to elicit histories that will support an alternative (and preferred) present and future (Madanes, Keim, Lentine, & Kiem, 1990; Monk, Winslade, Crocket, & Epston, 1997; White, 1993a). Seeking a "history of the present recovery" may be more salutary than the conventional psychiatric "history of the present complaint."[18] As the poet David Whyte (1997, p. 46) wrote:

> Let my history then
> be a gate unfastened
> to a new life
> and not a barrier
> to my becoming.
> Let me find the ghosts
> and histories and barely
> imagined future
> of this world

And, as Wendel Berry (1982, p. 244) wrote:

> Ended, a story is history;
> it is in time, with time
> lost. But if a man's life
> continue in another man,
> then the flesh will rhyme
> its part in immortal song.
> By absence, he comes again.

One also can assist clients to imagine future times (in a kind of "forward to the present" rather than "back to the future"), which then will give better meanings to current life as it is lived (Furman & Ahola, 1992b; Penn, 1985). Thoreau advised in *Walden* (1854/1975, pp. 562–563):

> If one advances confidently in the direction of his dreams, and endeavors to live the life which he has imagined, he will meet with a success unexpected in common hours. . . . If you have built castles in the air, your work need not be lost; that is where they should be. Now put the foundations under them.

☐ Opening Doors

Our remedies oft in ourselves do lie.
—William Shakespeare, *All's Well That Ends Well*
(Act 1, Scene 1, line 216)

Albert Einstein (quoted in Watzlawick, 1994) noted: "Theories do not come from observations; rather, observations come from theories." There are many ways to look, and how we look—a process shaped by our theories and stories—determines what we see.

There is nothing either good or bad,
but thinking makes it so.
—William Shakespeare, *Hamlet*
(Act II, Scene 2, lines 249–250)

Events may happen, but what meaning will be given? As Marcus Aurelius (A.D.167/1964, p. 64) recorded in his *Meditations*:

Among the truths you will do well to contemplate most frequently are these two: First, that things can never touch the soul, but stand inert outside it, so that disquiet can arise only from fancies within; and secondly, that all visible objects change in a moment, and will be no more. Think of the countless changes in which you yourself have had a part. The whole universe is change, and life itself is but what you deem it.

For better or worse, the beliefs and expectations that result from the processes of attribution (see Collins & Hoyt, 1972; Frank, 1961; Furman & Ahola, 1989/1992a; Jones et al., 1972; Kirsch & Lynn, 1999; Olson, Jackson, & Nelson, 1997; Sherman & Lynn, 1990; Taylor, 1989) can have great influence. Long ago, Alfred Adler (1931/1968; see also Carlson & Sperry, 1998) anticipated de Shazer's (1993) observation that we always "mis-read" as well as some of the ideas about narrative construction subsequently expressed by cognitive-behaviorists (e.g., Ellis, 1990, 1998; Meichenbaum, in Hoyt, 1996d; Mahoney, 1991; Neimeyer, 1993a, 1993b, 1993c, 1998a; Ramsay, 1998). Adler wrote (1931/1968, p. 4):

Human beings live in the realm of *meanings*. . . . We experience reality always through the meaning we give it; not in itself, but as something interpreted. It will be natural to suppose, therefore, that this meaning is always more or less unfinished, incomplete; and even that is never altogether right. The realm of meanings is the realm of mistakes.[19]

A related idea also was expressed by George Kelly (1955, p. 43; see also Neimeyer & Neimeyer, 1987) in *The Psychology of Personal Constructs*:

The universe is real; it is happening all the time; it is integral; and it is open to piecemeal interpretation. Different men construe it in different ways. Since it owes no prior allegiance to any one man's construction system, it is always open to reconstruction. Some of the alternative ways of construing are better adapted to man's purposes than are others. Thus, man comes to understand his world through an infinite series of successive approximations. Since man is always faced with constructive alternatives, which he may explore if he wishes, he need not continue indefinitely to be the absolute victim either of his past history or of his present circumstances.

Uncertainty and indeterminancy can open the door for a "re-telling" or "reconstruction." As Gregory Bateson (1980, p. 159; see also White, 1986/1989a) wrote: "Change will require various sorts of relaxation or contradiction within the system of presuppositions." Fixed meanings can be questioned, challenged, undermined; they can become fluid, perhaps even suspect; and this can create an opportunity for a "re-telling" or "double-description," a "thickening" (Geertz, 1973a) or "folding over" (L. Hoffman, 1998). As Mary Catherine Bateson (1994, p. 11), Gregory's daughter (!) put it, there can be a "multiple layering," a "rejecting . . . [of] the belief that questions of meaning have unitary answers."

How one "looks at it" occurs through language. Gergen (1993, p. x) explains:

> In this context a major aim of therapy becomes one of freeing the client from a particular kind of account and opening the way to alternatives of greater promise.

In therapy, we (clients and clinicians) decide what to highlight, what to bring forward (and what to ignore). Shawver (1996, p. 382) explains:

> Derrida's term *differance* . . . is a key term in postmodernity and it will help explain how language creates and deconstructs "being" through vernacular poetizing.
>
> The word differance, spelled with an "a," is a coined term, and Derrida contrasts it with the vernacular *difference*. Patterns of "Difference," he explains, "[are]... 'produced—deferred—by 'differance'" (Derrida, 1982, p. 14). But what does this mean? That difference is deferred by differance?
>
> Imagine observing a quilt on the wall with patches of yellow, blue, and white. If you notice the yellow and the nonyellow, you see a pattern of concentric boxes. If you notice the blue and the nonblue, you see a checkered design. Each pattern is a play of differences, but it is a different set of differences when yellow is differentiated from nonyellow than when blue is differentiated fron nonblue, a different set of differences that shows us different patterns.
>
> What is interesting about this shift from one pattern to the other is that it not only calls our attention to a new pattern, but that it suppresses our awareness of the other pattern. Differance defers a pattern of differences (say the pattern of differences between the blue and the not-blue). That is, one pattern of differences pushes into the background another possible play of patterns. You cannot study the pattern of yellows and the pattern of blues at the same time because differance causes one or the other patterns

to be "deferred." Differance is the hidden way of seeing things that is deferred out of awareness by our distraction with the imagery that captures our attention. Because it contains this other way to see things, "Differance is the . . . formation of form" (Derrida, 1976, p. 63). It is the "historical and epochal 'unfolding' of Being" (Derrida, 1982, p. 22).

A gateway into this perspective was neatly opened in the statement by Milton Erickson: "Not everything you see is the way you see it is" (quoted by Carl Hammerschlag in the videotape by Haley & Richeport, 1993[20]). Solution-focused and solution-oriented therapists "open doors" through use of the well-known "Miracle Question":

> Suppose that one night, while you were asleep, there was a miracle and this problem was solved. How would you know? What would be different? (Steve de Shazer, 1988, p. 5)

and by the highlighting of "exceptions" (times when the presenting problem is not present) and the use of language that emphasizes clients' endemic strengths and possibilities. In *Putting Difference to Work*, de Shazer (1991a, pp. 90–91) elaborated:

> Although exceptions are frequently read as related to the clients' complaints, they can also be read as precursors to goals (language games that lead the client toward setting and achieving goals), and solutions (a language game that marks the termination of therapy). That is, times when the complaints are unexpectedly absent can be seen as (a) times when the goal-state is approximated and/or (b) the raw material for constructing the solution.

Reading what de Shazer (1988, p. 10) wrote, that "This process of solution development can be summed up as helping an unrecognized difference become a difference that makes a difference." I hear my haiku muse whisper (see also Chapter 9, this volume):

> Focusing language
> On solutions, not problems
> Miracles happen

Some examples of the shift toward "solution talk" can be in Table 3.3.
We also may "open doors" via what Watzlawick, Weakland, and Fisch (1974, p. 95) call "the gentle art of reframing":

> To reframe, then, means to change the conceptual and/or emotional setting or viewpoint in relation to which a situation is experienced and to place it in another frame which fits the "facts" of the same concrete situation equally well or even better, and thereby changes its entire meaning. The mechanism involved here is not immediately obvious, especially if we bear in mind that there is change while the situation itself may remain quite unchanged and, indeed, even unchangeable. What turns out to be changed as a result of reframing is the meaning attributed to the situation,

TABLE 3.3. Solution-building vocabulary

In	Out	In	Out
Respect	Judge	Forward	Backward
Empower	Fix	Future	Past
Nurture	Control	Collaborate	Manipulate
Facilitate	Treat	Options	Conflicts
Augment	Reduce	Partner	Expert
Invite	Insist	Horizontal	Hierachical
Appreciate	Diagnose	Possibility	Limitation
Hope	Fear	Growth	Cure
Latent	Missing	Access	Defense
Assets	Defects	Utilize	Resist
Strength	Weakness	Create	Repair
Health	Pathology	Exception	Rule
Not Yet	Never	Difference	Sameness
Expand	Shrink	Solution	Problem

Note. From "Introduction: Competency-Based Future-Oriented Therapy," by M. F. Hoyt, in *Constructive Therapies* (Volume 1, p. 4), by M. F. Hoyt, Ed., New York: Guilford Press. Copyright 1994 by Guilford Press. Reprinted with permission.

and therefore its consequences, but not its concrete facts—or, as the philosopher Epictetus expressed it as early as the first century A.D., "It is not the things themselves which trouble us, but the opinions that we have about these things."

As Rainer Maria Rilke (1904/1962, p. 71) wrote in his *Letters to a Young Poet*:

> One must be so careful with names anyway; it is so often on the name of a misdeed that a life goes to pieces, not the nameless and personal action itself, which was perhaps a perfectly definite necessity of that life and would have been absorbed by it without effort. And the expenditure of energy seems to you so great only because you overvalue victory; it is not the victory that is the "great thing" you think to have done, although you are right in your feeling; the great thing is that there was already something there which you could put in the place of that delusion, something true and real.

And, as Walt Whitman wrote in *Leaves of Grass* (1891–1892/1940a, "Song of Myself," Stanza 21):

> I am the poet of the Body and I am the poet of the Soul,
> The pleasures of heaven are with me and the pains of hell are with me,
> The first I graft and increase upon myself,
> The latter I translate into a new tongue.

There may be "facts" that must be accommodated (see Bandler & Grinder, 1982; Cade, 1986; Coyne, 1985; Gale, 1999; Held, 1995, 1999; Reamy-Stephenson, 1983; Rennie, 1994; Sluzki, 1998), but there also is room for different understandings. "The story needed to be doctored, not her: it needed reimaging" (Hillman, 1983, p. 17). To be effective, reframing needs to speak to the "emotional truth" of the symptom (Ecker & Hulley, 1996, p. 31), honoring one's intentions and "preferred view of self" (Eron & Lund, 1989, 1996). "Thus, although the person is always constructing the meaning of the experience by a synthesizing process, the elements of the synthesis have an experiential validity, and can be more or less accurately symbolized" (Rice & Greenberg, 1992, p. 207).[21] Shakespeare advised both:

> This above all: to thine own self be true,
> And it must follow, as the night the day
> Thou canst not then be false to any man.
> (*Hamlet*, Act I, Scene 3, lines 78–80)

and

> Words, words, mere words, no matter from the heart;
> Th' effect doth operate another way.
> (*Troilus and Cressida*, Act V, Scene 3, lines 108–109)

Narrative therapists also commonly invite "family members to participate in the construction of new descriptions of the problem itself—an externalized description" (White, 1988/1989b, p. 37). This is part of the "restorying" or "re-authoring of lives" (White, 1995a; White & Epston, 1990):

> Stories are full of gaps which persons must fill in order for the stories to be performed. These gaps recruit the lived experience and the imagination of persons. With every performance, persons are reauthoring their lives. The evolution of lives is akin to their process of reauthoring, the process of persons' entering stories, taking them over and making them their own. (White & Epston, 1990, p. 13)

Sometimes only a small (albeit significant) pattern change is wanted or needed; a client may revise some "viewing and doing" (O'Hanlon & Weiner-Davis, 1989), but is looking only for some simple problem solving and does not have life-encompassing problems that require an "identity overhaul" (O'Hanlon, 1994, p. 28; White, 1989e). Other times, however, for clients to achieve his, or her, or their goal, one may need to engage the narrating function more fully, broadening the scope to assist in a "reauthoring" or "retelling" of a life (Freeman, 1993; Goulding & Goulding, 1979; Hudson & O'Hanlon, 1991; Parry & Doan, 1994; Polster, 1987; Schafer, 1992; Spence, 1982; Steiner, 1974; White, 1995a, 1997; White & Epston, 1990).

As is their wont, Berg and de Shazer (1993, p. 7) put it simply:

> Change is seen to happen within language. What we talk about and how we talk about it makes a difference and it is these differences that can be used to make a difference (to the client).

In this regard, narrative therapists and solution-focused therapists (or at least two of the originators) clearly agree (quoted in Duvall & Beier, 1995, p. 65):

> **Michael White:** . . . . *this is only one interpretation about what Insoo's doing and I wouldn't want to impose this, but, my guess is that Insoo makes it possible for people to talk differently about their lives, differently about themselves. It perhaps makes it possible for people to relate to themselves with compassionate ways. Would that fit for you, Insoo, that in some way people come along to see you and do wind up talking a bit differently about who they are and about other people?*
>
> **Insoo Kim Berg:** *Differently than, than what?*
>
> **Michael White:** *Than the ways that have them judging themselves harshly and measuring themselves against some way they should be.*
>
> **Insoo Kim Berg:** *I should hope so. Isn't that what we all try to do?*
>
> **Michael White:** *Yes.*

☐ Persons Versus Problems

> Methinks I see these things with parted eye,
> Where every thing seems double.
> —William Shakespeare, *A Midsummer Night's
> Dream* (Act IV, Scene 9, lines 189–190)

Like Dorothy in *The Wizard of Oz* when she looked behind the curtain, questioning underlying assumptions sometimes can puncture domineering illusions and defrock authority.[22] Hence, McGoldrick (1995, p. 56) suggests "jostling" your view of your family. Writing within the context of architecture, Papadakis, Cooke, and Benjamin (1989, flyleaf) say: "Deconstruction is characterized by an essential distrust of the authenticity of apparent meaning and form and the traditional distinction between the two."[23] According to Goolishian (quoted in de Shazer, 1991a, p. 50), "to deconstruct means to take apart the interpretive assumptions of the system of meaning that you are examining, to challenge the interpretive system in such a manner that you reveal the assumptions on which the model is based. At the same time, as these are revealed, you open the space for alternative understanding."[24] As Lynn Hoffman (1993a, p. 104) remarked:

> Postmodern and poststructural thinking has allowed us to look afresh at all prized or sacred writings and to "deconstruct" them. The purpose behind

deconstructing a text is basically one of political emancipation: by laying bare the relations of domination and submission embedded in the text, one (hopefully) weakens its power to oppress.

Michael White (1991/1993b, pp. 34–36) elaborates the implications of *deconstruction* for narrative therapy:

According to my rather loose definition, deconstruction has to do with procedures that subvert taken-for-granted realities and practices: those so-called "truths" that are split off from the conditions and the context of their production; those disembodied ways of speaking that hide their biases and prejudices; and those familiar practices of self and of relationship that are subjugating of persons' lives. Many of the methods of deconstruction render strange these familiar and everyday taken-for-granted realities and practices by objectifying them. In this sense, the methods of deconstruction are methods that "exoticize the domestic". . . . Deconstruction is premised on what is generally referred to as a "critical constructivist" or, as I would prefer, a "constitutionalist" perspective on the world. From this perspective, it is proposed that persons' lives are shaped by the meaning that they ascribe to their experience, by their situation in social structures, and by the language practices and cultural practices of self and of relationship that these lives are recruited into. . . . This constructionalist perspective is at variance with the dominant structuralist (behavior reflects the structure of the mind) and functionalist (behavior serves a purpose for the system) perspectives of the world of psychotherapy.

Inherent in this view is the narrative therapy motto, "It is not the person who is . . . the problem. Rather, it is the problem that is the problem" (White, 1989e, p. 6; see also O'Hanlon, 1994). Redekop (1995, p. 317; see also Madigan, 1992) quotes Michel Foucault (1988) as saying: "*Problematization* [italics added] is the 'totality of discursive and non-discursive practices that introduces something into the play of the true and false and constitute[s] it as an object for thought (whether in the form of moral reflection, scientific knowledge, political analysis, etc.).'"[25]

> Out, damned spot. Out, I say!
> —William Shakespeare, *Macbeth*,
> (Act V, Scene 1, line 35)

The consequent practices of *externalizing the problem* are steps toward reclaiming autonomy:

"Externalizing" is an approach to therapy that encourages persons to objectify, and at times, to personify, the problems that they experience as oppressive. In this process, the problem becomes a separate entity and thus external to the person who was, or the relationship that was, ascribed the problem. Those problems that are considered to be inherent, and those relatively fixed qualities that are attributed to persons and to relationship, are rendered less fixed and less restricting. (White, 1989e, p. 5)

White (1991/1993b, p. 39) again elaborates:

> These externalizing conversations "exoticize the domestic" in that they encourage persons to identify the private stories and the cultural knowledges that they live by; those stories and knowledges that guide their lives and that speak to them of their identity. These externalizing conversations assist persons to unravel, across time, the constitution of their self and of their relationships. Externalizing conversations are initiated by encouraging persons to provide an account of the effects of the problem on their lives. This can include its effects on their emotional states, familial and peer relationships, social and work spheres, etc., and with a special emphasis on how it has affected their "view" of themselves and of their relationships. Then, persons are invited to map the influence that these views or perceptions have on their lives, including on their interactions with others. This is often followed by some investigation of how persons have been recruited into these views.
>
> As persons become engaged in these externalizing conversations, their private stories cease to speak to them of their identity and of the truth of their relationships—these private stories are no longer transfixing of their lives. Persons experience a separation from, and an alienation in relation to, these stories. In the space established by this separation, persons are free to explore alternative and preferred knowledges of who they might be; alternative and preferred knowledges into which they might enter their lives.

Following White's description (see also Freedman & Combs, 1996; Hart, 1995; O'Hanlon, 1994; Redekop, 1995; Roth & Epston, 1996), externalizing in narrative therapy typically involves separating the person from the problem by naming the problem and exploring the person's relationship to the problem, including ways the problem may achieve influence over him or her and ways he or she sometimes resists the problem's attempts. Unlike classic psychodynamic theory, which construes externalization as a "defense mechanism" that "distorts reality" by the disowning of personal responsibility, narrative therapy construes the process as the externalizing of the problem and the internalizing of personal agency (Tomm, 1989). Robert Neimeyer (1998b, pp. 145–146) provides a nice thumbnail description:

> For authors such as White and Epston (1990), culturally predominant *internalizing* discourses attribute blame for problems to individuals, not only conferring on them narrow and pathological identities, but also separating them from important persons in their lives who might otherwise be sources of support and tangible assistance. The role of therapy is then to muster resistance to the *dominant narrative* of such problematic identities, typically by (a) *externalizing* the problem, (b) examining its *real effects* on the lives of the individuals who are subjugated to it, (c) searching for unique outcomes

or 'sparkling moments' when dominated persons resist its influence, and (d) *historicizing* their exceptional accomplishments and recruiting a supportive *audience* for these welcome developments (Monk et al., 1997). . . . Overall, the goal of such counselling is to help the client win freedom from the dominant problem narative, and achieve genuine authorship of his life.

Neimeyer (1998a) also warns of the "STDs (Serious Theoretical Discrepancies)" that may result from casually commingling therapies infused with contradictory core epistemological and ontogical values:

In the case of cognitive and constructivist therapies, of course these commitments are fairly explicit and carry concrete implications for the practicing therapist [Neimeyer, 1998a, p. 60]. . . . What would be problematic from the standpoint of a theoretically progressive integration of psychotherapy would be indiscriminate gallimaufry of deconstructive rules deriving from incompatible metatheories, leaving the therapist eliciting a fragile and almost inarticulate self-awareness on the part of the client at one moment, only to critique its logical or empirical warrant the next. Simply put, the affirmative, respectful, and celebratory spirit of constructivist therapists in relation to client narratives . . . clashes at fundamental levels with the more critical, suspicious, and editorial attitude of traditional cognitive therapists and researchers toward the same material. A perspective that promotes the aggregation of strategies deriving from both perspectives may increase the gross number of techniques available to the therapist, but only at the expense of coherence in case conceptualization and guiding principles. . . . If problems are more usefully "externalized," and viewed as inscribed in social systems rather than individuals (as White argues), then the attempt to identify "cognitive distortions" as the source of emotional distress, and their "rational reconstruction" as the cure, is problematic on several accounts. Not only does this traditional perspective artificially situate problems *within* people, thereby encouraging them to adopt a distrustful attitude toward themselves, but it extends the general [W]estern preoccupation with the control of deviance by external regulatory agencies to a pattern of self-monitoring and self-control which in essence represents the most pernicious form of internalized totalitarianism (White & Epston, 1990). (Neimeyer, 1998a, pp. 62–63)

Keeping these cautions in mind, there also are methods drawn from other theoretical approaches that can be seen, through the narrative lens, as forms of externalization. For example, Scott Miller (1994; see also Bateson, 1972b) notes the externalizing function of substance "addiction" models, Hoyt (1994d/1995k) calls attention to the externalizing function of Gestalt therapy two-chair work ("Put your guilt in that chair and tell it how you feel"), Allen and Allen (1998) portray the "early scenes" reworking of self-esteem in redecision therapy, and L. L. Havens (1986, p.

6) describes Harry Stack Sullivan as sometimes sitting next to a patient so that they could look out together at the problem that was troubling the person. Aspects of psychodrama, mindfulness meditation, mask and play therapy, and various "alternative" healing practices could be added to the list.

Although not all cases require exposition of mystified sociocultural power/knowledge factors (Foucault, 1980; Laing, 1967; White, 1989e), clinicians need to be careful that they do not simply adjust clients to more of the same rather than assisting them toward "exceptions" (de Shazer, 1985), "new directions" (O'Hanlon & Weiner-Davis, 1989), or "unique outcomes" (White & Epston, 1990). There is the risk—as Lerner (1995) has passionately argued—that health care policies may, in effect, seal off awareness of such factors if therapists are restricted to managing immediate symptomatology and are enjoined from looking at antecedent or systemic issues (see Chapter 4, this volume). In this regard, Salvador Minuchin (1991, p. 49) cautioned:

> Families of poverty have been stripped of much of the power to write their own stories. Their narratives of hopelessness, helplessness and dependency have been cowritten, if not dictated, by social institutions. When the institutional and societal coauthors of these stories are made invisible, when the family narratives are presented as if constructed by the families alone, family members become even more depressed, potential helpers are confused, and everybody becomes less effectual.

"'History' is written by the winners," as they say, with the dominant culture's voice (or discourse) given privilege and recognition over the voices of others. The warning sounded by Marshall McLuhan (quoted in Karrass, 1992, p. 78) is worth noting: "For any medium has the power of imposing its own assumptions on the unwary. But the greatest aid is simply in knowing that the spell can occur immediately upon contact, as in the first bars of a melody."

> Re-vision—the act of looking back, of seeing with fresh eyes, of entering an old text from a new critical direction—is for women more than a chapter in cultural history: it is an act of survival. Until we can understand the assumptions in which we are drenched we cannot know ourselves. . . . We need to know the writing of the past, and know it differently than we have ever known it; not to pass on a tradition but to break its hold over us. (Adrienne Rich, 1979, p. 35)

With this understanding, "resistance" can be seen quite differently from the conventional psychiatric pejorative. Not identifying and honoring the client's values and treatment goals may make it necessary for the client to "resist" (de Shazer, 1984; see Chapter 14, this volume) lest their realities be "extinguished in expression or anesthetized in experience" (A. Singer, 1994). Clients who are described as "noncompliant" or "resistant" may be in a power-politics struggle (see Albee, 1997; Tomm, 1993), a "reality contest" (G. Miller & de Shazer, 1998), engaged in counteroppressive practices to refuse being psychologically colonized or bent in directions they do not wish to go. In such cases, *vive la resistance!*

A metaview of some of the broader pragmatic implications of a constructivist or postmodern perspective for psychotherapeutic practice— in which (following Neimeyer, 1995) therapy may be conceived as a form of personal science, selfhood development, narrative reconstruction, or conversational elaboration—is presented in Table 3.4.

TABLE 3.4. Selected strategic and technical preferences of constructivist therapies

Area	Strategic preferences	Representative interventions
Assessment	Exploration of personal narratives, autobiography, personal and family construct systems and hierarchies	Identification of central metaphors, life review, repertory grids, laddering techniques
Goal of therapy	Creative rather than corrective; promotion of meaning-making and personal development	Fixed-role therapy, stream-of-consciousness technique, facilitation of meaningful accounts
Interpretation of emotion	Treatment of negative emotion as integral to constructive change; to be respected rather than controlled	Reprocessing of emotional schemata, systematic evocative unfolding, psychodramatic exploration
Level of intervention	Attention to selfhood processes, core role structures, family constructs or premises	Movieola technique, enactment of deep role relationship, circular questions, ritual prescription
Style of therapy	Personal rather than authoritative; empathic grasping of client's outlook as basis of negotiation	Credulous approach, adoption of "not-knowing" approach, elaboration of metaphor or story
Approach to resistance	To understand as a legitimate attempt to protect core-ordering processes; modulate pace of change	"Allowing" resistance, externalizing of the problem, identification of unique outcomes

Note. From "Constructivist Psychotherapies: Features, Foundations, and Future Directions," by R. A. Neimeyer, in R. A. Neimeyer & M. J. Mahoney (Eds.) 1995, *Constructivism in Psychotherapy* (p. 17). Washington, DC: American Psychological Association. Copyright by the American Psychological Association. Reprinted with permission.

☐ Whose Therapy Is It? Whose Story Is It? Whose Life Is It?

> To be or not to be.
> —William Shakespeare, *Hamlet*
> (Act III, Scene 1, line 56)

"To intervene or not to intervene" is *not* the question, as Duncan, Hubble, and Rusk (1994) have pointed out: *How* is the question. While strategic therapists—such as Haley (1963, 1977), Madanes (1981), Fisch, Weakland and Segal (1982), and Rosenbaum (1990)—have been explicit in assigning to the therapist responsibility for making something happen, in practice all clinicians wield considerable power. As John Weakland (1993, p. 143) wrote:

> Just as one cannot *not* communicate [see Ruesch & Bateson, 1951; Watzlawick, Beavin,& Jackson, 1967], one cannot *not* influence. Influence is inherent in all human interaction. We are bound to influence our clients, and they are bound to influence us. The only choice is between doing so without reflection, or even with attempted denial, and doing so deliberately and responsibly. Clients come seeking change which they could not achieve on their own; expertise in influencing them to change usefully seems to us the essence of the therapist's job. Therefore, we give much thought—guided, of course, by what a client does and says—to almost every aspect of treatment: To whom we will see in any given session, to the timing of sessions, to what suggestions we will offer as to new thoughts and actions, to responses we make to clients' reports of progress or difficulties encountered, and especially not just to the content of what we say, but to how we will phrase it. This strategic emphasis, however, does not mean that we propose or favor any arrangement in which a therapist has all the power, knowledge, control, and activity, while the patient is just a passive object of therapeutic actions—if indeed this were possible, which is very doubtful.

Writing from a solution-focused perspective, Michele Weiner-Davis(1993, p. 156) comes right to the point: "Since we cannot avoid leading, the question becomes, 'Where shall we lead our clients?'" Gale Miller (1997, p. 183) elaborates:

> Solution-focused therapists . . . use their questions to construct mutually satisfactory conversations with clients. The questions are not designed to elicit information about worlds outside ongoing therapy conversations, but to elicit information in building new stories about clients' lives. Within solution-focused brief therapy discourse, then, all questions are constructive. They are designed to define goals and to construct solutions that solution-focused therapists assume are already present in clients' lives.

Similarly, in *Narrative Solutions in Brief Therapy*, Eron and Lund (1996, p. 34) highlight the intentionality of narrative therapists:

Michael White and David Epston provide a map for the therapist to navigate an effective conversation. There's purpose to the therapist's comments and questions, and a direction to the search for alternative stories. White and Epston view therapists as accountable for what they do. Although the client is seen as the expert and primary author, and the therapist as the secondary author in the restorying process, it's the therapist who assumes primary responsibility for change. Therapists restory with the specific aim of deconstructing the problem, changing its meaning, and loosening its hold over people's lives. . . . [White and Epston have] brought the person back into the system—by affirming that an individual's preferences, intentions, stories, and experiences are relevant to the process of change. Like strategic family therapists of the 1970s and 1980s, however, these postmodern therapists have a plan for changing problems.

White (in Hoyt & Combs, 1996; White, Hoyt, & Zimmerman, 2000) also agrees that we are "influential" and that there is a "power differential" and suggests the following:

We can't pretend that we are not somehow contributing to the process. We can't pretend that we are not influential in the therapeutic interaction. There is no neutral position in which therapists can stand. I can embrace this fact by joining with people to address all of those things that they find traumatizing and limiting of their lives. . . . And, because the impossibility of neutrality means that I cannot avoid being "for" something, I take the responsibility to distrust what I am for— that is, my ways of life and my ways of thought—and I can do this in many ways. For example, I can distrust what I am for with regard to the appropriateness of this to the lives of others. I can distrust what I am for in the sense that what I am for has the potential to reproduce the very things that I oppose in my relations with others. I can distrust what I am for to the extent that what I am for has a distinct location in the worlds of gender, class, race, culture, sexual preference, etc. And so on. (in Hoyt & Combs, 1996, pp. 38–40)

Constructive therapists—who frame their practices in terms such as *collaboration, coparticipation, intersubjectivity,* and *cocreation*—pay special attention to issues of causation, control, power, influence, and direction. Unless cognizance is truly given to honoring "narrative intentions" (Combs & Freedman, 1994), "inviting," "wondering," and "questioning" could be used disingenuously to offer indirect (controlling) hypnotic suggestions (see Freedman & Combs, 1996, p. 6; O'Hanlon, 1994; Schmidt & Trenkle, 1985)— manipulation could be "cloaked in transparency," so to speak.[27]

In contradistinction, as part of their commitment to respectful collaboration, constructive therapists avoid usurping power. Extra care is taken to include multiple points of view, to "hear" (and sometimes evoke) the "voice" of the "marginalized," to create space for the recognition and expression of oppressed, sometimes inchoate experience. As essayist and playwright, Tony Kushner (1995, pp. 7–9) has said:

> The truest characteristic of freedom is generosity, the basic gesture of free-
> dom is to include, not to exclude. . . . Listing the full catalogue of the com-
> plaints of the disenfranchised is sure to raise howls decrying "victimology"
> and "political correctness" from those who need desperately to believe that
> democracy is a simple thing. Democracy isn't simple and it doesn't mean
> that majorities tyrannize minorities.

Thus, for some constructive therapists, therapy is an explicitly Political
act, a place for exposing the trapping of power and for giving "privilege
to" the special "knowledges" of the subjugated or disenfranchised (often
persons of color, women, children, older people, gays and lesbians, the
poor and homeless, people who are physically or mentally "different,"
and so forth). Personal problems are seen as often resulting from pernicious cultural practices, both blatant social injustices and the subsequent
(and perhaps more subtle) internalization of deleterious institutionalized
attitudes (see Albee, 1997; L. Brown, 1997; Markowitz, 1997; Waldegrave,
1990). For others (e.g., G. Miller & de Shazer, 1998), the clinical situation
is not construed in conventional political terms, but there is still keen
concern for who determines how we talk and what we talk about, for
what R.D. Laing (1967) called "the politics of experience." Imelda
McCarthy (quoted in Sharry, 1998) reminds us to stay mindful of "the
ethics of speaking and the politics of listening." As Efran, Lukens, and
Lukens (1988, p. 32) articulate:

> Because constructivists regard the language community as all important,
> therapists working from this point of view must get used to the idea that
> they are engaged in an essentially political endeavor. Like other human
> pursuits, therapy fosters the establishment, exchange, and maintenance of
> particular traditions and language formulations. Issues of personal respon-
> sibility and ethics can neither be ducked nor masked by objective-sound-
> ing terms like "treatment," "mental health," "the normal family," "family
> loyalties," and so on. . . . For constructivists, the *entire therapeutic venture* is
> fundamentally an exercise in ethics—it involves the inventing, shaping,
> and reformulating of codes for living together. In other words, from this
> point of view, therapy is a dialogue about the interlocking wants, desires,
> and expectations of all the participants, including the therapist.

Constructive therapists meet their clients somewhere "in the middle."
Clients may seek the therapist's assistance and expertise, but one side is
not superior or the arbiter of what is valid, legitimate, or right. (Or, one
is—but, ultimately, it is not the therapist.) The approach is "mutualistic"
(Griffith, 1997); the therapist is a "true participant" (Cantwell & Holmes,
1994). Matthews (1985) likens the relationship to the Escher painting of
one hand drawing the other.

> I learn to swim in the
> wetness of you.
> —E. Ethelbert Miller (1992, p. 160)

And, of course:

> O chestnut-tree, great-rooted blossomer
> Are you the leaf, the blossom or the bole?
> O body swayed to music, O brightening glance,
> How can we know the dancer from the dance?
> —William Butler Yeats (1928/1989, p. 217)

Drengenberg (1996, p. 52) described an encounter evocative of both Buber's (1958) I and Thou and Gergen's (in Hoyt, 1996c) "relational sublime"[28]:

> ...we meet in a shared space...non-hierarchically...
> respectfully...afloat in a sea of recursivity...seeing more
> clearly who we are and what we do and need...
> our encounter of exchange...activating innate potentials
> for growth...each never again to be the same...

Scrupulous attention must be paid to identifying and serving *clients'* goals. Hence, White (1995a; see also White, in Hoyt & Combs, 1996) calls for "accountability structures" to help keep us keenly alert to the politics of the therapeutic situation; Tom Andersen (1991, 1992) invites families to hear "reflecting teams" and Madigan (1993) "situates" the therapist's curiosity and motivations before the family; de Shazer (1984, 1985, 1988; see also de Shazer, in Hoyt, 1996c; de Shazer & Weakland, in Hoyt, 1994b) and Berg (1989) assert that "resistance" can be "dissolved" if we form relationships that honor what the client is a "customer" for; H. Anderson and Goolishian (1992) suggest that "the client is the expert"; Rosenbaum (Rosenbaum & Dyckman, 1996) silently bows to his clients as they enter his office to help orient himself to the upcoming encounter; and Tomm (1991a; see also Bernstein, 1990; Freedman & Combs, 1996, pp. 269–272) calls for greater awareness of "ethical postures" that "open space" without imposing upon clients.

Many examples of ways that these intentions can be promulgated, nuanced, and often achieved are to be found in *Constructive Therapies, Volumes 1 and 2* (Hoyt, 1994a, 1996b) and *The Handbook of Constructive Therapies* (Hoyt, 1998). With rootstock in the adjoining fields of brief therapy and family therapy, however, these books (like this chapter) strongly emphasize solution-focused, narrative, and Ericksonian perspectives at the relative expense of other constructivist ideas and approaches. "Most notably absent," as Michael Mahoney (1999, p. 424) commented in his thoughtful review of the *Handbook*, "are contributions from European, Central and South American, and Asian constructivists." I agree with Hugh Rosen (1999, p. 74) that "it is time to broaden the dialogue across conceptually localized knowledge contexts." For surveys of these important contributions I would especially recommend four well-edited volumes,

Therapy as Social Construction (McNamee & Gergen, 1992), *Constructivism in Psychotherapy* (Neimeyer & Mahoney, 1995), *Constructing Realities: Meaning-Making Perspectives for Psychotherapists* (Rosen & Kuehlwein, 1996), and *Constructions of Disorder: Meaning-Making Frameworks for Psychotherapy* (Neimeyer & Raskin, in press); as well as Mahoney's (in press) *Constructive Psychotherapy.*

☐ Responsibilities

> O, it is excellent
> To have a giant's strength, but it is tyrannous
> To use it like a giant.
> —William Shakespeare, *Measure for Measure*
>   (Act II, Scene 2, lines 107–109)

At its finest, a constructivist approach increases our sense of empowerment and participation, and reminds us that the essence of being human is that we are "meaning makers" and that no one can remain neutral in the "art of experience" (L. Hoffman, 1990/1995; E. L. Johnson & Sandage, 1999; Prilleltensky, 1997; Rosenbaum & Bohart, 1994; White, 1995). James Hillman (1996, p. 55) and Bill O'Hanlon (in Hoyt, 1996e, p. 106) both refer to Martin Heidegger's (1962) idea that we are "thrown" into a culture that shapes us. Jay Efran (1994, p. 219) describes our linguistic devices as "necessary and useful, [although] they also tend to entrap a person in a social cocoon of shared explanatory fictions." He goes on (p. 221) to explain:

> There is no fully effective way to break the spells our abstractions weave. . . . It is therefore essential for us to recognize that whenever we think we are looking at something outside ourselves . . . we are actually experiencing some aspect of our own organismic and communal organization. In the words of [novelist] Anais Nin, "We don't see things as they are, we see them as we are." In that sense, all our perceptions are, literally, *in*-sights, including the illusion that is hardest of all to shake—that we are able to see an independent, external reality.

Recall the Fundamental Postulate of George Kelly's (1955, p. 46) Personal Construct Theory: "A person's processes are psychologically channelized by the ways in which he anticipates events." We are always part of the equation: "There is no end to belief in meaning and reality. We thirst after them. We are natural ontologists but reluctant epistemologists" (Bruner, 1986, p. 155).

> But men may construe things after their fashion,
> Clean from the purpose of the things themselves.
> —William Shakespeare, *Julius Caesar* (Act 1, Scene 3, line 34)

We bring our "lenses" with us. As Hillman (Goulding & Hillman, 1995; see also Hubble & O'Hanlon, 1992) commented: "Your counter-transference is there long before the transference begins." O'Hanlon (O'Hanlon & Bertolino, 1999, p. 148) expounds:

> I maintain that there are no such "things" as therapy problems. I think therapists, for the most part, give their clients problems. That is, therapists negotiate problem definitions out of the raw material of clients' concerns by conversing with clients. They either come up with a problem definition that is agreeable to both client and therapist or they try to convince the client that he or she has a problem of the type the therapist says he or she has. . . .
>
> Clients do not usually decide which theory will work best for them and then seek out that kind of practitioner. They come in complaining about something, concerned about things, and the therapist helps shape those complaints into therapy problems, i.e., some problem that therapy can solve and some problems that this particular therapist with this particular approach knows how to solve.
>
> We advertently or inadvertently influence the descriptions our clients give us of their situations. We do not enter therapy neutrally, finding the "real" problem or problems. We usually only elicit or allow descriptions of problems that fit our theories, that we know how to cope with, make sense of, or solve.

This awareness only heightens our personal responsibility. Neutral "objectivity" is a myth. To borrow McBride's (1996) phrase, only God is "the color of water."[29]

There are numerous perils potentially lurking when one forgoes the safety of the positivist or objectivist shore. Beware of shoals and undercurrents. One can slide into an antiscientism or lack of standards of knowledge or critical thinking (M. A. Bernstein, 1998; Gergen, 1994c; Gross & Levitt, 1994; Held, 1995; Lazarus, 1997a; Leary, 1994; Lincoln, 1990; Lyotard, 1984; Rosenau, 1992; M. B. Smith, 1994; Woolfolk, 1992). The application of logic and rationality to shared meanings is important, lest chaos reign if we imitate the mind-boggling March Hare and Mad Hatter in Lewis Carroll's (1865/1997) *Alice in Wonderland* as they redefine terms willy-nilly. Even if more prosaic or straightforward,

> There are circumstances in which people are just wrong about what they are doing and how they are doing it. It is not that they lie . . . but that they confabulate; they fill in the gaps, guess, speculate, mistake theoretizing for observing. The relation between what they say and whatever it is that drives them to say what they say could hardly be more obscure. . . . [They] are unwitting creators of fictions, but to say that they are unwitting is to grant that what they say is, or can be, an account of exactly how it seems to them. (Dennett, 1991, quoted in Fancher, 1995, p. 1)

Others worry that we may overlook the inevitability of our influence, as well as the miserable circumstances of some individuals and families, especially amongst the poor and disadvantaged (see Woolgar & Pawluch, 1985a, 1985b). Coale (1992, p. 19) says a lot when she says, "Reframing hunger has no usefulness to poor families."[30] Fuchs and Ward (1994, p. 483) note: "The political implications of deconstruction are uncertain and controversial. There are those who think deconstruction is an ally of democratic social change, while others see deconstruction as part of a neoconservative reaction against the Enlightenment." Thus, while acknowledging "the richness that the constructivist movement contributes to our understanding of language, stories, and co-construction" (p. 10), Minuchin (1992; see also Held, 1995) argues:

> I am extremely concerned about the preservation of strengths that, I think, are vitiated by the constructivist framing [p. 5]. . . . When the constructivists equate expertise with power . . . and develop a new technology of interventions that avoid control, they are only creating a different use of power. Control does not disappear from family therapy when it is renamed "cocreation." All that happens is that the influence of the therapist on the family is made invisible. Safely underground, it may remain unexamined. Therapy is a temporary arrangement. Hierarchies are mutually organized for a period of time and for a "more or less" specific purpose. Temporary as it is, this arrangement would be a sham if the therapist were not an expert—that is, a person of informed uncertainty—on the human condition, the variety of family systems, family and individual development, processes of change, and the handling of dialogues, metaphors, and stories. . . . The bottom line is that the constructivist approach, by bracketing the idiosyncratic story, obscures the social fabric that also constructs it [pp. 7–8]. . . . Constructivist practice, with some exceptions, binds the therapist to the procrustean bed of talking and meaning, robbing the therapist of human complexity. [p. 10]

In their *Fashionable Nonsense: Postmodern Intellectuals' Abuse of Science*, Alan Sokal and Jean Bricmont (1998, pp. 274–275) debunk the pretensions of those who would attempt to gain authority by wrapping themselves in the mantle of science while, at the same time, denying the very existence of an observer-independent reality:

> Epistemological agnosticism simply won't suffice, at least not for people who aspire to make social change. Deny that non-context-dependent assertions can be true, and you don't just throw out quantum mechanics and molecular biology: you also throw out the Nazi gas chambers, the American enslavement of Africans, and the fact that today in New York it's raining. . . . [F]acts do matter, and some facts (like the first two cited here) matter a great deal.

Especially because meaning is so fluid, there are marked risks of (perhaps unknowingly) imposing one's own values. Michael Mahoney (1995;

in press) wisely cautions that the psychological demands of being a constructive psychotherapist are many and that a great degree of openness to self-examination and ambiguity is required. Accepting the validity of multiple viewpoints requires that we embrace, not erase, inevitable tensions. Writing within the context of race relations, Cornel West (1993, pp. 150–151) suggests jazz as a useful metaphor:

> I use the term "jazz" here not so much as a term for a musical art form, as for a mode of being in the world, an improvisational mode of protean, fluid, and flexible dispositions toward reality suspicious of "either/or" viewpoints, dogmatic pronouncements, or supremacist ideologies. . . . The interplay of individuality and unity is not one of uniformity and unanimity imposed from above but rather a conflict among diverse groupings that reach a dynamic consensus subject to questioning and criticism. As with a soloist in a jazz quartet, quintet, or band, individuality is promoted in order to sustain and increase the creative tension with the group—a tension that yields higher levels of performance to achieve the aim of the collective project.

There also is the danger of those who are deliberately misleading or nefarious, including actual perpetrators as well as persons who knowingly ignore or dismiss claims of individual or societal abuse (e.g., incest, the Holocaust). Hence, Frank Pittman decries those who hide behind "It's all in your mind"[31] or "That's just how *you* look at it" to justify an irresponsible "It's not my fault." He rails against anyone who would sophistically change words rather than right wrongs:

> Postmodernism entered family therapy in the form of constructivism, espousing that reality is in the eye of the beholder, and that it doesn't matter what people do, only what story they tell about it. What a breakthrough! People don't have to change what they do! They can just use different words instead! Constructivism is fun intellectual masturbation, until we notice that the world constructivism is defining away is a cruel, unsafe, unfair place that hurts real people. (Pittman, 1992, p. 58)

In addition, there is the perhaps more subtle but also pernicious practice of reducing experience to explanation (Hillman, 1975/1989), with a resultant loss of purposefulness, passion, and soul. "Text" or "narrative" are social constructions, not life:

> [T]houghts and definitions may annul one's own experiences even before they have been taken in: as, for instance, "Can this that I feel be love?" "Is it allowed?" "Is it convenient?" Ultimately, of course, such questions may have to be asked, but the fact remains—alas!—that the moment they arise, spontaneity abates. Life defined is bound to the past, no longer pouring into future. And, predictably, anyone continually knitting his life into contexts of intention, import, and clarifications of meaning will in the end find that he has lost the sense of experiencing life. (Campbell, 1972, p. 129)

Theorizing and categorizing experience can produce "petrification" (Polster, 1992, p. 144; also see Whitaker, 1982). Empathy and human relatedness can get short shrift if attention is too centered on the technologies of adjusting the calculus of cognition.

> A mind all logic is like a knife all blade.
> It makes the hand bleed that uses it.
> —Rabindarath Tagore (1861–1941)

As Cornel West (1993, p. 22) comments:

> Nihilism is to be understood here not as a philosophical doctrine that there are no rational grounds for legitimate standards or authority; it is, far more, the lived experience of coping with a life of horrifying meaninglessness, hopelessness, and (most important) lovelessness. The frightening result is a numbing detachment from others and a self-destructive disposition toward the world. Life without meaning, hope, and love breeds a cold-hearted, mean-spirited outlook that destroys both the individual and others.

The Jungian analyst Robert Moore (1994, p. 9) counsels us to take the high road:

> Is there an understandable reason why contemporary Western culture seems to be deconstructing itself into nihilism and anarchy? Careful reflection . . . can help us to understand some of the primary reasons for our deep—and contagious—disease. The culture of modernism with its attendant secularization and de-emphasis on the role of ritual in human adaptation has been dominated by the archtype of the magician and its shadow or dysfunctional forms. One might say that our culture is 'possessed' by the immature shadow-magician. When human beings use their magical potentials in the service of healing and community, the deconstructive and sociopathic energies of the immature magician—the trickster—are transformed into a mature, shamanic form that heals both self and the larger community.[32]

☐ Stories for the Good

> Liberty! Freedom! Tyrany is dead!
> Run hence, proclaim, cry it about the streets!
> —William Shakespeare, *Julius Caesar*
> (Act III, Scene 1, lines 78–79)

James Hillman (1983, p. 46) highlights the creative and healing powers within:

> I have found that the person with a sense of story built in from childhood is in better shape than one who has not had stories, who has not heard them, read them, acted them, or made them up. . . . Story coming early on puts a person into familiarity with the validity of story. One knows what

stories can do, how they can make up worlds and transpose existence into these worlds. One maintains a sense of the imaginal world, its convincingly real existence, that it is peopled, that it can be entered and left, that it is always there with its fields and palaces, its dungeons and long ships waiting. One learns that worlds are made by words and not only by hammers and wires.

C. P. Estes (1993, p. 30) also reminds us of the value of stories that open possibilities as they ensorcell:

Though none of us will live forever, the stories can. As long as one soul remains who can tell the story, and that by the recounting of the tale, the greater forces of love, mercy, generosity, and strength are continuously called into being in the world, I promise you . . . it will be enough.

Consider the constructive implications of statements such as these:

They were real to *me*. . . . Remember it's *belief* we're talking about here, and belief is the cradle of myth. I think that myth and imagination are, in fact, nearly interchangeable concepts, and that belief is the wellspring of both.
    —Stephen King (in *The New Yorker* profile, M. Singer,1998, p. 67)

I discovered I had no resentment toward my mother, as I had believed, and could remember her with the goodwill that neither of us was able to express while she was alive. I no longer had to invent a [mother] that suited my needs, and anyway, we shape our own past and build memories of many fantasies.
    —Isabel Allende (*The Infinite Plan*, 1993, p. 347)

She had indeed stepped from the road which seemed to have been chosen for her and cut herself a brand-new path....Each of us has the right and the responsibility to assess the roads which lie ahead, and those over which we have traveled, and if the future road looms ominous or unpromising, and the roads back uninviting, then we need to gather our resolve and, carrying only the necessary baggage, step off that road into another direction. If the new choice is also unpalatable, without embarrassment, we must be ready to change that as well.
    —Maya Angelou (*Wouldn't Take Nothing for My Journey Now*, 1993, p. 24)

"A warrior is aware that the world will change as soon as he stops talking to himself," he said, "and he must be prepared for that monumental jolt."
    "What do you mean, Don Juan?"
    "The world is such-and-such and so-and-so only because we tell ourselves that that is the way it is. If we stop telling ourselves that the world is so-and-so, the world will stop being so-and-so. At this moment I don't think you're ready for such a momentous blow, therefore, you must start slowly to undo the world."
    —Carlos Castaneda (*A Separate Reality: Further Conversations with Don Juan,*
    1971, p. 264)

Black Elk, a very famous Sioux Medicine Man, was asked, "Are these stories true?" He answered, "Well, I don't know if they happened exactly that way, but if you listen to them long enough, you will hear how they are true."
>   —Susan Strauss (*Coyote Stories for Children: Tales from Native Americans,* 1991, n.p.)

When you play songs, you can bring back people's memories of when they fell in love. That's where the power is.
>   —Johnny Mercer (songwriter, quoted in John Berendt, *Midnight in the Garden of Good and Evil,* 1994, p. 90)

You can't stop the waves, but you can learn to surf.
>   —Jon Kabat-Zinn (*Wherever You Go, There You Are: Mindfulness Meditation in Everyday Life,* 1994, p. 30)

Happiness lies in the endowment with value of all the things you have.
>   —Dad

>   —Milton H. Erickson (birthday card message to his daughter-in-law, Kathy Erickson, March 19, 1980; Kathy Erickson, personal communication)

Death ends a life, not a relationship.
>   —Morrie Schwartz (quoted in Mitch Albom, *Tuesdays with Morrie: A Old Man, A Young Man, and Life's Greatest Lesson,* 1997, p. 174)

☐ Two Images[33]

>   We need to reinvent ourselves continually,
>   weaving new themes in our life narratives,
>   remembering our past, revising our future,
>   reauthorizing the myth by which we live.
>   —Sam Keen (quoted in R. Simon, 1998, p. 61)

Some years ago, it was my good fortune to visit the village of Don José Rios Matsuwa, the venerable Huichol shaman, high in the Mexican Sierra Madre Mountains. While I was there, participating in the annual harvest festival, I became intrigued by the motif of a two-headed eagle with a special star-like figure in its breast that was repeated in many weavings (Figure 3.1). I inquired and was told (in Spanish and Huichol) that the figure was called *welika* (see Berrin, 1978). When I asked, "Why two heads?" I was informed, "When the heart opens, one can see the past and the other can see the future, at the same time. This is how we make our lives."[34]

More recently, I was viewing a videotape of Insoo Kim Berg (1994a; see Chapter 8, this volume) working with a married couple. On the tape, in her introduction to the session, she commented on the importance of

FIGURE 3.1. Soar like an eagle: Huichol representation of the two-headed eagle, *welika*. *Note.* From "Introduction: Some Stories Are Better than Others" by M. F. Hoyt, in M. F. Hoyt, Ed., *Constructive Therapies, Volume 2* (p. 22). New York: Guilford Press. Copyright 1996 Guilford Press. Reprinted with permission.

attending to language and the value of using a "not-knowing" (H. Anderson & Goolishian, 1992) posture in which the clients' expertise is especially respected and supported. This combined in my mind with the idea that all questions are, in effect, leading questions (Epston, 1995; Tomm, 1988). Watching Insoo work, I suddenly had the image of the compassionate Buddha (perhaps prefigured by her Asian countenance), who holds up his palm facing the viewer so as to reflect back whatever is offered. (As Levin, 1987, notes, such hand postures are called *mudras* in Buddhist iconography and embody an overall attitude and way of being.) However, I had the idea that the therapist's hand, rather than simply "reflecting and clarifying" like a flat miror à la Carl Rogers (1951),[35] was a special kind of mirror that could become convex or concave and swivel this way and that—expanding or shrinking the reflected image, opening parts of the story and closing others! Isn't this what (constructive) therapists do? Questions draw interest here or there, inviting one to focus attention and consciousness in (it may be hoped) more helpful ways.

One might speak of "panning for gold" (Wylie, 1994a) and finding and expanding a "unique outcome" or "sparkling moment"; or one might think of these gems as "exceptions" and "symptoms of solutions" (S. D. Miller, 1992). Myriad images are possible, of course. Furman and Ahola (1992b), for example, refer to "latent joy." Perhaps we are photographic processors trying to bring forth a latent image with our special developing bath (Greenleaf, 1994, p. 253); if that metaphor is appealing, it is good to remember the words of Richard Avedon (1994, p. 9): "All photographs are accurate. None of them is the truth." If a picture is worth a thousand words, this image suggests that, with skillful inquiry, parts of the picture can be elided or contracted into a mere mote, or perhaps can be expanded into the gateway to a new life story.

☐ R.S.V.P.

Dear Reader,
   Suppose tonight, while you are sleeping, a miracle occurs . . . and when you awaken tomorrow, you find that you're an even more constructive therapist than before! How will your story about how therapy works be different, and how will that affect your clients—and how will they affect you? What will be the first thing you (and your clients) notice? And then what? What might you "see" when you try some new "lenses"? How will your thinking get stretched? What bright ideas, new methods, and interesting conversations will you and your clients be delighted to have?

Paralleling the processes of constructive therapies, each person takes his or her own (multiple) meanings. This is not a new idea:

Each era has a predominant configuration of the self, a particular foundational set of beliefs about what it means to be human. Each particular configuration of the self brings with it characteristic illnesses, local healers, and local healing technologies. These selves and roles are not interchangeable or equivalent. Each embodies a kind of unique and local truth that should not be reduced to a universal law, because such reductions inevitably depend on a particular cultural frame of reference, which in turn inevitably involves an ideological agenda. (Cushman, 1995, p. 3)

Zen Master Rinzai warned his students several centuries ago: "All I am talking about is only medicine appropriate for curing specific ailments. In my talks there is nothing absolutely real" (quoted in Schloegl, 1976, p. 48). The Native American teacher, Rolling Thunder (quoted in Boyd, 1974, p. 92), also advised:

I want to warn you not to copy me, but to work out your own method. Our people tell us to be original. If you can watch the method, though, and the way I go about it, maybe that would give you some thoughts about what to follow, what it's all about. Then you work out your own substance, your own songs, your own prayers and things to go with it.

   I encourage readers to be receptive and generative, to apply their own insights and experience, to learn more than is printed, and to find ways to help clients change their stories in ways that bring them more of what the clients prefer.

☐ Notes

[1]Modern mass media make this feedback loop all the quicker. An article in *Newsweek* (Cowley & Springen, 1995) entitled "Rewriting Life Stories" not only heralded the narrative therapy approach, but also directed public consciousness toward a different way of thinking, with large type (p. 70) declaring, "Instead of looking for flaws in people's psyches, 'narrative therapy' works at nurturing their forgotten strengths." This is part of the "technology of saturation" described by Gergen (1991).

[2]As Campbell (1972) wrote in *Myths to Live By*, archtypal stories instruct and inspire as they pass from generation to generation. In books such as Robert Bly's (1990) *Iron John*, Allan Chinen's (1992) *Once Upon a Midlife*, Jean Shinoda Bolen's *Goddesses in Everywoman* (1984) and *Gods in Everyman* (1989), and Bly and Marion Woodman's (1998) *The Maiden King: The Reunion of Masculine and Feminine*, to name but a few from the Jungian fount, stories are recast and retold and new myths evolve and emerge to fit the times, mirroring and illuminating important social developments (changing roles for women and men, the aging population, the growth of technology, and so forth).

[3]As Hillman (1983, p. 18) noted, therapists also tend to do this: "We miss a lot of what we could be doing. Our ways of narration are limited to four kinds: epic, comic, detective, social realism. We take what comes—no matter how passionate and erotic, how tragic and noble, how freakish and arbitrary—and turn it all into one of our four modes."

Serving as a kind of Linnaeus of tormented tales as well as a cartographer of routes to territories less twisted, Gustafson (1992, 1995a, 1995b; see also McGoldrick, 1995; Omer, 1994; Omer & Alon, 1997; Roberts, 1994; Sluzki, 1992; Sternberg, 1998) presents numerous interesting nosologies. He situates the main stories of helping within the first world of objectivity, the second world of subjectivity, and the third world of narrative; he then categorizes (with many variations and nuances) the main stories of persons on fields of power into those having to do with subservience, bureaucratic delay, and overpowering. I particularly like Gustafson's description (1992, p. 76) of the themes of marital conflict: "The first dilemma is whether to be in or out. The second is whether to be top or bottom. The third is whether to be near or far." To which I might add: "A fourth is whether to be hot or cold."

[4]To cite one example, the *customer, complainant,* and *visitor* distinctions made in solution-focused therapy (see de Shazer, 1988, pp. 85–90) refer more to therapist-client *relationship* patterns than to individuals. The use of terms like *cooperation* and *fit* imply that *system, connection,* and *context* are the units of analysis.

[5]Something about the (non)essence of the discussion of *first-order* and *second-order* levels of reality seemed to be captured in a theater production I once saw of *Robin Hood.* Two characters were wandering in Sherwood Forest (quoted in Watzlawick & Hoyt, 1998, p. 190):

First Character: *Where are we on the map?*

Second Character: *We're not on the map; we're in the forest!*

[6]Hence, my protoconstructivist *bubbe* (grandmother) was on to something when she asked, "A Ph.D.? So what kind of disease is philosophy that it needs a doctor?" (Hoyt, 1994a, p. 77).

[7]While usually referring especially to trance phenomena when discussing *utilization* (see de Shazer, in Short, 1997, p. 19; Gilligan, 1987; Goldfield, 1994), Milton Erickson (1980a, p. 540) prefigured much when he recommended

the fullest possible utilization of the functional capacities and abilities and the experiential and acquisitional learnings of the patient. These should take precedence over the teaching of new ways in living which are developed from the therapist's possibly incomplete understanding of what may be right and serviceable to the individual concerned.

[8]It should be noted, however, that while there is much to recommend Held's (1995) cogent book, her repeated characterization of the work of Steve de Shazer and Michael White (among others) as "antirealist," which would seem to imply a disregard for the actualities of clients' lives, is very much at variance with my experience of their practices based on numerous direct observations and conversations (see Hoyt, Miller, Held & Matthews, in press). White himself (in White, Hoyt, & Zimmerman, 2000) has commented:

> In the literature I have read accounts of my thought and practices that represent me as "anti-realist," despite the fact that I have little sympathy for what is proposed in this tradition, and despite the fact that I believe the realist/anti-realist debate to be irrelevent to what I know of poststructuralist inquiry and narrative practice.

[9]Deconstruction of the very terms *patient, client, doctor, therapist, clinician* (and such related terms as *therapy, treatment, intervention, consultation, conversation*) reveals implicit and powerful assumptions about the process, its purpose(s), and the roles of the participants (see Hoyt, 1979/1995c, 1985/1995e; Chapter 5, this volume). Workers in medical and managed care settings tend toward the traditional term *patient*, although most constructive therapists seem to prefer the term *client* to emphasize the egalitarian and minimize the medical connotation of sickness or pathology and the doctor–patient hierarchy. Whatever one calls the participants and the process helps to establish a meaning context (frame) and influences their work together.

[10]Somewhere in the basement of time, around 1930, Rabindranath Tagore and Albert Einstein met and had a fascinating conversation about the nature of reality (see Chakravarty, 1961, pp. 110–113). Einstein began by asking the great Indian poet and religionist if he believed there was a Divine isolated from the world. When Tagore asserted that beauty and truth were human bound, Einstein allowed that beauty was, but contended, "I cannot prove scientifically that truth must be conceived as a truth that is valid independent of humanity; but I believe it firmly." Realizing that belief in a truth independent of human consciousness was an unprovable act of faith, at the end of their colloquy Einstein concluded: "Then I am more religious than you are!"

For an interesting discussion of how modern scientists grapple with subjectivity and the limits of knowledge, see Horgan (1996).

[11]Following Wallace Steven's poem, "Thirteen Ways of Looking at a Blackbird," Shafarman (1996, p. 25) described "Thirteen Ways of Looking at How a Poet and a Therapist are One":

> 1. The ability to sustain accurate attention. 2. The power to use language and the silences that surround language as the medium of change. 3. The vision to perceive the possibility of transformation that rests within the next moment. 4. Experience with subtle transitions that guide one towards skillful beginnings and appropriate endings. 5. The development of a skilled intelligence that can shape what is emerging into a communicable form. 6. The ability to speak, act, and witness truth with compassion. 7. An appreciation of the power of pacing, time, and rhythm in choreographing change. 8. A respect for the capacity of form to contain and transmute suffering into wisdom. 9. A regard for lineages and the power of our ancestors. 10. Skills that inspire humor, growth, and play. 11. A recognition of the beauty of form—and the need to judiciously break form. 12. The creation of something that endures over time. 13. A sense of the mystery that exists within the ordinary acts of everyday life.

[12]Susan Sontag (1964, p. 5) quotes Nietzsche: "There are no facts, only interpretations." A related view was expressed by W. T. Anderson (1990, p. 3) in his aptly named book, *Reality Isn't What It Used to Be: Theatrical Politics, Ready-to-Wear Religion, Global Myths, Primitive Chic, and Other Wonders of the Postmodern World*: "If there is anything we have plenty of, it is belief systems. But we also have something else: a growing suspicion that all belief systems—all ideas about human reality—are social constructions. This is a story about stories, a belief about beliefs."

[13]Hence, with twisted tongue in cheek, Berger and Kellner (1979, p. 308) wrote: "Not being convinced, however, that theoretical lucidity is necessarily enhanced by terminological ponderosity, we shall avoid as much as possible the use of the sort of jargon for which both sociologists and phenomenologists have acquired dubious notoriety."

[14]The use of the term *languaging* as a gerund (as in H. Anderson and Goolishian, 1988; Maturana, 1988) emphasizes both the activity of language and the power of The Word to give shape to being. Thus, in *The Jerusalem Bible* (Evans, 1966) story of *Genesis 1:3*, "God said, 'Let there be light,' and there was light"; and, as Shlain (1998, p. 84) notes, God's first instruction to Adam (Genesis 2:20) was to give names to the animals. Being as a process more than an event, an activity more than an entity, is highlighted in book titles such as Buckminster Fuller's (1970) *I Seem to Be a Verb* and O'Hanlon and Hudson's (1995) *Love Is a Verb*. If Rene Decartes (1637, *Le Discours de la Methode*) wrote "I think, therefore I am," and Professor Higgins' motto (in G. B. Shaw's 1913/1967 *Pygmalion*) was "Speak that I may know you," the social constructionist might say, "Speak that we may be."

[15]Several writers (see Abram, 1996; Eisler, 1987; Gimbutas, 1989; Jaynes, 1990) have suggested that a major shift in consciousness occurred in the mists of early history. In his recent book, *The Alphabet Versus the Goddess: The Conflict Between Word and Image*, Leonard Shlain (1998; see also Illich & Sanders, 1988) argues that the advent of literacy, the process of reading itself, fundamentally influenced brain anatomy and function, with far-reaching consequences including how "the story" is conceived and told (and who tells it).

[16]Gregory Bateson (1972a, p. 272) made a similar observation. This also is reminiscent of the statement quoted below (on page 43) from Saint Augustine's *Confessions*. The present-centered construction of all time may also have inspired the famous opening lines of T. S. Eliot's (1943a, p. 13) "Burnt Norton":

Time present and time past
Are both perhaps present in time future
And time future contained in time past.

There is no time but the present; or, as C. S. Lewis described it in *The Screwtape Letters* (1941/1982, pp. 80–81), the present is where time and eternity meet. "[T]ime is the moving image of eternity" Joseph Campbell (1972, p. 164) quotes Plato from the *Timaeus*. "Time is the substance I am made of" is the way Jorge Luis Borges (1964, p. 234) put it. How we experience time varies. As Marcel Proust wrote in *Remembrance of Things Past* (1919/1981): "The time which we have at our disposal everyday is elastic; the passions that we feel expand it, those that we inspire contract it; and habit fills up the rest." Eric Berne (1972, p. 205), the originator of transactional analysis, observed many people organizing their life story in terms of an approach to time:

Winning or losing, the script is a way to structure the time between the first Hello at mother's breast and the last Good-bye at the grave. This life time is emptied and filled by not doing and doing; by never doing, always doing, not doing before, not doing after, doing over and over, and doing until there is nothing left to do. This gives rise to "Never" and "Always," "Until" and "After," "Over and Over," and "Open-Ended" scripts.

For other perspectives on time and therapy, see Boscolo and Bertrando (1993), Hoyt (1990/1995g), Hoyt and Miller (Chapter 14, this volume), Melges (1982), and Ricoeur (1983).

[17]I am grateful to John Italia (personal communication, 2000) for calling my attention to the long Robert Browning (1868/1989) poem, as well as to this passage from *Moby Dick: Or, the Whale*, wherein Herman Melville (1851/1979, pp. 443–445) has a character say:

> Book! You lie there; the fact is, you books must know your places. You'll do to give us the bare words and facts, but we come in to supply the thoughts. . . . There's another rendering now; but still one text. . . . I look, you look, he looks; we look, ye look, they look.

As Italia also noted in his discussion with me, projective psychological testing (Rorschach, Thematic Apperception Text, etc.) is designed to explore how each individual manifests the ubiquitous phenomenon of meaning–making.

[18]Two examples of calling on the past for useful constructions:

1. a patient of mine, a former fashion model who over a decade has become severely afflicted by multiple sclerosis (bed bound, incontinent, barely able to speak) sent me a holiday card with the following inscription (she had an attendant write it): "Memory is what God gave us that we might have roses in December";

2. in the powerful scene near the end of the film *Amistad*, when facing what could be the daunting challenge of appearing before a biased U.S. Supreme Court, the African leader Cinque declares: "We won't be going in there alone . . . I meant my ancestors. I will call into the past, far back to the beginning of time, and beg them to come and help me at the judgment. I will reach back and draw them into me; and they must come, for at this moment I am the whole reason they have existed at all."

[19]While it may be true, as Shakespeare wrote, that "a rose by any other name would smell as sweet" (*Romeo and Juliet*, Act II, Scene 2, lines 43–44), in the world of meaning we are socially constructing *sense*, not *scents*. Thus, Weakland (1991, p. viii) questioned de Shazer's usage, asking "Does not 'misreading' itself imply the existence of some 'correct' reading, rather then simply saying that messages always and necessarily are *interpreted*?" Hoyt (1996a, pp. 347–348) similarly questioned Gergen about his use of the term "*perversity*" rather than "*diversity*," the former implying a deviance from a "normal" or "right" way.

[20]At another point on the same videotape, *Milton H. Erickson, M.D.: Explorer in Hypnosis and Therapy*, a dog barks in the background while a woman is recounting her experiences with Erickson. It seems incidental, until one recognizes the naturalistic style and human context of Erickson's approach. The work is done in life, as part of life. Along the same vein, writer-photographer Will Baker (1983, p. 262) remarked on his two attempted encounters with conventional psychiatry during times of despair:

> Both times, and only those times, I had gone to see the shaman of my own culture, the psychiatrist. I learned, this past night [spent around the fire with Indian friends], what had been missing from those sessions—which I very soon abandoned—missing from those offices with their polished wood, filing cabinets, soft lighting and black leather. There was nothing to drink. There was no singing. There was no ring of honest old friends with a yen to talk. There were no small boys to occupy the lap, or to tickle the feet.

[21]As Anne Lamott (1994, p. 178) noted, "If your wife locks you out of the house, you don't have a problem with your door." Assuming that there is an underlying unitary reality, however, be it historical or psychological, that needs to be recaptured or restored (what White, 1992a, refers to as the "essentialist project"), may lead to characterizations of reauthoring as "defensive distortions" (see Freud, 1937/1964a, and 1939/1964c especially pp. 127–132) or "switching maneuvers" and "sliding meanings" (Horowitz, 1976). This is complicated, of course, but there are realities outside the individual and it would be inauthentic and disingenuous "to escape from history and enter the vast playground of myth" (O'Toole, 1998–1999, p. 97) by simply ignoring or fabricating as one finds convenient.

Even in the most dire of circumstances, one may still have some choice regarding how to construe one's experience, as Victor Frankl (1963) illustrated so well in *Man's Search for Meaning: An Introduction to Logotherapy*, his personal account of experiences in a World War II Nazi concentration camp. This also may have been an intended meaning in the recent film, *Life is Beautiful*, although the repeated insertion of slapstick comedy and the downplaying of the prolonged horror (in his *Family Therapy Networker* review, Frank Pittman [1999, pp. 74], called it a "sugar-coated Holocaust") left me feeling manipulated and aggravated.

[22]In *The Wisdom of the Zen Masters*, Irmgard Schloegl (1976, p. 78) recounts: "A monk asked of Master Sosan: 'Please sprinkle the compassion of your teaching so that I may be liberated.' 'Who has put you under restraint?' asked the Master. 'No one.' Master Sosan said: 'Why then do you ask to be liberated?' At this, the monk awakened fully.'"

[23]Art criticism and literary criticism have yielded fertile ground for variegated development of this concept. As Bennington (1989, p. 84) expounds:
1. Deconstruction is not what you think.
. . . .
1.3 Deconstruction is not what you think. If what you think is a content, present to mind, in "the mind's presence-room" (Locke). But that you think might already be Deconstruction.
2. Deconstruction is not (what you think if you think it is) essentially to do with language.
2.1 Nothing more common than to hear Deconstruction described as depending on "an extension of the linguistic paradigm." "There is nothing outside the text" (Derrida): proves it, obviously.
2.1.1 Everyone also knows this is not quite right. "Text" is not quite an extension of a familiar concept, but a displacement or reinscription of it. Text in general is any system of marks, traces, referrals (don't say reference, have a little more sense than that). Perception is a text.

[24]de Shazer (1991a, p. 50) noted that "destruction," not "deconstruction," is the opposite of "construction"; and Shawver (1996, p. 383) commented that the similarity between the sound of "destruction" and "deconstruction" unfortunately may lead some critics to mistakenly assume that postmodernism is a philosophy of despair and nihilism when, "from another perspective, deconstruction is a way of freeing ourselves from the trap of ineffective language patterns." Fuchs and Ward (1994, p. 481) noted that

> As with "postmodernism," there is much confusion and uncertainty about the main message of deconstructionism. . . . [T]he situation comes to exemplify one of deconstructionism's main points: there are no firm "principles" and "doctrines" that could produce some stable and lasting order in the boomin' and buzzin' noise that is reality. More specifically, deconstructionism is skeptical about what it perceives as the universal foundations of modern culture—rationality, emancipation, autonomy, and progress.

[25]Constructive therapists truly respect their clients' own capacities. Hence, H. Anderson and Goolishian (1992) write of "the client as expert"; Lipchik (1994) describes solution focus as a basic attitude or orientation rather than a set of techniques; and Michael White (Wylie, 1994a) is noted for his "congruence" rather than harboring a privately disrespectful view that would put words into clients while elevating therapist authority. Similarly, Gergen (1994b) and Tomm (1990) reveal some of the many ways therapists have developed a clinical language that reinforces and disseminates deficit; and de Shazer and Weakland (quoted in Hoyt, 1994b, p. 20) commented that the activity of many professionals is "not a mental health industry; it's a mental illness industry." (For an antipathologizing exercise, see Dickerson & Zimmerman, 1995.) A fundamentally healthy attitude was expressed by

Carl Rogers (quoted in Satir, 1993, p. 75) when he declared: "What I am is good enough if I would only be it openly."

[26]See Duncan, Hubble, & Rusk, 1994; Goolishian and Anderson, 1992; Nichols, 1993. To my mind, London (1964, pp. 14–15) finessed the argument long ago:

> Either therapists can successfully influence behavior or they cannot, and they have little choice of what to claim. If they wish to say that they cannot do so, or may not do so in just those areas where human concern is greatest, and are therefore not at all responsible for the behavior of their clients, one must ask what right they have to be in business.

Others have made similar arguments.

[27]Constructive therapies also can extend to the use of psychopharmacological intervention. *Restoring restorying* is the term I prefer for the appropriate use of medication to support clients' self-empowerment. While there is great room for abuse (mind control), there also are patients for whom medication may allow thinking to focus and mood to abate enough for them to get on with the "reauthoring" and living of their lives. I am not in agreement with those who would not offer or suggest medication if the client had not first brought it up, anymore than I would ignore or abstain from mentioning alternatives to oppressive social circumstances if these situations were apparent. This may be part of our expertise that we can bring to the clients' service. People sometimes need input (information). What will be most important, of course, is full respect for informed consent, with invitation, not imposition, being the key.

[28]Gergen commented (in Hoyt, 1996c, pp. 364–365):

> As we move in this constructionist and narrational direction, we sometimes fix on the words as ends in themselves. We try as therapists to generate a new sense of meaning, new narratives, new constructions, as if a new set of words would "do the trick." In fact, I tend to talk that way myself at times. However, this is to miss the ultimate concern, which is relatedness itself—out of which meanings are generated. In effect, relations precede meaning . . . we might develop a sense of ourselves as fully immersed in relatedness—with all humanity, all that is given— and that we might conceive of this awesome sensibility of pure relatedness (itself born of relationship) as approaching what we might mean by the domain of the spiritual.

[29]Lyddon and Bradford (1995) noted how trainees' personal philosophical beliefs influence their preferences for different therapy approaches. In an *American Psychologist* article, Madigan, Johnson, and Linton (1995) also noted that how we are trained to tell the story (i.e., the forms we learn to follow in professional writing) teaches us how to think and thus inculcates a particular viewpoint, which in turn shapes what we see and report, and so forth. Lest we think that "scientific" writing is exempt from subjective influences, Stephen Jay Gould (1987, p. 85) cautioned:

> Scientific papers are polite or self-serving fictions in their statements about doing science; they are, at best, logical reconstructions after the fact, written under the conceit that fact and argument shape conclusions by their own inexorable demands of reasons. Levels of interacting complexity, contradictory motives, thoughts that lie too deep for either tears or even self-recognition—all combine to shape this most complex style of human knowledge.

[30]This is an apparent allusion to Gandhi's famous statement, "God comes to the hungry in the form of food." On a lighter note, in *Love's Labor's Lost* (Shakespeare, Act V, Scene 3, lines 39–41), Avon's Bard doth wrote:

> I marvel thy master hath not eaten

thee for a word, for thou art not so
long by the head as honorificabilitudinitatibus.

[31]Like the proverbial Zen teacher who whacks you and says, "Is that real?" the all-in-your-mind view has never really recovered from the kick it received from Samuel Johnson more than two centuries ago:

> After we came out of the church, we stood talking for some time together of Bishop Berkeley's ingenious sophistry to prove the non-existence of matter, and that everything in the universe is merely ideal. I observed, that though we are satisfied his doctrine is not true, it is impossible to refute it. I never shall forget the alacrity with which Johnson answered, striking his foot with mighty force against a large stone, till he rebounded from it, "I refute it *thus!*" (Boswell, 1791/1980, p. 333).

Or, as Woody Allen (quoted in Lahr, 1996, p. 70) once joked, "I hate reality, but, you know, where else can you get a good steak dinner?"

[32]Halifax (1993, p. 148) also described the "deep interconnectedness" of traditional peoples as a corrective to the dualistic view of reality often dominant in contemporaneous constructions:

> The wisdom of the peoples of elder cultures can make an important contribution to the postmodern world, one that we must begin to accept as the crisis of self, society, and the environment deepens. This wisdom cannot be told, but it is to be found by each of us in the direct experience of silence, stillness, solitude, simplicity, ceremony, and vision.

But how "real" is "real"? How "natural" is "nature"? (Pollan, 1991)? Is it ersatz if media mediate? In *The Age of Missing Information,* McKibben (1992) reported an interesting experiment in which he compared what is experienced over 24 hours sitting in nature with what is experienced over the same 24 hours in front of a television. In *The Spell of the Sensuous,* Abram (1996) eloquently described the disconnection of the body from the natural world. In *Life the Movie,* Gabler (1998) further explored the infiltration of pop culture entertainment values into our sense of reality.

[33]"Imagine," as John Lennon (1971) said.

[34]I am reminded of the lines W. H. Auden (1939/1989, p. 92) wrote about Freud after he died:

> All that he did was to remember
> Like the old and be honest like children.

[35]Even Roger's "mirror" was not so flat: All therapists select (consciously or not) what to attend to, what to highlight (by inquiry, interpretation, reinforcement, etc.) or to ignore, what to "privilege" and what not (see Hare-Mustin, 1992, 1994; Rorty, 1979). Even if the therapist remained somehow "blank" or only gave grunts on a random schedule, the client would still be in the position of deciding what meanings to attribute to these events. And, the therapist would concurrently and sequentially respond in kind, and so on and so on. Hence, the therapeutic reality is cocreated; we cannot *not* communicate.

CHAPTER

Likely Future Trends and Attendant Ethical Concerns Regarding Managed Mental Health Care

Meno: "What is good and what is not good?"
Socrates: "Need we anyone to tell us this?"
—Plato *(c. 428–348 B.C.E.) The Dialogues: Meno*

Compassion is what makes our lives meaningful.
It is the source of all lasting happiness and joy.
And it is the foundation of a good heart, the heart
of one who acts out of a desire to help others.
Through kindness, through affection, through
honesty, through truth and justice toward all
others we ensure our own benefit. This is not a
matter for complicated theorizing. It is a matter
of common sense. . . . [W]e can reject everything
else: religion, ideology, all received wisdom. But
we cannot escape the necessity of love and
compassion.
—His Holiness the Dalai Lama (1999), *Ethics for a New Millenneum*

Part of the material in this chapter was presented under the title, *Brief Therapy and Managed Care: Prospects for the Future*, as the First Annual Continuing Education Distinguished Speaker Seminar at the American Psychological Association annual convention in Chicago, August 1997. Additional material was presented as part of a panel, *Brief Therapy and Managed Care*, at the "Brief Therapy: Lasting Impressions Conference" sponsored by the Milton H. Erickson Foundation in New York, August 1998. Other panelists were Simon Budman, Nicholas Cummings, and James Prochaska.

We have seen the extraordinary growth of managed care, which may be defined as various "arrangements that regulate the utilization, site, and costs of services. . . . [in which] the nature and length of mental health treatment is determined partially by parties (insurers and reviewers) other than the clinician and patient/client" (Hoyt, 1995a, p. 1). From humble beginnings in the first years after 1900 involving collectives of loggers in the Northwest and Cuban-émigré cigar makers in Florida, through the nascency of the Loos-Atkins Clinic in Los Angeles during the 1920s and the advent of the Kaiser Permanente medical program in the late 1930s and 1940s (Henricks, 1993; Smillie, 1991), early prepaid insurance and not-for-profit health maintenance organizations (HMOs) were established to provide fixed-cost services for the masses.[1] Many of the patient-subscribers (often union members) and many of the health care providers in these plans joined as part of their social commitment to quality care through cooperative efforts.

In the past two decades, there has been an incursion of for-profit plans into the marketplace. They have emerged, often opportunistically, in response to the escalation of health care costs. There has been a conversion (some would say a *sub*version) of the early HMO ideals into business arrangements driven by the bottom line—a monetarization of motive that M. J. Bennett (1988) referred to as "the greening of the HMO." Many therapists have found this shift demoralizing and discouraging, a "bitter pill" (Lipp, 1980), and attribute at least some of their sense of despair and "burnout" to "developments in service delivery that are being increasingly dictated by the economics of the 'free' marketplace, not by what might be in the best interests of persons according to criteria that are important to them" (White, 1997, p. vi). Increasingly, clinicians are being required to practice "with one eye on economic indicators; measurements of productivity and cost compete with, and sometimes threaten to overshadow, the experience of working intimately in the service of a human being in pain" (Rosenbaum, 1998, p. x; see also Phelps, Eisman, & Kohout, 1998).[2] As the poet David Whyte (1994, p. 7) has cautioned, if these trends continue, corporations "will be forced to rely on expensive management pyramids to manipulate their workers at the price of commitment. Adaptability and native creativity on the part of the workforce come through the door only with their passions. Their passions come only with their souls. Their souls love the hidden springs boiling and welling at the center of existence more than they love the company."

Entrepreneurship has ascended.[3] While large-scale surveys of different HMOs still place the quality ratings of not-for-profit organizations above those of the for-profits ("America's Top HMOs," 1997; "Best HMOs," 1998; "How Good Is Your Health Plan?" 1996; "How HMOs Measure Up," 1999, Himmelstein, Woolhandler, Hellander, & Wolfe, 1999), the not-for-profits have responded to the competition in necessary and sometimes not-so-flattering imitation by various belt-tightening and cost-cutting measures (see Zinser, 1997). Throughout American health care delivery, including mental health care, both for-profit and not-for-profit HMOs and related managed care schemes have expanded exponentially and now cover approximately 150 million people, while traditional indemnity insurance correspondingly has dwindled.

The economic imperative has provided an environmental pressure that has opened new evolutionary niches. There have been greatly increased pressures for efficacy, efficiency, and accountability—trends that have been paralleled in many facets of modern economic and fiscal life. We have had to work smarter, not just harder; the alternative has been to do less of the same. Innovativeness has been rewarded. In the area of mental health services, eight features have characterized evolving approaches to managed behavioral health care: specific problem solving, rapid response and early intervention, clear definition of patient and therapist responsibilities, flexible and creative use of time, interdisciplinary cooperation, multiple treatment formats and modalities, intermittent treatment or a "family practitioner" model, and an overriding orientation toward results and accountability (Austad & Hoyt, 1992/1995; Hoyt & Austad, 1992; see Chapter 5, this volume). While some companies have tried to take the "high road" of assuring quality, the overriding raison d'être has been the control and reduction of costs associated with providing clinical services.

☐ The Drive for Cost Containment

As managed care has developed, different mechanisms have been used to contain costs. As seen in Table 4.1, these have focused on ways to reduce utilization (the number of sessions) and ways to control the price per session. All of these mechanisms are, by definition, designed to effect clinical practice by introducing outside (beyond client and clinician) influences, and all are subject to various ethical strains. Two of the most significant, each designed to limit the cost of services, are the continued insurgence of (1) *capitation* and (2) *case-rate* arrangements. Under capitation, a purchaser's cost is fixed (predetermined) by establishing prepayment for a list of contracted potential services. Payment is pre-set, administrators negotiating "per member per month" ("pm-pm") capitation rates that determine how much a company will get "per capita" for covering a set or catchment of "insured lives." Getting paid "up front" has resulted in insurers needing to calculate and bid carefully, since they may be assuming considerable risk and potential liability (see Crispin, 1999; Zieman, 1995)—some of which may be passed on to providers and to the patient-

---

TABLE 4.1. Total Costs = Units × Price

Primary mechanisms to reduce utilization

  A. Pretreatment authorization (certification);
  B. Carefully delimited range of what (diagnoses and treatment length) is covered;
  C. Concurrent utilization review, allowing piecemeal strictly limited numbers of additional sessions;
  D. Benefit plans designed to provide financial incentives or constraints to receive care from "efficient" providers;
  E. Copayments, increasing requirements for greater employee-user cost sharing.

Primary mechanisms to control price

  A. Capitated payments for a defined group of beneficiaries;
  B. Lower fee-for-service payments to "preferred providers";
  C. Case-rates, prospective fixed payments for diagnostic related groups (DRGs);
  D. Claims review;
  E. Insurance coverage extended to less expensive but supposedly equally (or at least adequately) effective treatment alternatives (e.g., groups, medications).

---

recipients themselves via strategies such as patient co-payments and the withholding of some therapist payments until end-of-the-year profits are calculated and assured (see Clay, 1998a; Hall, 1994a, 1994b; Stone, 1995). The fewer sessions the company authorizes and actually provides, the more it keeps as profits, so there is an inherent pressure toward undertreatment. Berwick (1996, p. 1227) sees both the potential benefits and the potential dangers:

> Capitation and decapitation have nothing to do with each other, but you could hardly tell the difference when observing the intense debate over the value and risks of capitation in health care payment.[4] Those who favor capitation seem to regard it as the sine qua non of effective containment of health care costs; those who oppose it suggest that it will spell nothing less than the end of medicine's commitment to patient advocacy and the Hippocratic oath. Meanwhile, health care coverage for more and more Americans is paid for in this way.

Under case-rate arrangements, therapist-providers agree to accept a certain fixed payment for the treatment of a particular case. Here, the managed care company's risk is fixed. For example, in exchange for a fee of $400, a therapist may agree to assume responsibility for the care of a patient diagnosed with panic disorder. If the therapist is able to resolve the patient's problems in four to five sessions, she or he realizes an effective payment of $100–$80 per session. If it turns out, however, that 20 sessions are required, the therapist makes only $20 per session—or may be liable for continuous care if the patient's problems are not resolved (again, especially see Hall, 1994a, 1994b)—a situation fraught with possibilities of countertransference resentment, acting out, and so forth. With the managed care organization absolved of all fiscal responsibility (except for the therapist's fixed payment), the brunt falls squarely upon the therapist. Of course, if only one session is required, the therapist realizes a small bonanza ($400 per hour!), but this also may be fraught with ethical strains, such as very strong temptations to curtail treatment prematurely (especially if there are other cases that are "lagging") and may yield the unseemly appearance of getting paid excessively for *not* seeing the patient. Particularly egregious situations may arise if a managed care company combines capitation arrangements with purchasers and case-rate arrangements with providers—it may appear as a "double-dip," so to speak, the contractually limited extent of services not being honored but actually being further limited in the agreement with the treating therapist.[5]

☐ Likely Trends

As well as developments in the areas of psychotherapy and psychopharmacology, there have been various administrative and structural changes directed primarily toward the containment of costs. The "macro" trends outlined in *Brief Therapy and Managed Care: Readings for Contemporary Practice* (Hoyt, 1995a) have continued and intensified:

1. *More outcomes measurement,* particularly assessment of resolution of the presenting complaint and determination of patient satisfaction. Quality improvement requires evaluation of results, with the various problems of who determines what is to be valued and how it is to be measured. This intrinsically impacts clinical performance as well as provides information on which business (purchasing) decisions will be based.
2. *More treatment planning* (see Goodman, Brown, & Deitz, 1992; Jongsma & Peterson, 1995; Jongsma, Peterson, & McInnis, 1996; Sauber, 1997; Seligman, 1998) and more attention to differential therapeutics and the integration of techniques drawn from varying theoretical backgrounds (see Prochaska & DiClemente, 1984; Prochaska, DiClemente, & Norcross, 1992), asking "What would be the best approach with this patient with this problem in this setting at this time?"
3. *Greater involvement of mental-health services in primary care,* based partly on fuller recognition of the connection between physical and mental well-being that was demonstrated by the many studies showing unnecessary medical utilization to be reduced when emotional and psychological issues are addressed professionally. This "medical utiliza-

tion offset phenomenon," which N. A. Cummings (1991a, 2000; N. A. Cummings and Follette, 1976; Follette & Cummings, 1967, 1991; see also N. A. Cummings & Sayama, 1995; Fraser, 1996, 1998; Georgoulakis, 1998; I. J. Miller, 1998; B. Miller & Farber, 1996; Mumford & Schlesinger, 1987; Mumford, Schlesinger, Glass, Patrick, & Cuerdon, 1984) first researched at Kaiser Permanente, is part of the current surge of interest in "mind-body" approaches (see Blount, 1998; Strosahl, 1994) that help "carve-in"[6] or "horizontally integrate" (N. A. Cummings, Cummings, & Johnson, 1997) psychology into the general medical enterprise, a strategy that has been recommended (N. A. Cummings, 1986, 1988, 1995; N. A. Cummings, Pallak, & Cummings, 1996; N. A. Cummings et al., 1997; Hersch, 1995) for the survival of psychological practice.

4. *Increasingly organized, vertically integrated systems of care,* the ideal being that the patient could move as needed to the appropriate level of care (outpatient, intensive outpatient, partial hospitalization, inpatient; individual, group, family; regular, episodic-intermittent, or continuous).

5. *Fewer and larger managed care companies,* consolidations and mergers incorporating smaller firms as we move toward national (or international) entities.

6. *More group practices and fewer solo practitioners,* with therapists joining existing multidisciplinary organizations or forming new ones (see Budman & Steenbarger, 1997).

7. *More care provided by masters-level clinicians, psychiatric nurses, and various certified counselors,* in keeping with the managed care cost-saving principle of having the least expensive workers do most of the labor.

8. *More group therapy,* including more psychoeducational programs on a variety of topics (e.g., stress reduction, parenting skills, communication training for couples), which will require administrative and financial support to make group referrals available and attractive (see Budman, Simeone, Reilly, & Demby, 1994; Hoyt, 1995h; MacKenzie, 1994; Norcross, Alford, & DeMichele, 1992; Steenbarger & Bulman, 1996). As Spitz (1996, p. x) has wrote: "There will be a 'marriage,' albeit in some cases an arranged marriage, between the requirements, regulations, and restrictions imposed by managed care and the technical flexibility, facility with time adjustments, and ability to reach almost any patient population that group therapy provides."

9. *Much less inpatient care,* with what there is mostly emphasizing rapid stabilization and return to the community as soon as possible (see Sabin, 1995; Schuster, 1995).

10. *Greater reliance on computer technology,* for both *telehealth* (the use of telecommunications to provide information and treatment across

distances, including interactive on-line services—see Nickelson, 1998; Stamm, 1998) and *data processing and research*, with both various advantages as well as heightened risks to privacy and confidentiality (see N. A. Cummings, 1999; Hoyt, 1999; L'Abate, 1999).

11. *Less utilization review*, at least in the outpatient arena, as education, certification, and credentialing of efficient providers moves forward.

12. *More emphasis on "constructive therapies"* (Hoyt, 1994a, 1996b, 1998), ones that are user friendly (client and clinician) and particularly consistent with the ideas of *health maintenance* in that they focus on clients' competencies and resources and are time-sensitive, future oriented, and collaborative.

In themselves, these trends are all reasonable and potentially laudatory. Measuring outcomes to increase efficacy and efficiency, avoiding costs incurred by unnecessarily long treatments and unnecessary hospitalizations, providing more access to group therapy, using a range of skilled professionals, emphasizing treatments that tend to be brief, and striving for an overall better coordination of services all are goals worthy of our support. However, as virtuous as they may seem, in practice they may give rise to various ethical dilemmas. Before addressing some of these challenges, consider what concerns may fuel the following.

☐ Did You Hear the One About . . . ?

The Director of a managed care company died and got up to heaven. At the Pearly Gates, Saint Peter met the Director and said, "We have good news and we have bad news."

"What's the good news?" the Director asked

"You can come in," replied Saint Peter.

"And the bad news?"

"You can only stay for two days!"

Later, a clinician died and was met by Saint Peter at the Pearly Gates. Recognizing a virtuous therapist, Saint Peter whisked the therapist directly to an audience with God. Before the Throne, the therapist nervously asked, "Will there always be managed care?"

God replied, "We have good news and we have bad news."

"What's the good news?"

"Someday there won't be managed care."

The therapist sighed with relief, then asked: "But what's the bad news?"

To which God replied: "But it won't happen in my lifetime!"

A managed care company president was given a ticket for a performance of Schubert's "Unfinished Symphony." Since he was unable to go, he passed the invitation to one of his managed care reviewers. The next morning, the president asked the reviewer how he had enjoyed it, and he was handed a memorandum, which read as follows:

MEMORANDUM

1. For a considerable period, the oboe players had nothing to do. Their number should be reduced, and their work spread over the whole orchestra, thus avoiding peaks of inactivity.
2. All 12 violins were playing identical notes. This seems unnecessary duplication, and the staff in this section should be drastically cut. If a large volume of sound is required, this could be obtained through use of an amplifier.
3. Much effort was involved in playing the sixteenth notes. This seems an excessive refinement, and it is recommended that all notes should be rounded up to the nearest eighth note. If this were done, it would be possible to use paraprofessionals instead of experienced musicians.
4. No useful purpose is served by repeating with horns the passage that has already been handled by the strings. If all such redundant passages were eliminated, the concert could be reduced from 2 hours to 20 minutes.
5. This symphony has two movements. If Schubert did not achieve his musical goals by the end of the first movement, then he should have stopped there. The second movement is unnecessary and should be cut.

In light of the above, one can only conclude that had Schubert given attention to these matters, his symphony probably would have been finished by now.

A couple was having difficulty getting pregnant, and sought consultation with an infertility specialist.

"As part of our assessment, we'll need a sperm specimen, Mr. Smith. Please go to the room at the end of the hall. In a few minutes a nurse will come to assist you."

An attractive nurse soon appeared and proceeded to give Mr. Smith an expert hand-job. Collecting the required specimen, the nurse accompanied Mr. Smith back to the waiting room and then departed.

In a short while the doctor reappeared and asked Mr. Smith to come back into the office to discuss the results. Upon entering, Mr. Smith said, "Doctor, I'm eager to find out the results of the test, but first I have to ask you something. When I was coming back down the hall, I passed a room with an open door. I looked in and there was a bunch of men looking at old *Playboy* and *Penthouse* magazines. They were all masturbating. My question is, well, why did I have such a nice assistant and they had to do it themselves?"

The doctor replied, "Oh, they're with an HMO!"

Davenport and Woolley (1997; see also Davenport, 1998; Anonymous, 1995) presented portions of a new tongue-in-cheek treatment manual for "Innovative Brief Pithy Psychotherapy: A Contribution from Corporate Managed Mental Health Care"—with sections on Selection and Training of Therapists, Principles of Training (including three-word, two-word, and one-word interventions), Fillers, and Diversity Issues—that should not be missed. Because of space limitations, we can provide only a fragment. Here's a typical session of pithy therapy:

Th: *Hi. Name?*

Pt: *Uh, my full name is Jonathan Michael Smith, but I guess you can call me Jonathan. My mom calls me Johnnie, but . . .*

Th: *I'll call you John, it's shorter. Why are you here? How do you feel about being here? What other feelings do you have?*

Pt: *Well, I guess I've been a little depressed. At least my wife says I'm depressed. I guess I am. I'm not eating, not sleeping. I don't go to work . . .*

Th: *(interrupts) Bummer. Life sucks. What else?*

Pt: *Well, I'm about to get fired, our 15-year-old ran away, and my wife says she's in love with someone else. (cries)*

Th: *Hold up! Get a grip! What are you doing wrong?*

Pt: *I beg your pardon?*

Th: *Well, this is someone's fault, John. Probably yours. What's your major malfunction?*

Pt: *(confused) I thought you were supposed to be nice to me. My mother was in therapy and her shrink was really nice.*

Th: *Must have been years ago. So what is your problem? How come everyone hates you?*

Pt: *Well, I think maybe I have a self-estem problem. My dad used to call me really bad names and he beat me whenever I made a mistake, so maybe I'm a little too dependent on others to make me feel good. Sometimes . . .*

Th: *Keep it brief, keep it brief. So you're a wimp. I'd say it's time to get off that bus.*

Pt: *Well, I've really tried. I've been to men's groups; I've read some books on assertiveness; I've seen another therapist; nothing seems to work. (cries) I just feel so bad about myself . . .*

Th: *Build a bridge!*

Pt: *I'm sorry, what?*

Th: *That's old stuff, that self-pity crap. That dog don't hunt here. Just grow up.*

Pt: *But what am I supposed to do? I don't know what to do! (getting upset)*
Th: *Have a clue. Move on already.*
Pt: *(confused, silent)*
Th: *Pouting?*
Pt: *No, I just didn't expect this. I think you should help me feel maybe a little better about myself before I move on.*
Th: *Objection overruled. No wonder you feel inadequate!*
Pt: *So you don't think my problems stem from early influences? I thought all therapists thought that. I've read some books . . .*
Th: *Spare me.*
Pt: *No, really, I've really thought about it. Every time someone gets mad at me, I remember my dad's face! Are you saying I should just stop feeling that way?*
Th: *Duh . . . !*
Pt: *You mean just like myself?! Just like that? No middle steps?*
Th: *(looks bored, raises eyebrows)*
Pt: *(brightens) Maybe you're right! Maybe I can just say no to the bad feelings!*
Th: *You're on it!*
Pt: *Maybe I can quit being a wimp and stand up for myself, huh?*
Th: *I'm thinkin'! Go boy!*
Pt: *(springs from chair) Yes! I'll do it! I'll be my own man! I'm the master of my fate, the captain of my . . .*
Th: *Yay you. Next?* (Davenport & Woolley, 1997, pp. 199–200)

Cartoonists also have expressed their views about changes in health care delivery. What does Figure 4.1 say about brief treatment?[7] Figure 4.2 might serve as the illustration for Davenport and Woolley's (1997) satire. There also has been a series of cartoons highlighting the dominance of insurance reimbursement practices on how and for what treatment may be provided,[8] as typified in Figure 4.3.

FIGURE 4.1. By Jerry Van Amergon. Reprinted with permission of Creators Syndicate.

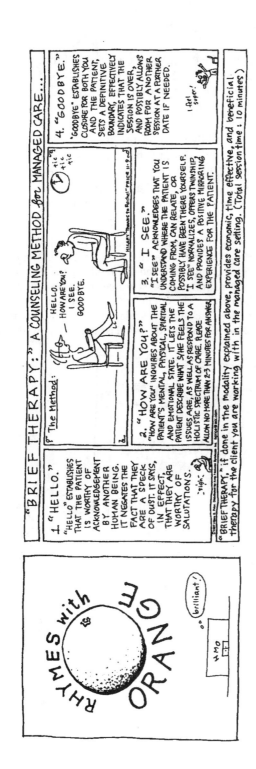

FIGURE 4.2. Reprinted with permission of King Features Syndicate.

All of this augers ill for the continued livelihood of many practitioners. There have been numerous suggestions (e.g., see Bobbitt, Marques, & Trout, 1998; N. A. Cummings, 1995) that, in the future, there will be less need for "routine" (continuous, outpatient, one-on-one) psychotherapy and more service demand for treating the severely mentally ill, the culturally diverse, and the rapidly expanding geriatric population. There are many competent and compassionate therapists (see Benedict & Phelps, 1998; Hunter & Austad, 1997), and not all dyed-in-the-wool Freudians, who could voice the thoughts of Irvin Yalom's psychoanalytic protagonist in his otherwise often comedic novel, *Lying on the Couch* (1996, pp. 160–161):

> But deep therapy was losing the battle: the barbarian hordes of expediency were everywhere. Marching to the starched new banners of managed care, the battalions of brief therapy darkened the landscape and hammered at the gates of the analytic institutes, the last armed enclaves of wisdom, truth, and reason in psychotherapy. The enemy was close enough for Marshal to see its many faces: biofeedback and muscular relaxation for anxiety disorders; implosion or desensitization for phobias; drugs for dysthymia and

FIGURE 4.3. Reprinted with permission of Harley L. Schwardon (illustrator).

obsessive/compulsive disorders; cognitive group therapy for eating disorders; assertiveness training for the timid; diaphragmatic breathing groups for panicked patients; social skills training for the socially avoidant; one-session hypnotic interventions for smoking; and those god-damned twelve-step groups for everything else!

The economic juggernaut of managed care had overwhelmed medical defenses in many parts of the country. Therapists in subjugated states were forced, if they wished to stay in practice, to genuflect to the conqueror, who paid them a fraction of their customary fee and assigned them patients to treat for five or maybe six sessions when in actuality, fifty or sixty sessions were needed.

When therapists used up their meager allotted rations, the charade began in earnest and they were forced to beg their case managers for additional sessions to continue treatment. And, of course, they had to document their request with mountains of phony, time-consuming paperwork in which they were forced to lie by exaggerating the patient's suicidal risk, substance abuse, or propensity for violence; those were the only magic words that caught the attention of the health plans—not because administrators felt any concern for the patient but because they were cowed by the threat of some future litigation.

Thus, therapists were not only ordered to treat patients in impossibly brief periods, but also had the added, humiliating chore of placating and accommodating case managers—often brash young administrators with only the most rudimentary knowledge of the field. . . . Not only was the dignity of psychiatrists being assaulted, but their pocketbooks were, as well.[9]

The rendering shown in Figure 4.4 may have been made at a conference on managed care survival tips for seasoned mental health professionals.[10]

☐ Realms of Ethical Concern

The vast majority of mental health professionals, both within and outside of various managed care arrangements, are no doubt well intended and concerned about "doing the right thing" (Hoyt, 1992a, 1992b, 1994e/1995l). There are enormous quotidian pressures, however, to make a living, to comply, and to get along—especially in these times of downsizing and relative economic austerity. Particularly with the cacophony of theoretical claims among different schools of psychotherapy and the somewhat vague standards of what constitutes quality in the area of mental health care, there seem to be fewer and fewer easy answers.

The shifting of more fiscal risk on to providers (both individuals and managed care organizations) through increased capitation arrangements, coupled with the increasing use of large information management systems to regulate and shape therapists' practice patterns (Berwick, Baker,

FIGURE 4.4. Reprinted with permission of L. J. Kopf.

& Kramer, 1992; Bologna, Barlow, Hollon, Mitchell, & Huppert, 1998; German, 1994; Hoyt, 1994e/1995l; Stone, 1995; Sperry, Grissom, Brill, & Marion, 1997), strongly encourages providers to internalize the values and practices promulgated by managed care.[11] While many of the values and goals of managed mental health care may be meritorious, their application needs to be done thoughtfully, lest it occur in an unreflective, uncritical "whole-cloth" manner, in which cooperation may blur into cooptation.

Older practitioners, including those who have chosen to work in salaried positions in clinics and staff model HMOs in order to avoid some of the business vicissitudes and exigencies of private practice, now often find themselves buffeted "27/7" by the very forces they sought to escape. I also have been concerned by the reactions I have observed in some young therapists who express interest in working within HMOs and other managed care settings. At times, they seem like clinical myrmidons, oblivious or barely having an inkling into the complexity of ethical and technical issues—which allows them, unlike their more seasoned colleagues, to practice without much recognition or concern for what may be getting lost or given short shrift.[12] I nodded with recognition when I read the following report from an esteemed colleague, Hanna Levenson, who is an expert teacher (see Levenson, 1995) and practitioner of time-limited dynamic psychotherapy:

> [I] had a startling and impactful realization . . . while giving an introductory seminar on time-limited therapy to third-year psychiatry residents at a prestigious medical school recently. At the beginning of the first class, [I] gave clinical examples and research findings to suggest that briefer interventions could be helpful. Instead of the usual onslaught of resistance from trainees who had been indoctrinated in long-term therapy, [I] was faced with rather ho-hum acceptance. Upon inquiry, the students informed [me] that they had never done any type of therapy other than brief, focused therapy of approximately ten sessions combined with psycho-pharmacological interventions! (Levenson & Burg, in press)

Don't get me wrong. I love the field of brief therapy (especially constructive approaches) and make my living practicing, studying, and teaching it. I am concerned, however, by the disdain I sometimes hear toward all things having to do with long-term therapy (such as transference dynamics, the desire for an extended relationship, enduring childhood trauma, and so forth). This may just be brief therapy enthusiasm, but the disregard for 100 years of psychotherapy developments sometimes reminds me a bit of the story in the preface to *The Gulag Archipelago*, wherein Solzhenitsyn (1973, p. ix) reported that upon finding "frozen specimens of prehistoric fauna some tens of thousands of years old . . . those present immediately broke open the ice encasing the specimens and devoured them *with relish* on the spot."

The issues are not simple (see Alperin & Phillips, 1997; Holleman et al., 1997; Lavizzo-Mourey & Mackenzie, 1996; Moffic, 1997; Nowack et al., 1989; Rimler & Morrison, 1993; Small & Barnhill, 1998; Waymack, 1992; Werhane, 1992; Zieman, 1998). Writing about the importance of informed consent, Acuff et al. (1999, p. 568) outline some of the problems:

> [T]he cost containment incentives embodied in managed care arrangements may require precertification of specific treatments, as well as initial and ongoing authorization for therapy. The manner in which these utilization procedures are implemented by some MCOs [managed care organizations] may be overly intrusive and thereby disrupt the therapeutic process. The MCO may limit the primary therapist's ability to refer to specialists, require release of confidential patient information in excess of that needed to process claims, authorize reimbursement for fewer sessions than the number stated in the health care plan, or impose other conditions that a patient would not generally anticipate.

To keep our "balance" on today's clinically and ethically "slippery slopes," therapists (and administrators, managers, purchasers, policymakers, and patients) need to remain cognizant of the following issues.

Undertreatment and Patient Abandonment

Just as in traditional fee-for-service arrangements there is the inherent risk of overtreatment (the more one does, the more one makes), in prepaid managed care arrangements; the incentive structure may encourage undertreatment (the less one does, the more the company keeps). The drive for cost containment needs to be constantly balanced against our prime obligations for quality patient care mandated by the ethical codes of all the major mental health professions (Sabin, 1994a, 1994b). As Stephen Blum (1992, p. 245) noted, "In their briefest form, the ethical issues that arise with the development of managed mental health services have to do with the nature of the relationship between the money spent on such services and the quality of the care provided." As the trenchant titles of Wylie's (1995) *Family Therapy Networker* article "Diagnosing for Dollars?" and Kirk and Kutchins's (1992) book *The Selling of DSM: The Rhetoric of Science in Psychiatry* would suggest, money drives much of the diagnosis and treatment industry.

Is psychotherapy a right or a privilege? An entitlement or a commodity? How do we balance the wants and needs of the individual with those of society? Not providing (or not continuing) services to someone who requests them is unsavory, but so is the practice of providing extensive services to some while others go without. We need to move toward a social ethic, a reconsideration of the strong focus on the individual—which is so much a part of American culture—with what is good for the commonweal. Given the reality of limited resources, it seems important to ask, as did Carol Shaw Austad (1996a, 1996b; see also Austad, Hunter, & Morgan, 1998), "Can psychotherapy be conducted effectively in managed care settings?" and "Is long-term psychotherapy unethical?"

Many who would sound the tocsin and claim the high moral ground of unlimited services seem to have little grasp of how to pay for what they would promulgate. While I am in sympathy with many of the concerns I detect in some colleagues' jeremiads and doomsday rhetoric (see R. E. Fox, 1995; Karon, 1995; Pipal, 1995, 1996; Shore, 1995; also see Hoyt & Budman, 1996), I am more impressed with the theoretical and clinical discussions of session effects and therapeutic integrity provided by Stern (1993) and Herron et al. (1994). I also appreciate the views articulated by I. J. Miller (1996a, 1996b, 1996c, 1996d) in a series of articles on the inappropriate limiting of therapy.[13] He describes the practice of *"invisible rationing,* a treatment allocation process that reduces mental health services without informing the client of the reduction" (I. J. Miller, 1996d, p. 583). Such restrictions can occur through Procrustean application of time-limited brief therapy to *all* clients as well as through systematic staffing patterns that effectively limit the number of sessions that can be provided. I. J. Miller (1996d, p. 585) elaborates:

> Managed care uses complex incentives to orchestrate the implementation of time-limited brief therapy. These incentives include capitation, bonuses, report cards, and dismissal from provider panels for providing long-term treatment. By and large, these incentives are invisible to the consumer, and professionals are often prevented from revealing these incentives by policies that gag the professional. Ethical principles require disclosing the details of these invisible incentives.[14]

Holleman et al. (1997, p. 350) note another common strategy:

> In lieu of physician bedside or clinical rationing, many managed-care organizations are engaged in rationing by exhaustion, in which physicians are permitted to appeal managed-care administrations for appropriate tests and treatments not covered by the plan, but the amount of work required to succeed in this process is designed to deter physicians from attempting the appeal or from carrying it through to its conclusion. Thus the 'hassle factor,' not medical judgment, determines whether a particular test or treatment is given. The beneficiaries of this strategy are stockholders and chief executive officers of the managed-care companies.[15]

Restricting the number and frequency of treatment sessions may have a variety of adverse effects. The therapeutic alliance may be attenuated as a vehicle for support and change (see Barron & Sands, 1996; Bracero, 1996; N. A. Cummings, 1977; Dyckman, 1997; Edbril, 1994; Elder, 1997; J. L. Feldman, 1992; Gabbard, Takahashi, Davidson, Eauman-Bork, & Ensroth, 1991; Goldensohn & Haar, 1974; Lipp, 1980; Sabin, 1991, 1992; Chapter 15, this volume). Concluding that the (inadequate) treatment they have been offered or given is all that is possible, patients may become unnecessarily discouraged and give up. An overreliance on the use of medication may develop if there is a dearth of available psychotherapy—a tendency toward the "medicalization of life" and "pharmaceutical invasion" about which we were warned a quarter century ago in books such as *The Myth of Mental Illness* (Szasz, 1974), *Medical Nemesis: The Expropriation of Health* (Illich, 1976), and *Prognosis Negative: Crisis in the Health Care System* (Kotelchuck, 1976).[15]

While there is useful information to be found in *Listening to Prozac* (Kramer, 1993), recent volumes such as *Talking Back to Prozac* (Breggin, 1994) and *The Anti-Depressant Era* (Healy, 1997) also provide troubling detailed documentation of the shaping of public perception by financial and marketing interests. Psychoactive medications can be very helpful, although popular slogans such as "Better Living through Chemistry" and "The Prozac Generation," linkages between the biologically-oriented *DSM-IV* (American Psychiatric Association, 1994) and prescription patterns, and the extraordinary growth of the use the tranquilizers, sleeping pills, antidepressants, Ritalin, and so forth bespeak the worrisome rise of the hegemony of the psychiatric–pharmaceutical industrial complex.

The inappropriate restriction of services may also be shortsighted in terms of its ostensible goal of cost containment—inadequate treatment may simply squander limited resources if patients have to return for treatment of the same problem because it was not addressed adequately.[16] Particularly egregious is the likelihood that undertreatment and potential abandonment (the discontinuation of services that leaves the patient at significant risk for major adverse consequences) may fall disproportionately on that very vulnerable portion of the population, the chronically and persistently severely mentally ill, who may be both the most needy and the least able to advocate for themselves (see Bailey, 1999; Bonstedt, 1992; Eist, 1998; Gerson, 1994; "Managed or Mangled," 1997; Norris, Molinari, & Rosowsky, 1998; Schlesinger, Dorwart, & Epstein, 1996; "Who's Reaping the Benefits?", 1999). Such folks may get caught in the "revolving door" of repeated emergency room visits, brief hospitalizations, and premature discharges—without ever receiving sufficient assistance—until someone writes a chart note such as "4th hospitalization in last 18 months," declares the patient "intractable," and seeks to "exclude from" (i.e., cut off) psychiatric insurance coverage. Affixing the pejorative term *recidivist* adds umbrageous insult to injury, the word coming from the criminology (not mental health) literature and meaning "a falling back into criminal habits, especially after punishment." It would be more respectful to use terms such as *repeat presenter* or *continuing care client* (or *"veteran,"* following Duncan, Hubble, & Miller, 1997b). Providing services for these often stigmatized and shunned people—who typically have multiple problems and a paucity of internal and external resources—is unlikely to pay for itself or to be seen as "cost effective" when gauged against the standard of a company's short-term fiscal bottom line. Who will pay? Why?

Professional Autonomy

I. J. Miller (1996b, pp. 567–568) writes:

> Frequently, managed care imposes time limits, incentives, or both to decrease the length of time in therapy. These policies are intended to overrule the judgment of the clinician and client, and consequently, they undermine the important safeguard of the clinical determination of treatment length.

As Tulkin and Frank (1985) noted, therapists working within an HMO (or other managed care) setting have less autonomy and less control of their practice. There is the danger of clinicians being turned from autonomous professionals who use their training and expertise to determine and do what would be best for the client into technicians who simply are employees of the insurance industry performing closely monitored routines. Efforts to improve efficacy and efficiency through the standardization of care may suggest useful guidelines (see Sauber, 1997; Strosahl, 1998; Wilson, 1998), but also threaten to replace clinicians' individualized judgments in favor of "cookbooks" and "paint-by-numbers" formulas (Silverman, 1996). Efforts to "manualize" or prescribe treatments on the basis of a few descriptors would appear "premature" (Drozd & Goldfield, 1996; Nathan, 1998). Moreover, as Arthur Bohart (1999, p. 3; also see Bohart & Tallman, 1999) writes:

> The problem with this suggestion [that there should be a detailed treatment plan and a concrete intervention plan for each patient session] is that it is based on a model of therapy that not all of us share, namely that therapy is akin to medical "treatment" and that "interventions" are the major reason it works. Many approaches do not view therapy as treatment. Treatment plans are antithetical to client–centered therapy (for which there is considerable empirical support).
>
> Many clients prefer exploratory approaches in which interventions arise out of therapist–client dialogue rather than being targeted and planned in advance by the therapist. In fact, the research shows that most clients value having a time and place to talk more than they do therapists' interventions. Finally, research also seriously questions the idea that interventions play an important role in therapy's effectiveness.

The legitimate use of solid research to ensure and enhance quality is important. Many suspect, however, that the managed care industry may be, "cherrypicking" research, selectively applying findings to justify limiting therapy (see Sleek, 1997). As one senior researcher, Hans Strupp (1997, p. 91), made clear: "I take strong exception to the manner in which research has been used, if not to say co-opted, as a tool for undergirding the rationing of therapeutic services." Another respected commentator, Kenneth Gergen (quoted in Hoyt, 1996a, p. 355) similarly remarked, "Personally, I think outcome evaluations are no more than window dressing for a given school of therapy, and the entire concept is misleading."

The frequent requirement of managed care to affix clients with psychiatric labels and diagnoses also raises other issues. Mirowsky and Ross (1989) likened psychiatric diagnosticians to stargazers somewhat arbitrarily connecting points to find different constellations and clusters depending on their concepts. Jeffrey Blum (1978) documented how diagnoses historically shift to fit available treatments. Quick "assessment" may result in "thin descriptions" (Geertz, 1973a; White, 1997), ones devoid of the nuances and subtle meanings on which therapeutic activity is constructed. Hoyt and Friedman (Chapter 5, this volume; see also Patterson & Lusterman, 1996) note some of the therapeutically counterproductive binds that may occur when one is required to provide a *DSM* diagnosis (e.g., the focus shifts from competence to pathology, from systemic to unilateral, from curiosity to certainty, from collaborative to expert-driven). Recognizing the "diffusion of deficit" (Gergen, 1994b) created by pathologizing diagnostic labels, Gergen, Hoffman, and Anderson (1996) asked "Is Diagnosis a Disaster?"; Tomm (1990) referred to the dehumanizing "spiritual psychosis" that may result from casting clients into the language of the *DSM*. Family therapist Carl Whitaker (1989a, pp. 190–191) advised: "One of the most difficult tricks is to avoid the process of diagnosis. All efforts, all tendencies to define the other character by individual diagnosis or, if you will, system diagnosis, are cop-outs. . . . Whenever you start pinning somebody down, the person disappears and you're dealing with your own fantasy."[17] Susan Sontag (1964, p. 29) also cautioned: "It is the same with our own lives. If we see them from the outside, as the influence and popular dissemination of the social sciences and psychiatry has persuaded more and more people to do, we view ourselves as instances of generalities, and in so doing become profoundly and painfully alienated from our own experience and our humanity."[18]

Competence

A related point involves the use of less skilled providers. Efforts to economize are worthy if they maintain quality while saving money and thus allow more services to be provided. If greed overtakes accountability, however, what is provided may not be enough, either in quantity or quality. Less-trained caregivers may be adequate for some tasks, but there is the danger of "dumbing down" and rote formulas replacing differential clinical judgment (see Howard, 1998). M. E. P. Seligman and Levant (1998, pp. 211–212) explain:

> In the past decade, health care corporations have been aggressively driving down costs. Psychological expenditures are increasingly restricted by routing patients to less well trained caregivers and by only authorizing brief therapy[19] . . . Today, psychotherapy is seriously threatened by MCOs' [managed care organizations] drawing inferences from efficacy studies about appropriate treatment to justify business practices. Only by overlooking the questionable external validity of efficacy studies can MCOs justify brief and inexpensive treatment. No one benefits by this misuse of the efficacy data, except stockholders—and then in the short run only. Psychotherapists have their autonomy and livelihood diminished. Skill, experience, and training become handicaps, rather than virtues. Patients receive briefer therapy from less-skilled providers . . .
>
> Some have claimed that the *CR* [*Consumer Reports;* "*Mental Health,*" 1995; see also M. E. P. Seligman, 1995] study "confirmed what we already knew": that increasing levels of experience, skill, and education do not make for

better therapy. The *CR* study did nothing of the kind, nor do "we already know" it. The *CR* data are conflicted on this. . . . In our judgment, the scholarly argument for less-qualified providers is seriously flawed. It wholly relies on studies where manuals are used, mild and uncomplicated clinical problems are diagnosed (by doctoral-level providers), and duration of therapy is very brief and fixed. This is precisely where clinical judgment, experience, and education matter the least . . .

Thus, (a) If a case is simple, if a manual must be followed, and if treatment must be very brief, less-qualified providers may do as well as doctoral-level specialists; (b) in therapy as commonly practiced in the field, where cases are more complicated and severe, where manuals are not used, where diagnosis is an ongoing process, and where therapy is long and clinical judgment is important, the use of highly trained and experienced providers improves outcomes; and, (c) effectiveness studies that examine level of educational training and experience of providers who treat different disorders, degree of severity of disorders, and co-morbidity are urgently needed, as are cost-benefit analyses.

This raises other issues. While studies of effectiveness and efficacy are important to improve quality, there has been a tendency—perhaps driven by marketing efforts—to confuse *patient satisfaction* with *therapeutic change.* As Pekarik and Guidry (1999, pp. 476–477) explain:

> [M]any mental health agencies, both public and private, have operated under the assumption that "consumer satisfaction" translates directly into "treatment efficacy". . . . [R]ecent studies reveal this to be an erroneous belief. With the absence of a significant relationship between satisfaction and problem change, treatment policies primarily based on consumer satisfaction are misdirected and may fail to effectively target symptom relief. . . . The high priority given to satisfaction results by behavioral health care organizations (Lambert et al., 1998) suggest that satisfaction data may be widely misunderstood or misrepresented as indicative of superior treatment impact. Bilbrey and Bilbrey (1995) reported, for example, that behavioral health care organization representatives view consumer satisfaction data as the most helpful of all 'outcome' measures. Psychotherapy researchers also sometimes load outcome measures with satisfaction questions, producing data that may be misleading if they are presented as indicators of symptom or pathology change (as implied by terms such as *outcome* or *effectiveness*). This was done in the oft-cited *Consumer Reports* study (Seligman, 1995), which used a satisfaction question as one of the three items that assessed outcome. It is important that clinicians, administrators, and consumers (including entities that contract for mental health services) have a realistic understanding of the implications and limitations of consumer satisfaction.

There is also the related managed-care practice of rigidly restricting psychiatrists (and nurses) to management of biological treatments—*if* any other treatment (such as talking therapy) is provided, a separate counselor or therapist is involved. While this may appear to be a good use of focused expertise, it may also result, unless very carefully coordinated, in frequent splitting of the therapeutic relationship. It may also serve to diminish job satisfaction for psychiatric physicians who want to be involved in the more comprehensive care of their patients—a concern that dovetails with the astounding observation that psychiatry residencies are increasingly omitting any expectation or requirement for significant psychotherapy training!

Keeping with the managed care principle of having the least expensive workers do most of the labor, some companies are heavily staffed with entry-level therapists, who seek to move on to better paying and more satisfying positions as soon as they have a bit of seasoning (which may seem to them to be a sort of "baptism by fire") . . . only to be replaced by a new issue of freshly minted beginners. In addition to a dearth of the clinical acumen that comes with extended practice, this rapid staff turnover results in there being little continuity of care—instead of benefitting from the HMO therapy principle of a "family practitioner" who provides intermittent treatment throughout the life cycle (N. A. Cummings & Sayama, 1995; Hoyt, 1995a), clients who recontact the managed care organization after a treatment hiatus often are perfunctorily told that their former therapist "no longer works here."

Managed care organizations often are requiring their providers to see more and more patients. Assuming the American standard of the 40-hour work week, how many is too many? When does more become less? Is there an asymptote? What happens to treatment planning, reflection, case consultation? When do "compassion fatigue" and "burnout" set in? Whence and whither quality?

During this time of increasingly heavy caseload demands, therapists fees and salaries frequently are being frozen and even, in some situations, significantly reduced. In addition to its demoralizing effect, a shrinking income also may increase the temptation to "take on" any client that appears rather than accepting referrals only within one's genuine scope of expertise. Some managed care organizations may encourage this by hiring less-qualified therapists and pressuring them to practice at the margins of their licensure, and by requiring therapists to be "generalists" that treat all comers (children, adolescents, adults, older people, couples, families) regardless of diagnosis or presenting problems.

Dual Relationships and Conflicts-of-Interest

"You work for the company, and they want you to keep it short and get rid of me as soon as possible" is a challenge clients could pose to providers working under managed care. Professional adherence to high-quality standards of care is imperative, and any so-called "gag rules" that attempt to restrict therapists advising clients about other (and more expensive) treatment options should be vigorously opposed. At the same time, it should be recognized, as part of informed consent, that clients have purchased potential therapy with various limitations, such as what kinds of problems will be treated and for how long. The limits of their managed care coverage need to be explicit and discussed openly and frankly, just as someone working in private fee-for-service would candidly discuss what might be possible or available if the client indicated having limited funds for payment. Any misleading statements or exaggerated claims made by the managed care organization need to be opposed (Bilynsky & Vernaglia, 1998; Geraty, Hendren & Flaa, 1992; Rabasca, 1998a, 1988b; Thomas, 1999).

It is a somewhat paradoxical "perverse incentive" that under a preferred provider arrangement, the payment of a reduced fee may at times actually serve to encourage the therapist to hold on to the client longer, in order to make a reasonable wage from a given case. While salaried, staff-model clinicians will not be susceptible to this particular pressure, they will have to safeguard appropriate quality against institutional pressures to end too quickly (see Chapter 15, this volume). In a related vein, it will be important for case managers and utilization reviewers to be salaried and not have their payment tied to the length of any particular case, lest it give the appearance, real or not, that they are paid to withhold treatment.

Confidentiality and Privacy

By definition, managed care involves the potential oversight or regulation of treatment by someone other than the client and therapist. Case managers may require clinical data for treatment authorization, quality control, research, and clinician profiling—and may seek it in the ways that C. H. Browning and Browning (1993; quoted in Wylie, 1994b, p. 24) characterized as the "*three i's* of managed care," namely, "intrusion, invasion and inquisition." Key concerns involve what kinds of information may be revealed, and to whom (including re-release). While well-run managed care organizations generally strive to handle confidential material appropriately, a *Nightline* (1996) ABC television program with Ted Koppel exposed disturbing examples of sensitive information being stored in relatively open databases and handled casually by clerical workers. Davidson and Davidson (1995) also highlighted some of the ways information may inadvertently "leak." Michael Freeny (1998) has written a novel, *Terminal Consent*, that vividly depicts managed care companies using computers to limit patient care and compromise confidentiality. Along related lines, Freeny's (1995) article in the *Family Therapy Networker* brought to many therapists' attention the existence of the Medical Information Bureau—a kind of "Big Brother" insurance company storehouse in which computerized information about millions of persons—possibly including you, dear reader, if you have ever applied for insurance—is already available for public scrutiny.

Psychotherapy clients may (mistakenly) expect total privacy, and advisement of the limits of confidentiality (due both to legal requirements as well as the possible involvement of managed care) may have a "chilling" effect on their candor and participation. In this regard, Kremer and Gesten (1998, p. 557) provide some suggestions for ethical practice with managed care clients:

1. Provide your clients with a first session discussion of the information requirements and utilization review practices governing their therapy.
2. Be certain your clients are informed by actively questioning their understanding of requirements and practices.
3. If the managed care organization provides forms that delineate requirements and procedures, carefully review them with your clients before signing.
4. Inform your clients about potential repercussions from disclosure of sensitive material.
5. Plan for utilization review, provide only the necessary minimum of information required to secure appropriate treatment for your clients—avoid dramatic details and extensive explications.
6. Advocate for your clients by working to change managed care practices which limit or interfere with treatment.
7. Always document interactions with utilization reviewers or managed care officials.

Acuff et al. (1999, p. 569) also emphasize practitioners' ethical obligation to gain clients' *informed consent*, including discussion of any financing limitations on services that may be anticipated:

It is helpful for psychologists [and other professionals] to understand and be able to convey to their patients such information as (1) the MCO's provisions related to the number of authorized sessions, (2) the method and timing of utilization review, (3) the nature of the information required by the MCO to authorize services, (4) the amount of reimbursement provided, (5) the patient's share of any expenses (deductible or copayment), (6) the services that are covered or excluded, (7) the responsibility for payment if the MCO determines that a particular service is not covered under the patient's plan, and (8) any other foreseeable financial matters.

Social Responsibility

The idea that organizations could better provide mental health treatment services is not new. Long ago, Sigmund Freud (1919/1961b, p. 167) wrote:

At some time or other the conscience of society will awake and remind it that the poor man should have just as much right to assistance for his mind as he now has to the life-saving help offered by surgery; and that the neuroses threaten public health no less than tuberculosis, and can be left as little as the latter to the impotent care of individual members of the community. When this happens, institutions or out-clinics will be started.

It would appear, however, that in many situations, industrialization and monetarization have pushed aside other values. (See Stone, 1995, for an extensive review of how market forces have preempted the transformation of American psychiatry.) As Tischler and Astrachan (1996, p. 959) wrote in their trenchant article, "A Funny Thing Happened on the Way to Reform":

> Corporate policy now dominates where public policy once ruled. The advocates of managed competition vanquished the champions of health rights. Marketspeak has become the lingua franca capturing the cost of caring for the ill in a simple phrase, "the medical loss ratio." As we stand on the threshold of the 21st century, much of what we once identified as social goods are now regarded as commodities. Economic issues dominate where social issues once held sway. In a world where human service agencies are regarded as market entities, the health care sector is little more than a microcosm of a larger universe that is being battered by change.

They went on to suggest (p. 962):

> In meeting this challenge, it is imperative that we speak, not out of guild or personal interest, but in support of change that is aimed at meeting the basic health needs of all Americans. If medicine is to play a meaningful role in the debate, it must challenge the notion of health care as a market-driven commodity and offer in its stead an alternative vision.
>
> The first step in articulating the vision is a return to the Aristotelian view of societal obligation and of health care as a social good.[20]

Others, such as former Surgeon General C. Everett Koop (1996; see also Fancher, 1995), have also suggested that we need to clarify our values before plotting strategy. In his book *Kinds of Power: A Guide to Its Intelligent Uses,* James Hillman (1995, p. 43) notes that a *both-and* solution is possible:

> There are businesses today dedicated to "the double bottom line"—profit *and* social responsibility. These companies are attempting to yoke the motive of profit together with other motivations. They are harnessing efficiency with concern for nature (material cause), aesthetic values (formal cause) and spiritual principles (final cause). They still seek efficiency (profit) but not at the cost of the well-being of their employees, the communities where the business is located, the implications for the wider world. The double bottom line protects against efficiency as an autonomous and isolated cause just as it recognizes that a company is not an autonomous power isolated within its property lines.

☐ What Are We to Do?

> Clinicians, now called providers, are mobilized in both constructive and questionable ways. Many are accepting the changes and are trying to create ways of working within the current system in a manner that allows them to maintain their professional and economic integrity. Others are vehemently opposed to managed mental health care in any form and are either trying to propose realistic alternatives or "bucking the system" in a variety of ways.
> —Henry I. Spitz, 1996, p. x

I do not recommend waging a retrograde battle for an economic yesteryear, but I also do not recommend that we simply capitulate or "get on board while we can." We need to advocate, as individuals and through our various professional associations and societies, for what we think is right. "He (or she) who pays the piper calls the tune," and special efforts have to be made to educate the public and private purchasers of health care. Public opinion polls (Church, 1997; Clay, 1998b; Rabasca, 1998c) show that consumers' initial enthusiasm toward managed care has cooled considerably, and the appeal for reform should be made both to finances and to greater social values.

Companies who violate their legal, ethical, and moral responsibilities should be avoided and, when necessary, confronted and exposed. In *Brief Therapy and Managed Care: Readings for Contemporary Practice* (Hoyt, 1995a), I drew from both personal experience and the literature (see American Psychological Association, 1996; Austad et al., 1998; C. H. Browning & Browning, 1993; N. A. Cummings, 1991b; Gottlieb, 1992; Haas & Cummings, 1991; Hall, 1994a, 1994b; Newman & Bricklin, 1991; Poynter, 1994; the industry newsletters *Practice Strategies* and *Psychotherapy Finances*; Small, 1992; see also Moffic, 1997; Poynter, 1998; Small & Barnhill, 1998; Zieman, 1998) to provide a discussion of "Twenty-Five Questions to Ask Before Joining a Managed-Care Organization." A list of warning signals about which companies to avoid includes

- unqualified reviewers;
- cumbersome and intrusive paperwork;
- inappropriate discharges (Is it more important to get them out than to get them well?);
- absent review criteria and absent appeals process;
- inappropriate short-term models for high-risk clients;
- punishing providers who challenge reviews;
- low fees, seeming lack of office staff, and long payment delays; and
- bad reputation, based on recent events.

Some writers have suggested ways of developing practices independent of managed care (e.g., Ackley, 1997; F. Brown, 1994; L. Brown, 1997; Kovacs, 1998; Perrott, 1998); others, in high dudgeon, (e.g., Moldowsky, 1990; Pipal, 1995, 1996; Sank, 1997; Shore, 1995; Welch, 1994; Wooley, 1993; R. H. Wright, 1992) have portrayed it as essentially evil and have suggested various ways to confront and attempt to destroy it; yet others have acknowledged difficulties but have chosen "constructive engagement" as a way of attempting to shape its continuing evolution (e.g., Bilynsky & Vernaglia, 1998; Broskowski, 1991; N. A. Cummings et al., 1996; Franko & Erb, 1998; Giles & Marafiote, 1998; Hoyt, 1995a; Moffic, 1997; Poynter, 1998; Schwartz, 1997; Todd, 1994; Zimet, 1989). As T. A. Kelly (1997, p. 320) wrote: "I have been impressed with the fact that policy is decided by those who show up, participate constructively, and build their credibility. Those who refuse to join the process are simply left behind." Shueman (1997, pp. 557–558) has drawn the battle lines:

> Those of us involved in the development of accountable health systems retain little hope that constructive discourse on issues surrounding the changes in health services organization and financing will occur in the climate prevailing within organized psychology. It is particularly discouraging that much of what is frequently presented in professional journals as informed discourse is offered by persons who appear severely deficient in their command of the fundamentals of health care organization, financing, and provision. Absent this knowledge base, discourse is too often characterized by unseemly and vituperative posturing in the interests of the guild and manifestly not of the public at large.
>
> Psychologists and other mental health professionals need to decide whether or not they wish to continue accepting the health care dollar. Those who do so have a clear responsibility to reconfigure both their competency profile and their practice structures to meet the requirements of the health services industry. Without accepting the imperatives essential to the conduct of a productive and responsible professional life within the evolving world of health care, traditionally trained psychological providers are better advised to target alternative areas of professional endeavor.

The dilemmas of health care reform and financing are more complicated than a simple *either-or* answer will allow. *Both-and* solutions must be sought. We always are practicing within an ethical context. As Feldstein (1998a, p. 15) wrote:

> Now, in this current era of managed care and managed competition, the physician, along with the team of providers, must:
>
> 1. satisfy the requirements of multiple stakeholders. . . . The original focus on the patient has expanded to encompass satisfying a group of stakeholders including patients, their families, patient representatives, employers, and purchasing groups as well as other providers (consultants,

nurses, etc.), the health plan, professional standards, and governmental regulations.

2. according to multiple ethical principles. . . . The ethical principles of beneficence and non-maleficence are expanded to include respect for patient's autonomy (including informed consent), and distributive justice (to allocate time and resources fairly, be fiscally responsible). Now as individual practitioners and as organizations, we must aim to do good and avoid harm, as defined by the patient, their representatives, our professional and organizational standards and policies, while at the same time be stewards of finite resources and act consistent with the broader ethical context. . . .

3. and do so explicitly. Satisfaction has become a requirement that care providers meet and it is being measured.

Priorities must be set and the needs of particular individuals balanced against the needs of society. Everyone cannot have their way; tensions are inevitable. It is strongly advised that clinicians consult a qualified heath care business attorney before signing any contract, since joining a managed care plan may involve legally binding obligations. The active and ongoing participation of interdisciplinary mental health practitioners is essential to assure that attention be focused on the quality of care (Abrams, 1993; Berwick, 1989; Hoyt, 1994e/1995l; Feldstein, 1998a, 1998b). As Bilynsky and Vernaglia (1998, p. 66) have suggested, proactive strategies should include "a thorough understanding of the managed-care principles, clear communication with the client, additional training, advocacy, and placing psychologists [and other clinically sophisticated practitioners] in charge." Training programs (M. J. Bennett, 1994; Budman & Armstrong, 1992; Carleton, 1998; S. Feldman, 1997; P. D. Fox & Wasserman, 1993; Moffic, 1997; Nahmias, 1992; Schuster, Lovell, & Trachta, 1997; VanDyck & Schlesinger, 1997; see Levenson & Burg, in press, for a good review) have barely begun to address these shifts, including much needed explicit attention to the many attendant ethical issues.

Those who care to manage must manage to care—about people *and* profits. We need to continue moving toward managed *care*, not just managed *costs*. Gandhi, when he was once asked, "What do you think of Western civilization?" replied, "It would be a good idea!" I submit that *true managed care*—arrangements to regulate the costs, site and utilization of services in an ethical and clinically appropriate manner—would be a good idea, too. Collaboration involving a four-way partnership—provider, patient, manager, purchaser—will be necessary if we are to do what is good and get the job done. As clinicians and as citizens, we need to meet this challenge.

☐ Notes

[1] I will restrict my discussion here to American developments, recognizing that other countries (e.g., Great Britain, Canada, Sweden, Japan) have initiated various national health plans that in some ways address issues similar to those in the United States (see A. Bennett & Adams, 1993; Wedding, Ritchie, Kitchen, & Binner, 1993). The cultural contexts and histories are different, however. It can also be noted that "managed care" can be traced back to circa A.D. 1300, when a young doctor in a Catalonian village agreed, for the payment of 5 to 20 sous a year, to treat several dozen men of modest means and their wives, children, and servants "for every illness that requires the art of medicine" (Stix, 1994, p. 20).

[2] During a slow staff meeting, I penned "The Managed Care Blues":

I've got the blues
The managed care blues
I just got the news
They're turning the screws
I gotta see more
They've taken off the door
They've pulled out my chair
Gotta be quick, still gotta care
I've got the blues, the managed care blues.

[3] Holleman, Holleman, & Graves, (1997, p. 350) report: "In 1994, the chiefs of the seven largest for-profit health-maintenance organizations averaged $7 million each in cash and stock pay packages."

[4] See Donald and Wampold (1986) and Steenbarger and Greenberg (1996).

[5] I am grateful to Anthea Fursland (personal communication, 1999) for clarifying some of the issues regarding case-rates.

[6] "Carve-out" (and "unbundle") are terms used to designate the practice of disassembling a comprehensive health care system into its component parts, as when a single-specialty company assumes responsibility for providing a sector of services (e.g., mental health treatment). While appearing to offer the advantage of focused expertise, this engenders a variety of problems such as reification of the Cartesian idea of mind-body dualism and a tendency toward cost shifting and risk avoidance between departments rather than an overall coordination of care (see Strosahl & Quirk, 1994).

[7] I was one of the originators (and the principal investigator) of the approach that has come to be called "single-session therapy," in which we sought to determine how and for which patients one treatment meeting might be helpful and sufficient (see Hoyt, 1994b/ 1995j; Rosenbaum, Hoyt, & Talmon, 1990/1995; Talmon, 1990). I was distressed—although not surprised, given that some managed care organizations may have misapplied our research to suggest that one session should be forced on patients and that "failure" to achieve results in one session is indicative of patient and/or therapist resistance or ineptitude—to see the possibility of potential one-session therapy being depicted in such a distorted and grotesque manner.

[8] Long ago, in *The Devil's Dictionary*, Ambrose Bierce (1906/1957, p. 36) offered this definition: "*Diagnosis*, n., A physician's forecast of disease by the patient's pulse and purse."

[9] Several recent movies have also caught the scent. In *Coma*, hospitalized patients are robbed of body parts and murdered to reduce lengthy stays; in *John Grisham's The Rain-*

maker, venal insurance company executives withhold expensive treatment from a boy dying of leukemia; in *As Good as It Gets*, Helen Hunt's character curses HMOs to the frequent cheers of movie house audiences; in *Dr. Doolittle*, Eddie Murphy's title character refuses to sell out to a medical corporation ready to pump profits by cutting services; and in the extraordinary *Bullworth*, Warren Beatty lays the rap on insurance industry profiteering and their nefarious efforts to block health care reform.

I'm not opposed to a fair payoff nor expecting an upsurgence of eleemosynary corporate largesse. Recently, however, I came across what Robert Frost (1942/1979, p. 363) penned long ago—writing about "Kaiser" the German ruler, not "Kaiser" the highly rated not-for-profit HMO:

> It is as true as Caesar's name was Kaiser
> That no economist was ever wiser
> (Though prodigal himself and a despiser
> Of capital, and calling thrift a miser).
> And when we get too far apart in wealth,
> 'Twas his idea that for the public health,
> So that the poor won't have to steal by stealth,
> We now and then should take an equalizer.

[10]When APA past-president Nicholas Cummings was informed that the American Psychological Association had prevailed (at great cost) in its fight to have psychologists given full privileges at psychoanalytic institutes, he responded, "Congratulations on winning the right to train dinosaurs!" Our Juraissic brethren in Figure 4.4 are about to experience "future shock" (see N. A. Cummings, 1999).

[11]This trend has been described by VandenBos, Cummings, and DeLeon (1992, p. 92):

> Initially, managed mental health care relied on two mechanisms of cost control: benefit limitations and utilization review. This can be viewed as the first-generation model of managed mental health care. The second-generation model added was unmanaged provider networks, administered through the traditional fee-for-service model but permitting the providers to deliver services to plan members at a discounted rate (paid by the centralized management system). Third-generation managed care models are currently using a defined continuum of care, clinical case management of outpatient services, on-site hospitalization utilization review, more open benefits, life-style management programs, and networks of providers trained in managed care. In the first- and second-generation models, practitioners were simply subjected to the sentinel effect as a means of ensuring efficiency. In third-generation models, the responsibility of efficiency and effectiveness shifts fully to the provider.

It is important to recognized that, while innocence through ignorance and "just following orders" have been exposed as non-excuses since Nuremberg and My Lai, extensive social psychological research on "forced compliance" (see Collins & Hoyt, 1972) has demonstrated that persons are especially likely to embrace new attitudes if they are induced to engage in new behaviors under conditions with seemingly inadequate external justification (e.g., little pay). A related idea about promoting internalization through modern information management, in which computers closely track clinician's "treatment profiles," was suggested to me by a colleague who refers to the "HMO Panopticon," an allusion to the eighteenth-century architectural form initially developed by Jeremy Bentham for prisons (see Foucault, 1977). In such a structure, a central figure has constant visual inspection access to a collection of subjects. As White and Epston (1990, pp. 68–69) explain:

> However, while the persons in these spaces were ever visible to the guardians in the tower, the guardians were never visible to the persons in the individual spaces.

The tower was designed so that, through a careful arrangement of windows and doors, those in the individual spaces could not see in to the tower. Those persons in the spaces could never detect whether they were being observed at any particular point in time. Such persons had little choice but to assume that they were the subject of a guardian's gaze at any time. Thus, they experienced themselves as the subjects of the ever-present gaze. This mechanism of power has the effect of "inciting" persons to act as if they were always being observed. This was to be a very effective system of surveillance, as well as a very economic one, in that relatively few guardians, moving from one observation window to another, were required for its functioning.

(White and Epston use this image to illustrate how normalizing judgments and the "gaze" are used to promote self-survellience in anorexia and other conditions of self-subjugation; Madigan and Epston [1995] aptly call this top-down stance a "spy-chiatric gaze.") While consistency of effort promotes efficiency (Deming, 1986), the disenchanted and disgruntled might extend this analysis and metaphorically situate "The Birth of the Managed Care Organization" somewhere between Foucault's (1973) *The Birth of the Clinic: An Archeology of Medical Perception* and his (1977) *Discipline and Punish: The Birth of the Prison*.

[12]These sardonic lines from e. e. cummings (1925/1972, p. 204) might give pause:

Humanity i love you
because you would rather black the boots of
success than enquire whose soul dangles from his
watch-chain which would be embarrassing for both.

[13]We are far from being in complete agreement, however. I. J. Miller seemed to favor dismantling rather than reforming managed care. He also seemed to conflate brief therapy with sparse or truncated treatment; *brief therapy*, as I use the term, refers to time-effective intervention based on certain principles of clinical epistemology, not on the length of treatment.

[14]Delaying payment of claims can be very lucrative. A recent PriceWaterhouse–Coopers study sponsored by the American Psychological Association and the Center for Patient Advocacy "found that insurance and managed-care industries could generate up to $280 million each year in interest if as few as 1 percent of claims are denied, and then reversed, following an independent review process" (Rabasca, 1999, p. 20).

[15]I also have observed many times, particularly amongst hurried physicians (psychiatrists as well as internists), a process that I have termed *projective medication*, wherein a sad patient is depressing to the doctor and quickly gets prescribed an antidepressant (or a nervous patient makes the doctor anxious and gets an anxiolytic, or a scattered or intensely ambivalent patient makes the doctor feel "crazy" and gets a mood stabilizer or antipsychotic). These prescriptions may be technically accurate and even useful, but sometimes they seem premature and perhaps not even necessary if the doctor would (could?) have taken the time to listen, understand, and talk with the patient.

[16]One colleague (C. Preston Sullivan, personal communication, 1998) likened such practices to providing patients with enough penicillin for two doses a day for 5 days when what is really needed is three doses a day for 10 days—having the patient call back later and perhaps providing another 2 × 5 course may temporarily reduce the clinical problem (until treatment resistance develops), but it is neither well managed nor caring.

[17]Whitaker wasn't opposed to clear thinking, as I learned during a year of supervision with him. Indeed, after an intake interview he would sometimes even question me closely about possible diagnoses. His concern, however, was that the therapist be present as a person in therapy rather than as a theoretician or technician, a position he stated perhaps

most clearly in his 1976/1982 paper, "The Hindrance of Theory in Clinical Work." If one does not bind anxiety by adherence to theory or prescribed method, one's humanity, creativity and intuition are more available to stimulate flexibility and growth for the family. As another family therapy master, Salvador Minuchin, wrote in his Foreword (1982, p. ix) to Whitaker's collected papers, *From Psyche to System: The Evolving Therapy of Carl Whitaker* (Neill & Kniskern, 1982):

> Any statement presented as complete is turned into a fragment; like James Joyce, Whitaker creates a revolution in the grammar of life. . . . Though seemingly random, his interventions all are directed to challenge the meaning that people give to events. Whitaker's assumption seems to be that out of his challenge to form, creative processes in individual members as well as in the family as a whole can arise. Out of this experiential soup, a better arrangement among family members can result. . . . By the end of therapy, every family member has been touched by Whitaker's distorting magic. Each member feels challenged, misunderstood, accepted, rejected, or insulted. But he has been put in contact with a less familiar part of himself.

[18]William Blake (1804/1965a, p. 687):

> Let the indefinite be explored, and let every man be judged
> By his own works. Let all indefinites be thrown into demonstrations,
> To be pounded to dust and melted in the furnaces of affliction.
> He who would do good to another must do it in minute particulars:
> General good is the plea of the scoundrel, hypocrite and flatterer,
> For art and science cannot exist but in minutely organized particulars
> And some in generalizing demonstrations of the rational power.

[19]Like I. J. Miller, Seligman uses the term *brief therapy* to refer to treatments of relatively few sessions rather than to intervention approaches based on certain theoretical principles.

[20]Proposals for health care reform, such as the one unsuccessfully promulgated by the Clinton administration (see *Health Security*, 1993), generally have featured the following characteristics (as described by MacKenzie,1994, p. 409):

1. Health care coverage as a right of every citizen;
2. Individual responsibility to join a delivery plan;
3. Universal access;
4. No exclusion because of preexisting health risks;
5. Guaranteed comprehensive basic benefits;
6. A choice of plans;
7. Portability;
8. Considerable local responsibility for program design.

In the next few years, we can expect to see a range of legislative, judicial, and commercial initiatives, including proposals for physical and mental health care parity, various Patients' Bills of Rights (see Cantor, 1999) and debate about what forms of legal redress (such as lawsuits) may be sought. There also will be attempts by provider groups to self-administrate (so-called "provider-sponsored health plans"—see Bredesen, 1999) and growing calls for unionization of health care professionals (see Volz, 1999). These may be of some help in protecting the quality of health care available to the masses, although they may be a rearguard manifestation of the paradox (as L'Abate,1997, noted) that mental health professionals expect their clients, not themselves, to have to make changes. This is not the time for internecine (guild) bickering. I recall, in his describing the difficulties clinicians are having in responding organizationally to the challenges of the times, another of Nick Cummings's perceptive remarks (personal communication, 1999): "If asked to form a firing squad," quipped Cummings, "a group of therapists would probably form a circle!"

CHAPTER 5

with Steven Friedman

Dilemmas of Postmodern Practice Under Managed Care and Some Pragmatics for Increasing the Likelihood of Treatment Authorization

I swear by Apollo Physician, by Asclepius, by Health, by Panacea, and by all the gods and goddesses, making them my witnesses.
—Hippocrates (c. 460–377 B.C.), "The Physician's Oath" (in Lyons & Petrucelli, 1987)

Therapists increasingly are encountering the challenge of working with managed care. These different insurance arrangements—which all regulate the costs, site, and utilization of services (Hoyt, 1995a)—now cover more than 150 million Americans, with numbers expanding rapidly. For better or worse, they provide a context for treatment. In addition to collaborating with clients on goals and direction for therapy, mental health providers often must negotiate with case managers and utilization reviewers from managed care companies in getting authorization to imple-

Written with Steven Friedman.

Part of the material in this chapter was presented at the Therapeutic Conversations 3 Conference in Denver, June 1996, and at the Therapeutic Conversations 4 Conference in Toronto. May 1998.

From *Journal of Systemic Therapies*, by M. F. Hoyt and S. Friedman, *17*(3), pp. 23–33. Copyright 1998, by Guilford Press. Adapted with permission of the publisher.

ment treatment plans. Moreover, therapists are being asked more and more by managed care companies to demonstrate their effectiveness with outcome data (see Pincus, Zarin, & West, 1996; Rainer, 1996; Sperry, Grissom, Brill & Marion, 1997; VandenBos, 1996). Some of the basic characteristics of psychotherapy under managed care are outlined in Table 5.1.[1] Therapists who identify themselves as "postmodern" or "constructive"—including those who may situate their practices under the rubrics of solution-focused, narrative, possibility, and neo-Ericksonian approaches—usually work with clients in a collaborative, competency-based manner (see Friedman, 1993, 1995, 1997; Hoyt, 1994a, 1996b, 1998/1998). (Some strategic, cognitive-behavioral, and other therapists also might include themselves in this broad category.) While there are important technical differences between various postmodern therapies, they share certain assumptions: the belief in a socially constructed reality with an emphasis on the reflexive nature of client-therapist dialogue, a move away from hierarchical distinctions in favor of greater client-therapist egalitarianism, and a search for and utilization of client competencies rather than a pursuit of putative pathology and the reification of diagnoses of deficit and dysfunction.

☐ Four Dilemmas

While postmodern approaches (such as solution-focused and narrative therapies) would appear to be compatible with the managed care metagoals of efficacy and cost effectiveness, there are certain inherent contradictions or dilemmas between the theoretical underpinnings of postmodern therapy and common managed care practices:

1. *Possibility versus certainty.* Postmodern practices are based on assumptions of curiosity rather than certainty (Hoyt and Nylund, Chapter 13 this volume), embracing an "emergent epistemology" (Lankton & Lankton, 1998) that is open to "possibilities" (Friedman, 1993, 1995; Friedman & Fanger, 1991; O'Hanlon & Beadle, 1994), looking for "what works" (Berg, 1994b; de Shazer, 1985, 1988; DeJong & Berg, 1997; Hoyt and Berg, Chapter 8, this volume; Quick, 1996) rather than "uncovering" an objective "truth." Remembering that we are peering through various "lenses" (L. Hoffman, 1990/1995) can help to maintain some perspective on our perspective. In contradistinction, managed care practice often requires a quick diagnosis and intervention (which may tend to totalize the client and foreclose space for marginalized capacities to take form). Intense pressures toward brevity of treatment, which may result in what Wells and Phelps (1990, p. 16) have called the "Survival of the Shortest," also may counterproductively limit thoughtful reflection and further clinical de-

TABLE 5.1. Characteristics of psychotherapy under managed behavioral health care

Features	Comments
1. Specific problem-solving	Why now has the patient come to therapy? Identification with patient of achievable, measurable goals.
2. Rapid response and early intervention	Therapy begins right away, engaging the patient as soon as possible, including amplifying useful pretreatment progress.
3. Clear definition of patient and therapist responsibilities	The therapist structures treatment contacts, conducts particular interventions and involves significant others as needed. The patient is encouraged to participate actively, including doing "homework assignments" and making behavioral changes outside of therapy sessions.
4. Time is used flexibly and creatively	The length, frequency and timing of sessions vary according to patient needs, with the ideal being the most parsimonious intervention likely to have positive effects in a given situation.
5. Interdisciplinary cooperation	Medical and psychological involvement blend into a more holistic view of the patient. Allied health professionals may be used as indicated, as may appropriate psychopharmacology.
6. Multiple formats and modalities	Individual, group and/or marital/family therapy may be used in sequential or concurrent combinations and participation in various community resources (including self-help, 12-step, and support groups) may be vigorously encouraged.
7. Intermittent treatment or a "family practitioner" model	The idea of once-and-for-all "cure" gives way to a more realistic view that patients can return for "serial" or "distributed" treatment as needed, often focused around developmental issues throughout the life cycle. The therapist-patient relationship may be long-term although frequently abeyant.
8. Results orientation and accountability	Is treatment helping? Outcomes measurement helps define what works best. Utilization review and quality assurance function as complementary procedures, efficacious relief of symptoms being in the best interests of the patient as well as the company.

Note. From "Characteristics of Psychotherapy Under Managed Health Care," by M. F. Hoyt, 1995, *Behavioral Healthcare Tomorrow, 3*(5), 59–62. Reprinted with permission from Manisses Communications Group.

velopments. While the idea of guidelines for efficient (or cost-effective) treatment would seem laudatory, especially in times of insufficient resources, a false sense of certainty[2] may lead to the hidebound idea that "algorithms," "best practices," and "clinical pathways" can invariably specify "If X, do Y."[3]

2. *Egalitarian versus expert.* A corollary of the assumption of certainty is the idea that the clinician is "The Expert," able (and often required by managed care arrangements) to make rapid and definitive assessments—and provide rapid and curative "treatments." This is not to deny that therapists do have various expertises and that they can perform with varying degrees of skillfulness, but elevating therapists' knowledge to a position of High Authority may result in client "disempowerment" and, from a postmodern perspective, may go against the notion of collaboration and "leading by following." Even (or especially) if we do not embrace a radical "not knowing" (H. Anderson & Goolishian, 1992) posture, beware hubris! "Treatment plans" are more respectful and more likely to yield desired results if they are intentionally and explicitly cocreated or conegotiated (Whitson & Sexton, 1993). Consistent with this spirit, postmodern therapists may find the very word *treatment* problematic, and may prefer to describe their work using terms such as *consultation, collaboration, conversation,* and so forth.

3. *Competency versus pathology.* Brief therapists usually are "in search of solutions" (O'Hanlon & Weiner-Davis, 1989), whereas the managed care utilization reviewer may require extensive (and often counterproductive) "problem talk" related to *DSM-IV* (American Psychiatric Association, 1994); diagnoses, symptoms, and "impairments" (Goodman, Brown, & Deitz, 1992). Similarly, most postmodern therapists prefer the term *client* rather than *patient*, the latter carrying a medical connotation of sickness (Gergen, 1994b; Gergen, Hoffman, & Anderson, 1996; Hoyt, 1979/1995c, 1985a/1995e). Even the term *managed behavioral health care* points to "where the money is": a focus on control or a melioration of presenting symptomatology.[4]

4. *Systemic versus unilateral.* While brief therapists usually open their "lenses" wide enough to see a broader picture, managed care has tended to focus on the "identified patient" at the expense of more inclusive conceptualizations. Insurance coverage often is contingent upon an individual receiving a *DSM-IV* Axis I diagnosis to support "medical (or clinical) necessity." Such diagnoses are individualistically based and may be of dubious value for couple, family, or parent-child relationship-based therapy (Kaslow, 1996; Patterson, 1993; Patterson & Lusterman, 1996; Tomm, 1991b; see also Haley's remarks in Chapter 12, this volume); moreover, their pathological slant overlooks the endemic strengths and competencies that a "wellness" model of family psychotherapy would draw on (Fried-

man, 1991, 1997). As Austad and Hoyt (1992, p. 113) noted, many practitioners have found that *DSM* "diagnoses are often not as promising as they had assumed they would be in understanding and actually helping the patient."

☐ Ten Tips for Communicating with Managed Care Case Managers

These dilemmas notwithstanding, it is our experience that postmodern/constructive/brief therapists can—and do—apply their professional skills (alliance building, goal co-construction, intervention, outcome assessment) in order to formulate and articulate "user friendly" (patient, therapist, case manager) treatment plans and authorization requests. The following guidelines, garnered from personal experience and discussion with other therapists and case reviewers, are intended to enhance that process.[5]

1. *Build alliance.* As with almost any relationship, it usually is far more pleasant and productive if one proceeds in a courteous and respectful manner. Avoid adversarial positions. Case reviewers have a job to do; communicate with the purpose of creating what solution-focused therapy calls a "customer" (rather than "complainant" or "visitor") relationship (see Berg, 1989; de Shazer, 1985, 1988; Hoyt and Miller, Chapter 14 this volume; S. D. Miller, Duncan, & Hubble, 1997). When possible, develop a relationship with someone in particular at the company.

2. *Be bilingual.* Part of developing a good alliance is to appreciate the other person's worldview and, at least to some extent, to speak their language. *¿Habla usted managed care?* It usually is helpful in securing appropriate authorizations for treatment if some of the following terms are a prominent part of the clinician's working vocabulary: *brief, cost-effective, focused, goals, symptom reduction, active, structured, homework, behavioral, self-help, time-limited, monitoring, accountability.*

3. *Be organized and specific.* It is important, if one is going to operate effectively within the managed care world, to determine what specific information a particular company requires before authorizing clinical services. There is considerable variation in prerequisites, with some companies providing coverage without any plan being filed, to others that require a treatment plan and authorization request if it is expected that a certain number of sessions will be exceeded, to others that micromanage by erecting frequent (and usually inappropriate) barriers to care. Most companies that require treatment plans will want the following questions answered (Goodman et al., 1992; see Wolf & Bistline, 1998, for an excellent review of the application of solution-focused therapy to care management):

A. Please tell me about the patient?
B. What is the patient's diagnosis? What specific "target symptoms" or "impairments"[6] are there? (These can be quantified using scaling questions; see Berg & de Shazer, 1993; Quick, 1996.)
C. What are the goals and objectives of treatment?
D. How are you planning to treat the patient? For how long?
E. Can the patient be treated with more cost-effective alternatives (e.g., outpatient instead of inpatient, group therapy instead of individual therapy)? Is treatment medically/clinically necessary?
F. How is the patient progressing? How is outcome assessed? (Again, scaling questions can be useful.)

4. *Be timely, neat, and complete.* Remembering that case reviewers have a job to do, too, make specific requests with good rational support. Answer required questions or be prepared to explain why certain information is inappropriate or unavailable.

5. *Be accurate.* Do not "upcode" or "downcode," that is, do not exaggerate or minimize diagnostic information. While postmodern perspectives may deemphasize both pathology and the notion of absolute or objective "truths," therapists can exercise "good faith" by providing data that is accurate to the best of their knowledge. Diagnoses are defined by the presence (or absence) of specific symptoms. Although some find such discourse anathema (see Gergen, 1994b; Gergen et al., 1996; Tomm, 1990), the necessity may exist for the therapist working with managed care to wear two hats and be able to shift from one to the other, depending on context.

6. *Offer education.* Be willing to provide case managers with information about more preferred (i.e., time-effective) ways to do therapy with clients, including brief written summaries, recent articles, workshop brochures, and book references. This will enhance the provider's credibility, and expanding their knowledge base will make it easier for managers to say "Yes" to what the clinician thinks is appropriate.

7. *Be sure to secure clients' informed consent for release of information.* It also is important to chart any *informed refusal* (see Giles, 1993, p. 12), that is, treatments or recommendations that the client declined (such as medications, family meetings, hospitalizations, specific therapeutic techniques). This documentation can be very useful if the therapist has to later defend her or his professional conduct and attempted treatment of the client.

8. *Make appeals in writing in a timely manner.* If the company declines authorizing services that you believe are justified, file a written appeal and follow up with a phone call. It may be useful to restate the request, including careful attention to documenting symptoms and impairments that support a (covered) diagnosis and clinical/medical necessity of treat-

ment, along with a clear request for authorization within a specific period of time. It also can be helpful to ask that someone with specific expertise in the area of concern (e.g., eating disorders with teenagers, dissociative disorders, family therapy with a particular ethnic group) do the review, and that they contact the therapist to discuss details of the case before seeing the client.

9. *Let the case manager know when you finish.* Clarify what the policies are for terminating a case (including those instances when a client may "drop out" or fail to keep an appointment). When a client completes therapy in fewer sessions than were authorized, the clinician should be sure to let the company know—it helps construct a reputation as a "preferred provider" and may be useful if additional sessions are sought in another case.

10. *Ask for feedback—don't wait for problems.* Gardens grow better when weeded occasionally; good relationships require some cultivation.

☐ Caution: More Turbulence Ahead

As anyone who has not just awakened from a decade-long coma surely has noticed, we in the health care field are going through a time of great upheaval and uncertainty. Vital issues of quality of care, professional autonomy, and benefits preservation are at stake. As discussed in Chapter 4, there are great dangers of poor and inadequate treatment, violations of confidentiality, and discontinuation of needed therapy and patient abandonment. While there may be a need for greater efficiency, our hope is that *true managed care* will entail various arrangements to regulate the costs, site, and utilization of services in an ethical and decent, fiscally viable, and clinically sound manner (see Hoyt, 1995a)—a considerably different picture than the all-consuming drive for *cost containment* that impels most insurance nowadays. We have fallen into the maw of the money monster. As Tischler and Astrachan (1996, p. 959) eloquently put it:

> Corporate policy now dominates where public policy once ruled. The advocates of managed competition vanquished the champions of health rights. Marketspeak has become the lingua franca capturing the cost of caring for the ill in the simple phrase, "the medical loss ratio." As we stand on the threshold of the 21st century, much of what we once identified as social goods are now regarded as commodities. Economic issues dominate where social issues once held sway. In a world where human service agencies are regarded as market entities, the health care sector is little more than a microcosm of a larger universe that is being battered by change.

We agree with former U.S. Surgeon General C. Everett Koop (1996, p. 69) when he wrote: "Before we can enact the reform we need in health care, we should agree on the basic values and ethics upon which our health-care system—indeed, our society—is based, and from which it derives its moral power." We share with M. J. Bennett (1988) his concerns about the "greening [i.e., monetarization] of the HMO" and with Tischler and Astrachan (1996, p. 962) in their desire to "return to the Aristotelian view of social obligation and of health care as a social good." To move "toward a social ethic in an era of managed care" (Austad, 1996b) will require a *both/and* perspective, with attention to both stewardship responsibilities and to profits. As Sabin (1994a, p. 328) succinctly put it, "we must 'care about patients' and 'care about money.'" We need to take on this challenge, as professionals and as citizens, and not enter into internecine guild warfare at the expense of the greater good. The alternative will be "mangled care," not "managed care."

Notes

[1]As the titles of several recent and useful books have it, we are increasingly practicing *Psychotherapy in the Age of Accountability* (L. D. Johnson, 1995) where we need to know *Brief Therapy and Managed Care* (Hoyt, 1995), *Psychotherapy in Managed Health Care: The Optimal Use of Time and Resources* (Austad & Berman, 1991), and *Time-Effective Psychotherapy: Maximizing Outcome in an Era of Minimized Resources* (Friedman, 1997). We also need to know about *Managing Managed Care: A Mental Health Practitioner's Survival Guide* (Goodman, Brown, & Deitz, 1992), *How to Partner with Managed Care* (C. H. Browning & Browning, 1993), *Surviving and Prospering in the Managed Mental Healthcare Marketplace* (Todd, 1994), and *Maneuvering the Maze of Managed Care: Skills for Mental Health Practitioners* (Corcoran & Vandiver, 1996). For an extensive bibliography, see Hoyt (1995).

[2]In a felicitious turn of phrase, O'Hanlon (1991; Hubble & O'Hanlon, 1992) referred to "delusions of certainty" as he cautioned against closing down possibilities via "theoretical countertransference."

[3]Improving the quality of psychotherapy can result from the integration of science and practice (L. D. Johnson & Shaha, 1996; O'Donohue & Szymanski, 1994; Steenbarger, Smith, & Budman, 1996), but the data are so far from conclusive that efforts to "manualize" or prescribe treatments would appear "premature" (Drozd & Goldfield, 1996; see also Strosahl, 1998) and likely to result in therapists being required to forsake individualized judgments in favor of "cookbooks" and "paint-by-numbers" (Silverman, 1996). As Tischler and Astrachan (1996, pp. 960–963) noted:

> Algorithms and decision trees provide digital wisdom in the form of practice guidelines and disease management profiles that create a facade of empiricism based on normative judgments. . . . As information is shared, one must guard against standarization of practice becoming an end in and of itself. . . . [I]t is imperative that the vision must strive to preserve innovation.

[4]See Wylie's trenchant (1995) article, "Diagnosing for Dollars?" in the *Family Therapy Networker* issue, "The Power of *DSM-IV*." Long ago, Ambrose Bierce offered this definition from *The Devil's Dictionary* (1906/1957, p. 36): "*Diagnosis*, n., A physician's forecast of disease by the patient's pulse and purse."

[5]These are general suggestions, and need to be considered within the specific contexts (clinical, medicolegal, ethical, and so forth) in which one works. For more information, see also Browning and Browning (1993), Goodman et al. (1992), and Hoyt (1995a, especially Chapter 2, "Twenty-Five Questions to Ask Before Joining a Managed-Care Organization"); plus Chapter 4, this volume.

[6]As Goodman et al. (1992, P. 31) wrote:

Impairment describes a worsening, lessening, weakening, damaging, or reduction in ability to function and, in turn, anticipates a potential for repair, improvement, enhancement, and strengthening. . . . [They] signal the appropriateness for treatment and frame the documentation and communication of not only the treatment plan but also the patient's response to treatment interventions. . . . Impairments are the reasons why a patient requires treatment. They are not the reason(s) for the presence of the disorder, nor are they the disorder itself. Rather, they are observable, objectifiable manifestations that necessitate and justify care.

with Jon Matthew Carlson

Interview I:
Brief Therapy and Managed Care

> I want to be seen here in my simple, natural, ordinary fashion,
> without straining or artifice; for it is myself that I portray.
> —Michel Eyquem de Montaigne (1580)
> *Essays*, Book 1, "To the Reader"

The following interview took place in November 1995 over the kitchen table at my home in Mill Valley, California. Matt Carlson and I discussed issues regarding brief therapy, some of the promises and problems of managed care, and several likely future trends and their implications for marital and family therapists and counselors.

Carlson: *It is evident today that psychotherapy in the 1990s and beyond will be increasingly influenced by financial forces. The shift seems to be moving from the traditional fee-for-service model to health maintenance organizations (HMOs) and managed care. What trends do you see from working with a large HMO?*

Hoyt: *I think we are going to see more and more a push toward efficiency and accountability. Because there are limited resources, we need to find out what works and do more of what works. Why are you doing what you are doing? Is it helping clients achieve their goals? Is it the most direct route?*

Managed care, generically speaking, can be defined as various arrangements to regulate the costs, site, and utilization of services, with treatment decisions par-

---

Written with Jon Matthew Carlson.

From "Interview: Michael F. Hoyt," by J. M. Carlson, *The Family Journal: Counseling and Therapy for Couples and Families, 5*(2), pp. 172–181. Copyright 1997. Adapted with permission of the publisher.

tially determined by parties other than therapist and client/patient. Whatever one's particular theoretical orientation and health care delivery system, there seem to be eight characteristics of therapy under managed care:

1. *specific problem solving*
2. *rapid response and early intervention*
3. *clear definition of therapist and client responsibilities*
4. *time used flexibly and creatively*
5. *interdisciplinary cooperation*
6. *multiple treatment formats and modalities*
7. *intermittent treatment or a "family practitioner" model*
8. *results orientation and accountability.*

There is going to be lots more emphasis on time-sensitive or time-effective therapy, which sometimes is called "brief therapy." Actually, I do not particularly like the word "brief," even though it has been used in the title of some books I have been involved with, because "brief" suggests rapid or quick. I prefer the idea of time sensitivity or making the most of each session. "Efficient therapy" might be the best term.

Carlson: *It seems that the next psychotherapy "wave" or shift is being pushed by financial forces.*

Hoyt: *The third Evolution of Psychotherapy Conference was held in mid-December 1995. Although I was not on the faculty at the conference, I have been thinking a lot about the field. To have evolution, we need to have two factors: One is genetic variability, and the other is environmental pressures. The financial part certainly is an environmental pressure. We also have multiculturalism and postmodern conceptions suggesting there are different ways of looking at problems and looking at solutions. We also are in the information processing era, so there is much more thinking about things in terms of information processing and cognitive therapy; similarly, there are cybernetics and systems thinking motifs in both environmental ecology and family therapy. In another era, Freud's time, we were looking at things through the hydraulic model. There is a lot of interaction between the culture and models of psychotherapy.*

Carlson: *So, therapists are not necessarily being pushed by finances, but they are being influenced by what works and also by what society is telling them.*

Hoyt: *Well, I think the financial forces are paramount. Initially, managed care was about cost containment. It really has not been managed care; it mostly has been managed cost. I think some of the better companies are now recognizing the importance of emphasizing quality of care rather than just trying to hold down costs.*

Carlson: *Managed care systems often work on an individual diagnostic model. How do you think they accommodate families?*

Hoyt: *That is a very complicated and important question. Of course, we should* *recognize that there is no one entity called "managed care." Different companies approach it in different ways. Generally, however, there was a movement toward it being very individualistic, and marital or family therapy often was not a covered benefit. Some of the more enlightened companies have now come to realize the importance of family and couples therapy. Oftentimes, however, they still insist that at least one of the family members must have an Axis I DSM-IV diagnosis, a diagnosable psychiatric condition, for which conjoint or family therapy is seen as the treatment of choice. This, then, raises questions about the identified patient versus a more systems or interactional perspective.*

Again, it depends on the particular service delivery system that you are involved in. Some will say that whoever is willing to come to therapy can be treated, and they will not require a psychiatric diagnosis, at least not if the problem can be resolved relatively quickly. Sometimes there is an apparent psychiatric diagnosis, but then we enter into a doublespeak, where we may tell the clients that we need to put one person's name down on the form to get treatment authorized, although it involves all of them equally. So, we wind up having to explain unilateral versus systemic thinking. We also get into doublespeak if insurance requires pathology-based diagnoses and we think therapeutically more in terms of learning or growth.

Carlson: *One of the keys to doing therapy in a managed care organization seems to be planned or best use of available resources within the facility, within the therapist, and within the patients themselves.*

Hoyt: *I think we are seeing a shift toward what I have been calling* constructive therapies, *those that are collaborative and competency based. This very much keeps with the HMO idea of* health maintenance—*looking for health, resources, and strengths, not just pathology, defects, and weaknesses. I think there are some very good advantages. One is that it is much more user friendly. Clients like to be seen as whole people, not just as diagnoses or defects. I also think it is more user friendly for therapists. It helps reduce the problems of burnout, when you are looking not only for problems but rather at the entire person or family. There has not yet been enough systematic research on the newer forms of brief therapy, but we already have seen that many of the solution-focused, solution-oriented, narrative, and other competency-based therapies get good results.*

Carlson: *What attracts you to solution-focused therapy?*

Hoyt: *It's simple, optimistic, respectful, versatile, and effective. It appreciates clients' own resources and worldviews. I am interested in helping clients to achieve their goals, so I like to use whatever works. This is not an either/or situation; it is a both/and situation. I also find a lot of value in other approaches, particularly those that can be termed* constructive—*including narrative, strategic, Ericksonian, and others yet to be determined.*

Carlson: *Do the brief therapies have common characteristics?*

Hoyt: *In their own ways, and to varying degrees, they all seem to emphasize certain features:*

1. rapid and positive alliance;
2. focus on specific achievable goals;
3. clear definition of client and therapist responsibilties, often with tasks or assignments to be carried out between sessions;
4. emphasis on strengths and competencies, with an expectation of change;
5. novelty and assisting the client toward new perception and behaviors;
6. here-and-now (and next) orientation
7. time sensitivity.

Carlson: *In* Brief Therapy and Managed Care *(Hoyt, 1995a), you discuss ways that time can be seen more as an attitude than just as the number of sessions. How do you look at time?*

Hoyt: *I think we are coming to realize that there is only now. If we talk about history or memory, we are still in the present remembering or looking backward. If we talk about the future, we are looking forward; it is expectation. But there really is no time but the present. So, I think of time as a perspective or medium in which we work. To give a very specific and practical example, we can think about the length and spacing of sessions. Traditionally, we oftentimes have seen patients for 50 minutes, week after week after week. That sometimes may be the best model. Other times, it may be better to see patients maybe twice in the first week and once or twice in the second week: Then they will have some skills and support and there will be some things they need to do before we see them again.*

Carlson: *Structuring time concentrates the focus.*

Hoyt: *Right. There also is Parkinson's Law in psychotherapy (Appelbaum, 1975), which says that work expands or contracts to fit the time allotted. Sometimes if we tell people that they have 20 sessions, they will start to get down to it in the eighteenth session. You tell them they have five, and they will begin to focus on the second or third or fourth. Most of us studied the night before the exam.*

We also may not always want to have every session be 50 minutes. Particularly with a family or couple, it may be useful to have a 75- or 90-minute session. We could say, "Let's roll up our sleeves and talk until you have some ideas about what you need to do next. And then, after you've done it, call me." Notice the language: It's not that "we're going to talk until we solve all of this" but rather "until you have some ideas of what you need to do next." I think of this as an empowerment model in the sense that we are helping people find their power and assuming that they can make some changes without having to be in weekly contact with the therapist.

Carlson: *This is a new approach to therapy.*

Hoyt: *For some people, yes. I think Nicholas Cummings (1990; N. A. Cummings & Sayama, 1995) was one of the first to talk about intermittent therapy or therapy throughout the life cycle, where people will come when there is a particular problem for a period of time, but then they may not be seen for long periods of time.*

Carlson: *Therapy is used at certain times, much like you use a family practitioner.*

Hoyt: *Oftentimes, people will come in around developmental crises, during passages or life cycle transition points. For example, when people get married, it may raise issues that were not salient until then; or when a child is born; or the so-called "empty nest syndrome"; or if there is a divorce or a bereavement. Thinking this way, we sometimes also can normalize some of the problems that bring people to therapy as developmental challenges, noting that they already may know some of the skills but that they also may need to learn some new skills in order to deal with a particular problem. It is very different from the traditional cure model, where we are going to find a problem, get to the root of it, work it out, and be rid of it once and for all.*

Carlson: *So, treatment may be more focused and specific?*

Hoyt: *Well, some research evidence has been coming out lately. For example, Neil Jacobson's (1995) article in* The Family Therapy Networker *suggested that therapy may be helpful at the time, but we should not always assume that it has permanent long-term effects. So, I think what we try to do is help clients get unstuck or back on track, not necessarily expecting that we will solve this problem for all time. It is like the family practitioner model, where when I am ill, I go and see my doctor. I have not seen her in a couple of years, but I will have episodes of care when there is a particular problem. The fact that I go back to see her does not mean that we did not do a good job. Quite the opposite. I go back when the time is right for more therapy.*

Carlson: *In the meantime, the problem may have changed a bit, so you can adapt and change your approach.*

Hoyt: *Therapy is very powerful, but I think we have overestimated the power of therapy. There are many other factors that help people make changes—friendships, spirituality and religion, life circumstances, maturation, or the psychotherapy of everyday life. Salvador Minuchin, in his fine book* Family Healing *(Minuchin & Nichols, 1993), says therapy may take place in the office, "but change takes place at home" (p. 84). It is interesting to ask clients later what was most helpful in their therapy and hear what they report. Sometimes, it is not what the therapist felt was most important. And, sometimes, it can be a humbling experience to find out that it was something not so clearly related to our "brilliant" interventions.*

Carlson: *This also seems to be a shift in therapy, decreasing the authority of the therapist and making the relationship between the therapist and the client more equal. Therapists become more like guides and less directive.*

Hoyt: *Well, this is a controversial area. I think we are seeing a general shift toward being egalitarian or coequal rather than hierarchical or authoritarian. It is not "I'm an expert and I'm going to fix you." However, I do think that we have certain expertises or skills that we need to call on. I was involved in a conference at one time where a very well-known therapist who is an M.D.—a psychiatrist—*

worked with a family. Later, I asked him why he had not suggested medication and he said that, because the clients had not brought it up themselves, he did not want to impose on them. I thought it might have been wise for him to suggest medication, not to insist on it perhaps, but at least to use his expertise and say, "This is a resource I know that might be helpful. Are you interested in it?" So, I think we have to be careful that, in the move toward not taking over clients' lives, we do not let it swing too far and forget that we do have certain training and expertise they may not know about.

Carlson: *After all, there is a reason why the client is seeing you in the first place.*

Hoyt: *Yes, although I think part of our real expertise is also knowing how to ask questions in a way that will help the client realize his or her own competency or expertness. A number of people have written about the importance of asking good questions. Socrates recognized how important it is to ask questions that help people see what they have.*

Carlson: *So, the purpose of the question, in this respect, would be to lead, not simply to elicit information?*

Hoyt: *Well, all questions are leading questions. If I ask you how old you are, or your marital status, or what you do for an occupation, or how many times you have been in the hospital, or how often you feel depressed, all of those questions are leading your consciousness, your attention, in one direction rather than another. So, I think there is a balance where we have to ask questions that are going to lead (or, perhaps, "invite" would be a better word, as Freedman and Combs [1993] have used it) to help people to consider alternatives or possibilities. We are not insisting, but we are inviting them. This also ties in with some of the interesting work being done with reflecting teams. Friedman (1995) edited a book on reflecting teams in family therapy that beautifully illustrates ways wherein, by hearing the reflections of the therapeutic team, clients are in a position to choose different options, different constructions of reality, that may suit them. We should not be manipulative in the sneaky, self-serving sense of the word, but inevitably we do influence. It is our job as therapists to promote change.*

Carlson: *So, it goes back to the basic skills of listening, reflecting, and good questioning.*

Hoyt: *While Carl Rogers (1951) talked about "reflecting and clarifying," he of course did more than simply reflect and clarify. He chose what we would reflect and clarify, to what he would pay and call attention. An image that I have become fond of lately is the image of the compassionate Buddha. In Buddhist iconography, the compassionate Buddha is holding his hand up; it is called a mudra, which is a hand position that depicts an overall attitude toward life. The idea is that the compassionate Buddha is just reflecting back what is given. However, I think that when therapists hold a hand up, so to speak, the hand is a convex and concave mirror on a swivel, and we can turn it and open or close certain parts of the story. So, for example, when clients tell us that they have been having problems for 10 years but the past couple of weeks have gone well, we have to choose: Do we talk* *about the past couple of weeks that have gone well or the 10 years of history of the problem? Perhaps both, but we may want to open part of the story and shrink part of the story. Oftentimes, when we talk about taking history, I think it would be better to realize that we are making history. As Michael White (1993a) has put it, there are many "histories of the present." It would be interesting, I think, for therapists to take not only a history of the present complaint but rather a history of the present recovery.*

Carlson: *You are talking about what is happening with the client right now. Constructivist approaches also are based on the idea that people create their own meaning. Michael Lerner (1995) has spoken about how we currently are in a crisis of meaning. In the face of this crisis, why are these approaches so popular with therapists and clients?*

Hoyt: *First, let me say that I do not know. It is an interesting question: Why now does something come up in the culture? Is there some collective unconscious or need that is being filled? There does seem to be a breakdown in meaning, at least in terms of one overarching worldview that provides organization and purpose. Some of the impetus is the information saturation that Gergen (1991) has written about so well. Everything seems relative nowadays. I am worried that there is a kind of alienation or anomie or breakdown in basic values. The recent O. J. Simpson trial got an enormous amount of attention. Whatever you think of the verdict, the whole thing did not seem to reduce anybody's cynicism. We also see right now a reactionary right-wing movement that is going under the banner of family values. The issues are complicated, although sometimes their values seem as oxymoronic as the idea that one can "kill for Christ."*

Carlson: *How about in the therapy realm?*

Hoyt: *Many therapists, like Alfred Adler and Viktor Frankl, have long talked about how we build our understanding and search for meaning. The philosophical idea—traceable through Epictetus and Marcus Aurelius, through Vico and Kant, through Husserl and Merleau-Ponty, amongst others—that we are putting together our sense of reality rather than just knowing an objective "truth" is central to constructivism. This, I think, also is manifesting itself in a positive way in the idea that there are many different schools of therapy now, that there is not an orthodoxy anymore, be it psychoanalysis or cognitive-behavioral or a certain form of family therapy. This is one of the overarching messages in* Constructive Therapies, *Volumes 1 and 2 (Hoyt, 1994a, 1996b, also see Hoyt, 1998). We are recognizing that there are many different ways to look at reality. I think we and our clients have to find ways of looking and making meaning that have the basic values that we believe in, values of justice and cooperation—values that hold up human beings as being most important. In that wonderful movie* Smoke, *I love the line when, in ambiguous circumstances, the female character says, "It's your call, Augie."*

Carlson: *What is another overarching message from the* Constructive Therapies *volumes?*

Hoyt: *Responsibility: Our perceptions and practices have consequences. One implication is that, because all approaches are not equally effective, therapists need to find out and do what works best—with all the attendant problems of who defines "best."*

Carlson: *In constructive therapy, you are finding what is meaningful for the client. What do you think is meaningful for therapists themselves?*

Hoyt: *I think most therapists have gone into this field for very positive reasons. In* Constructive Therapies, *Volume 2 (Hoyt & Combs, 1996), Michael White speaks very eloquently about efforts that have sometimes been made to undermine or pathologize therapists' own motivations for becoming helping professionals. We sometimes are questioned if there are some unresolved issues in our families, if we are working on some problems with our mothers or our fathers, if we are codependent, if we are on some kind of power trip, and so on. I do not think that is why most therapists go into this field. I think we have gone into this field because we have basic values—wanting to see the world be a better place, wanting to make things right, trying to help people. We have to resist being undermined in our commitment and our motivation. Having said that, I do think that therapists sometimes are enticed by a certain kind of process. There is a certain kind of intimacy, there are certain status and perhaps financial payoffs for being a therapist, and sometimes there is a need to be needed. I think we have to be honest with ourselves about what our motivations are to make sure we are serving the best reasons rather than others.*

Carlson: *As therapists continue to search for meaning in their work, there has been some debate about where therapists and therapy will fit in managed care. Will it still be good therapy? As someone who works in an HMO and writes about managed care, how do you address those critics?*

Hoyt: *I think therapists working in HMOs generally see it as a positive experience. They enjoy the stimulation and the challenge. They enjoy the idea of trying to be effective with a wide range of clients, although the work is hard and the caseload volumes are not easy. They value efficacy and efficiency in getting the job done. Those therapists who primarily are long-term process-oriented, however, may find it too frustrating, and most therapists, working in HMOs and in private practice, are feeling financially pinched nowadays. So, if those are the primary motivations, they may be dissatisfied.*

Carlson: *Some people who have been highly critical of managed care have not seen it as having positive values.*

Hoyt: *Michael Bennett (1988) wrote an interesting article called "The Greening of the HMO" where he talked about how, when HMOs initially were formed, they were seen as almost revolutionary: the therapists who went to work for them and the patients who enrolled in them had a social mission of wanting good treatment for the masses. Recently, some of the HMO ideas have been taken over by the rest of managed care and there has been "greening" or monetarization. Some of the ini-*

tial prosocial values have been lost, and it is being seen as just another business enterprise. For me, the positives of managed care and HMOs are accountability, availability, and an emphasis on quality of care. The negatives have to do with greed. And sometimes we hear stories—unfortunately, sometimes they are true— that are shocking about patients being denied care that they truly need. This should not be tolerated. But it raises another issue, which is, Who is going to pay for all of this? It has been very easy for therapists to take the high moral ground and say we are not involved in a business, we are involved in a special human service calling. The fact is that there also is a financial aspect. Somebody has to pay for all of it. Everyone wants more care to be provided, but very few people want to raise their taxes enough to pay for it. In California, voters in 1995 rejected Proposition 186, a single-payer health care reform initiative. When I have consulted with people in some of the other countries that have been held up as models, such as Canada, Great Britain, and Japan, they have told me that they are not so satisfied with their health care delivery systems—there are oftentimes long waiting lists, and therapists are not accustomed to being as well paid and having the standard of living that we have in the United States. There seems to be no free lunch. Somebody is going to pay for it.

Carlson: *It also is very interesting that therapists are being held accountable for some of their work, maybe where they have not been in the past.*

Hoyt: *There are ethical and medical-legal abuses by some companies, to be sure, but some therapists and clients also contributed to the current situation by submitting billing for a lot of dubious "treatment." We are going through a "correction" right now, and I expect the pendulum will swing back toward meeting a broader range of true clinical needs. I certainly hope so, for the sake of our patients and our professions. We all have heard stories about "mangled care." I am not an apologist or even entirely a supporter, but I do not see managed care as the "Evil Empire" either.*

Carlson: *When people voice their concerns, their problem with managed care can be viewed in terms of profit versus people or money versus service. Yet, it seems that what is lost here is the idea that there is some very good work being done, very effective work being done.*

Hoyt: *Everything cannot be cost effective or pay for itself. I do think there is some good work being done. There are some good innovations that question some of the very basic ideas of how therapy should be delivered. Is it best that it be one-on-one, week after week? Would it be better to have more group therapy? Would it be better to have more focus on natural systems such as families or work groups? Sometimes innovations will come only when there is pressure requiring an innovation. At the same time, I am concerned that there is a great temptation toward greed, particularly if the managers of the managed care company are only interested in the next quarter—if their basic purpose is to show that they have held down costs for 3 months so that they can get promoted and move up to headquarters, and they do* *not have an interest in the long-term relationship and the long-term outcomes for clients. Then we are going to have a problem.*

Carlson: *In* Brief Therapy and Managed Care, *you wrote two chapters on single-session therapy, one coauthored with Robert Rosenbaum and Moshe Talmon. How do therapists create pivotal moments in single sessions?*

Hoyt: *I think one way we create a pivotal moment is by listening for the moment in the therapy where the client brings up a past success—the ideas that Steve de Shazer and Bill O'Hanlon have written about as "exceptions" and "solutions" and that Michael White and David Epston have written about as "unique outcomes" and "sparkling moments"—and trying to amplify the positives. That is one way. Another, as I learned from Bob and Mary Goulding, is to confront the moment when the client tries to "con" himself or herself into thinking they don't have responsibility (or authorship) for their own experience (like when they say that someone "makes" them feel a certain way) or when they disingenuously say they will "try" to do something (meaning they will not really do it in good faith). Not letting these slip by can help clients take a big step toward autonomy. Introducing humor is another way to help the client get "unstuck." One time, I was obsessing about something and one of my mentors, Carl Whitaker, remarked, "Don't worry. Whatever you decide, you'll regret it!" Pop! That was Carl! We also can look for strengths in the client's complaint. The client comes in and is unhappy about something, but we can hear the positive intention. For example, not long ago, I saw somebody who had made a suicide attempt in an effort to get a life insurance payment to help his family members, who were suffering financial hardship. As he told me about it, I said to him, "You know, in some ways you're a hero." He said, "What do you mean, a hero?" I said, "Well, you're a hero." And he said, "I heard you, doctor, but what do you mean? Why do you say I'm a hero? I couldn't even do that right." And I said, "Well, have you ever heard the term 'deadbeat dad'? Many men in your situation would have run away, but you even were willing to consider giving up your life to try to feed your children and keep a roof over your family. Your technique, the way you went about it, I don't think was particularly good, but I think it sounds like your heart is in the right place." He and I both were very touched by this recognition. We went on to talk about some other ways that he could help his family and also talked about what he was going to need to do to cope until he could find a job again. So, I think that looking for the strength, even in the problem or even in the complaint, is very helpful. Most clients are doing the best that they can. The technique of a mother or a father who is very domineering or very passive might not be good, but they are trying as best they know how and I think we have to recognize that, if we are going to respect clients and get them to engage in therapy. We have to hear what they are trying to accomplish, give honor to that, and then offer them some other ways of going about doing it.*

Carlson: *So, it seems that the basic skill not only is listening but also knowing* *what to listen for. In addition, you are looking to reframe the past experience and create an optimistic idea that better things are possible.*

Hoyt: *While my wife and I were walking out of the theater after seeing* La Bamba, *the movie about singer Richie Valens, we started to talk about his brother, who I thought had been quite destructive in Valen's life. In response, my wife said, "He had such heart and such passion; too bad he couldn't find a positive way to use it." My wife often sees the light while I'm still cursing the darkness.*

Carlson: *Single-session therapy certainly fits well with the current tendency toward shorter and shorter treatments.*

Hoyt: *Sometimes it can be done in one session. If therapy requires more than one session, however, it does not mean that it was a failure; it just means it took more than one session. Our finding that some clients could make a useful, constructive shift in one session and did not require more therapy sometimes has been misquoted or misused. It has been held up to say that therapy should take only one session. That was not our intention at all. Our intention was to say that some clients can get enough in one session, that they can get unstuck, empowered, and go on. If clients need more therapy, I think they should have more therapy.*

Carlson: *One of the keys to the constructive approaches is looking for positives, looking for the light in the person, maybe in the past or maybe in his or her story.*

Hoyt: *Sometimes we "see" the other person and we make a healthy connection, which may be both a corrective experience in itself and the start of bringing forward something good. It sure makes therapy more enjoyable. In an interview we did together (Hoyt, 1994b), John Weakland and Steve de Shazer said that most therapists are not mental health professionals; rather, they are mental illness professionals. We spend a great deal of time being trained to look for illness, pathology, and so forth. I think clients will respond much more positively if they see that we are looking for their strengths. If we keep focusing on what the clients feel badly about, we tend to move more and more to a shame-based therapy. That is not to say we should ignore problems or pretend they are not there, but I think many clients expect therapy to be getting dragged through the mud or being reminded of all their failures and flaws rather than a more balanced view.*

Carlson: *So, what you are doing is acknowledging the past but, at the same time, looking toward the future so there is some place that the client wants to go to.*

Hoyt: *Yes. Otherwise, we do not have a message of hope. By taking too much terrible history and focusing too much on the past, we can give clients the message, "You've got this enormous bag of problems you're carrying around. How could you ever be different?" I think the real question is not how far back the problem goes but, rather, how much farther forward the client is going to carry it. And, the idea of hope is that something can be different. We have a saying, "If you don't change directions, you're going to wind up where you're heading." More of the same does not make a change. We are trying to help clients change something in their "viewing and doing," to use O'Hanlon's excellent phrase. Sometimes, we can* *do this by reframing, by giving different meanings to things that have happened. Other times, we can do this by helping clients begin to construct a different idea of their future that will give a different meaning to what they are going through in the present.*

Carlson: *Looking back at the past, you are not eliminating it or glossing it over. You just are looking at it in a different way.* In Brief Therapy and Managed Care, *you highlight the distinction between being a "shrink" versus an "expander."*

Hoyt: *Right. Oftentimes, I think clients are so stuck in one view of the past that we need to help them get some degrees of freedom to look at themselves differently. The brief therapy principles of co-creating achievable goals, focusing on strengths and exceptions to the problem, and looking forward can be especially useful with clients who have had terrible pasts. So-called chronic and persistently and severely mentally ill clients can be very discouraged and discouraging if the therapist does not help them focus on the possible.*

Carlson: *In constructing the future, constructing an individual's life, how do clients deal with problems outside of the self, problems of society, and social problems that they are facing? How do those filter in?*

Hoyt: *Well, I think it is very important for clients to recognize that some of the problems they experience personally are larger social problems such as ageism, racism, sexism, homophobia, and economic displacement. Sometimes, we can help clients recognize how they may have internalized certain beliefs—how they were indoctrinated or "recruited" (to use the narrative therapy term) into certain self-limiting or self-defeating beliefs. Sometimes, this happens very subtly and people do not even recognize that they have been in a trance or politically oppressed. Much of the good work done in feminist therapy, for example, gets patients to recognize how some of their oppression is not originally intrapsychic but rather is politically based. We need to help clients see what their own roles in their problems may be and what options they may have, but we also need to recognize that many clients live in a pernicious world. Some problems need to be addressed on a political or socioeconomic level.*

Carlson: *How does a family conflict, for example, create or prefigure their reality, their future?*

Hoyt: *One time I asked R. D. Laing what he thought about transference, and his response was, "It is posthypnotic suggestion with amnesia." I think we get programmed to see things a certain way, and we do not even know where the program came from. So, in that sense, we truly are doing consciousness raising in therapy. We are helping clients become conscious of some unconscious scripts or trances that they have been put into.*

Carlson: *What trends do you see with psychotherapy and managed care?*

Hoyt: *There are 12 likely trends, as outlined in* Brief Therapy and Managed Care *(Hoyt, 1995a; see also Chapter 4 this volume):*

1. *more outcomes measurement*
2. *more treatment planning*
3. *greater involvement of mental health services in primary care*
4. *increasingly organized and integrated systems of care*
5. *fewer and larger managed care companies*
6. *more group practices and fewer solo practitioners*
7. *more care provided by masters-level clinicians, psychiatric nurses, and various certified counselors*
8. *more group therapy*
9. *much less inpatient care*
10. *greater reliance on computer technology, with information processing and research advantages as well as "Big Brother" risks to confidentiality*
11. *less utilization review, especially in the outpatient arena, as education, certification, and credentialing of efficient preferred providers move forward*
12. *more emphasis on constructive therapies, ones that are collaborative, future oriented, and based on clients' competencies and resources.*

I am concerned, however, that managed care may prematurely foreclose some of the creativity in the field. Some of the companies, wanting therapy to be as efficient as possible, have begun to authorize certain treatments and not other treatments. This may be premature. I do not think it has all been worked out. People are much too complex. We cannot have a simplistic formula—here is the diagnosis, and here is the treatment. There has to be room for individual differences, therapist autonomy, and new innovations. I also am very concerned about those clients who truly need longer or ongoing therapy and support. Managed care has not managed to care for these people. Intensive and continuous care arrangements will have to be made, at considerable expense, if we really are going to reform health care.

Carlson: *What do you think therapists can do right now to address these needs or these concerns?*

Hoyt: *I think there are several things. Who pays the piper calls the tune, so I think it is very important that we spend a lot of effort, both as individuals and through our various professional societies and associations, educating the purchasers of health care about good health care, including psychotherapy, so that they do not just buy the cheapest and later find out that it was not adequate. I think therapists also need to pay more attention to the purpose of therapy and be able to document that we are achieving successful outcomes with patients so we can demonstrate that what we are doing has value (Carlson, Hinkle, & Sperry, 1993). We know as therapists that what we are doing adds quality, meaning, purpose, and beauty to life. The purchasers of health care, more and more, are interested in symptom resolution, patient satisfaction, reduced absenteeism, and so-called bottom-line ideas, and I think we are going to have to pay more attention to that. If we do not, the risk will be that companies will insure only so-called catastrophic illness. They will say that this other kind of therapy, although nice, is not clinically* *or medically necessary. They will say people can pay for it if they want it, but that it should not be insured.*

Carlson: *Do you see therapy with families falling into this category?*

Hoyt: *I hope not. I think family therapy needs to be held up as one of the more valuable approaches. But, again, I think we are going to have to ask, "What is the problem that is being treated? Why are they in family therapy?" Otherwise, the risk is that it will be seen as enrichment or personal growth, which companies will say is laudatory but not something they should insure. They are trying to define what insurance is going to cover very narrowly in terms of clinical or medical necessity.*

Carlson: *What do family therapists working within HMOs need to do?*

Hoyt: *Well, I think one of the problems has been that most of the diagnoses for which managed care organizations and insurance companies have agreed to pay are individual psychopathology diagnoses. Family distress, family dysfunction, and parent-child conflict oftentimes have been excused as a "V" code or "problems in living" and have not been seen as things legitimately needing intervention, therapy, treatment, or whatever you want to call it. So, I think we need to advocate that these are human interactional problems which are as important as anxiety disorders or depression. Clients often request "marriage counseling," so this can be a selling point for market-oriented companies. HMOs also increasingly need to recognize that, unless treated, family problems often will eventuate in expensive medical and psychiatric cases. This is the idea of the "medical utilization offset phenomenon," the well-documented finding that mental health services reduce the need for medical care. Family therapy needs to be seen as an integral part of the overall health enterprise.*

Carlson: *Do you think it is important for therapists to be more open, to break down some of their walls around their theoretical orientation and look at others?*

Hoyt: *When a new school is forming, it is important to highlight differences to sharpen thinking, to distinguish it from other schools, but, eventually, I think we discover that most good schools of therapy have certain things in common. We need to look for the common factors and draw from whatever works for a particular client rather than saying, "I'm only going to do narrative or solution," "I'm only going to do Bowenian or Ericksonian," "I always use hypnosis," or "I always make psychodynamic interpretations." I like to ask myself, What would be the best treatment for this client with this therapist in this situation at this time? I try to what I call* multitheoretical, *drawing from different theories and different approaches. I think we need to have some kind of overall thinking structure of what we are trying to accomplish so that we do not simply throw techniques at clients willy-nilly or helter-skelter, but I think it is important that we be technically heterodox instead of orthodox and draw from whatever seems most likely to work. There also is an increased need to take a serious look at what does work best for certain problems and not just say "anything goes." What treatments are most likely* *to give good results given certain kinds of problems? Everything does not work equally well.*

Carlson: *Where do you see us heading?*

Hoyt: *It is very hard to predict where the field is going. There are so many different things going on. There are the economic pressures, and there is managed care. There are a lot of new theoretical approaches being developed. There is multiculturalism. As Jay Haley has commented (see Chapter 12, this volume), much of therapy as most of us understand it was developed on a white European population. Now we are facing new waves of immigrants from other places. There may be important differences in how people go about understanding problems and solving problems if they or their ancestors have come from Asia or South America or from Africa or Europe, so I think the field is open now. It is a very exciting time. Of course, there is an old curse: May you live in an interesting time. I think this is both an opportunity in a positive sense and a very challenging time. We have to be careful that we do not look for a simplistic answer just to reduce the complexity.*

Last week a woman who was Hawaiian came to my office having certain conflicts or problems about having family members living with her. The solutions that made sense to her in her cultural milieu were somewhat different, I think, than those for someone who might have had a European background or a background from another continent. Another one of my patients, who came from the Philippines, approached the therapy, the doctor, and her sense of self somewhat differently than might someone from another ethnic group. I think this is going to be an interesting challenge for us to recognize, while we are working with lots of different people, that we all *have ethnicity. I would be concerned if we decided we could work only with clients of our own group. I would hate to see African Americans treated only by African Americans, Jewish Americans treated only by Jewish Americans, Hawaiians treated only by Hawaiians, Hispanics treated only by Hispanics, and so forth. So, I think we are going to have to learn from one another much more.*

Carlson: *Where are your professional interests right now?*

Hoyt: *I have several things going that I am very excited about. I am involved in teaching workshops on brief therapy and managed care, for which there has been a lot of response, so that is continuing. In 1995, I had a wonderful opportunity to go to Japan with some colleagues and do some presentations there. I also have spent a couple of weeks in Austria, Hungary, and England doing some teaching on brief therapy. Having contact with colleagues in other countries, and seeing both how their health care systems work and how they conceptualize psychological processes differently, has really brought home to me more the idea of how much of what we do is constructed. Particularly in Asia, I became aware of how much of what we normally take for granted—ideas such as the self, family, love, authority, and emotion—how much of that is constructed, and we need to deconstruct it or at least see it in its cultural context.*

I am pleased with the publication of the two volumes of Constructive Therapies *[and with* The Handbook of Constructive Therapies, *1998]. I was the editor and, although I made certain contributions, major kudos go to the authors. I think that they are incredibly exciting books in terms of the ideas they present about different ways of working with clients. I expect that professional audiences will find the books very, very helpful. I certainly have.*

My job at Kaiser Permanente is a constantly stimulating challenge. I also am working on several other endeavors, including a couple of new workshops, some conference presentations, more teaching abroad, and a number of writing and editing projects.

Carlson: *You sound busy.*

Hoyt: *There is a lot to do.*

Carlson: *In the book* Constructive Therapies, Volume 2 *(Hoyt, 1996b) you have a chapter that draws on your passion for golf and baseball.*

Hoyt: *In addition to writing an introductory chapter and doing some interviews with a number of colleagues, I wrote a chapter entitled "A Golfer's Guide to Brief Therapy (With Footnotes for Baseball Fans)" (see Chapter 2, this volume). It contains my favorite explanation of constructivism, which is not a theoretical disquisition but, rather, a joke that many people already may have heard. But, let me repeat it. It is about the three baseball umpires who are disputing their acumen. The first umpire says, "Well, I call 'em the way I see 'em"—he's the honest, ethical ump. The second ump says, "Well, that's not bad, but I call 'em the way they are"—he's the objective, accurate guy. And, finally, the third ump says, "You know, they ain't nothin' until I call 'em!"—he's the narrative constructivist. I think what we need to do as therapists is to recognize that we have to help clients "call 'em" in a way that will be constructive and productive and will allow them to move into the healthier ways of being that they want.*

Carlson: *Thanks for the interview.*

Hoyt: *I am honored to be asked.*

Interview II: Autologue: Reflections on Brief Therapy, Social Constructionism, and Managed Care

How sweet I roam'd from field to field,
And tasted all the summer's pride,
Till I the prince of love beheld
Who in the sunny beams did glide.
—William Blake (1769–1778), *Poetical Sketches*

For the past several years, I have had the good fortune to be involved in doing a series of published interviews with some of the leading figures in the field (see Hoyt, 1994a, 1995b, 1996b; Tomm, Hoyt, & Madigan, 1998; Watzlawick & Hoyt, 1998; see also Chapter 6, this volume). This experience has suggested to me a number of questions which I would like to be asked and have a chance to answer. So, here goes:

Interviewer: *I understand that you specialize in brief therapy. What do you mean by* brief?

Hoyt: *When I asked Jay Haley why he and his 1950s–1960s pioneering colleagues called it "brief," he told me (personal communication, 1995) it was mostly to distinguish it from the then dominant (psychoanalytic) theoretical perspective that treatment should be "long term." So one part of the definition is "less than long or extended." Actually, I prefer the terms "efficient" or "time sensitive," and*

From "Autologue (Self-Interview): Reflections on Brief Therapy, Social Constuction, and Managed Care" by M. F. Hoyt, *Journal of Psychological Practice, 3*(2), pp. 1–6. Copyright 1997. Adapted with permission of The Northamerican Association of Masters in Psychology.

sometimes subtitle my "Brief Therapy and Managed Care" workshops, "Making the Most of Each Session." Statistics tell us that most therapy is relatively brief, a handful of sessions (averaging three to eight, with the mode being one), so time specification is not really all that defining. There are certain characteristics that seem to cut across different schools of "brief therapy": a positive therapist-client alliance; clear goals, with a focus on resolving the presenting problem or complaint; an emphasis on increased activity (both therapist and client) and appreciation of the client's strengths and resources; an expectation of change which helps to engender hope and energy; the rapid introduction of novelty to help the client change the problematic pattern; a predominantly here-and-how (and next) orientation; and a heightened sensitivity to issues of time, with the corollary of episodic or intermittent treatment replacing the notion of a once-and-for-all "cure."

Interviewer: *How did you get interested in brief therapy?*

Hoyt: *That's complicated. Let me begin by quoting my answer to that same question from the book,* The First Session in Brief Therapy *(Hoyt, in Budman, Hoyt, & Friedman, 1992, p. 81):*

> *I was born to be a brief therapist. My mother, a loving and wonderful woman bless her soul, was a major-league worrier. I often consoled her, and soon learned to do it quickly. When the story got old, I told her not to be such a worrier (my first second-order intervention) and began to find ways to enhance her self-understanding as well as to anticipate, outflank, and redirect her. My academic pedigree includes a Yale Ph.D. [1976], extended training with Whitaker, Horowitz, and the Gouldings, numerous long-term and short-term therapy courses and workshops, plus lots of side trips through various psychospiritual schools of enlightenment (est, Zen, the Sufis, Hasidic Masters, etc.), bodywork, and personal therapy. By temperament and attention span, I prefer the "action" and excitment of brief therapy. As staff psychologist and [former] Director of Adult Services at a large HMO (Kaiser), my delight in new problems, stimulating contact and human experience is constantly aroused. Now, if I could only get my mother to stop worrying!*

Interviewer: *What else?*

Hoyt: *I'm generally interested in* what works—*which is part of my strong affinity for solution-focused therapy (see Chapters 8 and 9, this volume). I don't think, however, that there is one best approach for everyone. I think it is better to ask, "What would be most useful with this patient and this therapist with this problem in this situation, today?" We need a* both/and *(not* either/or *) perspective. We need to be organized in our approach(es), drawing useful techniques from different traditions.*

I'm deeply interested in efficient service that reduces suffering and enhances the quality of life. Let me say that I agree with Michael White (in Hoyt & Combs, 1996) about the dangers of overly psychologizing and pathologizing our honorable commitments to doing therapeutic work. I've always been interested in mind and culture—when I was a child, I was interested in people, art, literature, and anthropology, and never really cared about how cars worked or stuff like that. The

Norwegian sculptor, Gustav Vigeland (Hale, 1968), said about himself, "I was born to be a sculptor. No matter how hard I tried to turn away, I was always called back." I think the same is true about my interest in psychology; it seems to call to my daimon, as James Hillman (1996) might say.

Interviewer: *How did you get interested in narrative therapy and social constructionism?[1]*

Hoyt: *Generally speaking, I look for three things in an approach: (1) aesthetics, (2) ethics, and (3) effects. Is it interesting, does it capture the ear? Is it respectful and empowering, or does it make people feel smaller and shut down? And, does it work, does it get results that people want?*

As far as social constructionism (under with I would include both narrative and solution-focused therapies, as well as some neo-Ericksonian, strategic, and language systems approaches), there never was one moment, an a ha!, but I can see lots of clues. There always was lots of storytelling in our house when I was growing up, and my older brother and I used to sharpen our verbal skills on one another. My parents had friends of some diversity, as did my grandfather, and I attended a racially mixed school—so I got some idea that there was more than one way to look at things. My father was interested in archeology and anthropology, and we went to museums together. He also was antiracist. I remember one time as an early teenager when I came home and told a racist joke. My father immediately took me aside and said, "You sound like a Nazi (we're Jewish). If you talk that way or think that way, you can't be my son."

Interviewer: *That was clear.*

Hoyt: *Yes. I got "multi-versed" (to use a phrase I heard from Rob Doan, personal communication, 1996) early on. And, I think that being aware of being Jewish, even though we were not religious, made me more sensitive to an "outsider's" perspective. My favorite line in the Bible is from* Exodus 23:9: *"Remember that you, too, were once a stranger in the land of Egypt."*

Interviewer: *What other events stand out?*

Hoyt: *I remember when as an intern (at the University of Wisconsin-Madison, 1974–1975) I was being supervised by Carl Whitaker. I also was presenting the same case to another supervisor—without telling either what I was doing. Finally, I told Carl that Dr. G. had been giving me very different advice. Carl laughed and said, "Well, I guess you'll have to think for yourself!"*

In the mid-1970s I did est *[Erhard Seminar Training]. At the end of the training they went around the room and asked each person, "Did you get it?" (It was the understanding that we were constructing our "reality" and thus were "responsible" for our construction.) When the trainer came to me and asked, "Did you get it?" I told him, "I brought* it *with me!"*

When I attended the first Evolution of Psychotherapy Conference in Phoenix in 1985 (see Hoyt & Ordover, 1988; Zeig, 1987), the first speaker was brilliant and right on. The second speaker was equally brilliant and convincing . . . and contra-

dicted the first! The third also was brilliant and convincing . . . and contradicted both of the others, etc., etc. By the time I was on the way back to the hotel, I was having a kind of "manic" episode—my mind would not stop and was sort of spilling out on the floor. It was mind-blowing. I experientially realized that all of my cherished theories were just that—theories, ways of thinking, constructs but not "real." I really got it! It can give you a lot of freedom to know that thoughts are just tools or working assumptions—you do not have to take your perceptions so seriously. Since then, I've been a constructivist. I do believe that there is an external reality, a there *out there, so I probably am technically more of a social constructionist—I am interested in the interpersonal construction of meaning and "reality." As I tried to emphasize in my Introduction in* Constructive Therapies, Volume 2 *(Hoyt, 1996b; also see Chapter 3, this volume), it's also important to recognize that it's not "all in your head" so as to maintain social consciousness and an awareness of the terrible social circumstances in which some people are compelled to live.*

They say that travel "broadens" the person. I think that is especially true when (from an American perspective) you go to places that are non-Western. Some time in Japan, or in a tiny village high in the Mexican Sierra Madres, or on a walkabout in India can help deconstruct some of our usually taken-for-granted assumptions about culture and reality. Rapidly going from one environment to another to another can add to a postmodern sensibility, as can the tumultuous electronic media infusion and subsequent "multiphrenic" rush that Ken Gergen (1991) describes so well in The Saturated Self: Dilemmas of Identity in Contemporary Life.

Interviewer: *Is social constructionism a postmodern development?*

Hoyt: *As an* ism, *essentially yes. One can argue, however, that the process of social construction is integral to being human. We're meaning makers. Let me give two disparate examples. One can think of jurisprudence in terms of the social construction of reality—there are rules for what information is admitted (privileged) as "evidence," "facts" are tried and determined, and meanings are negotiated and assigned until a consensual version/vision of the "truth" is developed. Another example might involve grief and mourning—we recount the story over and over, incorporate perspectives and reflections from other people, sift and shift memories and meanings, processing toward some personal way of knowing. "Working through" may have very different norms and pathways in different cultures, but it seems universal that we very much try to make sense of the pain and the mystery. If it has not already been used, "Constructing Death" would make a good title for an account of different mourning practices.*

Interviewer: *Let's go on . . .*

Hoyt: *Not quite yet. To mention one other experience that specifically pertains to narrative therapy: When Gene Combs and I were having our conversation with Michael White that was published in Volume 2 of* Constructive Therapies, *there was a moment when we were discussing how we do not just walk a path but, rather, create our path as we walk it—and something in this image crystallized* *and helped change my life. I know that is dramatic but, again, I just got it, that sense of heightened personal responsibility, that I really* could *choose which way I want to be and want to go. It is interesting to me that in the* Milton H. Erickson Foundation Newsletter, *there is the transcript of a speech by Viktor Frankl (Short, 1996) in which he reports that prisoners at San Quentin really liked it when he told them they have choice and responsibility both for their crimes and their futures, as men, and that they are not just the inevitable products of their horribly disadvantaged and abusive childhoods.*

Interviewer: *The books* Constructive Therapies, Volume 1 and 2 *[and* The Handbook of Constructive Therapies*] have been very well received. What stimulated you to produce them?*

Hoyt: *To help get out the good news. Kudos to the authors for developing and sharing so many clinically useful, innovative, competency-based, and respectful ideas and methods. I've done my job as editor, but I've been blessed by working with such fine colleagues, most of whom even get things in on time! I've had a great time and have learned a lot, too. One Kaiser colleague told me, "Michael, I see what you're doing. You get interested in something and become an editor so that the experts in the field will each write a report to you on their approach, which you then discuss with them until they make it clear to you. Then you publish it and get paid for your tutorial!" I think that she is on to something, although I can assure you that being an editor is not a big moneymaker.*

Interviewer: *By the way, why the name "constructive therapies"?[2]*

Hoyt: *As I mentioned earlier, I generally use the terms* brief *(or* time sensitive *or* efficient*) and think they're fine. "Brief," however, simply means "not long" or "short" or something like that. "Brief" doesn't really indicate anything theoretical. When I edited the first volume of* Constructive Therapies *I was initially going to call it* Building Solutions. *The publisher wanted a different title, something broader (not sounding like it only covered solution-focused therapy). My thinking was* Building = Constructive *and* Solutions = Therapies, *plus "constructive" refers to the theoretical basis of constructivism and social constructionism and also has the connotations of positive, productive, creative, etc. "Constructive therapies" are based on the recognition that we are constructing, not simply uncovering, our psychological realities.*

Interviewer: *You also have presented many workshops on aspects of brief therapy and managed care—why?*

Hoyt: *There are a number of reasons. Most important, I see it as part of my commitment as a therapist—it is a way of helping people help people. If I help attendees to each better help just one client, that's a big leveraged (multiplier) effect. I was blessed to have some great supervisors and mentors, so it's a privilege to do some "payback." Given the enormity of managed care and the potential for abuse, it is important that ethical people don't abandon ship. I also learn a great deal while presenting—people give me all sorts of useful information and I have to* *keep sharpening my knowledge and skills. The "crosstraining" keeps me sharp and away from boredom. I also get to meet lots of nice people and see different places. I also like getting paid!*

Interviewer: *What are the bad parts of being a workshop presenter?*

Hoyt: *Being away from my family a lot. Jet-lag—that feeling of being slightly exhausted and out of whack, with sudden waves of dizziness and fatigue in the middle of the afternoon. Presenters become targets for all sorts of "transference" phenomena, especially if you are talking about something as controversial and problematic as managed (and often mismanaged) care. Last year I had to tell one woman that, "As hard as it might be for you to believe it, I really don't make health care policy for the United States!" I read every word of every conference evaluation as part of my commitment to quality assurance and continuous quality improvement. I appreciate the feedback, including constructive criticisms. However, sometimes a cruel evaluation can really hurt—participants occasionally think that attending a workshop gives them license to make all sorts of personal observations and interpretations about the presenter (see Hoyt & Budman, 1996).*

Interviewer: *What has been your worst workshop experience?*

Hoyt: *I've had really good experiences, and don't want to dwell on problems. I had something of a disaster, however, one time when I was presenting a couple of years ago in Las Vegas. I had the flu and a 102° fever, actually threw up once during lunch, the audiovisual equipment kept malfunctioning, an important videotape broke, and there was a muffled din coming from the hotel casino.* Brief Therapy and Managed Care *meets* Leaving Las Vegas! *Quick, let's change the topic!!*

Interviewer: *Where do you think the field is going? What should therapists be focusing on nowadays?*

Hoyt: *Obviously, managed care is a major force to be reckoned with. Therapists need to know how to deal with it—how to communicate to get appropriate treatment authorizations (see Chapters 4 and 5, this volume). More attention will need to be paid to targeting psychiatric symptoms and to clearly defining and achieving outcomes. At the same time, we should be careful to not become overly specialized or too focused on symptom management and abatement at the expense of the bigger, systemic picture. We also should not capitulate if we see indecent or unethical practices—it is important that we advocate, as individuals and through our various professional associations and societies, for what we think is good quality care. I also see a number of trends which are likely to continue, including more use of mental health services in primary care, more group practices and fewer solo practitioners, more care being provided by various masters-level clinicians, more group therapy, and much less inpatient care. I've discussed this further in* Brief Therapy and Managed Care *(Hoyt, 1995a; also see Chapter 4, this volume).*

Interviewer: *In closing, what is your purpose or mission in teaching?*

Hoyt: *Good question: Hey, you can almost read my thoughts!*

Interviewer: *I knew you were going to say that! So, what would you like readers to take away from your work?*

Hoyt: *I think what is most important is that the person shows up, that he or she is present. It is good to learn more skills, of course, but I think the main impediment is inhibition, not ignorance. We've all had the experience of being "on" and "in the zone." We need to "step up" and to "throw down hard," to put it in street parlance. Carl Rogers once said (quoted in Satir, 1993, p. 75), "What I am is good enough if I would only be it openly." Truly.*

Interviewer: *Thanks for the interview.*

Hoyt: *I couldn't have done it without you. Let's do lunch sometime!*

☐ Notes

[1]Thanks to Rob Doan for suggesting this question.

[2]Thanks to Tatsumi Kojima for suggesting this question.

with Insoo Kim Berg

Solution-Focused Couple Therapy: Helping Clients Construct Self-Fulfilling Realities

> What we talk about and how we talk about it makes a differ-
> ence (to the client). Thus reframing a "marital problem" into
> an "individual problem" or an "individual problem" into a
> "marital problem" makes a difference both in how we talk about
> things and where we look for solutions.
> —Steve de Shazer (1994), *Words Were Originally Magic*

Solution-focused therapy is an intervention approach that has been described and applied in a wide variety of situations (see de Shazer, 1982,
1985, 1988, 1991a, 1994; Berg, 1994a; Berg & Miller, 1992; Berg & Reuss,
1997; DeJong & Berg, 1997; Dolan, 1991; George, Iveson, & Ratner, 1990;
S. D. Miller & Berg, 1995; S. D. Miller, Hubble, & Duncan, 1996; J. J.
Murphy, 1998; Walter & Peller, 1992). Initially, the approach emerged in
an inductive manner; that is, from studying what clients and therapists
did which preceded their declaring problems "solved." It was noticed that
problems were described as "solved" (or resolved, dissolved, or no longer

Written with Insoo Kim Berg.

The case dialogue in this chapter is drawn from a professional training videotape, copy-
right 1994 by I. K. Berg. Adapted with permission. Versions of this chapter appeared in *Case
Studies in Couple and Family Therapy*, pp. 203–232, by F. M. Dattilio, Ed., 1998, New York:
Guilford Press, Copyright 1998 by Guilford Press; and in *The Handbook of Constructive Thera-
pies*, pp. 314–340, by M. F. Hoyt, Ed., 1998, San Francisco: Jossey-Bass, Copyright 1998 by
Jossey-Bass. Adapted with permission of the publishers.

problems) when clients began to engage in new and different perceptions and behaviors vis-à-vis the presenting difficulty. This recognition led to de Shazer's "basic rules" of solution-focused therapy (see Hoyt, 1996c, p. 68):

1. If it ain't broke, don't fix it.
2. Once you know what works, do more of it.
3. If it doesn't work, don't do it again; do something different.

Following from these rules, some basic heuristic questions can be derived: What is the client doing that works? What does the client want? What can the client do toward what is wanted? What can help keep the client going in the desired direction? When should therapy end?

☐ Focus on Solutions, Not Problems

Solution-focused therapy can be understood as a constructivist, postmodern, poststructural approach (de Shazer & Berg, 1992), one that conceives therapy as a process whereby the client and therapist co-construct more desirable "realities." The basic guiding principle is that as therapists we are actively involved—whether we realize it or not—in helping clients construe a different way of looking at themselves, their partners, their situations and their interactions. How we look influences what we see, and what we see influences what we do—and around and around the process goes, recursively. All questions are leading questions, directing attention and consciousness here rather than there, there rather than here. Solution-focused therapy is just that: intervention that purposely directs attention and energy toward the expansion of desired outcomes. *Building solutions* is not simply the reciprocal or inverse of *having problems;* indeed, development of a solution often involves a reformulation or different construction such that the former "position" loses its relevance or simply "dis-solves."

A "problem" arises and a couple seeks therapy (intervention) when the partners view their situation in such a way that they do not have access to what is needed to achieve what they consider reasonable satisfaction. While support can be given and skills taught, the primary emphasis in solution-focused therapy is on assisting clients to better utilize their own existing strengths and competencies, with a recognition that how clients conceive their situation will either empower them or cut them off from existing resources. The solution-focused therapist thus interviews purposefully (Lipchik, 1987; Lipchik & de Shazer, 1986) in order to "influence the clients' view of the problem in a manner that leads to solution" (Berg & Miller, 1992, p. 70). As de Shazer (1991a, p. 74) wrote:

The therapeutic relationship is a negotiated, consensual, and cooperative endeavor in which the solution-focused therapist and client jointly produce various language games focused on (a) exceptions, (b) goals, and (c) solutions (de Shazer, 1985, 1988). All of these are negotiated and produced as therapists and clients misunderstand together, make sense of, and give meaning to otherwise ambiguous events, feelings, and relationships. In doing so, therapists and clients jointly assign meaning to aspects of clients' lives and justify actions intended to develop a solution.

☐ Orientation

A few general points about solution-focused therapy may be highlighted in preparation for the case to be described below:

1. There is usually a "future focus," with the therapist drawing attention toward what the client(s) will be doing differently when they have achieved a desired outcome or solution. The language presumes or presupposes change ("After the miracle . . . "). Questions are designed to evoke a self-fulfilling map of the future (Penn, 1985; Tomm, 1987). The purpose is therapy, not archeology; blame talk and escalation of negative affect are avoided in favor of eliciting movement in helpful directions.

2. The therapist assumes a posture of "not knowing" (H. Anderson & Goolishian, 1992), allowing the clients to be the "experts" rather than having the therapist tell the clients what is "really" wrong and how to fix it. This is not to say that the therapist abdicates his or her role as skillful facilitator, but it does imply that the clients' language and ideas—their way of "storying" their lives—will be given full respect and seen as valid and real.

3. Focusing on strengths, exceptions, solutions and a more favorable future inspires clients (and therapists) and promotes empowerment. The therapist-client relationship is evolving and dynamic. Flexibly renegotiating goals, and appreciating and working with clients' sense of their situation, maintains therapist-client cooperation and vitiates the concept of *resistance* (Berg, 1989; de Shazer, 1984; see Chapter 14, this volume).

4. Well-formed goals have the following general characteristics: They are small rather than large; salient to clients; articulated in specific, concrete behavioral terms; achievable within the practical contexts of clients' lives; perceived by clients as involving their own hard work; seen as the "start of something" and not as the "end of something"; and treated as involving new behavior(s) rather than the absence or cessation of existing behaviors (de Shazer, 1991a, p. 112).

5. Questions are asked and responses are carefully punctuated to build or highlight a positive reality facilitative of clients' goals. All questions, in

effect, are leading questions, inviting clients to organize and focus their attention and understanding in one way rather than another (Tomm, 1988; Freedman & Combs, 1993). As discussed in Chapter 3 of this volume, the therapist functions like a special kind of mirror that can become convex or concave and swivel this way or that. Rather than providing a "flat mirror" that simply "reflects and clarifies," the solution-focused therapist purposely and differentially expands and contracts the reflected image, so to speak—opening parts of the story and closing others, making "space" for (or "giving privilege" to) discourses that support the realization of clients' goals. The therapist endeavors to help the couple build a solution. Recalling the story in Chapter 2 (pp. 15) and Chapter 6 (p. 134), about the three baseball umpires disputing their acumen, in the following interview, we want to show the details of how a solution-focused therapist selects what to highlight, how the therapist and clients co-create how they will "call 'em," and what results.

☐ The Case of Bill and Leslie[1]

Bill and Leslie had been married for approximately 7 years and had two children, ages 5 and 3. Bill also had another child from a previous marriage, but he rarely saw this child, even though he made child support payments. Bill was an attorney working for a large law firm and Leslie was a consumer-services director for a large telephone company. Leslie initiated therapy; when she told Bill she was "unhappy" and wanted "marriage counseling," he agreed to attend. This was their first session, held at the Brief Family Therapy Center (BFTC) in Milwaukee, Wisconsin. Insoo Kim Berg (IKB) was the therapist.

The session began with socializing and joining, in which the therapist and clients introduced themselves and started connecting. The couple quickly began to present their conflict, in both words and action. Leslie complained that Bill worked a great deal entertaining women clients, while Leslie did her full-time job outside the home and also maintained the children and household; Bill countered that he was working 70 hours a week to make partnership in his law firm and thus provide better for his wife and family. Tensions mounted.

IKB: *How long have you been together?*
Bill: *Seven years.*
Leslie: *Seven long years.* [rolling her eyes]
IKB: *And so, it sounds like you both are feeling very frustrated about what's going on or what's not going on with the two of you.*
Bill: *Yeah, I mean she has zero understanding about what's going on.*

IKB: *Right.*

Bill: *It makes it very difficult. We used to communicate.*

Leslie: *See, that's part of the problem.*

Bill: *But now . . .*

Leslie: *See, it's always me. I have the zero understanding. He understands it all. That's the problem.*

IKB: *Uh-huh.*

Leslie: *He . . . I don't think he is frustrated. We wouldn't be here if it weren't for me making the appointment.*

IKB: *Right.*

Leslie: *I think he's happy that it just goes on and on and I just work myself to a frazzle.*

Bill: *I'm frustrated, but I think it's our responsibility.*

IKB: *Mmm-hmm.*

Bill: *You know. I mean we should be able, as two adults, to sit down and talk about our problems.*

Leslie: *Well, as two adults we ought to be able to do a number of things.*

Bill: *When we do, it goes just like this. She just goes on and on and on and I don't have an opportunity . . .*

Orienting Toward Progress

Following Gergen and Gergen (1983, 1986) and de Shazer (1991a), we think of three types of narratives: *progressive narratives,* which justify the conclusion that progress is being made; *stabilizing narratives,* which justify the conclusion that life is unchanging; and *digressive (or regressive) narratives,* which justify the conclusion that life is moving away from goals. The storyline Bill and Leslie were enacting did not seem to be taking them to where they wanted to go so, at this juncture, the therapist interrupted the escalating cycle of complaints and problem talk to elicit the clients' view of a desirable outcome of therapy. This redirected attention to progressive narrative by refocusing the interaction on constructing solution talk.

IKB: *What do you suppose needs to happen as a result of your being here today, so you can look back—oh, let's say a few months from now, when you look back at this period in your life—so you can say to yourselves: "That was a good idea that we went and talked to Insoo, that was helpful." What needs to happen?*

Leslie: *I would hope that Bill could come up with some kind of understanding of what are his responsibilities and that, in these sessions, he could really hear what*

I am saying—because, at home, he really doesn't listen and, therefore, he could change his behavior so that we could be as we were earlier in the marriage.
IKB: *Really?*

The therapist's question responded to an indication of a more satisfying life in the past. In her reply, Leslie laid out her complaints: When Bill understands his responsibility, he will change his behavior and they will return to how they were earlier in the marriage. Notice how the therapist then builds consensus between the couple.

Leslie: *You know. Listening to one another and communicating.*
IKB: *Right.*
Leslie: *But he seems to have strayed from that.*
Bill: *That's what, that's what we need.*
IKB: *What?* [trying to refocus the conversation]
Bill: *Communication.*
IKB: *Okay.*
Bill: *If we can come out of this with some ground-level communication, I will think that it has been successful.*
IKB: *Okay.*
Leslie: *You know, I appreciate him as a husband. I do love him.*
IKB: *You do?* [emphasizing this positive aspect of their relationship]
Leslie: *And, I know he does work hard.*
IKB: *You do love him.* [further highlighting of positive]
Leslie: *Yes, I do. I do.*
IKB: *Okay. When he is more responsible, what will he be doing that he's not doing right now, that will let you know he's being more responsible?* [presupposing change with "when" rather than "if"]
Leslie: *He will take more responsibility for our children. He will take more responsibility for his own son, whom I love very much, too.*
IKB: *Okay.*
Leslie: *He will take responsibility to include me—have respect for me. Include me in his activities and have respect for me.*

Getting Specifics

Having identified a positive in general terms, the therapist now asks for a specific behavioral description.

IKB: *What will Bill be doing exactly that will let you know that he is being* *responsible around the house with his children, with his son?* [establishing behavioral indicators that Bill is more "responsible"]

Leslie: *Well, right now I'm always reading the bedtime stories because he's out doing whatever.*

IKB: *Okay. So, he will be doing some of those?* [refocusing on behavioral criteria]

Leslie: *Yes. Especially on weekends when you don't have to carry the load that you carry during the week.*

IKB: *Okay.*

Leslie: *I would like some help around the house. He thinks that I'm the built-in maid, it feels like.*

IKB: *What would he be doing?*

Leslie responded by complaining that she did all the washing, ironing, and cooking. Bill suggested hiring someone to do housework, Leslie replied that they could not afford it, and Bill rejoined the argument with a comment about Leslie not wanting anybody else taking care of the children. At this point, the therapist refocused on the thread of Leslie's small but specific behavioral goal that Bill help at bedtime. She tried to amplify the positive possibility, rather than the complaint, to build a shared vision of their life.

IKB: *So, he will be reading bedtime stories?*

Leslie: *Yes.*

IKB: *He will be doing what else?*

Leslie: *He would be helping with the shopping. He would be helping with household duties, the cleanup.*

IKB: *Like what? You mean washing dishes?*

Leslie: *Yes. He could help once in a while.*

Bill: *Hold it.*

Leslie: *Once in a while, you could help wash the dishes.*

Bill: *Wait a minute. I'm going to be frank.* [pointing out a different path to the shared vision]

IKB: *Okay.*

Bill: *If I work 70 hours a week, I do not have time to wash dishes!*

Leslie: *But, I have time 'cause I work 50 plus hours. I have all the responsibility of . . .*

Bill: *That doesn't even make sense.*

Leslie: *. . . the children.*

Bill: *Look. That doesn't even make sense.*

Leslie: *Well, we have a dishwasher. It's not that difficult. You could help.*

The therapist persisted in attempting to refocus the conversation toward the desired outcome. It is common for couples to become distracted and embroiled in "problem talk" when their trigger words are used. Therefore, it is particularly helpful for the therapist to focus on what the client wants and not on what may interest the therapist.

IKB: *I need to know from both of you what needs to happen so that I am helpful to both of you. So, let me come back to this. What would he be doing different? Let's say 6 months down the road?*

Leslie: *I think even though it's important that he is building a partnership and I realize it takes time and I try to be supportive . . .*

IKB: *Right. Okay.*

Leslie: *He also has to build a relationship at home. We have little ones that don't even know you.* [to Bill] *We have little ones that don't even know you.*

IKB: *So, what would he be doing to build a relationship at home?*

Leslie: *He would be communicating more with me.*

IKB: *Okay.*

Leslie: *He would be taking an active role with our children. Our children. He is just someone who comes in during the morning and leaves. I mean, they don't even have a concept of who you are. And, I think that's a shame.*

IKB: *Okay. Now . . .*

Bill: *Uh—you—uh.* [starting to argue back]

IKB: *Let me come back to you, Bill, on this. I'm assuming you want to have this relationship with Leslie also?* [returning to the shared vision and refocusing toward the goal]

Bill: *Yes, of course. I love her as well.*

IKB: *You do.*

Bill: *Yeah.*

IKB: *Does she know how much you love her?*

Leslie: *Do I know?*

Bill: *She should. I mean, you know.*

IKB: *Yeah? What do you think? Does she know?*

Bill: *You know. We've been together for 7 years. I love her and I haven't left her. I wouldn't leave her. This is my wife. I love her. I love my children as well.*

Leslie: *Do you see this?* [she holds up Bill's left hand, which is ringless] *He has a wedding ring. I wear mine. He doesn't wear his. He doesn't wear his.*

IKB: *Uh huh.*

Bill: *I figure that they're* [the children] *3 and 5 years old, that if I put in these* *hours now, when they are older they'll be able to appreciate me more, that I will then have more time to spend with them.*

IKB: *I see.*

Bill: *That's the principle that I'm operating on. Either I can stay at home and wash dishes or I can spend 70 hours a week trying to build up this practice so that, as an eventuality, you won't even have to work, and you don't seem to have any patience or understanding or cooperation.*

Leslie: *I won't have to work?*

IKB: *Oh, wow. So you really are working for the future.* [building the shared vision once more]

Bill: *Yes. Absolutely. I'm trying to secure a future, not just for myself, but for all of us.*

Using the Miracle Question

As the interview proceeded, the therapist then introduced the "Miracle Question"(de Shazer, 1988). Notice how, as common goals began to emerge, the affect changed. Also notice how detailed and specific were the elicited behavioral descriptions of what would indicate the beginnings of a desired outcome.

IKB: *Okay. I'm going to ask both of you some very strange questions that will take some imagination on both of your parts. Let's say as a result of a miracle, the problem that brought you here today is gone.* [snaps her fingers] *Just like that.*

Leslie: *That would be a miracle!* [laughs]

Bill: [laughs]

IKB: *That would be nice. Wouldn't it? But, this miracle happens in the middle of the night when both of you are sleeping. Like tonight, for example. So, you don't know that this has happened.* [both Leslie and Bill chuckle] *So, when you wake up tomorrow morning, what will be the first small clue to you that: "Wow! Something must have happened during the night! The problem is gone!" How will you discover this?*

Bill: *I'll smile first thing in the morning, instead of avoidance.*

IKB: *You will smile at Leslie.*

Leslie: *He would put his arm around me.*

IKB: *He'll put his arm around you. Okay.*

Leslie: *That would be a real sign of a miracle at this point.*

IKB: *Okay. All right, so suppose he does. What will you do in response to that?*

Leslie: *I won't turn my back to him.* [laughs]

IKB: *All right. Okay. Is that right? Is that what she would do? Would that be a miracle for you?*

Bill: *Yeah. That definitely would.*

IKB: *That would be a miracle for you.*

Bill: *It would be very different.*

IKB: *It would be different. Okay.*

Bill: *Yeah. It would be a miracle.*

Leslie: *Mmm-hmm.*

IKB: *Okay. So when she turns her back towards you, I mean, so she's facing you. When you smile at her, she'll face you instead of turning her back towards you. What will you do when you see her do that?*

Bill: *I don't know. I suppose I'll embrace her, probably.*

IKB: *Uh-huh. So you will give her a hug.*

Bill: *Yeah.*

IKB: *What about you, Leslie? What will you do when he gives you a hug?*

Leslie: *Well, if he hugs me, I'll hug him back.*

IKB: *Uh-huh. Okay. Okay. What will come after that?*

Leslie: *Tomorrow's Saturday, you never can tell!* [said sexily; Bill and Leslie laugh]

IKB: [laughs] *Okay.*

Bill: *A miracle!*

Using an Exception Question

The therapist then posed an *exception question* to find recent problem-free times that the couple might already have achieved on their own. Once identified, such exceptions often can be built upon.

IKB: *When was the most recent time when you had a morning like that? Maybe not all of it, but just pieces of that, part of that miracle picture?*

Bill: *It's been a while.*

Leslie: *Probably right after Evelyn was born.*

IKB: *Is that right?*

Leslie: *That's almost 2 years, almost 3 years ago.*

IKB: *Wow. That was a long time ago.*

Leslie: *Yeah. I think so. Am I right? Can I be right sometimes?*

Bill: *Well, I don't know if it's quite that long; somewhere in that framework, but I wouldn't say it's been that long.*

IKB: *Well, not all of it, but just pieces of it?* [seeking a small positive exception rather than buying into bickering]

Leslie: *It's been a couple of years.*

Bill: *It's been a while.*

Leslie: *But, we've been avoiding. He's out a lot. I take care of the kids. I bury myself in my job. But, I don't—I'm not married to my job.*

IKB: *Right.*

Leslie: *You know. I'm married to him. And my job is important. My children are precious to me. But, I want the whole thing and I want to . . .*

IKB: *You want this relationship back.*

Leslie: *Right. I know it won't always be, you know, peaches and cream, but it's not supposed to be, you know . . .*

Not getting a more recent exception to build on, the therapist returned to their positive response to the "Miracle Question" by using *relationship questions;* that is, each client's perception of others' perceptions of him or her.

IKB: *So, let me come back to this tomorrow morning. When the children see the two of you tomorrow morning, what would they see different about the two of you that would tell them: "Wow! Something happened to Mom and Dad."*

Bill: *Wow.*

IKB: *I mean, if they could talk. I realize they're very young and they may not be able to have the right words for it, but if they could talk.*

Leslie: *Well, Carl knows something is going on, because he always asks me, "Why are you and Daddy always yelling at each other?" You know, I tell him not to yell at his little sister and—see, I haven't told you this—and then he says to me, "Well, you and Daddy are always yelling."*

IKB: *Yeah. So what would he notice different about the two of you tomorrow morning?* [persistently returning to image of desired positive outcome]

Bill: *Some warmth.*

Leslie: *Yeah. I don't think our kids have seen us embrace lately. They probably won't even remember it.*

IKB: *So he may see the two of you embracing. What else? What else would he see?*

Leslie: *We would go somewhere together. That would really be a miracle. You know, instead of me . . .*

IKB: *You mean the family of four.* [interrupting to maintain solution-building set]

Leslie: *All four of us.*

IKB: *All four of you will go somewhere. Someplace fun?* [focusing on solution, not problem]

Leslie: *Yeah. Someplace fun where we're not just dropping them off on the way to work, you know.*

IKB: *Okay.*

Bill: *Just all of us being in the same space would be a miracle.*

Leslie: *Not getting ready to go to the babysitter's or day care and not getting ready to go to bed. It would really be different.*

IKB: *That would be different.*

Building Interactional Bridges

The therapeutic task now was to bridge the emerging images of changes and possible solutions by highlighting the interactional aspect of this new and different vision. The partners' shared vision for how they want their lives to be—in concrete and behavioral, measurable detail—was examined from several points of view, including that of the children ("if they could talk").

IKB: *I'm not sure if this is realistic or not, but suppose you do, how would Leslie be different with you? What would she do different?*

Bill: *Well, I suppose, she'd be warmer.*

IKB: *She'll be warmer with you?*

Bill: *We'd get along better. We would communicate.*

IKB: *Okay. Say some more about this getting along. What would go on? What would go on between the two of you?*

Bill: *If we just try to get along we could get along but, if we have to get along at the cost of me suddenly, you know, not giving the time that I need to give to my job, as an eventuality it's going to affect us financially. I'm trying to look out for our future, and I think that we have to invest some time in that in order to make the whole thing work.*

IKB: *Got you.*

Leslie: *There are some ways that we could be investing and doing our money differently . . .*

Bill: *I love our children and I love you, you know, but I'm trying to build something.*

Leslie: *There are some ways we could be saving money and doing better financially that don't require you to be out of the house 70 hours a week and meeting with these female clients. "Clients" in quotes, okay?*

Bill: *Well, then, you tell me what it is then.* [angrily]

Leslie: *Because if you were home every night . . .*

Bill: *You tell me what it is, then.* [angrily]

IKB: *Hang on a minute. What has to come first? In order to do whatever you'd* *like to see happen between the two of you, what might be the first small step to help you move toward that?*

The therapist actively intervened to stop the negative escalation. She did not ignore the angry affect, but attended to Leslie's insistence that Bill become an active partner in raising the children and responding to her wishes. This was pursued by refocusing the discussion on what small steps would move them toward their vision of greater closeness and cooperation, rather than another round of accusations and rebuttals.

Leslie: *He could be honest.*

IKB: [to Bill] *What would it take, do you think, knowing Leslie as well as you do, what would it take for her to believe you that you are being honest?* [tracking Leslie's comment while highlighting progressive interaction and constructively using Bill's position as an expert on Leslie]

Bill: *I don't know. What would it take? I'm willing to try.*

IKB: *Oh, you are?* [highlighting husband's positive motivation with question]

Leslie: *It would help if you would call. If you would let me know about what time you're going to come home. I don't need to know every client that you're going to meet, but I would like to be included in your life in a way that I think is respectful.*

IKB: *Ahh. That's what you really want, isn't it?*

This was a good example of how partners often do not know initially what are the first small beginning steps toward better communication. The jump between the issue of "honesty" and Bill's calling to let Leslie know what time he will come home was not obvious.

IKB: *You want to be part of Bill's life.*

Bill: *I'll call. I can do that. That's not unreasonable. And, sometimes I get caught up in business and I don't call.*

IKB: *I see.*

Bill: *Okay. But, I can call. That I can do.*

IKB: [to Leslie] *What do you need so that you feel that Bill understands how hard you are working to make this marriage work? What do you need from Bill?*

Leslie: *I need some support from Bill. I work more than 8 hours a day also, and I come home. I mentioned that I needed him to take more responsibility with the child care arrangements, everything. Doctor appointments, shoes, clothes. I do all that. He doesn't even ask me any questions about how was the day with the kids. You come in and say, "How are the kids?" And, you know, sometimes you're not even listening. You walk right by.*

IKB: *So, his asking?*

Leslie: *I could say they had both been in a train wreck and you wouldn't even hear it.*

IKB: *So, his asking and being concerned—sounds like that's what you want.*

Bill: *Well, I mean she's made an assumption that I don't hear. I mean, if I didn't want to know, I wouldn't ask.*

Leslie: *I don't think so. When you come in the house, it's common courtesy, you're going to ask how your kids are, but one day I think I'll try that. You know, "The kids have been in a train wreck." I'm going to see if you hear me.*

Bill: *That's not common courtesy. These are my children.*

Leslie: *See, I'm female. I wouldn't come in the house without asking how are the kids. I mean, I guess you just expect that to happen, you know.* [possibly inviting the female therapist to join in a discussion against the husband; instead, the therapist attempts to refocus on what would be helpful]

IKB: *So, what . . .*

Leslie: *Okay. I know he loves the kids. I'm not accusing you of that.*

IKB: *Oh, you do! Does Bill know how much you love him?*

Leslie: *Well, earlier in the marriage . . .*

Bill: *No, not earlier. Let's talk about right now.*

Using Scaling Questions

Leslie went on to complain that she felt her husband no longer found her attractive; that she wondered if he had other "romantic or sexual interests"; and that he might be staying because, like the saying goes, "It's cheaper to keep her." When the therapist said, "You really want to change that," Leslie responded, "It's going to have to change or else I'm going to be someplace else." The therapist then posed a series of *scaling questions*, each designed to "make numbers talk" (Berg & de Shazer, 1993)—that is, to help the partners articulate their conceptions of their relationship and what would be needed to help it progress in the directions they desired.

IKB: *Let's say on a scale of 1 to 10, as things are right now—and you know what you've been through, the two of you know what you've been through, and you know what the issues have been and you know what the issues are better than I do right now—let's say 10 stands for that you will do just about anything humanly possible to make this marriage work. That stands for 10. Okay? And the 1 stands for you're ready to throw in the towel and you're ready to walk away from this. Where would each of you say you're at on this scale of 1 to 10?*

Bill: [pauses, thinks] *Hmm.*

Leslie: *Honestly?*

Bill: *Seven.*

IKB: *Seven. How about for you, Leslie?*

Leslie: *Well, the past year or so I think I've been at a 10, quite frankly, but the way I'm feeling now I'm probably—well, let's put it this way—I've talked to a lawyer. I've talked to a lawyer, just to inquire about what my rights would be. I'm probably about a 5.*

IKB: *About a 5.*

Leslie: *I'm in the middle somewhere.*

IKB: *Yeah.*

Leslie: *I don't want it to go to the 1, but . . .*

IKB: *You don't want to be at 1.*

Leslie: *No, but I can't . . . I feel like I'm pulling it alone.*

IKB: *Right. Uh huh.*

Leslie: [to Bill] *I'm surprised you're at a 7.*

IKB: *Now, I have another set of numbers questions here. Knowing how things are right now between the two of you, let's say 10 stands for you have every confidence that this marriage is going to survive. Okay? Ten stands for this marriage has every chance of making it. And 1 stands for the opposite—there's no chance this marriage is going to make it. Where would you say things are right now?*

Leslie: *Well, if we worked at it, I could say it would be more than a 5.*

IKB: *Really? So, you see a lot of potential in this?*

Leslie: *Well, we do love each other. I know it doesn't sound like it, but I think we do.*

IKB: *You do.*

Leslie: *I know I love him.*

IKB: *Does he know? Does Bill know how much you love him?*

Leslie: *He ought to.*

IKB: *Bill, what would you say the chances are of this marriage making it?*

Bill: *Uh. I would really say an 8.*

IKB: *Eight.*

Bill: *You know, I mean, I want this to work. I'm willing to try to make it. We have to find some kind of way to compromise, though. I mean, I didn't go through undergrad and law school, working in the mail—all that bullshit—just to now suddenly chuck it all away. I mean, we can't . . .*

Leslie: *I don't want you to chuck it all away.*

IKB: *What would it take, do you think, from your point of view, Leslie—what would it take for you to go from 5 to 6, so you can say it's just a little bit better? It's not perfect yet, it's not all the way up to 10, but it's just a little bit better. What has to happen between the two of you so that you can say that to yourself?*

Leslie: *Well, he could call like he said he would, and . . .*

IKB: *That would help?*

Leslie: *Yeah, if he could just make some effort with trying to share some of the responsibilities. I would recognize it. I know he has to work.*

IKB: *So, calling would help you a little bit.*

Leslie: *I mean, I don't know. Maybe if he could hug me sometimes.*

IKB: *He could what?*

Leslie: *He could hug me sometimes. To make me feel like a wife.*

IKB: *Okay. That would help also. Now what would that mean? What does that mean? How would that help? His hugging you and calling you and . . . I don't understand that. How would that be helpful for you?* [trying to understand Leslie's personal construction of what hugging and calling means in the context of their relationship]

Leslie: *Because for me, first of all, he doesn't believe it, but I do worry about him. It can be dangerous out there. And, two, I could, we could talk just about what his day has been like. I would know what time he was going to come home. Maybe I would sit up and we could have, you know, a late dinner together.*

IKB: *Uh-huh.*

Leslie: *Sometimes I sit up and I don't know what time . . . I just fall asleep and then he comes in and the next thing I know he's in the bed, but then he's asleep and . . .*

IKB: *So, some more personal and private time together.*

Leslie: *Right. The kids still go to bed relatively early, and I'm just, you know, doing some paperwork or I end up watching TV alone. I don't know what time he's coming in.*

IKB: *Okay. What about it will be helpful for you? Having those kind of private times between the two of you?*

Leslie: *We used to have those private times.*

IKB: *You used to have those.*

Leslie: *Before the kids were born, and it was something I looked forward to. You know, I mean, we—he was working long hours. But, that was our special time and we talked. I mean, I knew people at his office before—not always person-ally—but because we talked about those things, and I talked about problems on my job.*

IKB: *So, when you have this private time talking about what his day's been like, what his work is like, and he also asks you about what your day has been like and having this time without children . . . how would that be helpful?*

Leslie: *It was close. Your husband is your main confidant. We would have the relationship, and then I remember the times we would even go to bed and make love and it would be nice. And, it was beautiful.*

IKB: *Uh-huh.*

Leslie: *And, that doesn't happen anymore, either.*

IKB: *Right. So, that's what you're looking for. Some special moments with Bill that you feel close to him and you feel like he's your confidant.*

Leslie: [to Bill] *Didn't you like those? I mean, I thought it was fun. I looked forward to it. I mean, no matter how bad the day was, I could look forward to it at some point, you know, over salad or whatever. Maybe even a glass of wine. We would talk. We would have good times.*

IKB: [to Bill] *Is there something that Leslie can do to make it easy for that to happen?*

Bill: *Yeah!*

IKB: *What? What can she do to make it easier for that to happen?*

Leslie: *I'm listening. I'm all ears. What can I do? I'll do it . . . within reason.*

Bill: *Just be understanding.*

IKB: *What does that mean: "be understanding"?*

Bill: *I mean, don't pressure me.*

IKB: *Okay.*

Bill: *And, know that I love you and I love our children. You know, I'm really and truly trying, and it's difficult, and a lot of times I just don't have the time, you know, but that . . .*

Leslie: *You're going to be able to make time? Is that what I'm hearing?*

Bill: *I'm going to try the best I can, you know? But, I have a vision and you need to help me with this vision, and if the vision calls for you maybe to do a little more now, I guarantee you'll do a little less later.*

Giving Feedback and Suggestions

At this point the therapist took a 5- or 10-minute break, asking the clients to sit in the waiting room. This pause can be used to reflect upon what has occurred and to plan a message or feedback to present to the couple when the session is resumed. This time also can be used to consult with colleagues, including any team that may have observed the session.

The session presented here was difficult and not atypical. Both partners brought up important issues. For Bill, his way of caring about his family was to be a good provider and to be successful financially. He referred to his vision of the future, which was to be a good provider so that Leslie could even stay at home and not have to go to work—a view that, in some ways, was very traditional. At the same time, he recognized that there needed to be some balance. On the other hand, Leslie's issues had to do more with the here and now: the family relationship, time with the children, helping her out, doing things together, more intimate moments like they used to share earlier in their life together. What she wanted and what he wanted both had to do with the relationship; they were coming from very different angles, but were moving toward the same vision of their life. The therapist's task was to help them somehow figure out how they could see themselves working cooperatively together, incorporating both the vision of the future as well as what needed to happen in their current life. They would then be in a position to bring their skills and resources to bear in a more mutually satisfying way.

When a therapist invites a couple back into the room after taking a break, there are typically three components to what is said (de Shazer, 1985, 1988): *an acknowledgement and validation* of the clients' point of view; *a bridging statement* that leads to the suggestion or directive that is to be offered; and the *suggestion or directive*, a message designed to guide the couple toward perceptions and behaviors that are more consistent with their goals. In what follows, we will see how the therapist complimented and positively framed Leslie and Bill's coming to therapy and their expressed concerns as the beginning step. She then offered suggestions for each person to notice what the other was doing to make the relationship better, but not to tell the other what has been noticed. This task was carefully constructed to shift attention from what was wrong to what was right—to help the partners watch each other from a different point of view, each noticing positives about the other. The suggestion not to tell the other what had been noticed was given for two reasons: (1) to make the task interesting and capture the partners' attention and cooperation; and (2) to permit each partner to even give favorable credit to the other for something that was inadvertent.[2] Consistent with the social constructionist idea that we all make meaning and build "reality" out of ambiguous circumstances—that how we look determines what we see and what we see determines how we act, and that this feeds back self-recursively—this observational task purposefully focuses the partners' attention toward constructing a more mutually self-fulfilling relationship.[3]

IKB: *I really have to tell you that I think that your calling to set up this appointment was really good timing. It sounds like you both are very concerned about what's not happening between the two of you, and you want to do something about that. And I am very impressed, Bill, that you responded to Leslie's initiating this meeting and your willingness to take time from your very busy schedule, and obviously this relationship is very important to you.*

Bill: *Yes . . .*

IKB: *And that's why you are here, to do something about this. Both of you really care about this relationship a great deal. But both in a very different way. Let me explain to you about this. Bill, your way of caring about this relationship is to have this vision of the future—how you want things to be. That is, you're accustomed to* *sacrificing a lot for the future, and that's how you still see it, in order to have a better future, even to the point of maybe Leslie staying home one of these days.*

Bill: *Yeah.*

IKB: *That finally you could earn enough money so that she could stay home. And so you have this vision of the future, how you want things to be. And that's how you care about this relationship. On the other hand, Leslie, your way of caring about this relationship is to be paying attention to now, when the children are young.*

Leslie: *Mmm-hmm.*

IKB: *You want the two of you to do more things with the children. You want to share this experience of raising children together. You want to stay close and have more intimate moments and somehow try to make it—sort of like have it all, right? And that's how you care about this relationship. So, there's no question in my mind that both of you care about each other in a very different way. And, that gets misunderstood. And I think that both of you need both ways. Any relationship needs both—that is, to pay attention to here and now as well as the future. You need to do both. You need to—like Bill said, it's a matter of a balance. How to balance here and now, and also worrying about the future.*

Bill: *Mmm-hmm.*

IKB: *And so, I think that you two have a very good start because you're already thinking about right now as well as the future. So, the next task for the two of you is to figure out how to fit your concerns together.* [the bridging statement] *I don't think it's either your way or your way. It's the blending of the two. In order to do that, both of you have to work together to strike this balance. And, I really like the way that you want to get started on this. You have lots of ideas of how to get started on that—like sort of stealing those few moments here and there without the children, that certainly would help. So, what I would like to suggest to you between now and the next time we get together, is for each of you to keep track of what the other person is doing. For you* [to Leslie] *to keep track of what Bill does, and for you* [to Bill] *to keep track of what Leslie does to make things a little bit better for the marriage. And, it's important for you not to discuss it, but just keep track of them. And, when we come back together we will discuss this more, the details of them. But, I want you to sort of observe, file it away, and then when we get together we'll talk about it. Okay?*

The couple agreed to perform the task, a subsequent appointment was scheduled, and the session was adjourned.

Follow-up

When Bill and Leslie returned for their appointment 2 weeks later, they were smiling and looked relaxed. Bill announced that he had taken time off from his busy schedule to go with Leslie and the kids to the zoo on Saturday morning. The therapist complimented them on this and explored with them how they had managed to accomplish it. Consistent with the thrust of the first session, and in keeping with the second basic rule of solution-focused therapy—*Once You Know What Works, Do More of It*—throughout the session efforts were made to elicit, reinforce, amplify, and extend favorable changes (see Adams, Piercy, & Jurich, 1991; Weiner-Davis, de Shazer, & Gingrich, 1987). This included getting details of positive movement and exploring the meanings each partner assigned to favorable developments, complimenting each partner's efforts and accomplishments, asking scaling questions about their hopefulness and what would strengthen it, refocusing on goals and finding out what each person did do and could do to further solutions, and developing future goals to help them stay on track.

Throughout this session—and the therapy—the therapist worked to help the couple avoid escalating past complaints (which usually trigger a cycle of blaming-accusing-defending-blaming the other and so on). Instead, she asked questions and otherwise directed the clients forward, escalating the future by helping them create a view consistent with how they would like to be. Their communication style was reframed as "passionate" rather than "conflictual" to help them remain engaged and moving in a positive direction rather than falling into the stalemating perceptions of "right/wrong," "black/white," and "husband versus wife." As a task to keep them on track, Bill was asked to notice what Leslie did, in her own way, to stay in communication with him; and Leslie was asked to notice what Bill did, in his own way, to keep her included, thus shifting their "noticing" from "noncommunication and exclusion" to "communication and inclusion."

☐ Thinking About Practice: Some Questions and Possible Answers

The case we have reported here raises several issues:

There did not seem to be a lot of attention given to exploring underlying issues, including anger. Is this typical? Throughout the therapeutic interaction, the emphasis was on doing what works. The therapist repeatedly focused on those aspects of the clients' presentation that suggested movement in the direction (outcome) they wanted to go. It sometimes may be useful to facilitate the expression of anger and other so-called negative affects, especially if this is part of what the clients require to feel that therapy can be useful, although experience suggests that an "abreactive" approach often simply leads to more animosity and further alienation (see G. Miller & de Shazer, in press). In the case presented here, reinforcing Leslie's "victim" position would not have been likely to move things forward. The therapist, by word and demeanor, acknowledged the couple's frustration and unhappiness. Clients need to know that their experience has been heard and appreciated as valid. It may be more therapeutically helpful in the long run, however, to look for positive intentions that have not yet worked out and to highlight them.[4] Each case is unique, so guidelines have to be general.

Was Bill having an affair? Why wasn't this important issue focused on? It is important to be reminded of the "big picture" of what this couple wanted and how they imagined their lives could be different. Leslie—in her frustration and anger at being treated as if "It's cheaper to keep her" and feeling unappreciated for her own long hours of work—said many negative things such as that Bill was indifferent and unconcerned about her or his children. It is interesting to note that, when viewing the videotape of this session (Berg, 1994b), many therapists immediately become focused on the issue of affair/no affair and not on other issues such as why Bill thought he is too busy to wash dishes or help with the shopping or child care as Leslie wanted him to do. We believe that therapists tend to hear selectively, according to their own constructions of what leads to marital conflict (and resolution). What proved to be therapeutic in this case was to address what would help the couple move in the direction of greater trust in the here and now. Once the present reality improves, it is easier for clients to let go of what may (or may not) have happened—to let it be "past." We once heard John Weakland say to a client who was focused on a particular idea, "Would it be okay with you if we solve the problem and then come back to that if you're still interested?" This helped move the client into a present-to-future orientation and allowed therapy to occur. We also have to be careful, of course, that a client does not feel discounted. However, when we say that an issue is "important," we need to ask, "Important to whom?" Sometimes it is the therapist more than the client who feels something has to be "addressed" or "dealt with directly," and this may lead to the kind of either/or thinking that can produce a therapeutic impasse.

How does solution-focused therapy address issues of ethnicity and cultural diversity? By working within the goals, ideas, values, and worldview that clients present, solution-focused therapy is sensitive to the cultures that clients bring to the consulting room. It should be *their* therapy, not the therapist's. The solution must fit their frame of reference, not that of the therapist. Moreover, the therapeutic alliance is foremost, and is based on a high regard and respect for what makes sense to the client, not to the therapist. This means that, as therapists, we have to have skills to join and work with folks of varying ethnicities, and we also have to be clear about what our values (tacit as well as explicit) may be so that we do not impose them. In the case presented here, the couple was African-American; the therapist was Korean-American.

What are some similarities between solution-focused therapy and other therapeutic approaches? While a thoroughgoing review is beyond the scope of the present discussion, we are glad to acknowledge a few connections and related perspectives. As Shoham et al. (1995) noted, solution-focused therapy especially shares certain important commonalities with the strategic therapy (Fisch, Weakland & Segal, 1982; Watzlawick, Weakland & Fisch, 1974) practiced at the Mental Research Institute (MRI) of Palo Alto, California—such as a Batesonian interactional constructivist orientation that eschews normative/pathological theorizing, a preference for "minimalist" interventions, and an Ericksonian interest in utilizing whatever the client brings. However, the approaches are distinct in that MRI attends more directly to changing behaviors that maintain a problem, whereas the BFTC solution-focused model assumes that behavior change will follow naturally after clients see things differently. Summarizing the two approaches, Weakland and Fisch (1992, p. 317) wrote: "We focus primarily on attempted solutions that do not work and maintain the problem; de Shazer and his followers, in our view, have the inverse emphasis. The two are complementary."[5]

There also are connections between solution-focused therapy and narrative therapy (Freedman & Combs, 1996; White, 1995a; White & Epston, 1990), including a postmodern, nonpathological perspective and an emphasis on client-therapist collaboration. Although both approaches are interested in "exceptions" (solution-focused) or "unique outcomes" (narrative) as keys to "solutions" or "reauthoring life stories" (narrative),[6] there are major differences between the approaches in terms of perspectives, intentions, and procedures as outlined by Chang and Phillips (1993) as well as by the prime enunciators of the respective approaches themselves (de Shazer, 1993b; de Shazer & White, 1994; White, 1993a; White & de Shazer, 1996). Finally, there are similarities between solution-focused therapy and cognitive-behavioral couples therapy (Beck, 1988; Baucom & Epstein, 1990; Dattilio & Padesky, 1990; Jacobson & Margolin, 1979), since these latter approaches also are directly concerned with how clients may be constructing their psychological realities (although they may spend more time assessing deficits in thinking and acting, as well as teaching specific skills). Helping clients become aware that they have a choice in how to construe their reality is the most helpful task we can perform as therapists (as those cognitive-behavioral clinicians identified more with the "constructive" than "rationalist" wing especially know—see Ellis, 1998; Lyddon, 1990; Mahoney, 1991; Meichenbaum, in Hoyt, 1996d; Neimeyer, 1998a; Ottens & Hanna, 1998).

☐ Doing What Works

The solution-focused approach, because of its strong constructivist and antipathologizing slant, places emphasis on assisting clients to develop a new perspective that allows them to draw more effectively on existing resources and competencies (e.g., finding exceptions to help build solutions). In order to "problem solve" it is generally believed that one must understand the nature of the problem and then find the solution that will fit the problem. In contrast to this way of thinking, solution-focused therapy eschews the imposition of concepts of deficit or pathology (see DeJong & Berg, 1997; de Shazer, 1991a; Fish, 1995; Hoyt and Friedman, Chapter 5, this volume; G. Miller & de Shazer, 1998) and may even say that there may not be any relationship between the problem and solutions:

> For an intervention to successfully *fit*, it is not necessary to have detailed knowledge of the complaint. It is not necessary even to be able to construct with any rigor how the trouble is maintained in order to prompt solution . . . *any* really different behavior in a problematic situation can be enough to prompt solution and give the client the satisfaction he seeks from therapy. All that is necessary is that the person involved in a troublesome situation *does something different*, even if that behavior is seemingly irrational, certainly irrelevant, obviously bizarre, or humorous. (de Shazer, 1985, p. 7)

The therapeutic task is to construct a detailed description of what *solutions* might be like and to build consensus around these solutions, not to tear down barriers.

Examination of various effective brief therapies suggests that they all share certain basic characteristics (Budman, Hoyt, & Friedman, 1992; Hoyt, 1995a):

1. rapid and positive alliance
2. focus on specific, achievable goals
3. clear definition of client and therapist responsibilities and activities
4. emphasis on client strengths and competencies with an expectation of change
5. assisting the client toward new perceptions and behaviors
6. here-and-now (and next) orientation
7. time sensitivity.

Whatever one's particular theoretical orientation, as therapists it is incumbent upon us to join with our clients to notice and amplify what works for them in achieving their goals. At a conference held in Saratoga, California during March 1995 (see Chapter 12, this volume), a number of leading brief therapists of varying theoretical persuasions discussed the importance of acknowledging connections and collaboration rather than promoting a divisive pitting of one approach against another. We applaud the "both/and" idea that everything is not "revolutionary" and "completely different." Consistent with the solution-focused model, we are interested in what works and recognize that there are multiple perspectives and paths for constructing self-fulfilling realities.

☐ Notes

[1]The excerpts that follow are drawn from the first session of a reconstructed case presented on a professional training videotape by Berg (1994b). Particularly in the spirit of the postmodern perspective informing the work to be reported, it is important to realize that what follows is a construction about a construction, not "what happened." Therapy, as John Weakland (quoted in Hoyt, 1994b, p. 25) said about life, is made up of "one damn thing after another." Any report can be only a gloss, a few brush strokes that can suggest (or obscure). Still, some useful approximations (or misunderstanding or misreadings, since each person takes his or her own meaning—see de Shazer [1993] and de Shazer and Berg [1992] may be receivable. For additional applications of solution-focused principles to couple therapy, see de Shazer and Berg (1985), Friedman (1996), Friedman and Lipchik (1999), Gale and Newfield (1992), George, Iveson, and Ratner (1990), Hoyt (2000), Hudson and O'Hanlon (1991), C. E. Johnson and Goldman (1996), Lethem (1994), Lipchik and Kubicki (1996), Nunnally (1993), O'Hanlon and Hudson (1994), Quick (1996), and Weiner-Davis (1992).

[2]This observation task, in which each member of the couple is to notice what the other person is doing to improve the relationship (but not reveal what has been noticed), is somewhat similar to the "jamming" tactic a Mental Research Institute (MRI) strategic therapist (Fisch, Weakland, & Segal, 1982, pp. 156–158; Shoham, Rohrbaugh, & Patterson, 1995, p. 149) might employ—that is, having one partner randomly perform a negative behavior and having the other try to guess (without telling) when the behavior is "real" or "fake." The intention of the MRI strategy is to disrupt a problematic interactional pattern by reducing the informational value of interpersonal communication, whereas the Brief Family Therapy Center (BFTC) solution focused observation task (noticing the positive) is designed more to shape viewing in order to support a more favorable interaction.

[3]A related example is provided by Furman and Ahola (1992b, p. xix) in their book *Solution Talk: Hosting Therapeutic Conversations.* They tell of a woman who complained about the rudeness of a man she knew. A friend offered to intercede and, a few weeks later, the woman reported that the man was completely changed. When she asked her friend if the man had been confronted, the friend replied, "Well, not really. I told him that you think he is a charming man." If we see someone in a positive light, we are more likely to respond in kind; this may help produce a "virtuous" instead of a "vicious" cycle.

[4]After watching portions of the videotape (Berg, 1994b) depicting the case presented here, then-7-year-old Alexander Hoyt remarked, "Dad, that's good. Instead of letting them fight she's getting them to talk about ways they could be happier."

[5]Paul Watzlawick (Watzlawick & Hoyt, 1998, p. 192) commented: "Without claiming that I have fully understood these distinctions, I believe that my orientation is more interactional and system-oriented. My 'patient' is the relationship."

[6]Clients prefer both.

CHAPTER

Solution-ku

"Thank the Maker!"
—C-3PO (1977, in the movie, *Star Wars*)

> Solution focus
> Find exception and increase
> Otherwise stay same
>
> More of same, no change
> More of difference, not same
> When will you notice?
>
> Single session now
> Kill it, make it sing, or wait
> The cage is open

Note. Written July 1995 in Kyoto at 4 a.m. after being awakened by a small earthquake. Legend has it that three Japanese lords of old revealed their very different characters when asked what they would do with a nightingale that did not sing.

10

A Single-Session Therapy Retold: Evolving and Restoried Understandings

> Life can only be understood backwards; but it must be
> lived forwards.
>
> —Soren Kierkegaard (1843), *Journals*

When the book *Single Session Therapy: Maximizing the Effect of the First (and Often Only) Therapeutic Encounter* (Talmon, 1990) appeared, it contained an edited (and somewhat truncated) transcript of a case in which I was the therapist, involving a 29-year-old woman who had sought assistance in dealing with her highly intrusive father (Hoyt & Talmon, 1990).[1] While the case appears to have had a successful outcome, as assessed both by immediate feedback and longer-term follow-up, even in the initial report we wrote (p. 78): "In retrospect, we feel that the therapist could have done a few things differently."

My understanding of the therapeutic process and what may have been helpful has evolved over time. My continued peregrinations—including discussions with colleagues (some of whom will be cited below) and feedback from workshop audiences who have viewed the videotape—have yielded an expanded ("restoried") conceptualization, including a greater

Part of the material in this chapter is from "Single-Session Therapy in Action: A Case Example," by M. F. Hoyt and M. Talmon, in M. Talmon, *Single Session Therapy* (pp. 78–96), 1990, San Francisco: Jossey-Bass. Copyright 1990 by Jossey-Bass. Adapted with permission of the publisher.

appreciation of collaborative narrative construction. What follows is not definitive (nor is the therapy especially sterling). Rather, it is intended to serve both as an update and as a modest example of the stereoscopic advantage of using multiple "lenses" (L. Hoffman, 1990/1995; Zeig & Munion, 1990) to construct theoretical perspectives. I shall first provide a brief overview of the case, then present several portions of transcript with commentary, and conclude with several additional remarks.

☐ A Thumbnail Sketch of the Case

> A repetition of the experiment is impossible, for the simple reason that the original situation cannot be reconstructed. Therefore in each instance there is only a first and single answer.
> —C. G. Jung (1949/1977, p. xxix)

A woman contacted our HMO Psychiatry Department saying she needed to learn how to better deal with her father, who was in jail. Her mother had divorced her father when the client was a child. After some time he had drifted off and would not be heard from for long stretches, but would recontact the family when he was in trouble and wanted something (such as money or a place to stay). He had a reputation as a ne'er-do-well, a long history of alcohol and drug abuse, and had been in and out of jail on charges of petty theft, barroom fighting, and the like. One time, he had even threatened the life of the client's husband if he was not given a sizable loan, but quickly backed off when the loan was refused and police action was suggested.

The client, who had no prior psychiatric or psychotherapeutic treatment, called when she did because she recently had received a phone call from her father, who was in the local jail demanding that she visit. She said she did not want to see him or have anything to do with him, but that she felt "shaken up" and "guilty" if she did not do as he wanted. During our one therapy session, we explored some of the personal and familial difficulties her father had caused, and then role-played an instance in which she pretended opening a door, seeing her father, refusing him entry, and closing it. We also identified times when she had been able to stand up to her father, including when she was angered by a sexual proposition he had made to her a few years earlier (when she already was a woman—she denied that there ever had been sexual improprieties when she was a child). We then discussed ways she could recall this angry feeling to help her move away from feeling guilty. In response to my question about what would be her next steps, the client described how she would refuse her father's phone calls.

As she indicated to one of my coinvestigators during a follow-up research interview, a few days after the session she received a jailhouse phone call from her father during which she asked him, somewhat pleadingly, not to continue calling her because she found it upsetting. Her father did call her again, a few days later; and, during this second call she was much tougher, unequivocally stating her intention not to help him and telling (not asking) him not to call again. He subsequently did not bother her, and she did not feel guilty.

☐ The Session: Some Points of Departure

> The first cut is the deepest.
> —Cat Stevens (1974)

I had spoken with the client briefly on the telephone a few days before the session. During this initial contact, we confirmed the appointment, she agreed to having the session videotaped, and (after briefly hearing that "I get all shaken up and fall apart when I have to deal with him" and that she wanted to "learn how to deal with my father better") I suggested that she give some thought to times with him when she had been able to stand up for herself. This variant of the "Skeleton Key Question" (de Shazer, 1985) was intended to "seed" change by helping us identify "exceptions" and "clues to solution" (de Shazer, 1985, 1988, 1991a).

Building Alliance and Motivation

As described in Hoyt and Talmon (1990), the session opened with the client describing her predicament. I gathered information and responded to her appeal for assistance by highlighting and cultivating the client's motivation with a positive connotation of her call for help and an optimistic expression of the meeting's purpose. At the beginning of this passage, however, I inadvertently placed the client in a double bind.

Therapist: *The purpose of our meeting today is to find out what problems you are having, what brings you here, and then to figure out what solutions would be helpful.*

Client: *Yeah, that's what I need.*

Therapist: *Okay. Sometimes we can get everything solved in one visit. That is, if you are really motivated and want to get right down to figuring out what to do, we may be able to get everything dealt with today. If we are not able to, then we will figure out what the next steps are.*

Client: *Okay.*

While things seem to have worked out OK, this approach ran the risk of blaming the client and possibly stimulating "resistance." It might have been better to omit the reference to "if you are really motivated," and simply say that "We may be able to get everything solved in one visit but, if not, we will at least figure out the next steps." More attention might also have been given to explicating the client's construction of her preferences, both in terms of possible solutions ("What will you be doing differently when things are better?") and in terms of pace ("Do you think we should go right for a possible solution, or maybe spend more time understanding the history of this problem?").

Focusing on Goals

As the session progressed, I clarified with the client her treatment goals. By creating a therapeutic focus, I endeavored to help the client feel less overwhelmed and confused.

Therapist: *I know we spoke briefly on the phone the other day. Fill me in— what brings you here today? What's cooking?*

Client: *Actually, most of the problems started with my father. I grew up with a manic-depressive father, and we went through a lot of things as kids. I have three brothers, and my mom hung in there with us the whole time and has gone through it with us. And my dad comes around every now and then. He's living his own miserable life, and he puts a lot of it off on us, and he won't let go of the past—he keeps throwing it up. I had him staying with me from mid-January to late February, and there were a lot of things he said. And I've just tried to tuck it all in and erase it. Every time he's around or calls it gets all stirred up—I get in an emotional turmoil.*

Therapist: *So, what is it that you would like to accomplish today?*

Client: *It keeps eating away at me. I keep thinking about it and it makes me a nervous wreck. I want to take it out of me, deal with it and get it aside, and then learn how to handle him when he calls, when he comes to my door. For years, I just didn't let him know where I lived, didn't talk to him. And that worked, but he's not gone. You know, he finds out where you live, what's your number.*

Therapist: *It sounds like there are two things you really want to accomplish. One is the stuff from the past that is eating away at you—you want to finally get it out and be done with it.*

Client: *That's right. From childhood on he has dug it up. So now, I am flashing back, reliving a lot of it. I can't stop thinking about it. He just makes me so mad, so torn up inside—I can't eat, I can't sleep, my stomach is in knots.*

Therapist: *So, he was living with you, your husband, and your two kids. What* *kind of stuff does your dad do that you keep trying to bury and he keeps digging up?*

Client: *Just badmouthing my mother and saying everything is her fault.*

Therapist: *So, that is one thing: dealing with your childhood. The second is how to deal with your father* now *when he starts to intrude into your life.*

Client: *Yeah. I want to deal with it and learn how not to let him upset me. For years, I just did not let him know where I lived, did not talk to him, and that worked. But he is not gone. He finds out where I live. I just wish he would never come around. But he calls. He's in jail now; he's in and out of jail constantly. It's just his own manic state that puts him there. There's no institution for them to put him in. He knows the game so well. He's dealt with it since we were little kids. As soon as he goes to a psychologist, he straightens out his act.*

Therapist: *Just to give me the flavor, why did they put him in jail this time? What did he actually do?*

Client: *I don't know. I didn't want to know. One thing is he had a new car, so probably car theft for a start. He says they want to keep him there for 1 to 3 years. I feel relieved [laughs nervously] because I know he is not going to be knocking at my door for a while. Isn't that terrible?*

Therapist: *No, it's really not terrible, given what you have been through. It sounds like you care about him; you don't want anything bad to happen to him. You just want him to back off.*

Client: *Back off, that's fine. Even if he just wrote me letters, I could handle that, I think . . . but he keeps digging it up, constantly badmouthing and blaming my mother and my brothers.*

Therapist: *So, which problem do you want to deal with first, the past or the present?*

Client: *I don't know. I mean, I can't say one feels more important than the other. He still calls. He calls collect and tells me, "You are the only one who will talk to me. You are the only one." Last time he called, I blew up at him and said, "You know, ever since you were here and talked about Mom and the past, I am just torn up inside, my nerves are shot." He just said, "I am sorry," but he continues to do it. I do not know why I sat there and listened to it all, other than I have never given him a chance to speak his mind and say it all out. . . . And, when he was through, that is when I knew that this has gotten to me. I guess he just hit some point which tore me apart. He blames all of it on everybody but me, because I am the one opening the door. I let him come into my house.*

Therapist: *Opening the door for him, huh?*

Client: *When we had him living with us, he was on his best behavior, because he knows that my husband would just boot him out. But, he let him stay, because, as I told my husband, he has to give me justified reasons to boot him out. I cannot just, say, slam the door in his face. . . . Some days I say: "Yes, I could!" He just* *makes me so mad, so torn up inside. I can't eat, I can't sleep, my stomach is in knots.*

Therapist: *Before today, have you ever seen a counselor or a psychiatrist?*

Client: *No, I've just kept kind of tucking it away.*

Therapist: *So it's finally gotten bad enough that you've got to do something about it. You're ready.*

Client: *Yeah.*

In Search of Solutions (and How to Avoid Their Impediments)

Discussion then shifted to exploring ways the client had attempted to deal with the situation. This was undertaken for several reasons: to join with her and convey a sense of acceptance and validation, to enhance understanding of the client's predicament, to note and not repeat attempted solutions that had not been helpful,[2] and to identify and possibly amplify any attempted solutions that had been helpful.

Client: *I feel I'd still be running from it. He's hurt me, but to hurt him—I know how much it would hurt him. Yet, I know, I've had other people tell me, "Just don't deal with him. Just because he's your father doesn't mean you have to put up with it." And, I've told myself that, but he doesn't stop there. You close the door at home and he'll follow you to work, he'll follow you around in the car. He'll just have to get to you, and if there's a way . . . I mean, restraining orders, we've dealt with those . . .*

Therapist: *And what happened?*

Client: *It runs him off for awhile but . . . I don't know . . . I think it's because everyone else has kind of turned their back on him. And, like he says, I'm the only one left. Then it makes me feel guilty. If I just close the door . . . I get to a point where I could do that . . .*

Therapist: *That's how he gets his foot in the door: He says, "You're the only one" and you start feeling sorry for him.*

Client: *Like the collect calls. I told him, I can't afford the collect calls. I've been sending him money for cigarettes and commissary things. And, "I'm the only one, there's no one else". . . .*

Therapist: *What do you say in your mind to feel guilty? What do you hear?*

Client: [looks quizzical] *What do I hear?*

Therapist: [clarifying] *What do you think? Like: "Children should always help their parents" or "I've got to save my Dad"? What do you do to put yourself on a guilt trip?*

Client: *"I'm the only one." The only one he has to turn to. So, if I don't, then he* *has no one, and I'd hate that to happen to me—even though he's caused his own, it's his own fault. If he didn't live in the past so much we could all handle him, or deal with him.*

Therapist: *So, you know it's his fault.*

Client: *Yeah. He twists it all around. He puts the blame on everyone else—it's my brothers' fault, it's my mom's fault, everyone but his.*

Therapist: *So, what are you going to do? Are you going to keep feeling guilty and letting him disturb your kids and disturb you, or are you finally going to say enough its enough?*

Client: [nodding] *Yeah. I came to that point.*

Therapist: *So, what are you going to do?*

Client: *But, is turning my back on him handling it, you know?*

Therapist: *If you were in a house and the house caught on fire, and it was getting really hot and burning, what would you do?*

Client: [laughs] *Get out of the house!*

Therapist: *You'd get out. Would that be running away?*

Client: *No.*

Therapist: *Would that be cowardly?*

Client: *No.*

Therapist: *That would be, that would be . . .* [pauses³]

Client: *Survival!*

Therapist: *It would be survival. Would you say, "I've got to stay and face the heat" and have it burn your nose?*

Client: *No!*

Therapist: *You'd say "This is survival" and leave. That's what a normal, intelligent, sane person would do. And she'd take her kids, too. You wouldn't leave them in the house. Well, I think that's more of what you're dealing with. It's like a fire, it's consuming . . .*

Client: *Consuming, yeah.*

Therapist: *Yeah, and destructive. And, when you say you want to face it, I understand what you're saying, and I admire your devotion to him and your courage and your wanting to do the right thing, but trying to face somebody who is manic and uses alcohol and drugs and is obsessed with the past . . . it would be like if you put a record on and let it play and it went over and over and over . . .*

Client: *That's what he's like, that's what he's like!*

Therapist: *Well, you're like somebody who says, "I'm going to face the record player, I'm going to keep staring at it." Until what? The record player is never going to wear out: he's manic, he has a great deal of energy and has nothing better to do than to sit there and go over and over and over the past. And, if you're willing* *to sit there with him, he will do it forever. He'll do it until you're 90 years old.[4] He's shown that he's willing to make his whole life about the past and all of his problems, instead of getting on with it. So, I think that's where you're getting stuck with him. When you said you want to face him, I was wondering what you hope to accomplish. If it was giving him a chance to say his piece, that would be nice, sure, but there's no end to it because he doesn't want to solve it or get to the bottom of it or end it; what he wants to do is keep going over and over and over.*

Client: *He wants to switch it around and make me believe that it's all my mother's fault, that all the problems we dealt with are all her fault.*

Therapist: *And they're obviously not. She stayed there and took care of you while he went off and went wild.*

Client: *Yeah.*

Therapist: *So, letting him talk at you isn't going to help because he's never going to stop until you finally say, "You are right. Mom was terrible, and you're the only good parent I ever had." You're never going to say that.*

Client: *He's done that with my brother. And I hate that, because he's got him so twisted up that he's got him turned against my mom. And, for what?*

Therapist: *Yeah. Well, I'm sorry to hear that, but that's his problem.*

Client: *And my mom's.*

Therapist: *So, what are you going to do? You've got to really make a decision of how you're finally going to protect yourself, how you're going to put up some kind of a shield, something that will stop him.*

Planning and Practicing

We continued talking about what the client was going to do. Applying the idea of Prochaska (1999; see Chapter 14, this volume) that there is a progression of stages in the process of change (from *precontemplation* to *contemplation* to *preparation and planning* to *action* to *maintenance* to *termination*), we discussed ways she could refuse collect calls and not accept (or throw away) unwanted letters. At this juncture, using the image of "closing the door" that she had provided earlier, we launched into a more experiential venture as we practiced a possible solution—one that might also serve as a symbol or metaphor.

Client: *The phone calls will be easiest. When he comes to the door, that is going to be rough.*

Therapist: *That's going to be the hard thing.*

Client: *There was a period between them when things were pretty good. They had split up and gone back together so many times, trying to work it out and be a family. There was a period when . . .* [pauses, searching her memory] *. . . It* *had something to do with, oh, closing the door on him. I was probably 10 years old, and we used to live next to my dad's sister. We'd moved away from that house and to a different house, and there had been a few years when I never saw him or talked to him. My dad and my second-to-youngest brother went over to the house, and she just opened the door, saw him, and closed the door in his face. Just like that. And, I thought: "How could she do that?" I had that belief: "How could you do that? That was your brother at the door."*

Therapist: *So, other people in the family know how to do it.*

Client: *Yeah, but I used to think that was so wrong.*

Therapist: *Let's do an experiment, okay?*

Client: *Okay.*

Therapist: [directs client to the door of the interview room and stands behind her] *Open the door, look out, pretend that he's there, and close it on him.*

Client: *He's not there.*

Therapist: *Imagine standing there. You see him. What would you say to him? There he is.* [therapist raps on door with his knuckles] *He just knocked, and he's going to give you one of his . . .*

Client: *And he is going to start talking and walking in the door.*

Therapist: *So, you need to do something.*

Client: *I'll close the door.* [closes the door softly]

Therapist: *You did it!*

Client: *Then he is still going to be there, though.*

Therapist: *So, open it again. He's still there. Try it.* [she reopens door] *Now, what would you say to him if he was standing right there and you wanted him to go away?*

Client: [a bit louder, but still tentative] *I cannot talk to you. I can't deal with what you're going through and your problems. I don't want to see you.* [shakes her head and speaks under her breath] *I can't say that to him.* [closes the door; client and therapist return to their chairs]

Therapist: *All right. Let's talk about it. What are you thinking?*

Client: *I could!*

Therapist: *You could!*

Client: *I could.*

Therapist: *Of course you could. I mean, you said it. You could say it. But, how do you stop yourself? What goes on inside yourself?*

Client: *Guilt! There is my father standing at the door, and I am going to close the door in his face. I have grown up thinking how terrible that is, how terrible that would be, not even giving him a chance to talk or say anything.*

Therapist: *Of course, how old are you now, 29? You've given him a lot of chances.*

Client: *Yeah.* [nods slowly, as though she is realizing something] *But, hurting him . . . I mean, that is the bottom line. I know it would hurt him for me to just close the door. I'm all that is left. Yet, I don't want to deal with him, I don't want to see him. Now I know why my mom moved! It would take awhile for him to find where we moved—we wouldn't have to face him. If my husband's there I've got all the strength in the world. If he's not, I just melt. I feel just vulnerable. I feel like he's got* zing! [waves her hand Svengali-like] *control over me or something.*

Therapist: *You are a very loving, caring person.*

Client: *Yeah.*

Therapist: *That is what makes it hard. If you were coldblooded, you could do it with ease.*

Client: *That's it! But, you know, I have. I've gotten those feelings. After he said those* [looks disgusted] *things to me, that time I had him staying with me, it wasn't hard.*

Therapist: *What did he say to you?* [sees that she hesitates[5]] *What were the words?*

Client: *It wasn't a whole bunch of things. It was one phrase. He said I was laying on the couch one day and that I said to him, "Ball me," and that he just stood there looking at me. And, I'm like, "Huh?" I just stopped in my tracks. He had come home all beaten up and half-delirious and he was sitting in the chair almost bleeding to death and I'm patching up his eye. And, it just turned my stomach. And from that point on, I just could not forget. And when he called, that's when I got that cold feeling. No problem. Any man who could talk to his daughter like that, I don't care what state of mind you're in, there's no excuse. And I told him, "You are sick. I don't want to talk to you," and hung up. No problem. Now, I feel guilty, though, for that. And later, he threw that at me.*

Therapist: *What do you think? Why do you feel guilt?*

Client: *Because he said he called a couple of other times and needed my help, and I wasn't there.* [long pause] *Why should I be,* with all the pain he caused me? *Why should I be?* [said with angry protest]

Therapist: *Good question! Why should you be there?*

Client: *Because he's my father.* [sighs and stares off into space]

Therapist: *What are you thinking?*

Client: *He makes me mad. And it hurts. And I wish he'd just go away, and then I wouldn't ever have to deal with it. I mean, there are times when I just wish he were dead! I mean, that's pretty serious, to wish your father were dead.*

Therapist: *Do you feel mad now?*

Client: *Confused . . . I think what I've been going through, though, it would be easier—not easy, but easier—to start with not accepting the collect calls.*

Feedback and Moving Forward

The foregoing material was useful in the feedback portion of the session, during which time I attempted to convey an understanding to the client that, by highlighting her strengths and competencies, would help empower her in the direction she wished to go.

Therapist: *I think there are two problems. One problem is your father. In reality, your father sounds like bad news. He has threatened your husband's life. He has come on to you sexually. He's got all of his problems. He is bad news. So, one problem is how to protect yourself and your family from him: the restraining order, the hanging up the phone on him, the slamming the door, keeping him away, getting rid of him. But, the second problem, which interferes with solving the first, is the guilt that you keep putting yourself on. Where you say, "Oh, but he is my father. I'm his last one. I got to help him, poor guy. He'll be disappointed—it'll hurt his feelings." You know what you need to do to deal with him* [client nods in agreement], *but you keep stopping yourself because you think of things that make yourself guilty: "I am his daughter," "I have to take care of him," and all that stuff. So, there are really two problems—one is him, but the other is you.* [client nods] *You're defeating yourself, because if you would get yourself clear on what you want to do and do not stop yourself, you could deal with him. It would be hard, because he's obnoxious, but you can do it.*

Client: *I have. I know I have.*

Therapist: *You have these two memories . . .*

Client: *I want to erase that other one. I just want to clean it out, get rid of it, solve it or something.*

Therapist: *You can use one memory to fight the other one. One memory you have, which makes you very angry and when you get angry you are very strong, is the memory of his saying "I want to ball you" or whatever he said, some obnoxious, terrible thing to say to a daughter. When you think about that, you are ready to slam doors, hang up, tear up things, get rid of him. You're not guilty, you're angry! But then you have this other memory, and you think of the good times and "the poor guy" and "I'm his only daughter," and make yourself feel guilty—and you open the door and say, "Oh, he's my father." When you're angry, no one can mess around with you, can they?*

Client: *No one!* [nods firmly in agreement]

Therapist: *So, when you walk out in a few minutes, what are you going to say to yourself? What are you actually going to do when this meeting is over?*

Client: *Draw a line. Draw a line!*

Therapist: *How and where are you going to draw the line?*

Client: *I will start with the phone calls, because that is when I will hear from him next.*

Therapist: *And, what are you going to do?*
Client: *Not accept it!*
Therapist: *Perfect!*

Last-Minute Issues

As the session was about to end, I asked if there was anything else that needed to be discussed that day. (As noted in Hoyt and Talmon, 1990, pp. 92–95, it would have been preferable to inquire about last minute issues before attempting to conclude the session, rather than as an afterthought.) The client responded that she had been troubled by a "claustrophobic feeling" which, discussion revealed, had began shortly after her father's sexual come-on several years prior. It seemed that, with the momentum generated during the session, it was possible that this "additional symptom" could be resolved within the focus that already had been created. This was interpreted to her with a suggestion:

Therapist: *You felt like you were trapped by him. Here he was, coming on to you. One thing that is going to help this situation is if you really keep reminding yourself and keep drawing the line. Remind yourself that you are back in control instead of him controlling you and him trapping you. You can say things like "I am back in control. I am angry. I made up my mind. I will not take this anymore. I am in control."* . . . *The second thing that is going to help is when I call you in a month (or when you call me), I will ask you how things have changed, and you will be able meanwhile to do some practicing. What you need to do is every day, little by little, try going into situations where you are slightly uncomfortable. Just slightly uncomfortable. And then stand there until you relax.*

The client and I then spent a few minutes discussing various locations in which to do the practicing, using a variety of techniques (behavioral desensitization, cognitive affirmation, hypnotic suggestion) to help her feel "untrapped." We then concluded:

Client: *It makes me feel better already. . . . As long as I see the light.*
Therapist: *You can lighten the load you've got by taking control and not letting him run your life anymore. So you're not trapped.*
Client: *Exactly.*
Therapist: *Good.*
Client: *Be in control and not get trapped.*
Therapist: *All right. Let's speak in a month or so. . . . If something comes up before and it is a question that can wait, wait. But if it is something that you have got to know or have to ask, do not hesitate to call me.*

Client: *Like if he comes up with a new trick.*
Therapist: *You have got tricks, too. You can fight back.*
Client: *Yeah. Now that I know how!*
Therapist: *Yes!* [they shake hands]

Outcome

Follow-up phone interviews, done a couple of months and then more than a year post-therapy, indicated that the client had achieved her treatment goals. She reported:

Client: *It was helpful in talking it out, realizing the guilt feelings and that I don't have to take it anymore. I felt relieved in a big way. I am very satisfied.*
Interviewer: *Was the one session enough for you?*
Client: *Yes. Since that session, I confronted my father and drew a clear line with him. He has not tried to bother me since.*

☐ Thinking about Practice: Some Questions and Possible Answers

> The essence of epigenesis is predictable repetition; the essence
> of learning and evolution is exploration and change.
> —Gregory Bateson (1980, p. 52)

A number of issues may be raised:
Was this way of working typical of single-session therapy? It is useful to mention the possibility of one session being adequate to provide some structure and impetus, but the goal should not be to do therapy in a *single session* but, rather, to help the client achieve her goal as soon as possible. The client in this case had a fairly specific and circumscribed complaint and goal. Every case is truly unique, although a series of general guidelines (a couple of which were not followed in this case) can be offered (adapted from Talmon, Hoyt, & Rosenbaum, 1990, and from Hoyt, 1995a, pp. 146–147):

1. Seed change through induction and preparation. Engage the client via a presession phone call or letter encouraging a focus on goals and the collection of useful information about competencies, past successes, and exceptions to the problem. Ask, for example, the "Skeleton Key Question" of de Shazer (1985, p. 137): "Between now and when we meet, I would like you to observe, so you can describe to me, what happens that you want to continue to have happen."

2. Develop an alliance and co-create obtainable treatment goals (specific, measurable, achievable with effort). When getting started, inquire about change since initial contact and amplify accordingly. Introduce the possibility of one session being adequate, and recruit the client's cooperation.

3. Allow enough time. Most of us work in the 50-minute hour, which is usually adequate; but consider scheduling a longer session (especially with a couple or family) to allow for a complete process or intervention.

4. Focus on "pivot chords," ambiguities that may facilitate transitions into different directions. Look for ways of meeting the client in his or her worldview while at the same time offering a new perspective—respectful questioning, positive connotation, education, and reframing introduce possibilities of seeing or acting differently.

5. Go slow and look for client's strengths.

6. Practice solutions experientially. Rehearsing outcomes provides a "glimpse of the future," teaches and reinforces useful skills, and inspires enthusiasm and movement.

7. Consider taking a time-out. A break or pause during a session allows time to think, consult, focus, refocus, prepare, punctuate.

8. Allow time for last-minute issues. "Eleventh-hour" questions should be asked at about "six o'clock," to allow time for inclusion or prioritization. Unaddressed issues may impede a sense of the session being complete and satisfactory.

9. Give feedback. Information should be provided that enhances the client's understanding and sense of self-determination. Tasks or "homework" may be developed that will continue therapeutic work.

10. Leave the possibility of future sessions open. The decision to stop is usually best left to the client (see Chapter 15, this volume).

Therapeutic alliance often takes a long time to develop, particularly with clients who have experienced abuse. In the case discussed here, how were the two of you able to move along so quickly? The client and I were able to develop a clear *customer* relationship (de Shazer, 1985, 1988; see Chapter 14, this volume) by identifying and maintaining focus on what the client was hoping to achieve that was under her control. Recall, for example, the client's annoyance about the way her father had manipulated her brother against her mother—had I focused discussion on the father-brother relationship, about which the client could have little if any immediate influence, she would have lost her sense of instrumentality or self-efficacy and entered into a *complainant* relationship.

I did make several potential errors that could have been harmful to the alliance. As already noted, at the beginning of the session, I attempted to motivate the client by suggesting that, with hard effort, she might resolve her problems in one meeting. While this way of framing the situation may have been intended to serve as a "therapeutic double bind" (Bandler & Grinder, 1975; Erickson & Rossi, 1975/1980), in retrospect it seems unfair. It suggests that, if everything is not solved in one visit, it will be due to the client's not being "really motivated" and not wanting "to get right down to figuring out what to do," rather than allowing that the problem may simply require more time or that I, not the client, may lack the requisite skills to deal with things successfully in one session.[6] It also may be noted that this placed a demand on the client to "perform" for me—a possible recapitulation of the client-father situation.

I also made another potential "alliance error" when, mid-session, I imported some psycho-jargon and asked her, "What do you hear in your head?" (This literally asked the client to report any auditory hallucinations!) Her puzzled look signaled the breach, and I quickly returned to "speaking the client's language" by asking what her thoughts were that evoked her feelings of guilt. Finally, when giving feedback near the end of the session, I appropriately first reflected back the detailed problems that the client had recounted (her father threatening her husband, coming on to her sexually, and so forth) before offering my own ideas. This served to acknowledge and validate her experience rather than offering a radical recasting that would leave her feeling unlistened to.

The client also may have had a predisposition (transference) to follow the lead of a (male) therapist. It was important that such a tendency be used to the advantage of the client, not the therapist.

How might this case be understood from some different theoretical perspectives? As the client described it, there were issues of guilt, which can be understood from a variety of perspectives. Psychodynamicists, of course, would conceptualize this in terms of "conscience" or an "internalized super-ego figure." A redecision therapist, following Mary Goulding (1985), might ask, "Who's been living in your head?" Cognitive therapists would consider "maladaptive self-schemas," while a narrative therapist might wonder aloud if these are the client's preferences and how she was "recruited" (indoctrinated, brainwashed) into these particular beliefs.

All of those ideas more-or-less flitted through my mind, although in the moment I was mostly attending to what the client was saying. The transactional analysis concept (Woollams & Brown, 1978, pp. 201–205) of "Protection, Permission, Potency" (P.P.P.) framed my efforts to encourage her strength with remarks such as, "You just want him to back off" and "Other people in the family know how to do it." My "strategic Ericksonian mind" had me wanting to "make something happen" and looking for ways to utilize the client's ideas and motivations to help her move toward her goals. The particular action of going to the door and role-playing shutting out her father was especially influenced by my background in redecision therapy (Goulding & Goulding, 1997; Hoyt, 1992c, 1997; Hoyt & Goulding, 1989/1995). While we were not exactly doing an "early scene" redecision, I was inspired by the Gouldings' ideas of revivifying the problem and mobilizing the client. I also was conscious of the need to focus on a solution, à la de Shazer (1985, 1988), although—as I will discuss below—I think I missed a number of keys and clues.

Several years ago I participated with three esteemed colleagues in a conference that I found very instructive.[7] I was honored to be included with Donald Meichenbaum, Bill O'Hanlon, and Peter Sifneos, each a preeminent author and presenter. One day, we took turns before the large audience, each briefly describing our work, illustrated with a piece of video, with the other three then making comments. When my turn came, I outlined some of my ideas about the temporal structure of brief therapy (see Chapter 14, this volume) and then showed the videotape excerpts transcribed above. My colleagues were gracious and constructive. The first commentator was Peter Sifneos (see 1972, 1987, 1992), one of the originators of short-term psychodynamic psychotherapy. He opined that the success of the treatment would probably last, and noted—from his psychodynamic view that emphasizes so-called unconscious Oedipal dynamics—that the client might still be hoping for a relationship with an idealized father. He noted that she may have been partially protected by her good relationship with her stepfather, but suggested that, if she returned to therapy, it might be useful to frame the problem in terms of longing for her lost father and help her grieve her disappointment.

The next commentator, Donald Meichenbaum, also offered several useful ideas. One of the founders of the "cognitive revolution" in psychotherapy (see Meichenbaum, 1977, 1994; Meichenbaum, in Hoyt, 1996d), he noted that, as therapist, I had oftentimes moved quickly, perhaps too quickly. It would have been more collaborative to allow the client more time to process and respond.[8] Meichenbaum also noted that, unlike Sifneos, who would emphasize what the client seemed to be hoping to gain (the "lost father"), he would highlight what the client stood to *lose* by continuing the relationship: He suggested motivating her toward better self-care by repeatedly emphasizing to her "the cost, the price, the toll" of keeping her father in her life.[9,10] He also suggested that he would "pluck" (seize upon) certain key words and feed them back to her, noting that she said about her father, "He has *zing!* control—I just melt." It might be useful to go through that sequence when she "melts," nanosecond by nanosecond, since that is when she loses control or gives up her autonomy (or "goes unconscious" or "into trance" or "the old tapes play" or whatever theoretical metaphor you prefer).[11] Clients often are okay when they leave our offices but "lose it again" under stressful conditions, so relapse prevention, goal maintenance, or "inoculation training" (Meichenbaum, 1985; see Chapter 14, this volume) is very important.

The final commentator was Bill O'Hanlon, who also focused on the importance of collaboration and carefully listening to the client for possibilities that might be amplified. A peripatetic author and world-renowned brief therapy workshop trainer (see Bertolino & O'Hanlon, 1999; Cade & O'Hanlon, 1993; O'Hanlon, 1987; O'Hanlon & Weiner-Davis, 1989), Bill noted that the client had voiced various "exceptions" and possible solutions (such as when she commented that "Some days, I could," "I've come to that point," and "I used to think that was so wrong"), but that I had been theory or model-driven, not client-driven, and had pressed on right past these potentially useful clues. It also may be noticed, as I did when responding to Bill's cogent remarks, that the client had identifed two major exceptions to the pattern of her father's intrusion: when her husband was present, and when she became offended and angered by the incest proposal. In the feedback portion of the session, I had focused on the latter, involving her anger, perhaps underappreciating the value of drawing strength through connection and solidarity. (This may have been an effect of testosterone-driven male mentality poisoning!) It might have been helpful to highlight both exceptions.[12] I could have suggested she consider imagining her husband's presence when dealing with her father (perhaps using her wedding band as a reminder), or that she call her aunt and mom and discuss the situation with them; and/or I simply could have asked her how she might recall support when she needed it.[13]

Do you think there was a "critical moment" in the session? It is always interesting—and often surprising—to hear what clients recall and remember as important. In our standard research follow-up interviews (see Talmon, 1990, pp. 127–128), we asked what stood out for the client. I would have guessed that mobilizing her anger had been useful. She remarked that she had thought a lot about what we had discussed and had concluded that "I'm not dropping the ball—I've tried longer than anyone in the family to help him, but I can't keep doing this." This recognition—which may have been ticking when she nodded in response to my remark that she was 29 years old and already had given her father many chances—seemed to her to assuage her sense of guilt, not my push to get her to express her resentments.[14]

If you could, what would you "take back" or do differently? "Monday-morning quarterbacking" and "20/20 hindsight" are of limited value, as Heraclitus recognized in 513 B.C. (*On the Universe,* fragment 91) when he wrote, "You could not step twice into the same rivers; for other waters are ever flowing on to you." Having said that, in addition to prescience of my colleagues' suggestions that are reported above, it would have been nice to go back to the door (if the client was willing) and re-do the scene so that she could have a clearer sense of success.[15] Also, I do wish that I had raised doubts about her characterization of her father's problems as being due primarily to his being "manic-depressive," and more importantly, I think it would have been good to have discussed explicitly what to do if her father again made threats or someday began stalking her. Maybe I'm being overly careful or alarmist, since she had told him she would call the police if he made threats and he was incarcerated at the time of the session, but he had once tried to extort money by threatening to kill the client's husband.

It's important, especially in brief therapy, that the client feel listened to and not rushed or forced. What we did seemed agreeable to her and helpful. She can also return as needed.

What else? Ask me in 5 years!

☐ Notes

[1]The book also contained a coauthored chapter (Talmon, Hoyt, & Rosenbaum, 1990) outlining a series of guideline steps that had been originally presented (under the title "When the First Session May Be the Last") at the 1988 Brief Therapy Congress held in San Francisco. My colleagues and I have published other single-session therapy studies both collaboratively (e.g., Hoyt, Rosenbaum, & Talmon, 1992; Rosenbaum, Hoyt, & Talmon, 1990/1995) and separately (e.g., Hoyt, 1994/1995k, 1995a; Rosenbaum, 1993, 1994; Talmon, 1993).

[2]Recall the basic admonition of the Mental Research Institute (MRI) strategic interactional approach (Watzlawick et al., 1974; Fisch et al., 1982) that the attempted solution may serve to perpetuate the problem.

[3]Inviting the client to "fill in the blank" through such naturalistic pauses can be very helpful. One person's "memory lapses" can be another's "technique," as Peter Falk's TV character, the seemingly bumbling detective Lt. Colombo, so well demonstrated.

[4]An old Chinese saying: "If you don't change directions, you'll wind up where you're heading!" Again, following the MRI idea that the attempted solution actually continues the problem, becoming yet more compliant or passive (or, in other cases, more dominant or aggressive) will not help. From a solution-focused perspective (de Shazer, in Hoyt, 1996c, p. 68), there are three basic rules: (1) If it ain't broke, don't fix it; (2) Once you know what works, do more of it; and (3) If it doesn't work, don't do it again—do something different.

[5]The intention was to have the client recognize her experience and strengthen her resolve, not necessarily to have her emotionally abreact. Seeing her hesitation, the request to simply report the words allowed her some distance and control. It is interesting to note that Freud's (1913/1958, p. 135) original instruction for free association was as follows: "So say whatever goes through your mind. Act as though, for instance, you were a traveller sitting next to a window of a railway carriage and describing to someone inside the carriage the changing views which you see outside."

[6]As O'Hanlon and Wilk (1987, p. 107), among others, have noted, "The briefer successful therapy can be, the better," with the ideal being one session. As O'Hanlon (quoted in Hoyt, 1996e, p. 107) has remarked, however, "There's only so much leeway there, because of the physical reality and because of the cultural social practices and traditions." [Hoyt: "Not *tabula rasa*."] "No, not that kind of radical constructionism. Because if that were the case, I'm really good at creating therapeutic realities, and all my clients would be cured in one session. They're not. They bring their own traditions and their own narratives, and then we have to be co-narrative."

[7]The symposium, *The Future of Psychotherapy,* was held in Orlando, FL, February 1995. It was produced by the New England Educational Institute (NEEI), the sponsors of the annual Cape Cod Summer Symposia, and was very ably chaired by Robert Guerette, M.D., the NEEI director.

[8]I had been quite active and somewhat directive. While we remarked in the earlier report of this case (Hoyt & Talmon, 1990, pp. 78–79) that "Whereas therapists with a background in a very active form of therapy might want to learn more about being 'constructive minimalists' in SST [single session therapy], those who are more accustomed to acting mainly as 'privileged listeners' in therapy may learn more from this case," in retrospect a more balanced approach might have been best. "Less might have been more," as the Bauhaus architect Mies van der Rohe said.

[9]At a subsequent conference, an attendee who viewed the same tape noted that many women who are battered, when they finally leave the batterer, often cite their great concern for their children as the deciding factor that impelled them to get out and stay away. In the case presented here, I may have appealed to the client's "maternal instinct" when I reminded her that the father would keep "disturbing your kids and disturbing you" and commented that someone fleeing a burning building would "take her kids, too."

[10]I also have found it helpful when working with battered women who are still hoping that the brute will somehow magically change or telling themselves that "It's not really him, it's . . . [his childhood, alcohol, job stress, etc.], to offer the following metaphoric image to collapse the good-bad splitting: "Suppose we told you that we would give you a new Mercedes-Benz, a $100 thousand car, the one with the leather seats, the burled walnut interior, the works, and we would pay all of the insurance, the gas, repairs, etc. There's one little problem, however. Every now and then—and we can't tell exactly when—it explodes! Fire goes through the cockpit and burns whoever's inside. So, would you take it? Maybe just relax and go for a ride?" Presented this way, the answer invariably is "No." I then ask, "OK. With all due respect, how is your marriage different than that car?"

[11]One time, I asked R. D. Laing what he thought of transference and he replied, "It's post-hypnotic suggestion with amnesia." That's deep! He was suggesting that early on we get "programmed" (like the fellow in the movie *The Manchurian Candidate,* who suddenly felt impelled to kill when he saw a particular playing card) to respond certain ways to certain cues, and that the power of the programming is ensured (sealed) by our being unaware ("unconscious") of the programming (see Laing, 1970). Within this way of thinking, the client described here is struggling not to become "entranced" or "go on automatic" when her father attempts to manipulate her. It seems to me that one way he does this is by confounding in her mind the ideas of being *assertive* and *aggressive,* conflating *self* and *selfish,* so that she feels that she is doing something hurtful (and guilt provoking) when she simply is asserting herself—taking care of herself gets construed as going against him. In my observation, this kind of "guilt-tripping" is a common dynamic in so-called "co-dependency."

[12]Greater sensitivity to what makes sense to clients, honoring their values and worldviews, will become increasingly important as we move more toward recognizing and appreciating the values of cultural diversity and provide more services to people of differing ethnicities.

[13]Long ago, Blaise Pascal advised: "People are generally better persuaded by the reasons which they have themselves discovered than by those which have come from the minds of others" (quoted in Duncan et al., 1998, p. 301). A similar idea for getting cooperation was articulated by Dale Carnegie (1936/1964, p. 150): "Let the other fellow feel that the idea is his." In what may still be the best self-help book, *How to Win Friends and Influence People,* he repeatedly suggests ways to build alliances and elicit strengths and resources.

[14]It seemed to me that the client was still trying to be a "good daughter" even though her father had long since abandoned being a "good father."

Once when I presented this tape at a workshop in a religious area of the Deep South, an attendee who apparently had very strong so-called "traditional values" did not like my encouraging the client to assert herself so strongly vis-à-vis her father. The person politely raised a hand and, when recognized, remarked "Dr. Hoyt, I'm not too happy about this—it says in Ephesians 6:1 and 6:2 that children should be obedient and 'Honor your father and mother.'" Suddenly, someone on the other side of the room jumped up and said, "Yeah, but it says in Ephesians 6:4, 'The father should not outrage the daughter!'" [In my *Jerusalem Bible*, Ephesians 6:4 says "And parents, never drive your children to resentment."] I looked at them and said, "Why don't y'all go out in the hall and settle this and let us know who's right!"

[15]When we moved to the door—as viewers of the videotape can see—the client slumped her shoulders and spoke in an uncertain voice. (When we were not actively evoking images of her father, her posture and tone were much stronger.) This suggests the importance of attending to nonverbal behavior, and the possibility of doing *solution-focused body awareness* (eliciting times the client felt strong and confident, and having her incorporate these ways of being into her deliberate response repertoire). Recall, for example, that when her father called her the first time after the session, she wavered and essentially pleaded that he not bother her, and he called back. When she was much stronger and unequivocal on the second call, he backed off. We need to attend to the words *and* the music.

CHAPTER

What Can We Learn From Milton Erickson's Therapeutic Failures?

> You will realize that the strong must have their happy moments
> and their sad moments . . . [and] you are going to respect fully
> and appreciatively people who fail in some way here and there
> and elsewhere.
> —Milton H. Erickson, *The February Man:*
> *Evolving Consciousness and Identity in Hypnotherapy*
> (Erickson & Rossi, 1989)

We all recognize Milton Erickson as an extraordinarily innovative and
effective clinician, a master therapist nonpareil. Time and again he achieved
outstanding results, often in difficult situations where other professionals
had not succeeded or would not even have known where to begin.

Clearly, he was a genius. Given his skillfulness, I wondered if there
were cases where even he had not been therapeutically effective and, if
so, what might have caused these "failures"—and if there was anything
to be learned that might help the rest of us?

I first wrote to three colleagues each of whom had studied directly with
Erickson. They all indicated that they did not know of any published papers on Erickson's failures, and one wrote back: "Erickson only told me of

Part of the material in this chapter was presented as part of a panel, *Therapeutic Failures,*
at the "Brief Therapy: Lasting Impressions Conference" sponsored by the Milton H. Erickson
Foundation in New York, August 1998. Other panelists were Mary Goulding, Leigh
McCullough, and John Norcross.

cases that appeared at first to succeed or fail and, in the end, succeeded (often due to his continued attempts to approach things differently)."[1]

I then reviewed the compilation that O'Hanlon and Hexum (1990) have entitled *An Uncommon Casebook: The Complete Clinical Work of Milton H. Erickson, M.D.*, based on reports of "complete clinical cases, that is, cases in which there was a clear presenting problem and/or request for treatment and a conclusion, whether success, failure, or dismissal" (p. x). While O'Hanlon and Hexum recognized (p. x) that "there may be more case examples in Erickson's work than are reported here" (and welcomed additional information), they were able at the time of their 1990 writing to identify and summarize 316 cases. Of these, 15 were classified as "failures." They are summarized in Table 11.1.

☐ Discussion

Examination of the table leaves one curious and puzzled. No clear pattern emerges: There are cases involving men, women, and couples; there is a wide variety of presenting complaints; while many of the cases only lasted a session or two, Erickson also reported many successes in such brief treatments.

So, what can be learned?

Looking again at Table 11.1 (and reviewing the original reports that are summarized therein), I wonder how many of these "single-session" failures were cut short because Erickson's clinical judgment told him that he would not be able to help with the particular problem unless the client(s) followed his directives exactly. Perhaps it was a lack of psychologically binding conditions and an absence of high emotional tension that kept Erickson from being able to structure a "psychological shock" to galvanize the patients and help them move forward (see Rossi, 1973).[2] In Case 1, the man did not protest Erickson's prediction that he was not going to stop smoking.[3] In Case 2, the man who ostensibly wanted to stop smoking offered the rationalization that Erickson made it so easy to stop that he decided he didn't need to try (see Zeig, 1985, p. 80). The apparent severe characterological problems of the nasty woman with the headaches (Case 5), the paranoid man who would not compliment his wife (Case 13), and the couple with interlocking affairs (Case 15), as well as the seeming lack of motivation in the obese woman (Case 3) and the young couple who would not share a quart of ice cream (Case 14) would not bode well. In his original report about Case 6, Erickson (1985, p. 192) wrote: "She was a very nice hypnotic subject, and she listened to me very, very carefully. But I was afraid of the consequences, because I didn't quite

TABLE 11.1. Erickson's failures as listed in *An Uncommon Casebook: The Complete Clinical Work of Milton H. Erickson, M.D.* (O'Hanlon & Hexum, 1990)

Case no.[a]	Presenting problem	Techniques(s)	No. of sessions
1. (17)	Male, smoking and social anxiety[b]	Task assignment (repeat "I don't give a damn")	NA
2. (18)	Male, smoking	Reframing (Erickson linked this to revealing homosexuality); task assignment (behavioral—things to do with his hands)	1[c]
3. (30)	Female, obesity	Task assignment (behavioral—climb Squaw Peak)	2
4. (83)	Female, smoking[d]	Hypnosis	1
5. (89)	Female, headaches (patient very critical and negative)	Task assignment (behavioral—have patient write life story)	NA
6. (111)	Female, urinary retention	Hypnosis; posthypnotic suggestion (Erickson instructed husband to take patient directly home, but they stopped on the way to buy flowers)	1
7. (175)	Male, impotence[e]	Metaphor/implication (Erickson told stories and gave a Saturday appointment so that nothing would interfere with patient's job)	1
8. (178)	Male, gagging when anything in his mouth	Hypnosis; amnesia	1
9. (210)	Female, blind, desire to recall early visual images	Hypnosis; hand levitation	1[f]
10. (213)	Couple, indecision about operation for birth control	Hypnosis; future projection	NA
11. (218)	Male, unmanageable adolescent	Task assignment; pattern intervention (boy in hotel on budget; parents on vacation)	2 weeks
12. (231)	Couple, marital problems (did everything together)	Task assignment (Erickson suggested they go to separate movies and then meet for dinner; they disagreed with his advice, and eventually divorced)	1
13. (238)	Couple, marital problems (husband refused to compliment wife)	Direct suggestion (Erickson modeled by complimenting wife—paranoid husband said he wished he could have thought of it that way)	NA

(*continued*)

TABLE 11.1. *Continued*

Case no.[a]	Presenting problem	Techniques(s)	No. of sessions
14. (251)	Couple, marital problems	Task assignment (Erickson told them to share a quart of ice cream before next appointment; they did not, and subsequently divorced)	2
15. (258)	Female/couple, headaches, airplane phobia, marital problems (affairs)	Hypnosis	NA

[a]Case number used in O'Hanlon and Hexum (1990) appears in parentheses; see their book for references to original sources.

[b]Failure *and* success: The patient kept smoking, but stopped being anxious in social situations.

[c]O'Hanlon and Hexum (1990) indicate that length of treatment is not available, but Zeig (1985, p. 80) indicated that the patient was seen for one session.

[d]A year earlier, Erickson used four sessions of hypnosis to successfully treat the patient for fear of dental procedures—the subsequent one session for smoking did not work.

[e]Earlier, Erickson had successfully treated the patient's fear of heights in one session with metaphor and task assignments; this patient's wife (Case 4 above) referred the patient to Erickson after Erickson helped her overcome her dental fears.

[f]Total length of treatment (and possible benefit) is not clear. In the original case report (Erickson & Rossi, 1981, pp. 64–109), Erickson (p. 108) mentioned in his discussion with Ernest Rossi that "A week or so later she [the patient] casually remarked to Mrs. Erickson that for some unknown reason she was able to walk on the street more easily—walking down the street was different in some way. It was easier." Rossi reflected to Erickson, "She had learned to rely on unconscious mechanisms more. She learned to let go of conscious controlling. So you got through to her in this session after all!" and Erickson responded: "I got through! She was so pleased to have a totally new experience of walking on the street."

feel that she was being fair and honest with me. So I dismissed her from my office." The client's subsequent interruption of the therapeutic task assignment may have contributed to the failed outcome. Poor starts make subsequent efforts all the harder, as Erickson (1980b, p. 23; cited in Havens, 1989a, p. 128) noted: "Failure in attempts at hypnotic therapy always increases the difficulty of further attempts at therapy."

Erickson himself struggled to find explanations for why some cases did not succeed. Being a strategic therapist, he looked to himself to make something happen (or assumed responsibility if it did not); but, recognizing the cardinal importance of the patient's contribution (on which rests the principle of *utilization*) he also included the client's motivations and effort in his search. In 1965 (p. 254), he wrote:

Many times the author has been asked to publish an account of a failure in hypnotherapy when success was fully anticipated. To date, the author has hesitated to do so since there was no understanding of why the failures occurred (and there have been failures, as one should expect). Why this is so seems best explained in terms of either the therapist's lack of understanding or the patient's own purposes.[4]

Along related lines, in 1966 he reported the case of a man (Case 8 mentioned above) who had initially appeared to have been successfully treated for a severe dental phobia and gagging problem in a single demonstration interview but who, many months later, inexplicably stopped using dentures. Erickson (1966, pp. 64–65) wrote:

> The author has no understanding of the course of events with this patient. Successful therapy was apparently achieved, enjoyed for months by the patient, and then apparently abandoned for no known reason and without regret. . . . The family dentist and the psychiatrist and the psychologist friends all found nothing of note in their association with the man and his family that would be considered as offering even a semblance of an explanation of the patient's behavior.

As obvious as it may seem, I find it helpful to know that even the brilliant Dr. Erickson had failures. I have been concerned about the relative absence of reports of failure and negative therapeutic effects in brief therapy (see Hoyt, 1989). Perhaps I am not the only one who, at times, has felt "disempowered" by reading one miracle success after another. Even—or especially—if we cannot always explain *why*, I find it encouraging to know that even "The Master" did not hit a home run every time.

☐ Notes

[1]In a similar vein, in his Foreword to *Experiencing Erickson: An Introduction to the Man and His Work* (Zeig, 1985), Lewis Wolberg (1985, p. viii) wrote:

> Erickson loved challenges and he could not let this one go by, especially since the patient appeared negative to any more attempts to get him into a trance. . . . But Erickson never gave up and after two hours, to my astonishment and, I am sure, to that of the patient, Erickson succeeded in inducing a somnambulistic trance during which the patient hallucinated objects and animals at suggestion. I was as much impressed by Erickson's persistance in the face of failure as I was by his induction skills.

[2]Thus, in the final case described in *Uncommon Therapy: The Psychiatric Techniques of Milton H. Erickson, M.D.* (Haley, 1973, p. 273), in which Erickson had used unusual and somewhat shocking provocations to stir a patient into action, he reported that when the client's wife had recontacted him after many years, again hoping for what would have then required a miracle, Erickson recognized his therapeutic limits:

> I wrote to her and pointed out that he was past the age of sixty, and he had been badly damaged by the first stroke. Now the second one had left him unconscious

for several days. He was as helpless as he had been before. I told her I didn't think there was anything more I could do.

[3]Zeig (1985, p. 78) reported:

I helped a patient stop smoking. Years before, he had unsuccessfully seen Erickson to stop smoking, noting "Erickson told me that I wasn't going to stop smoking and, in fact, I didn't." On the same occasion he talked with Erickson about his anxiety in social situations. Erickson told him stories and suggested that when he went into a room full of people, he should think to himself, "Don't give a damn; don't give a damn; don't give a damn." The patient said, "I have used that technique to this day, and it works. I seem to feel better when I walk into a room."

[4]In the case reported in that article, "Hypnotherapy: The Patient's Right to Both Success and Failure," Erickson (1965, p. 257) honored the patient's very specific request and succeeded in helping him overcome a highly circumscribed kind of driving phobia, but also noted that otherwise "this man needs help, has a poor prognosis, and, to this author and a number of other psychiatrists he is therapeutically inaccessible, despite the fact that he is a good though completely passive hypnotic subject."

12
CHAPTER

Unmuddying the Waters:
A "Common Ground" Conference

> To lords and ladies of Byzantium
> Of what is past, or passing, or to come.
> —William Butler Yeats (1927), "Sailing to Byzantium"

Concerned about increasing confusion and possible divisiveness between various constructivist and interactionalist brief therapy approaches, Patricia Emard and Jim Keim met at the Sixth International Ericksonian Congress held in Los Angeles, December 1994. They formulated the idea for an "in-house" conference in which a number of participants could explore commonalities and differences. It was hoped—and largely achieved—that a spirit of nonaggression would be generated as a context for considering some strategies for promoting the common good offered by the various therapeutic approaches.

The meeting, entitled "Unmuddying the Waters," was held March 18–19, 1995, at Pat Emard's home in Saratoga, California (near San Francisco). While not everyone who was invited could attend, a worthy list of participants was gathered: Tom Ayers, Eileen Bobrow, Rhonda Burnaugh-Grove, Brian Cade, Sky Chaney, James Coyne, Wes Crenshaw, Lorraine

The author gratefully acknowledges the many contributions made by Patricia Emard of the Mental Research Institute, Palo Alto, CA, and James Keim of the Family Therapy Institute, Washington, DC, which have included organizing and hosting the conference reported in this chapter as well as providing useful summary information.

From "Unmuddying the Waters: A 'Common Ground' Conference," by M. F. Hoyt, *Journal of Systemic Therapies, 1997, 16*(3), pp. 195–200, Copyright 1997 by The Guilford Press. Adapted with permission of the publisher.

Douglas, Don Efron, Patricia Emard, Joseph Eron, Richard Fisch, David Grove, Jay Haley, Michael Hoyt, James Keim, Judith Landau-Stanton, Lynn Loar, Thomas Lund, Cloe Madanes, Skip Meyer, Scott Miller, Keiichi Miyata, Larry Palmartier, Jerome Price, Wendel Ray, Madeleine Richeport, Michael Rohrbaugh, Karin Schlanger, Varda Shoham, Carlos Sluzki, Terry Soo-Hoo, John Walter, Paul Watzlawick, and John Weakland.[1]

The welcoming statement, prepared by Pat Emard and Jim Keim, set the theme and tone:

> The idea for this meeting originated out of a desire to generate a greater sense of unity within the world of brief therapy at a time when the pressures toward divisiveness are great. Our hope in hosting this meeting is that some of the greatest talents in the field of brief therapy—theoreticians, writers, teachers, trainers, and researchers—could come together to discuss ways to clarify our ideas and build a spirit of cooperation and collaboration. Indeed, our waters are muddy. Unmuddying them can only take place in an atmosphere of mutual respect, willingness to listen without criticizing, minimizing, or ignoring one another's views. Our goal here is to reach a common ground; an agreement to work together to promote the *interactional view* for purposes of gaining support, inspiring intellectual curiosity, creating a commitment to something greater than ourselves as individuals: the kind of future we all believe brief therapy deserves.

This report can provide only a gloss of what transpired and is based on my perceptions; others might see and describe it differently.[2] A number of prominent commonalities or "agreements" were identified as principles that unify various brief therapies:

1. each clinical situation is unique
2. therapeutic influence is inevitable
3. an "interactional" view—the minimum unit of consideration is two people
4. language is an important map, but not the territory
5. we focus on what the client brings in
6. we focus on observable (concrete) behavior.

Discussions were open and, for the most part, paralleled the cooperative, resource-focused, and future-oriented processes valued in our therapies. There was emphasis on the need for collaboration, effective outcome research, more clearly speaking the language of therapy purchasers (insurance and managed care), proactive outreach efforts, and being more political. Smaller "break-out" groups discussed and reported issues having to do with disseminating information both publicly and within the profession (including the desire for conference directors and journal editors not to encourage the hype-ridden pitting of one approach versus another);[3] the need for expanded training, including more graduate school education; uses of the Internet; and the need to protect public and consumer interests, including political and economic action and the development of alternatives to the pathology-oriented *DSM-IV* (American Psychiatric Association, 1994); to name but a few. Additional initiatives can be anticipated, and readers are encouraged to carry these (and other) ideas forward.

Near the end of the second meeting day, the six senior "first-generation" participants were asked to provide some "words of wisdom." Their remarks were off the cuff, humorous, and suggestive:

Weakland: *It's very different now; things keep changing. So, the words of wisdom that I might have given you when I started don't apply anymore. So, you've got to take it yourself.* [Hoyt: *John, I asked you that question in an interview that was printed in* Constructive Therapies *(1994c), essentially the same question, and you said something that moved me greatly. You thought about it and then said:* "Stay curious."] *Okay, I'll be willing to repeat that.*

Sluzki: *My only words of wisdom are to remain fanatic, but only for a short period! You need to be fanatic to learn, to be enamored; but if you stick to it and stay fanatic, you will be forsaken.*

Haley: *You should be curious about exploring the limits of fanaticism!*

Fisch: *If you're going to make any kind of inroad anywhere, you need to think in terms of what is workable and sustainable rather than what's unique, because they're not necessarily the same. I'd be thinking in terms of what each individual could do, what could be done and could be done in a way that is sustainable. And, if you do anything that seems to get anywhere at all, then just convey that to other like-minded people:* "Here's what I did and it worked." *For example, any one of us could go home and find out who is the science editor of the local newspaper. And, if we could get that, we could think of the next step, which would be talking to that person:* "Would you be interested in a story?" *that has to do with whatever you think would be useful for them to print. And that person could be recontacted at some point later, if you want something else. It could be used in different contexts. That's just one quick example that could make some difference.*

Watzlawick: *There is the age-old saying:* "Publish or perish." *I think it is important for us to publish our ideas so that others can learn from them.*

Madanes: *Stay alert to change and refuse to be identified with the first generation of anything!*

Haley: *I don't think this is a good time to start being a first-generation therapist. When I went into therapy, you could hang out a shingle. There was no licensing. All you needed was referrals and the people paid you. It was so simple then compared with how complex it sounds today.*

As far as this group goes, it would be nice if there were more emphasis on what distinguished this group [brief therapists] *from other therapists. The outcomes we discussed are asking people what's the problem and then afterwards asking them if they got over it. I don't think that deals with the process in families, which would be a measure of changing interactions.*

One of the things I missed today, and we should have put it on the agenda, is ethnicity. Therapy was built upon European immigrants, and now we have the Asian immigrants and the South American immigrants. At a local elementary school near me they had a multicultural day and the kids all came in their costumes. There were 187 cultural groups! And a lot of those are heading for therapy. So, we're going to work with them just hoping they speak English. It's a whole new scheme. The population that people face today, they didn't used to face. We used to have middle-class "properly educated" people who came and paid on time, and so on. Now, we've got the poor and different ethnic groups, and violent people. There's another issue that didn't used to happen: compulsory therapy. The fact that the court orders people to go to therapy raises not only rights issues but the nature of therapy. I think it raises the question of "Whose agent are you?" We once were the agent of an individual and wouldn't even talk to the family on the phone. Then we were the agent of the family against the community in the 1960s. Now, when you are seeing people sent by the state to straighten this person out, you're an agent of the state. You can't get around it. I think some kind of a clear position should be taken on this. People treat it so often like it's just one more complication in life. There are whole agencies that only work with people ordered by the court— it's a new phenomenon.

I would like to see this group be more radical, and do something that others probably wouldn't do. Since, for example, the DSM-IV is only individual, I think this group should make a therapy DSM *in which the basic unit is two people and you formulate problems in a way that is helpful to a therapist. Instead of calling a kid a "school phobia" you call him a "school avoidance problem." That guides you to do something. It also guides you to think about why he is avoiding school. It would be interesting as a task to make a diagnostic manual that is for therapists, not for the institutions and insurance companies and so on (who might never accept it). But, it would be very good for training, because you would begin to find symptoms falling out in terms of certain ways to deal with them in order to get people over them.*

Weakland: *It could be very useful if you would just run up a sample of that to illustrate the difference. You wouldn't have to do the entire job to start with.*

Haley: *Somebody should do it, and somebody will do it. And the next obvious step is to recognize that somebody had the idea in the nineteenth century that therapy should be paid for by the hour, so everybody liked that and kept that—but there are different ways to pay for therapy and I think the day is approaching when you could take a certain fee for curing a particular symptom. In California, there were some people who said they would cure any phobia for $300, and they figured they'd make money on that because they'd do it in one session. You might not want to do it for all the problems that come in, but if you had a fee schedule for different symptoms. . . . I mean, we're in a situation where brief therapists need to put up.*

They claim they can cure people quickly. Well, why not put the money on the line—if you can cure them quickly, you predict how many sessions and set a fee. It would force you to formulate problems very quickly and would be a bonanza to the insurance companies, who would be happy to deal with you if you could set a fee and they didn't have to pay for therapy forever and ever and ever.

But anyhow, what I'm getting at is that the whole field of therapy is getting into a more exciting time, and if this group wants to be recognized as a group that is different from the others, they need to do things that are different from the others. So I recommend that.

☐ Coda

Some time has passed, dear reader, between the March 1995 "Unmuddying the Waters" Conference and today. Which recommendations have been heeded, which ones not? Are current developments positive or negative? In June 1996, the Therapeutic Conversations 3 Conference was held in Denver. There were many excellent presentations but, to my ear, there also was an undercurrent of growing factionalism. At one point, someone jarringly challenged me, "Are you Solution or are you Narrative?" People tended to follow instructional "tracks" that reified "schools" or "camps." I also overheard the following exchange, somewhat reminiscent of the famous story about the three monks declaiming the virtues of silence:

Person #1: *You're in denial. You have this neurotic need to nonpathologize.*

Person #2: *I do not! You're sick, the way you pathologize everyone.*

Person #3: *You people are both wrong. We're supposed to be collaborative.*

In October 1996, two major figures in the field, Michael White and Steve de Shazer, presented a conference together in Milwaukee to explore their commonalities and differences. They were *both/and*, excellent individually and together, but again it seemed that much of the audience often wanted to take "sides" and have an *either/or* of someone being more "right" or more "wrong."

I ask: Are these trends taking us where we want to go? Is it inevitable that we split into factions? How can we keep true dialogue (or "multilogue") open? As participants and consumers (and conference organizers), what shall we do?

☐ Notes

[1]There was a moment when Haley and Weakland were discussing something said to them by Gregory Bateson and Don Jackson. I looked around the room, glanced at the faces

(Milton Erickson's spirit also seemed to be hovering nearby) and at the names on the books lining the bookcases, and had a new (and more literal) appreciation of the saying: "The mind is not in the head."

[2]For another review of the conference, see Efron (1995). In a letter to the *Family Therapy Networker* a few weeks before his death, Weakland (1995, p. 16) wrote:

> Specifically, the meeting explored common premises and values shared at a general level despite specific differences, and avenues of cooperation and collaboration to present to colleagues and students. While not always easy, one of the strengths of the field from its earliest days has been constructive reflection and discussion of its diversity. The emphasis on having things "my way" and needing something new each year has distracted us from serious and useful dialogue about what aids people in distress and facilitates change. The participants of the meeting . . . hope this will reinvigorate this tradition of viewing diversity usefully.

[3]There seems to be contradictory tendencies in the field to both exalt the charismatic "gurus" of different schools and to act as though developments emerge de novo, without antecedents (e.g., whence Don Jackson?). As Efron (1995, p. 2) noted in his review of the conference, "Family therapy has a peculiar ideology that contributes to this trend. We revere the 'masters' in an almost sacred manner. . . . On the other hand, we do not actually cite their works, or the publications of anyone else, that are more than a few years old. Compared to other fields we actually diminish the importance of past works instead of honoring them!" This may, in part, be a kind of "parallel process" related to the ahistorical approach of some brief therapies, and also may stem from an overidentification of therapy with science: "Current developments have widened the ancient gap between science and philosophy. . . . While artistic and literary creativity incorporates and expands upon the past, scientific truth negates the past from which it derives. A medical textbook, even a decade old, is already outdated" (Lown, 1983, p. 24). In a related vein, Bly (1996, p. vii) attributes to adolescent shortsightedness an inability "to imagine any genuine life coming from the vertical plane—tradition, religion, devotion" He goes on to comment, "Even graduate students in science are said to share this problem," and quotes a neuroscientist as saying: "The ones I train to become scientists go at it like warriors, overturning reigning paradigms, each discovery a murder of their scientific ancestors."

CHAPTER

with David Nylund

The Joy of Narrative: An Exercise for Learning From Our Internalized Clients

One composed of many.
—Virgil (70–19 B.C.)
"Moretum," *Minor Poems*

A part of her still lives inside of me,
we've never been apart.
—Bob Dylan (1974), "If You See Her, Say Hello"

How therapists choose to conceive and construe their clients and their work together not only profoundly impacts the clients, but also the therapists. Especially in this "age of accountability" (L. D. Johnson, 1995) and "managed care" (Hoyt, 1995a), fatigue and demoralization can be common experiences for therapists. However, while the pressures are considerable, we agree with Michael White (1995a, 1995b, 1996, 1997) that therapist burnout is not inevitable but has to do, in part, with how the therapy project is structured. Approaches that allow therapists to work in ways consistent with their best intentions for entering the therapy field—

Written with David Nylund.
Part of the material in this chapter was presented at the "Therapeutic Conversations 3" Conference in Denver, June 1996.
From "The Joy of Narrative: An Exercise for Learning from Our Internalized Clients," by M.F. Hoyt & D. Nylund, *Journal of Systemic Therapies*, 1997, 16(4), pp. 361–366. Copyright Guilford Press 1997. Adapted with permission of the publisher.

ones that emphasize client autonomy and choice, that highlight respectful collaboration, that speak to issues of justice, and that avoid therapist isolation and conceptualizations of pathology and deficit—are more likely to avoid burnout in favor of an enhanced sense of what the dictionary defines as *joy*: "a feeling of delight, happiness, and gladness, and a source of pleasure." This invigorating aspect of human awareness (Schutz, 1967) is especially important in the face of the problems we confront.

As described by Friedman (1995, pp. 450–451), a postmodern or constructivist therapist:

- believes in a socially constructed reality
- emphasizes the reflexive nature of therapeutic relationships in which client and therapist co-construct meanings in dialogue or conversation
- moves away from hierarchical distinctions toward a more egalitarian offering of ideas and respect for differences
- maintains empathy and respect for the client's predicament and a belief in the power of therapeutic conversation to liberate suppressed, ignored, or previously unacknowledged voices or stories
- co-constructs goals and negotiates direction in therapy, placing the client back in the driver's seat, as an expert on his or her own predicaments and dilemmas
- searches for and amplifies client competencies, strengths, and resources and avoids being a detective of pathology or reifying rigid diagnostic distinctions
- avoids a vocabulary of deficit and dysfunction, replacing the jargon of pathology (and distance) with the language of the everyday
- is oriented toward the future and optimistic about change
- is sensitive to the methods and processes used in the therapeutic conversation.

These attitudes embrace an "emergent epistemology" (Lankton & Lankton, 1998) based on assumptions of curiosity rather than certainty, one redolent of "possibilities" (Friedman & Fanger, 1991; O'Hanlon, 1998; O'Hanlon & Beadle, 1994) and evocative of vocabularies of "solution" rather than "problem" (see Chapter 3, this volume). Acceptance of the construction that we are constructive, that we are actively building our stories and sense of self, yields some of the intrinsic awareness of freedom that is part of the energizing excitement of narrative and solution-focused approaches. It also de-centers the "objectivity" of the therapist and opens options for feedback and further learning.

The following exercise, which has been favorably received when presented at a number of workshops and conferences, is one such possibility. It offers an opportunity to experience the process of reflexivity, the construction of self via the internalization of significant others. Its purpose is to help us "re-member" our skills, abilities, and intentions (White, 1996, 1997), to help therapists use their empathy and connectedness as a source of instruction and renewal. It invites a greater appreciation that therapy is a two-way process wherein the therapist's life also is impacted, inspired, moved, and shaped by the interaction.[1] It is very much a work in progress, and our hope is that readers will experiment with it and improve it—and let us know.

☐ Surprised by Joy, or Were You Expecting Her/Him?[2]

Introduction

Karl Tomm (1992; MacCormack & Tomm, 1998; see also Epston, 1993; Fow, 1998; Goulding & Goulding, 1979; McNeel, 1976; Nylund & Corsiglia, 1993/1998; Tomm, Hoyt, & Madigan, 1998) has described the practice of *internalized other questioning*. This practice refers to the idea that the "self" is made up of a person's internalized community of significant others. One can "step into" the experience of the other by being addressed by the name of the other person and being asked a series of questions. What can our internalized clients offer to nurture and sustain us?

Invitation

Break into small groups. Now, think of a specific person (client) you have worked with that had a significant impact on you and your work as a therapist. Imagine that person as best you can—the way they talked, what they said, their intonation, the way they sat, how they looked, and so forth. Immerse yourself in the experience. Now, using the practice of internalized other questioning, have your partner interview you as your client. The interviewer should function like a reporter or journalist, simply trying to get "the story." He or she should attempt to draw out specific details and particulars to increase verisimilitude, but should not attempt to "therapize" (change or modify) the client-therapist interviewee.

The following are some questions that you may use as guideposts (feel free to devise and ask your own questions). Interview from the internalized other position for about 10–15 minutes.

- What impact did your therapist, _____, have on you? What did you value most about her or him, as a therapist and as a person?
- What would you want your therapist to know about your work together? Were there some things you wish you would have said to her/him? What else? What kept you from sharing this with your therapist?

- What did your therapist do that helped your sense of hope and optimism? What else?
- What submerged strengths and energy did your therapist touch? What "latent joy" (Furman & Ahola, 1992b) did she or he miss?
- Was there a "critical moment" or situation that especially captures or symbolizes how your therapist worked with you in helpful ways? What was said? What happened?
- If you were to tell your therapist something she/he may not have known (or fully appreciated) about her/his effect on you, what would that be? What would you say?
- Did your therapist share what positive effects your work had on her/him? If so, what was that like? If not, how would you have experienced that?

Now, step out of your client's experience and return to being interviewed as yourself (10–15 minutes). Have somebody ask these questions (or invent your own):

- When you get in touch with your client's experience of you, what counseling abilities do you most appreciate about yourself?
- What effect will it have on your work knowing how much you impacted your client's life?
- How does getting in touch with these abilities and effects fit with why you became a therapist ("your best intentions and purposes for getting into the therapy field"—see White, in Hoyt & Combs, 1996)?
- What colleagues/friends/previous supervisors/clients support these intentions? How? Who would be glad, even honored, to know of your work with the client? What would they say—what words might they use?
- What did your client stimulate in you that you want to nurture and expand? Where is your sense of humor in your clinical work? Your spirit of adventure?
- Do your clients get inspired by your sense of hope and passion? How?
- What about your client's experience invigorates you? What gives you joy?
- How will you remember and recall what you have been learning here? When you feel tired or frustrated, what about this client's experience will help encourage you? When you need it, how will you remember to remember?

Now, switch roles: The interviewer becomes the interviewee, and vice versa. Again, work through the internalized other questions for 10–15 minutes; then interview as self for 10–15 minutes.

☐ Before Closing

The exercise invites a greater awareness of one's influence and the need for accountability and clarity about personal ethics (see White, 1997; in Hoyt & Combs, 1996; and in McLean, 1994; White, Hoyt, & Zimmerman, 2000). It is not intended to be a solipsistic stroll through a hermetically sealed hall of mirrors, nor is it intended to indulge clinical incompetence or a self-congratulatory sense of grandiosity or arrogance.[3] While a balanced view often is useful, this exercise was especially designed to help therapists learn more about what they may be doing well, an alternative to the frequently dominant critical or even pejorative self-surveillance that we have seen occur in many case reviews and which may contribute to vitiation (not invigoration) and a sense of burnout rather than joy and excitement in therapeutic work. As White (1997, p. 142) has written:

> Narrative practices not only provide options for therapists to join in the identification and the exploration of the little events and acts that contradict the problem-saturated stories of persons' lives, but also provide the opportunity for therapists to join with these persons in celebrating the significance of these events and acts. The joy that is had by therapists in doing so contributes directly to their experience of their work, and invariably flows into other domains of their lives.

Discussing the experience of the exercise with colleagues is very important, lest one become isolated in a "mirrored room" (Hare-Mustin, 1994; Rorty, 1979) with no recourse to extra-self input. Questions to consider might include: Why was this client chosen to reflect upon? How do we know the client's wishes and autonomy were honored? What ideas might the interviewer and/or other colleagues contribute to help further the therapeutic endeavor? The ensuing discussion itself can be understood as a further opportunity to experience and learn from reflexivity, this time via a reflecting team (Andersen, 1991; Friedman, 1995; see also special issue Postmodern Supervision, *Journal of Systemic Therapies*, 1995) involving the listener choosing among external (rather than internal) "voices."

☐ Notes

[1]"One hand draws the other," as Matthews (1985) put it. The idea of mutual influence is not new, as seen in Carl Jung's (1929/1966, p. 72) comment: "Between doctor and patient, therefore, there are imponderable factors which bring about a mutual transformation . . . the doctor is as much 'in the analysis' as the patient. He [sic] is equally a part of the psychic process of treatment and therefore equally exposed to the transforming influences." From

an objectivist-modernist perspective, however, the client's impact is usually viewed as a deleterious distortion, a "countertransference" (Kahn, 1996).

[2]With a nod toward C. S. Lewis (1956) for his book title, *Surprised by Joy*.

[3]One participant doing the exercise commented that it felt too one-sided, that she could not allow herself to think of "positives" without also acknowledging "negatives." Another, however, commented that it seemed like an "oxygen tank." Yet another comment that seemed to capture the spirit of the exercise likened it to an "autogenous [self-generated] blood donation."

CHAPTER

with Scott D. Miller

Stage-Appropriate Change-Oriented Brief Therapy Strategies

A journey of a thousand miles
must begin with a single step.
—Lao-tzu (c. 604-531 B.C.E.)

We find it useful in brief therapy to think about what would be best in a given moment to identify, encourage, promote, amplify, and help maintain clients' desired changes. We seek collaboration and expect forward movement, a significant shift from earlier orientations. In 1904, Sigmund Freud placed the concept of *resistance* to change at the center of his evolving theory of therapy. Based on his observation that clients would frequently and often vigorously reject the interpretations he offered, he concluded that "patient[s] cling to [their] disease and . . . even fight against [their] own recovery." Overcoming these resistances by provoking and then "working through" them was, he came to believe, "the essential function of [treatment] . . . the only part of our work which gives us an assurance that we have achieved something with the patient" (Freud, 1915–1917/1961a).

While the concept of resistance has seen many modifications over time, the belief that people sabotage or otherwise subvert the change process survives (C. M. Anderson & Stewart, 1983; E. Singer, 1994; see Wile,

---

Written with Scott D. Miller.

A version of this chapter will also appear in *Brief Therapy Strategies with Individuals and Couples*, by J. Carlson and L. Sperry (Eds.), Phoenix, AZ: Zeig, Tucker, & Company. Copyright 2000. Adapted with permission of the publisher.

1993, p. 29). "Resistance," pioneering family therapist Lyman Wynne (1983, p. vi) once observed, "is a thorn that by any other name pricks as deep." *Secondary gain* (Freud, 1909/1959; Weiner, 1975), *habit strength* (Dollard & Miller, 1950), *homeostasis* (L. Hoffman, 1981; Jackson & Weakland, 1961), *self-protection* (Mahoney, 1991), *lack of motivation* (Malan, 1976; Sifneos, 1992), and the recent and popular characterization of people as *being in denial* are just a few of the terms used nowadays which reflect Freud's original concept. This belief, as Mahoney (1991, p. 18) noted in his massive and systematic review of psychotherapy process research, has led to "one of the most important points of convergence across contemporary schools of thought in psychotherapy: Significant psychological change is rarely rapid or easy."

☐ Shifting Toward Working *With*

It's easier to ride a horse
in the direction it's going.
—Cowboy adage

In 1970, Speer pointed out the irony of basing therapeutic approaches to change on theories of how people do *not* change. Some 14 years later, brief therapist de Shazer (1984) developed this insight in his now-classic paper, "The Death of Resistance," in which he argued that traditional theories of resistance were tantamount to pitting the therapist against the client in a fight that the therapist had to win in order for the client to be successful. In contradistinction, de Shazer suggested shifting the focus of therapeutic activity to the study of how people *do* change. From this perspective, clients could be seen as having unique ways of *cooperating with* rather than resisting the therapist in their mutual efforts to bring about desired changes.

Borrowing concepts from an earlier resistance-based framework, de Shazer and his colleagues (e.g., Fisch, Weakland, & Segal, 1982; Segal & Watzlawick, 1985) developed a rudimentary system for classifying different types of client-therapist cooperation. They described the therapeutic interaction as an active, doing type (referred to as the *customer-seller* relationship), a passive-reflective type (referred to as the *browser-listener* relationship), or an uncommitted, waiting type (referred to as the *visitor-host* relationship). The purpose of the classification system was to provide therapists with a "thumbnail" for cooperating with their client in the development of interventions that were tailored to each client (de Shazer, 1988). This system has evolved into the well-known solution-focused therapy taxonomy of *customer/complainant/visitor* (see Berg, 1989; Berg & Miller,

1992; de Shazer, 1988; S. D. Miller & Berg, 1991). As Shoham, Rohrbaugh, and Patterson (1995, p. 153) (italics added) explained:

> Here the distinction between customer, complainant, and visitor-type relationships offers guidelines for therapeutic cooperation or "fit" (de Shazer, 1988; Berg & Miller, 1992). If the relationship involves a *visitor* with whom the therapist cannot define a clear complaint or goal, cooperation involves nothing more than sympathy, politeness, and compliments for whatever the clients are successfully doing (with no tasks or requests for change). In a *complainant* relationship, where clients present a complaint but appear unwilling to take action or want someone else to change, the therapist cooperates by accepting their views, giving compliments, and sometimes prescribing observational tasks (e.g., to notice exceptions to the complaint pattern). Finally, with *customers* who want to do something about a complaint, the principle of fit allows the therapist to be more direct in guiding them toward solutions.

Recognizing that "imposition generates opposition" (see Chapter 1, this volume), the basic idea is that working *with* the client's stage of motivation, language, goals, and theories of change (Duncan, Hubble, Miller, & Coleman, 1998) often obviates or simply dissolves "resistance." We may know that we are helpers (or, at least, think that we are), but the client may not—or may not be ready or looking for what we think would be helpful. With this understanding, "resistance" can be seen quite differently from the conventional psychiatric pejorative. Not identifying and honoring the client's treatment goals may make it necessary for the client to "resist." Clients who are described as "noncompliant" or "resistant" may be in a power-politics struggle (Tomm, 1993), engaged in counteroppressive practices to refuse being psychologically colonized or bent in directions they do not want to go (see Chapter 3, this volume). In such cases, *vive la resistance!* The clients' response signals an opportunity to repair a mismatch.

☐ Stages of Change

> What is the hardest of all? That which you hold the most simple;
> seeing with your own eyes what is spread out before you.
> —Johann Wolfgang von Goethe (1749–1832)

Around the same time that de Shazer and his associates were developing their ideas, another group of clinicians in a very different setting were coming to a similar conclusion; namely, that traditional schools of therapy were "more about why people do not change than how people can change" (Prochaska, 1999, p. 228). Based on the realization that *most* people change *without* the benefit of formal therapy, Prochaska and his colleagues extended their analysis beyond the therapeutic setting that had been the focus of the de Shazer group and began studying how people change naturally, spontaneously, and on an everyday basis (DiClemente & Prochaska, 1982; Prochaska, 1995; Prochaska & DiClemente, 1982, 1983, 1984). In the nearly two decades of research that followed, they discovered

> a phenomenon that was not contained within any of the leading theories of therapy. Ordinary people taught us that change involves progress through a series of stages. At different stages people apply particular processes to progress to the next stage. (Prochaska, 1999, p. 228)

As Norcross and Beutler (1997, pp. 48–49) summarized, in this *transtheoretical model,* change unfolds over a series of five (or six) stages of motivational readiness:

> *Precontemplation* is the stage at which there is no intention to change behavior in the foreseeable future. . . .
> *Contemplation* is the stage in which people are aware that a problem exists and are seriously thinking about overcoming it but have not yet made a commitment to take action. . . .
> *Preparation* is a stage that combines intention and behavioral criteria. Individuals in this stage are intending to take action immediately and report some small behavioral changes. . . .
> *Action* is the stage in which individuals modify their behavior, experiences, and/or environment in order to overcome their problems. . . .
> *Maintenance* is the final stage in which people work to prevent relapse and consolidate the gains attained during action. . . . [M]aintenance is a continuation, not an absence, of change. . . . Stabilizing behavior change and avoiding relapse are the hallmarks.

Prochaska (1993, p. 253) added a final stage, perhaps more ideal than realistic: *Termination,* in which "there is zero temptation to engage in the problem behavior, and there is a 100 percent confidence (self-efficacy) that one will not engage in the old behavior regardless of the situation."

In their aptly named article, "In Search of How People Change," Prochaska, DiClemente, and Norcross (1992, p. 1107) focused on "*when* particular shifts in attitudes, intentions, and behaviors occur." Movement through these stages generally happens in two ways. First, change may advance linearly, proceeding gradually and stepwise through the stages from start to finish. The second, and by far the most common form of progression, is characterized by advance, relapse, and recycling through the stages. This is the process intimated in the popular saying, "Three steps forward and two steps back." Sudden transformations in behavior are possible, too, such as Jean Valjean's change from sinner to saint in Victor Hugo's *Les Misérables* (Alexander & French, 1946; Hoyt, Rosenbaum,

& Talmon, 1992) and the celebrated overnight conversion of Ebenezer Scrooge in Charles Dickens' *A Christmas Carol* (W. R. Miller, 1986).

Both Prochaska's and de Shazer's theories of the change process have the advantage of shifting the guiding metaphor for clinical practice from one which emphasizes therapist power to one that stresses collaboration and facilitation. Within both systems, therapy is not a matter of using "techniques, strategies, and other clever maneuvers . . . for the good of the clients" (de Shazer, 1986, p. 73). Rather, therapists are thought of as "joining with," "working together," or "cooperating with" clients in an attempt to facilitate their unique process of change. Prochaska's work is supported by a wealth of empirical data, a critical feature in today's health care environment that requires both individualized treatment and accountability from third-party payers (Hoyt, 1995a; Hubble, Duncan, & Miller, 1999; L. D. Johnson, 1995; S. D. Miller, Duncan, Hubble, & Johnson, 1999).

For the majority of people, reaching lasting change takes time and sustained effort. This does not mean, however, that treatment necessarily *must* be a long-term and intensive process in order to be successful. In their research, for example, Prochaska et al. (1992) found that people who moved from one stage to the next during the first few sessions of treatment doubled their chances of taking effective action to solve their problem in the next 6 months. A movement of two stages as much as quadrupled the chances of success (Prochaska et al., 1997).

From this vantage point, the traditional distinction between long and brief forms of therapy can be seen as a muddle. Indeed, the length of treatment is largely irrelevant to successful outcome. Rather, *effective* therapy is a result of working cooperatively with people to facilitate their movement to the next stage of change. Research shows that such movement generally occurs early in the treatment process or *not at all*. Nearly all large-scale, meta-analytic studies, for example, show that people's response in the first few sessions is highly predictive of eventual outcome (Hubble et al., 1999). In one representative study, J. Brown, Dreis, and Nace (1999) found that people *not* reporting movement by the third visit on average showed no improvement over the entire course of treatment regardless of the model of treatment their therapist employed (e.g., brief versus long-term, psychological versus medical).

Prochaska et al. (1992) demonstrated that stage of change is a better predictor of treatment outcome than the client's age, socioeconomic status, problem severity, goals, self-efficacy or self-esteem, and existing social support network—variables that continue to be used despite their low predictive power. As one example of the predictive power of the stages-of-change model, consider the results of a study on the moderating effects of stages of change in drug treatment for anxiety and panic disorder

(Prochaska, 1995). Following treatment, stage-of-change measures predicted more of participants' progress than assignment to either active drug or placebo conditions. In other words, the person's stage of change had more predictive power than the psychoactivity of anxiolytic medication (Beitman et al., 1994)!

Research to date has further shown that therapists improve the chances of success when treatment is tailored to the client's stage of change. For example, several studies have found that stage-appropriate treatment interventions result in greater recruitment and retention of people in the treatment process—two serious problems in outpatient practice (Prochaska, 1999). Other studies have shown that stage-appropriate treatments produce degrees of success equal to those observed in intensive programs but at much lower cost—outcomes of considerable importance for those interested in meeting current demands for efficiency and accountability (S. D. Miller et al., 1999; Prochaska et al., 1997).

☐ Illustrating Stage-Appropriate Practice

> The readiness is all.
> —William Shakespeare
> (*Hamlet,* Act V, Scene II)

Combining Prochaska's transtheoretical model of stages of change with strategic and solution-focused therapy (de Shazer, 1985, 1988; S. D. Miller, Hubble, & Duncan, 1996) suggests some differential intervention strategies, as discussed at length by S. D. Miller, Duncan, and Hubble (1997, pp. 88–104):

Precontemplation: Suggest that the client "think about it" and provide information and education;

Contemplation: Encourage thinking, recommend an observation task in which the client is asked to notice something (such as what happens to make things better or worse), and join with the client's lack of commitment to action with a "Go slow!" directive;

Preparation: Offer treatment options, invite the client to choose from viable alternatives;

Action: Amplify what works—get details of success and reinforce;

Maintenance: Support success, predict setbacks, make contingency plans;

Termination: Wish well, say goodbye, leave an open door for possible return if needed.

Let's take a closer look at some of these transtheoretical ideas and how they can help provide a framework for integrating techniques and practices developed by various schools of brief therapy.

Precontemplation

Prochaska (1999, p. 228) indicates that people in this first stage "are not intending to change or take action in the near future, usually measured in terms of 'the next six months.'" These are the people typically labeled "resistant," "in denial," or "character disordered" in traditional treatment approaches. In reality, however, these people may "not have a clue" that a problem exists. Alternatively, they may feel there is a problem but, as yet, they may not have made a connection between this problem and their contribution to its formation or continuation. Quite often, people in this stage actually have tried to change. Their lack of success, however, may have caused them to become demoralized. As a result, they avoid thinking, talking, or reading about ways to solve the problem. As might be expected, people in this stage often are not interested in participating in treatment (Prochaska, 1995). Most often, they come at the behest or mandate of someone else (e.g., parent, partner, probation officer, court). As such, they may portray themselves as under duress or the victim of "bad luck."

Ruth, a 52-year-old woman who was ordered into treatment after receiving a citation for driving under the influence of alcohol (S. D. Miller et al., 1997), is an example of someone in the *precontemplation* stage. Despite previous arrests on similar charges, Ruth indicated that she did not have a problem with alcohol.

Therapist: *Ruth, tell me just a little bit about what brings you in today?*

Client: *I got a, uh, ticket for driving under the influence.*

T: [nodding]

C: *Actually, I only had one or two drinks but I hadn't eaten much and probably some of the medication I had taken contributed to that.*

T: [sympathetically] *Yeah, and, so, you got a ticket?*

C: *Yeah, I got my license suspended and I have to come here or someplace for counseling. I've been evaluated, very unfairly I might add, as having a big problem.*

T: *A big problem.*

C: *Yeah, according to these tests, which I don't think are very reliable, uh, that's what they say, and there is no recourse. I have already tried to do something about it but the State says that if I want my license back I gotta come here.*

Contemplation

The process of change continues in the second stage. According to Prochaska (1999, p. 229), people in the *contemplation* stage "intend to change in the next six months." In traditional treatment approaches, these people frequently are referred to as the "Yes, but" clients—those who earnestly seek the therapist's help and advice only to reject it once it is offered. In reality, however, people in this stage recognize that a change is needed but are unsure whether it is worth the cost in time, effort, and energy. In addition, they are concerned about the losses attendant to any change they might make.

Consider the following dialogue from a first session with a woman who was experiencing difficulty making a decision about whether or not to marry (S. D. Miller et al., 1997). On the one hand, she knew that, in order to make this important decision, problems in the relationship must be discussed with her potential mate. At the same time, however, she worried about the consequences that might ensue from such a discussion:

Client: *I don't like the way things are right now but, I don't want to, we have a very nonconflictual relationship, so I don't want to fight with him. We always have a good time. I just want to figure out, you know, should we marry or, uh,* [laughing] *just be merry.*

Therapist: *Do you think that if people are assertive and let other people know what they want, do you think that makes conflict?*

C: [shifting in chair] *No, I don't, but it's difficult to do.*

T: *Well, perhaps.*

C: *I have tried to talk with Michael about this and tell him, you know, but . . .*

T: *Sometimes people mistake aggressiveness for assertiveness and they say things that thwart the other person, the conversation, and you don't want that to happen?*

C: *No, but I have tried to talk with him and tell him what I want. Like last week, we were coming home from this party we'd been to and I told him how I was feeling, how I wanted to talk about our, you know, relationship, where we were going.*

T: *Did he hear you?*

C: *Yeah, well, at least to start, but then the same old thing, the subject got changed.*

T: *What did you do then?*

C: *I just laughed to myself.*

Preparation

The third stage is *preparation*. According to Prochaska (1999, p. 230), people in this stage "intend to take action in the immediate future, usually measured in terms of 'the next month.'" Their main focus is on identifying the criteria and strategies for success as well as finalizing the development of their plan for change. *Preparation* is also characterized by the client's experimenting with the desired change—trying it on for size, noticing how it feels, and then experiencing the effects. For example, a person experiencing problems with drugs or alcohol may delay using temporarily or even modify the conditions under which they typically use (Prochaska & DiClemente, 1992). In contrast to the two previous stages—wherein the client's relationship with change is more tenuous and delicate—clients in the *preparation* stage rarely are given negative psychological labels. Indeed, these clients often are considered the ideal—their customership is on a surer footing and their intention to take action fits with traditional ideas about the change process (Prochaska et al., 1992).

The following dialogue from the fifth visit with a man struggling to overcome obsessive and compulsive thoughts and behaviors can be used to illustrate this stage:

Client: *Well, you know, working on my symptoms is where my head is at. I've really been working on setting up this behavior program.*
Therapist: *Uh-huh.*
C: *In many ways, though, the bottom line is that it is like a diet. You know?*
T: *Uh-huh.*
C: *You can do it this way or that way. But, anyway you do it,* if you do it, *you're gonna lose some weight.*
T: *Right.*
C: *But, you still gotta do it.*
T: *Right.*
C: *Right now, I am thinking about doing it, but I'm not doing it.*
T: *Uh huh.*
C: *It's like, I'm having a hard time moving from thinking about doing it to actually doing it.*

Action

Following *preparation*, the *action* stage commences. According to Prochaska (1999, p. 230), this "is the stage in which people have made specific, overt modifications in their life-styles within the past six months." Because of a tendency to equate the *action* stage with change in psychotherapy, many traditional treatment models erroneously identify this stage as the one in which *the* treatment takes place (V. E. Johnson, 1973, 1986; W. R. Miller, 1986; Prochaska et al., 1992). Research has shown, however, that in spite of the field's historical bias toward action, people are *least* likely to be in this stage at the onset of treatment. This mismatch goes a long way toward explaining the persistance of the concept of *resistance* in mental health discourse.

The following excerpt from the fourth session with a woman who sought therapy in order to regain contact with alter personalities that had been lost following a head injury is typical of dialogue in the *action* stage. (See Schwarz, 1998, for discussion of the collaborative treatment of dissociative disorders):

Therapist: *Have you had an opportunity to try any of the things that we've talked about?*

Client: *Yeah.* [slight laugh] *It was quite fun.*

T: *Good. I was hoping it would be.*

C: *Actually, we did not have to do many at all. Nat* [an alter personality] *left a note for everybody* [the other alters]. *I would say a lot of things changed after that talk with you. That evening and that next day some different things were tried, and then that next evening Joe* [her partner with whom she previously had been unable to speak with regarding her difficulties] *said, "Obviously something is wrong, so what gives?" Chris* [another alter] *was out and she told him. I think it's made a big difference because I'm out and Linda was out earlier in the week, also* [two alters that she had been out of contact with since the head injury].

Maintenance

In this stage, change continues and emphasis is placed on what needs to be done in order to maintain or consolidate gains. In contrast to those in the previous stage, people in the *maintenance* stage "are less tempted to relapse and are increasingly more confident that they can continue their changes" (Prochaska, 1999, p. 231). This is because they have learned from difficulties and temptations that they have encountered while passing throught the other stages.

A session with a man who had been treated for problems with alcohol and depression illustrates dialogue typical of someone in the *maintenance* stage:

Client: *I've been thinking that, well, I've really got a lot out of coming here.*

Therapist: *It shows.*

C: *Yeah, and, I thought about what we talked about last time . . .*

T: *Uh-huh.*

C: *About spacing out our sessions . . .*

T: *Uh-huh.*

C: *And, well, I think I'm ready.*

T: *What gives you that confidence, that you're ready?*

In the ensuing discussion, the therapist and client explored the reasons for the client's confidence as well as any circumstances he might encounter that would challenge it. This helped to reinforce and solidify the client's gains as well as prepare (inoculate) him for subsequent difficulties.

Termination

According to Prochaska (1993, p. 253), in this final stage, there is zero temptation to engage in the problem behavior regardless of the situation. So defined, this stage actually may be more of an ideal than a realistic or achievable stage of change, although over time some people move past "recovery" to a life and self-image that no longer contains the old problem (see Y. D. Dolan, 1998; Hoyt, 1994/1995). More than likely, however, most people stay in the *maintenance* phase. That is, they continue to be mindful of possible threats to their desired change and monitor what they need to do to keep the change in place.

☐ The Temporal Structure of Brief Therapy

There is a season for everything, a time
for every occupation under heaven.
—Ecclesiastes 3:1

Time is nature's way of not having everything happen at once. In the course of an event or process, some activities precede others; sequencing gives order and can provide direction. Recognizing that different issues and activities may be appropriate in the early, middle, and finishing phases of therapy also may help to organize and potentiate change interventions.

Therapy can be thought to have five interrelated phases or stages (see Hoyt, 1990/1995g; Chapter 15, this volume). In actual practice, the phases blend into one another rather than being discretely organized. The structure tends to be epigenetic or pyramidal, each phase building on the prior so that successful work in one preconditions the next. Each phase sets the stage for the following phase, for example, the client typically needs to elect therapy and be selected for treatment before an alliance and goals can be formed; goals need to be established before working through and refocusing can meaningfully occur; a sense of movement needs to precede discussions of homework, relapse prevention, and leavetaking; and

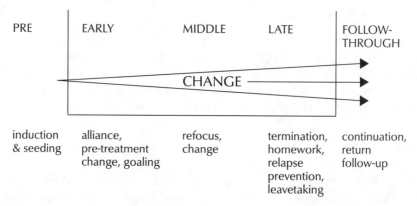

FIGURE 14.1. The temporal structure of brief therapy.

all of these anticipate change processes continuing past the formal ending point of treatment and the possibility of a return to therapy as needed. Schematically, the five phases look like those in Figure 14.1.

There often is an interesting parallel between the structure of the overall course of treatment and the structure of each individual session. As seen in Figure 14.2, there is a microcosm-macrocosm resemblance ("Ontogeny recapitulates phylogeny," say the biologists), the activities of each treatment phase mirroring the activities of each session, for example, the client elects (to return to) therapy, the first portion of each session (and treatment) emphasizes alliance building, the middle portion of each session (and treatment) focuses on accelerating change, the latter portion of each session (and treatment) emphasizes how to keep it going, and the follow-through after each session (and treatment) is a time of continuation and possible return. Each course of therapy thus can be schematically represented as comprising a chain or sequence of sessions, as seen in Figure 14.3.

It can be noted that when a single session comprises the entire course of therapy (as happens in approximately 20% to 50% of cases—see Hoyt, 1994/1995k, 1995a; Hoyt et al., 1992; Rosenbaum, Hoyt, & Talmon, 1990/1995; Talmon, 1990), Figures 14.1 and 14.2 collapse on to one another,

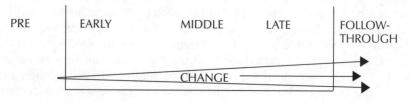

FIGURE 14.2. The temporal structure of each session.

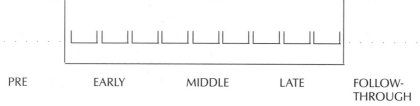

PRE   EARLY   MIDDLE   LATE   FOLLOW-
                                                     THROUGH

FIGURE 14.3. Therapy as a temporally structured sequence of sessions, each with a temporally structured sequence.

the structure of the individual session and the overall treatment, by definition, being selfsame (isomorphic).

One also can schematically depict, as in Figure 14.4, various arrangements in which sessions occur at variable intervals, such as (see Figure 14.4A) having sessions on a regular (e.g., weekly) periodic basis; or (Figure 14.4B) initially having sessions weekly, then biweekly, and then monthly (see Boegner & Zielenbach-Coenen, 1984); or (see Figure 14.4C) having sessions episodically or intermittently on an as-needed basis.

☐ Strategies by Temporal Stage

> Organizing is what you do before you do something, so that when you do it, it's not all mixed up.
> —Christopher Robin in *The Complete Tales of Winnie-the-Pooh*,
>   A. A. Milne (1926/1994)

There are various tasks to be accomplished at each stage or phase of a session (and treatment). While flexibility, innovation, and honoring the clients' theories, motivations, goals, and energies ("leading by following")

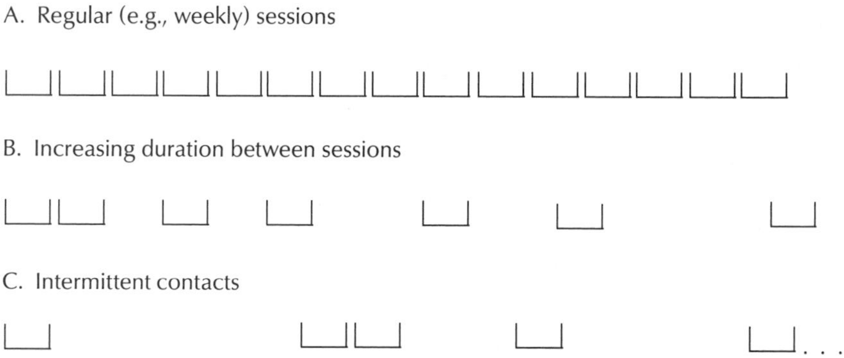

A. Regular (e.g., weekly) sessions

B. Increasing duration between sessions

C. Intermittent contacts

FIGURE 4.4. Some ways sessions can be temporally arrayed.

are paramount (Duncan et al., 1998; S. D. Miller et al., 1997), we find it helpful to have these ideas available to strategically organize our therapeutic activity across the course of working with clients. It should be noted that, as we use the term, *strategies* refers to purposeful, respectful activity; we accept our responsibility as therapists to help make something useful happen *with* the client (see Haley, 1977; Held, 1992; Solovey & Duncan, 1992; Weakland, 1993).

In what follows, we present a sampler of typical questions that might be useful at different phases of therapy. It should be noted that these are "questions (not answers)" (S. D. Miller, 1994); that we are looking for "symptoms of solutions" (S. D. Miller, 1992) that often are best accessed if we "step off the throne" (Duncan, Hubble, & Miller, 1997a),"recast the client as the star of the drama called therapy" (Duncan, Hubble, & Miller, 1998), and listen carefully to our clients' constructions of what would be helpful (Duncan et al., 1998).

Pretreatment

Change begins even before we have contact with the client: she or he or they have decided that there is a "problem" and that they would like assistance to resolve the difficulty. While making an initial appointment, we inquire (a receptionist or even a questionnaire can do this):

- What's the problem? Why now have you called?
- How do you see or understand the situation?
- Who's involved?
- What do you think will help?
- How have you attempted to solve the problem thus far?
- When the problem isn't so bothersome, what is going on differently?

During this initial contact, before the first session, we also recruit the client's cooperation and seed change by asking:

- Please notice between now and when we meet, so that you can describe it to me, when the problem you called about isn't so bad (when you're less or not depressed, when you're not having panic attacks, when you and your partner are getting along okay, etc.), what you're doing differently then? This may give us some clues regarding what you may need to do more of. (This is a variant of the "First Session Formula Task" described by de Shazer, 1985, p. 137; Weiner-Davis, de Shazer, & Gingerich, 1987):

We also may remark to the client:

- Therapy involves making some changes, not just talking about what's been wrong, so identifying exceptions to the problem that led you to call will help us focus on solutions that may be useful for you.

Early in Treatment and Early in Each Session

As we begin a session and a therapy, we attend carefully to developing a good alliance, inquiring about possible changes since our last contact, and establishing goals for the session and the therapy. Some useful questions include:

- Since we last spoke, what have you noticed that may be a bit different or better? How did that happen? What did you do? (This question regarding presession change follows up on the earlier request for the client to notice possible exceptions—it may provide information to build on and also conveys a metamessage of accountability, that the therapist will recall and inquire about agreed-upon tasks and homework.)
- When is the problem not a problem? When is the presenting complaint not present?
- What do you call the problem? What name do you have for it? (This personification is part of the "externalization" process described by Roth & Epston, 1996; White, 1989/1989d).
- When (and how) does [the problem] influence you; and when (and how) do you influence it? ("Relative influence questioning," following White, 1986/1989a.)
- What's your idea or theory about what will help?
- How can I be most useful to you? What kind of therapist would you like me to be? (See Norcross & Beutler, 1997.)
- What's on your agenda? What needs to happen here today so that when you leave you can feel this visit was worthwhile?
- What are you willing to change today?[1] (See Goulding & Goulding, 1979; Polster & Polster, 1976.)
- Given all that you've been through, how have you managed to cope as well as you have? (This acknowledges the seriousness of the client's complaints and situation while still looking for strengths, resources, and competencies.)
- If we work hard together, what will be the first small indications that we're going in the right direction?
- Suppose tonight, while you're sleeping, a miracle happens, and the problem that led you here is resolved. When you awaken tomorrow, how will you first notice the miracle has happened? What will be a first

sign that things are better? And the next? And the next? ("The Miracle Question," following de Shazer, 1988, p. 5.)

In the Middle of Treatment and the Middle of Each Session

Like a pilot checking the flight plan (the intended destination, the present location, the remaining fuel), we keep track of clients' goals and whether we are going in the right direction or if some course "corrections" need to be made. Possible refocusing is directed by the client's response to the following questions:

- How did that work? (If an attempted solution perpetuates the problem, something different that still honors the client's belief structures and view of reality is needed—see Fisch, Weakland, & Segal, 1982; McCloskey & Fraser, 1997.)
- Is this being helpful to you? What might make it more so? (See S. D. Miller, Duncan & Johnson, 1999.)
- Do you have any questions you'd like to ask me?

If the client is making progress that is adequate and satisfying to her, him, or them, we attempt to keep in mind the solution-focused principle, *"If it works, don't fix it"* (de Shazer, in Hoyt, 1996c). We offer encouragement and support, and try not to push. If the client is moving forward, we cheerlead rather than mislead, so to speak. We attend assiduously to empowering the so-called "common factors" (alliance and client contributions) that voluminous research (see Lambert, 1992; Lambert & Bergin, 1994; S. D. Miller et al., 1997) has shown accounts for most of the variance in psychotherapeutic outcomes. Remembering that the client-therapist alliance is the vehicle and not the destination, however, we do not necessarily focus explicit discussion on the therapeutic relationship unless something seems amiss. If we do not experience the client as experiencing us as helpful and supportive or if there is not movement in the direction of the client's goals, we may inquire:

- Are we working on what you want to work on?
- I seem to have missed something you said. What can I do to be more helpful to you now?

Late in Treatment and Late in Each Session

Nearing the end of a course of therapy and nearing the end of each session, issues of *termination* become central. This phase can be thought of as subtracting the therapist from the successful equation (Gustafson, 1986;

Hoyt, 1990/1995g; see Chapter 15, this volume), a basic heuristic being, "You've been doing well with me; how can you continue to do well without me?" There are a number of issues to be addressed, as the following guideline questions suggest:

Goal Attainment/Homework/Post-Session Tasks

• Has this been helpful to you? How so?
• Which of the helpful things you've been doing do you think you should continue to do? How can you do this?
• Between now and the next time we meet [or, to keep things going in the right direction], would you be willing to do____?
• Who can be helpful to you in doing _____? What might interfere, and how can you prepare to deal with those challenges? (See Kazantzis & Deane, 1999; Levy & Shelton, 1990; Mahrer, Nordin, & Miller, 1995; Meichenbaum & Turk, 1987; Mohr, 1995.)

Goal Maintenance and Relapse Prevention

• What would be a signal that the problems you were having might be returning? How can you respond if you see that developing?
• Suppose you wanted to go back to all of the problems you were having when you first came in? What would you need to do to make this happen, if you wanted to sabotage yourself? (While independently developed [see Hoyt, 1986, 1995a] this can be seen as a variant of Norm Reuss' "The Nightmare Question"—see Berg & Reuss, 1998, pp. 36–37.)
• How might [the problem] try to trick you into letting it take over again? (For some narrative therapy examples, see Madigan & Goldner, 1998; Nylund & Corsiglia, 1996.)
• What will you need to do to increase the odds that things will work out okay even if you weren't to come in for awhile?
• Who will be glad to hear about your progress? How can we circulate the good news? Who in your present or past would support your efforts? Which friends and family make up your community of positive concern? (See Madigan, 1997; Madigan & Epston, 1995; White, 1991/1993b, 1997.)

Leavetaking

• Would you like to make another appointment now or wait and see how things go and call me as needed? (See Chapter 18, this volume, for a number of variants.)
• What is the longest period you can imagine handling things on your own at this time?

- If you got stuck and wanted some help, but decided to try something other than therapy, what would you do? Who could you turn to, if not to therapy, if things get difficult again? (These questions come from Kreider, 1998, pp. 352–353.)
- How can you recall some of the helpful things we have discussed when you need them?

☐ Case Examples

Number 1: Stage-Appropriate Brief Therapy with an Individual

> Call me another thrower.
> —Loren Eiseley (*The Star Thrower*, 1978)

John was a 23-year-old in great distress. His relationship with his girlfriend, Jennifer, had continued to spiral downward. Despite many promises, she had been increasingly nasty and rejecting toward John. She had lost another job and was on the verge of being evicted from her apartment. John suspected that she had begun drinking and using drugs again, especially speed, despite her angry protestations to the contrary. Finally, during a late-night phone call, she admitted that she had been going to bed with Jeff, whom John had thought of as one of his best friends. She dumped John. Never before much of a drinker (nor into drugs), over the next several days John drank heavily, missed work, and felt miserable.

John's parents called and scheduled an emergency appointment. As I (M.F.H.) found out, John worked in a law office. He lived with his parents. He described himself as a Christian, dressed with style, and followed professional basketball closely. He had gone out with Jennifer for almost 3 years. He said that he loved her and that he had been aware of her "vices," but had hoped to reform her. She had not returned any of his recent calls. When John had begun talking about Satan and suicide, his parents had become understandably alarmed and had called the HMO Psychiatry Department.

I took their call and agreed to see John and his parents that day, then asked if I might speak with him on the phone. I introduced myself, saying I had heard he was having a rough time, and asked if he wanted some help. He said he did not know, that the call had been his folks' idea. When I asked why they were so concerned, he said he really needed to calm down and have someone to talk with. I told him that I felt I could be helpful with that, and added that we might also talk about "making some changes." I confirmed our appointment time later that day, asked him to think about what else I could do to be helpful, and then hung up.

When he and his parents arrived in the late afternoon, I brought them all into my office. Wearing jeans, running shoes, and a rumpled T-shirt, John looked like someone who had not showered or slept much in several days, which he had not. His parents were almost frantic. They had not liked Jennifer, but said they appreciated his concern about her and how hard breaking up was . . . but this was not the son they knew. "Should he be hospitalized?" they wanted to know.

I asked John if he felt he needed hospitalization to ensure his safety. He did not think so. "What would be most helpful right now?" I asked, adding that I could not influence Jennifer. "Something to help me get some rest and sleep," he responded. "If I get a doctor to come in and give you a prescription, will you promise not to drink and not to harm yourself, and will you come to see me again on Friday?" (It was Wednesday.) He said "Yes," we reviewed our no-suicide and no-drinking agreement in front of his parents, and I summoned the on-call psychiatrist who, after a brief evaluation, gave John a prescription for a couple of antianxiety pills. I did not want to go down the slippery slope of medicating life problems, but he was quite agitated and seemed sincere in his promise to not drink, and I hoped some immediate response to his request would provide some relief, help strengthen our alliance, and perhaps build some hope.

I also asked John what he did when he was not upset and found out some of his interests, including his avid attention to professional basketball. His affect brightened and he revealed a keen knowledge as we talked about some recent trades the local team had made. We also discussed Jennifer—he nodded and cried when I asked if he thought "it was over." When I asked about ways he had been able to cope successfully with stress in the past that he could use now, he mentioned several (prayer, exercise, talking with friends, reminding himself of what was best in the long run) and agreed to use these over the next few days. I also suggested that he think about the good times and the bad times with Jennifer to see what conclusions he might draw.

We met that Friday, and the next, and the next. He reevaluated his relationship with Jennifer, realizing more of the problems. He still felt very sad, but said he no longer felt that he had "failed." We discussed what he thought had gone wrong and what he might want to do differently in the future, once he was ready to move on and someday meet another woman. (He laughed when, utilizing sports jargon, I referred to his next girlfriend as "a player to be named later.") He decided that he had been too much of a "rescuer," that the relationship had been "too one-way—I gave and she took."

At our next meeting, John reported that Jennifer had called him, long-distance collect. He said he had been sympathetic, but that he did not get sucked back in. He promised to call her a couple of days later, but she was not there when he called at the appointed time. He then had heard through a friend she had lost yet another job because of continued lateness and absenteeism, and that she was living with another guy. This fortuitous ("extratherapeutic") sequence of events brought up more disappointment, but John said it also helped confirm his decision to let go and move on.

After a fourth weekly meeting, John said he felt he was doing better and that he did not need to come in so often—but that he still wanted to keep meeting for awhile. I asked what he thought would be a good schedule, and he suggested 3 weeks hence. Jennifer was still a topic, but John also brought up the situation with his folks. He felt "jammed" (cramped) by them. He said he was a good son, but that he needed to live his own way. He had been contemplating moving out, but feared his parents would be worried or hurt, especially after the way they had been there for him during his crisis. We discussed times when his parents had been proud of his independence—this "reframe," which allowed him to maintain a "preferred view" of himself (see Coyne, 1985; Eron & Lund, 1989, 1996; Watzlawick, Weakland & Fisch, 1974), relieved his guilt. It also prefigured his growing readiness to discontinue therapy. We considered several possible courses of action (e.g., living on his own versus roommates), to which John said he would give more thought and soon make a decision.

We met two more times, a month apart. He was maintaining his gains ("I'm sorry it had to end that way with Jennifer, but it did"). He was working, socializing, not drinking, and had moved in with roommates. I congratulated him on his good work. We discussed some possible temptations and "pitfalls," and how to avoid them. In leavetaking, he expressed his appreciation and said that he had liked the feeling that he had been given emotional support but had been allowed to work things out in his own way and at his own pace. We discussed what might be some possible indications to return to therapy. He agreed to recontact me if he felt the need. We wished each other well and said goodbye.

Number 2: Stage-Appropriate Brief Therapy with a Couple: From Changing Individuals to Changing Relationships

> Know what you see; don't see what you know.
> —Addie Fuhriman (personal communication, 1984)

While the stages-of-change model was originally developed to describe an individual's progression through the change process, it also is possible to apply the ideas to clinical work with couples and families. In such cases, the stages are applied to the relationship between the individuals in treatment rather than to the individuals themselves.

The following excerpts are taken from the fourth session of therapy with Marcus and Felicia, a married couple who sought treatment for "long-standing communication problems."[2] In their intake information, the couple reported having been in treatment on two prior occasions for the same problem without success. In the first three sessions of the present therapy, the couple was treated as if they were in the *preparation* or *action* stage of change. As such, treatment sessons were active in nature (e.g., teaching and practicing communication skills), and action-oriented homework assignments (e.g., "try out the skills you learned in the sessions") were given between visits. While the couple willingly engaged in the skill-building exercises during the sessions, they did not complete the homework assignments.

The fourth session began with the following exchange:

Therapist: *Well, welcome. I'm glad you both could get here. The first thing I'd like to know is, is there anything different that's been happening between you since the last time I saw you?*

Felicia: *I think, I think there is. I think there's less communication.*

Therapist: *Okay.*

Felicia: *Because, we haven't really spoken. Yesterday, we got into an argument before we left for work. So, we didn't speak all evening.*

Therapist: *Uh-huh.*

Felicia: *But, I think there's been less communication. So . . .*

Therapist: *There's been less communication.*

Felicia: *Uh-huh. I mean there hasn't been any communication about what we discussed at our last session.*

Therapist: *Okay.*

Felicia: *We've been avoiding it.*

Therapist: *How about you, Marcus? Anything different that you've noticed?*

Marcus: *Mmm-huh, nothing, other than what Felicia has noticed.*

Therapist: *You've noticed less communication also?*

Marcus: *Uh-huh, less communication.*

Therapist: *What do you think that means?*

Marcus: *That we have a problem.*

Therapist: *And, what's the problem?*

Marcus: *Uh, that we're not communicating and we don't have mutual objectives, I don't think.*

Both Felicia and Marcus recognized that a problem exists. At the same time, however, neither member of the dyad had *acted* to solve the problem in the time between the present and previous session. Rather, in the words of Felicia, the couple had been "avoiding it [the communication problem]." Such *in*action on the part of this couple might easily be viewed as "resistance" or, minimally, a "lack of motivation." This mind-set might, in turn, lead the therapist to engage in activities aimed at "breaking through" the resistance (e.g., confrontation) or getting the clients to *do* something (e.g., encouraging activity or the taking of responsibility, assigning homework tasks) to solve their problem.

When viewed through the lens of the stages-of-change model, however, the couple was considered neither resistant nor in need of a therapist-provided motivational "pick-me-up." Rather, emphasis was placed on identifying and cooperating with the clients' stage-of-change. In this case, the interaction between Felicia and Marcus was typical for people in the *contemplation* stage. As such, therapeutic activities that encourage new thinking, feelings, or observations were likely to be the most congruent with the activity level of the couple's current change process.

In the next excerpt, the therapist follows up on Marcus's comment about "not having mutual objectives" and attempts to help each member of the couple generate new thinking about their understanding of the problem as well as their goals for treatment. This represented a shift in approach from the previous visits during which the couple was treated as if they were in the *preparation* or *action* stages.

Felicia: *He's the only one who can answer that. I don't know what he wants. He doesn't ever communicate what he wants. So, I don't know what he expects or what he wants.*

Therapist: *What do you think, Marcus, is that a possibility?*

Marcus: *Uh, it's a great possibility. I think that when communication is taking place, one has to, I think, understand that you can't verbally abuse someone and expect them to have perfect communication. As a matter of fact, that type of behavior produces just the converse. That person doesn't want to communicate with someone that is verbally abusive.*

Therapist: *Mmm-huh.*

Marcus: *And, I think that behavior not only causes me individually, but I think that's probably a natural reaction for anyone. I don't know anyone that is positive to verbal abuse.*

Therapist: *Okay. But, is it possible that you could incorporate . . . some of, maybe, do you gesture, how does it happen?*

Marcus: [nodding]

Therapist: *When you perceive that she is being verbally abusive, she does what? She raises her voice?*

Marcus: *Well, she could raise her voice. Not necessarily raise her voice. She uses profanity. She uses it very inappropriately and sometimes very consistently.*

Therapist: *Mmm-huh.*

Marcus: *One thing that really gets me is the fact of how she displays this verbal abuse, and it's not setting a good example for our daughter. And, I guess that's what makes me so angry at the situation, because of the fact that it's not just impacting me individually any longer—it's impacting our child with this behavior. And, as I said, it was something that I saw early in our relationship. I felt that it would get better. Of course, as you know, this is not our first attempt at counseling. And I'm not beyond the fact that we, as a couple, may have problems. But I know fundamentally that we can't get to our joint problems unless I can get Felicia to look at the behavior that she is displaying because it's not only, you know, tearing me down, but it affects me when I see the impact on my daughter. And I think that's more the impact on me, because I'm an adult and can deal with it. But, at the same time, I react to her verbal abuse. But it really gets me when I have a daughter and now, you know, she's part of that whole behavior pattern that Felicia has, and I don't like it.*

Felicia: *Yeah, but you're part of the problem in this relationship, too, Marcus. It's not only my doing. You—it takes two people to work on a relationship. And, it's not only about me. It's just like we discussed the last time we were at the therapist's office. You always want to blame me for every damn thing. You never want to take responsibility for your actions. You don't want to be blamed for anything because you think that you can't do any wrong. My sisters see that about you, our friends see that about you, that you never want to be blamed for anything. And, you're always trying to impress everybody. You want to impress everybody else, except me. Your family should come before other people come into play about trying to impress people, Marcus.*

At this point in the session, the interaction between Marcus and Felicia turned into a heated argument. Each member of the dyad presented their view of the problem and attributed the cause to the other. Specifically, Marcus blamed the couple's difficulties on Felicia's "verbal abuse"; while Felicia, in turn, credited Marcus's "lack of responsibility" for their problems. Such behavior is not atypical for people in the *contemplation* stage of change. Indeed, a hallmark of this stage, as Berg and Miller (1992, p. 23) pointed out, is the belief that "the only solution is for someone other than themselves to change" *first*. At the same time, however, the key to maximizing the success of therapeutic intervention from the stages-of-change perspective is accommodating rather than changing this belief.

One brief therapy strategy that has proven particularly useful in such circumstances is *relationship-oriented* or *circular-style questions* (Tomm, 1988). Briefly, such questions "attempt to bring forth" patterns that connect "persons, objects, actions, perceptions, ideas, feelings, events, beliefs, contexts" (Dozier, Hicks, Cornille, & Peterson, 1998, p. 192). As such, these questions contrast sharply with the more common lineal-style questions that seek to uncover beliefs about the origin of the problem or goals for treatment.

In the excerpt that follows, the therapist switched from individually oriented to circular questions. The impact on the couple's interaction was immediate. Specifically, they stopped presenting their individual positions and opinions, and began to develop a vision of working together as a couple.

Therapist: *There's a question that's in my mind, and I've sort of been trying to twist my tongue and figure out exactly how to ask it of the two of you. I'm wondering, what would be signs to the two of you that you were* working together *at resolving these things that happen in your relationship? What would be signs to each of you that you were working together rather than at cross purposes? Does that question make sense?*

Felicia: *I'm not . . .*

Therapist: *Okay. When you actually had one of these episodes where you're obviously at a different place, my sense is that when you're trying to communicate each of you sort of talk and it's like, "What the hell?"*

Felicia: *Yeah, each of us doesn't listen to what the other says.*

Therapist: *Right, that's the point I'm getting at. So, what I'm looking for is what would be signs—when one of those episodes actually happens—what would be signs to each of you that you were working constructively around that difference rather than at cross purposes?*

Felicia: *Sitting down and talking about it, and each of us listening to each other instead of trying to out-do the other.*

Therapist: *Okay. And, let me ask you this, and* [pointing at Marcus] *you can't give any hints here, okay? What would Marcus say he would notice about you that would give him the idea that you were listening?*

Felicia: *My not interrupting, because he complains that I always interrupt when he tries to speak to me.*

Therapist: *Okay. Instead of interrupting, you would . . . ?*

Felicia: [thinking] *Hmm.*

Therapist: *Paint a picture for me.*

Felicia: *I would probably just sit there and listen.*

Therapist: *Yeah? And, how would he know? What would make him say, "She's listening to me!"?*

Felicia: *Probably just being relaxed and not making any gestures or facial expressions.*

Therapist: *Okay.*

Felicia: *Cause he says I roll my eyes or I sigh or I look away when he's talking.*

Therapist: *Okay. How about for you, Marcus? What would Felicia say or, in* *fact, what would be signs to you that you were working together at resolving these things when they came up rather than being at cross-purposes? What would be signs that your couplehood is working?*

Marcus: *I don't know . . .*

Therapist: *Okay.*

Marcus: *Because we have this way of communication that is different.*

Therapist: *Okay. Well, that's obvious to all of us . . .*

Marcus: *Yes.*

Therapist: *That your styles are different.*

Felicia: *Mmm-huh.*

Therapist: *What I'm trying to figure out is what it might look like when the two of you are working together at resolving the difference.*

Marcus: *I think she would say that I would look at her.* [looks at Felicia] *I guess that would be what she would say.*

Therapist: *Anything else that you can think of? Sort of looking at her, maintaining eye contact. Any other ideas?*

Marcus: *Uh. Probably tell her, "I'm listening."*

Therapist: [looking at Felicia] *Okay.*

Marcus: *Tell her, "I'm here, I'm with you."*

Therapist: *So it's not going to be enough just to look. You have to keep going, "I'm with you, I'm with you." Is that right?*

Marcus: *Yes. She says that—it's really frustrating—she says that I'm not listening when I am!*

Therapist: *Okay, so to give her the idea that you're listening, you* [pointing to Marcus], *you have to say, "I'm with you, I'm trying, I'm listening, I'm trying."*

Marcus: [nodding]

Therapist: *Anything else that would tell the two of you that?*

In the discussion that followed, circular-style questions helped the couple continue to add details to their vision of working together to resolve their difficulties.

As the session neared the end of the hour, the therapist used another strategy from brief therapy—*scaling questions*—as a way to assess the couple's stage of change. Such questions, which can be used at any temporal phase, are based not on normative standards, but rather on the clients' perception of self and others as well as their impressions of how others view them. As Berg and de Shazer (1993, p. 10; see also Kowalski & Kral, 1989; S. D. Miller, 1994; Chapter 8, this volume) point out, the questions serve to "motivate and encourage, and to elucidate the goals and anything else that is important."

Therapist: *So, Felicia, let me ask you: On a scale from 1 to 10, where 10 is the highest and 1 is the lowest, where would Marcus say you are in terms of your interest in having a different kind of conversation? In being interested in working at resolving these differences? Where would he say you are, on a scale of 1 to 10?*

Felicia: *Probably a 2 or 3.*

Therapist: *And where would Felicia say you are on a scale of 1 to 10, Marcus? Interested in having these kind of conversations we've been talking about?*

Marcus: *Probably a 1 or 2.*

Therapist: *And, Marcus, where are you? Where would you say you are in terms of your interest in having a different kind of conversation?*

Marcus: *My interest is probably about a 9 or a 10.*

Therapist: *And you, Felicia?*

Felicia: *I would probably say mine is probably a 5.*

Therapist: *Okay, a 5. So, Marcus thought you'd be a 2 or a 3; you're saying a 5?*

Felicia: *Mmm-huh.*

Therapist: *What is it that Marcus will be noticing more of once he gets the idea that you are actually more interested in having a different kind of conversation? What would he notice different about you that would tell him you are much more interested in having a different kind of conversation?*

Felicia: *Probably trying to sit down and talk to him when I'm not angry.*

Therapist: *Okay, trying to talk when not angry.*

Felicia: *Mmm-huh.*

Therapist: *Okay, that would be a big one.*

Felicia: *Mmm-huh.*

Therapist: *You mean, as opposed to trying to make the conversation work once things have already sort of plummeted?*

Felicia: *Yeah. Mmm-huh.*

Therapist: *All right. You're saying you're a 9 or 10?*

Marcus: *Mmm-huh. Felicia probably doesn't think so.*

Therapist: *You think she'd say you were a 1 or 2?*

Marcus: *Yeah.*

Therapist: *Okay. What is it that Felicia would be noticing more about you, once she gets the idea about how much more interested, how much more willing you are? What would she notice different about you?*

Marcus: *Probably, basically, to know that I am really listening.*

Therapist: *Really.*

Marcus: *If I look at her, hold her hand, while she was talking.*

Therapist: *Okay. You're* [pointing at Marcus] *saying you're a 9 or a 10. You're* [pointing at Felicia] *saying you're a 5. If the team behind the one-way mirror has some ideas—and I have some ideas—how interested or willing would you be to try them out? 10 being that, "Damn it, I'll do anything, once." A 1 is, "I'm outta here—straight to the divorce lawyer." I want you to be honest with me here. If the team has some ideas . . .*

Marcus: *A 9 or a 10.*

Felicia: *I would be 9 or a 10. I'd be interested, very interested.*

Therapist: *Okay. I'd like to take a break and go back and chat with them. I really appreciate your helping me fill in the blanks from here.*

Marcus: *This was really interesting.*

Felicia: *And helpful. I mean, you know, I mean it's like you said—we do, it's a struggle for us to work at it, but we both* [tearful] *really want it to work but, you know, I'm at the point where I'm not willing to work at it anymore.*

Therapist: *Right. And, I don't sense that that's what either of you want, actually.*

Felicia: *No, I don't. But, it becomes a job on a daily basis and I'm not willing to work at it anymore.*

Therapist: *Right. Give me 5 or 6 minutes, okay?*

At this point in the interview, the therapist took a break to consult with a team of therapists who had been observing from behind a one-way mirror. (The couple had briefly met this team at the beginning of the session.) Discussion centered around creating a between-session homework task that was congruent with the couple's stage of change. Whereas in previous sessions the therapist and team had conducted treatment as if the couple were in the *preparation* or *action* stage, the therapist and team now decided to treat the couple as if they were in the contemplation stage. Consistent with this stage, the couple was encouraged to "go slow"— even stop their problem-solving efforts altogether—and given an *observation assignment* to help them shift their viewing from conflict to cooperation.

Therapist: *We've had a chat behind the mirror with everybody that you saw. Sort of sharing ideas. At least my experience of it is that the consensus is how very hurt each of you has been. That there is a tremendous amount of pain, emotional pain. It shows in your faces. We thought about when you first started talking about how you got together, there was all this brightness; and now, there seems to be a distance and hurt and pain. At the same time, a desire to re-connect that hasn't seemed to work. But not for lack of trying. You've both come to individual counseling. You've both come here and tried things out. You both, in a painful way, I think, have tried to get your point across. The result is mostly, at best, frustration and, at worst, exhaustion.*

Felicia: [nodding] *Mmm-huh.*

Marcus: [nodding] *Mmm-huh.*

Therapist: *And so, it's not surprising to us to hear things like, "Oh, if this doesn't change quick, I want the hell out of this." I would say that makes you normal, that feeling. At the same time, I don't think that's what you want. At least, I don't get that experience yet. I get a thread of hope: around your children, how much you both mutually care about your family. Does this fit for you both?*

Felicia: [nodding affirmatively]

Marcus: *Yeah.*

Therapist: *When I was thinking about what we could offer, in terms of useful things, I did have some ideas, and the team and I talked about them. But, after reflecting with each other about it, our sense is that the amount of the pain, the depth of the pain, and the amount of exhaustion that's apparent, makes me think at least, and I think the team understands, what is required first is a vacation from the constant drive to solve this. Not a vacation where you move out. But a vacation so that each of you can replenish individually and then come back and work together. Because right now both of you are sort of like, "Oh, please don't give anything too much right now." And I think that's wise. What I think, my impression—and I'm willing to hear your feedback—maybe a few weeks vacation, where you stop trying to figure out and solve this. And you give the other person a vacation from that also. And you simply work quietly, observing the other person for signs that they are being replenished so that you can come back rested and work together, work at figuring out a way to resolve this, like I know both of you want to. Is that helpful?*

Marcus: *Makes sense.*

Felicia: *Yeah, it makes a lot of sense.*

Therapist: *I'm not talking about a* laissez faire . . .

Marcus: *Uh-huh.*

Therapist: *Not just not doing anything. Now, that's not a vacation. A vacation is, you go to Rome. And, you know the old saying, "When in Rome . . . " Looking for signs that the other is being replenished.*

A return appointment was scheduled for a month later. At that visit, Marcus and Felicia reported that they each felt rested and replenished. They also both reported noticing things their partner had done to facilitate their being rested and replenished. Coincidentally, both felt that they had been communicating better as a couple during the vacation period. Time was spent exploring and reinforcing this change in this session and in two subsequent sessions. By the last visit, the therapist and team were treating the couple as if they were in the *active* or *maintenance* stage.

☐ Doing What Works

> Every art and every investigation, and similarly every action
> and pursuit, is considered to aim at some good.
> —Aristotle (*Nichomeachan Ethics*, 1976, Book 1, Chapter 1)

Rather than following traditional psychiatric discourse—which tends to discount and exclude clients and places control within the therapist—we are interested in respectful collaboration that more fully appreciates and utilizes clients' strengths, resources, and competencies. Recognizing different stages of change, levels of motivation, and phases of treatment can help clinicians join with clients to empower and promote their active and efficacious participation in therapy.

☐ Notes

[1]In this one sentence, spelled out almost like a haiku for therapeutic effectiveness, we can see all the key elements of brief (efficient or time-sensitive) therapy (see Hoyt, 1990/1995g, 1997, p. xv):

What (specificity, goal, target, focus)

are (active verb, present tense)

you (self as agent, personal functioning)

willing (choice, responsibility, initiative)

to change (alter or make different, not just "work on," "try," or "explore")

today (now, in the moment)

? (inquiry, open field, invitation, therapist respectfully receptive but not insistent)

[2]This report is based on a case supervised by Scott Miller.

15
CHAPTER

The Last Session in Brief Therapy: Why and How to Say "When"

> So teach us to number
> our days that we may
> get us a heart of wisdom.
> —Moses (*Psalm* 90:12)

> Whoever loves, if he does not propose
> The right true end of love, he's one that goes
> To sea for nothing but to make him sick.
> —John Donne (1633),
> "Love's Progress"

> It ain't over 'til it's over.
> —Yogi Berra (Pepe, 1988)

Betwixt epigraphers times three lies the realm of termination.

Having previously written at length about the problems of a proper beginning in *The First Session in Brief Therapy* (Budman, Hoyt, & Friedman, 1992), I want here to discuss some aspects of a proper ending of treatment. Finishing well both completes and perpetuates the good work that has preceded it. While we can recognize that termination in some ways may be a pseudoevent in that the work continues and formal treatment can be intermittently resumed (M. J. Bennett, 1983, 1984; Budman, 1990; N. A. Cummings, 1990; N. A. Cummings & Sayama, 1995; Hoyt, 1990/

A version of this chapter will appear in *Brief Therapy: Lasting Impressions*, J. K. Zeig (Ed.), in press, Phoenix, AZ: Zeig, Tucker & Co. Adapted with permission.

1995g), it is important to end sessions and a course of therapy well. Done skillfully, we increase the likelihood that, while the therapy may be brief, the benefit may be long term.[1]

Termination simply means "extracting the therapist from the equation of the successful relationship" (Gustafson, 1986, p. 279). In effect, we ask and attempt to answer the question, session by session and therapy by therapy: "You have done well with me; how will you continue to do well without me?" My intention here is to provide a number of perspectives, drawing from both my personal experience and the literature, that address issues of *why* and *how* to say *"when."*

☐ Why Stop?

Knowing that therapy will stop provides structure and direction. It focuses the mind. It shows respect for the client's autonomy and competence (and his or her checkbook), and conveys the existential implication to "get on with it"—that therapy, like life, does not involve an endless proliferation of time (Goldberg, 1975; Hoyt, 1990/1995g).[2]

As Nick Cummings put it, our contract with clients should be that we will be available as long as they truly need us, and their contract should be to make us obsolete as soon as possible (N. A. Cummings & Sayama, 1995). Therapy can be brief by *design* or by *default* (Budman & Gurman, 1988, pp. 6–9); this also is what Bloom (1992, p. 3) meant by *planned:* "treatment that is intended to accomplish a set of therapeutic objectives within a sharply limited time frame." Unless it is forever, it will end—the pertinent questions then become *when?* and *how?*[3] Talking ourselves out of a job should be our intention.

At times, clients can become "prisoners of psychotherapy" (Minsky, 1987), especially if the therapist is adept at theory-driven one-upmanship (see Haley, 1969; Duncan, Hubble, & Miller, 1997a) and insistently views the client's attempts to terminate a nonproductive treatment as "premature" (see Hoyt, 1993, 1994c). Therapists may have a number of "resistances" toward "brief" therapy with its ever-present implication of ending, including the belief that "more is better," the confusion of therapists' interests with clients' interests, the temptation to hold on to that which is profitable and dependable, the need to be needed and difficulties saying goodbye, resentment of externally imposed limits, and the avoidance of the paperwork involved in closing cases and having to open new ones (Hoyt, 1985/1995f, 1987). With apologies to Paul Simon (1975), we might sing (or hum, for the exhibitionistically challenged):

"Fifty Ways Not to Leave Your Client"

You just insist they come back, Jack,
Make a new treatment plan, Stan
Avoid the topic of ending—be coy, Roy
Tell them they're not ready, Freddie
If they try to cancel, make a big fuss, Gus
They still need to discuss much
Before they can leave, Steve
("How could you do this to me?")
And don't forget your fee, Lee

However, while we want to avoid fostering needless dependency, the goal is not just to be "brief" or "quick." Some clients need and will benefit from more extended or longer-term approaches, and many of the skills of brief therapy may be applicable (e.g., see Duncan et al., 1997b; Kreider, 1998; O'Hanlon, 1990; Rowen & O'Hanlon, 1999; Yapko, 1990). Indeed, it may be more accurate, following Budman and Gurman (1988) and Friedman (1997), to use the terms "time-sensitive" or "time-effective" rather than "brief." Therapy should not be "long" or "short." It should be sufficient, adequate, and appropriate: "measured not by its brevity or length, but whether it is efficient and effective in aiding people with their complaints or whether it wastes time" (Fisch, 1982, p. 156). Effectiveness "depends far less on the hours you put in than on what you put into those hours" (Lazarus, 1997b, p. 6). The approach is characterized more by an attitude than a particular length: "as few sessions as possible, not even one more than is necessary" is the way Steve de Shazer (1991b, p. x) puts it. By its very nature, in brief therapy the issue of termination is always present. We need to "seize the moment" and "be here now." Time is of the essence. When we are thinking *brief*, "termination is our frame" (Goldfield, 1998, p. 243).[4]

I should note that while I use the term for continuity with the literature, I find the very word *termination* somewhat troubling. Derived from the Latin *terminus*, meaning "an end, limit, or final goal," it seems so heavy and ominous, conjuring images of Arnold Schwarznegger in *The Terminator* or, more darkly, of Final Solutions. We sometimes say that we are going to "terminate a case" or, even worse, "terminate a patient." What a different prospect, how more encouraging and respectful, if we speak of the ending phase as *completion* or *graduation* or *achievement*, or even simply as *stopping meeting*.[5]

The answer to *Why Stop?* also involves the issue of how best to use limited community resources, which one colleague, Carol Austad (1996b), highlighted in the provocative title of her book *Is Long-Term Psychotherapy Unethical? Toward a Social Ethic in an Era of Managed Care*. While the terms *brief therapy* and *managed care* need to be kept clearly distinct, I am in agreement with the need for greater efficacy and accountability (see Hoyt, 1995a; Chapters 4 and 5, this volume).[6] We need to be especially careful not to become overly enamored with the God of Efficiency, however— one only need read the section on devotion to efficiency in James Hillman's (1995, pp. 33–44) *Kinds of Power: A Guide to Its Intelligent Uses* to see where blind obedience to the calculated bottom line can take us.

☐ Literature Round-Up

I'd like here to highlight a few of the authors whose writings have contributed to my understanding of the process we call *termination*:

Sigmund Freud, known as the father of psychoanalysis, can in some ways also be thought of as a progenitor of brief therapy. His early cases (Breuer & Freud, 1893–95) ranged from a single session to several sessions to a few months, and his early techniques involved the frequent use of hypnosis, suggestion, directives, guidance, reassurance, and education—as well as interpretation (see Freud, 1910/1957, p. 111). Near the end of his career, he described analysis as "interminable" (Freud, 1937/1964). In his famous case of the "Wolf Man," Freud (1918/1953b) introduced the idea of setting a termination date, a time past which doctor-patient contacts would not continue, as a way of both stimulating the patient's work and of extricating himself from what seemed to be an interminable therapeutic quagmire—a technique which Freud (1937/1964b, p. 218) described as a "blackmailing device" likely, but without guarantee, "to be effective provided that one hits the right time for it."[7]

Franz Alexander and Thomas French, in their 1946 book *Psychoanalytic Therapy: Principles and Application*, described many groundbreaking innovations including varying the therapist's demeanor with different types of patients to help generate what they termed "corrective emotional experiences," the application of a learning model and a call for new theoretical perspectives, alterations in the frequency of sessions and the use of interruptions in treatment to prepare for termination, and the limiting of therapy to deliberately brief contacts in selected cases. In Alexander's last significant paper, published in 1965, he reviewed these developments and commented (pp. 90–91):

> Very long treatments lasting over many years do not seem to be the most successful ones. On the other hand, many so-called "transference cures" [see Oremland, 1972] after very brief contact have been observed to be lasting. . . . If one starts out treatment by saying to the patient that one can forget about time—that is the wrong emphasis. You encourage procrastination by this. Instead, one should say that we wish to complete treatment

as fast as possible. Of course, we are not magicians, but our intention is to make therapy as brief as we can. It may last longer than we hope, but at least we make an attempt at shortening treatment.

Lewis Wolberg (1965, p. 140), in *Short-Term Psychotherapy*, the first book published in America on the subject (almost four decades ago), recommended:

The best strategy, in my opinion, is to assume that every patient, irrespective of diagnosis, will respond to short-term treatment unless he proves himself refractory to it. If the therapist approaches each patient with the idea of doing as much as he can for him . . . he will give the patient an opportunity to take advantage of short-term treatment to the limit of his potential. If this fails, he can always then resort to prolonged therapy.[8]

James Mann (1973, p. 36), writing from an existential-analytic perspective in his book *Time-Limited Psychotherapy*:

It is absolutely incumbent upon the therapist to deal directly with the reaction to termination in all its painful aspects and affects if he expects to help the patient come to some vividly effective understanding of the now inappropriate nature of his early unconscious conflict. . . . Since anger, rage, guilt, and their accompaniments of frustration and fear are the potent factors that prevent positive internalization [of the therapist] and mature separation, it is these that must not be overlooked in this phase of the time-limited therapy.

Carl Whitaker, whose family therapy approach is sometimes called symbolic-experiential, emphasized the power of the moment. In his paper at the First Evolution of Psychotherapy Conference, he said (1987, p. 81):

It is important to maintain the therapist's conviction that each appointment is both the first interview and the last interview. The first interview is, in essence, a blind date; and every subsequent interview opens the possibility of divorce or at least the separation between the family as foster child and the therapist as foster parent.

In *Midnight Musing of a Family Therapist*, Whitaker elaborated (1989b, p. 166):

The ending phase is a process in which the family's participation is subtle and critical. Their message may be, "Enough already," "Things are better," "Things are worse"; or the exposure of outside transferences with or without the stories: that is, "I almost forgot to come," "My job is going better," "My boss is a wonderful guy," "I'm falling in love with my wife." Essentially, they are saying that life is more important than psychotherapy. The distortions that can occur during the ending phase include the family members' offer of new symptoms, their denial of change, the bribe of their fear of anxiety returning, a symbolic dropout . . . , the presentation of a pseudo-symptom, a symptom in the therapist, the discovery or the presence of concealed hostility in the therapist or the family, the lack of humility in the therapist, or the pride of the therapist in being humble. When ending is successful, there evolves the arrangement for a future alliance (if needed), a discussion of the lining of the therapist's empty nest, his request for direct therapeutic help from the family members, his learning from their case and the sharing of his real-life fragments in terms of persons, his work, new cases, the money, and his inner video replay of their joint experience together. Finally, ending includes the therapist's dream of greatness and his dream of craziness, and his sharing with them of Plato's famous summary of the *Dialogues*, "Practice Dying."

Aaron Beck and his associates, in their book *Cognitive Therapy of Depression* (1979, p. 317), made their view clear:

> Because cognitive therapy is time-limited, the problems associated with termination are usually not as complex as those associated with longer forms of treatment. . . . The issue of termination should be touched on periodically throughout therapy. From the beginning the therapist stresses to the patient that he will *not* stay in treatment indefinitely, and that he will be shown how to handle his psychological problems on his own. . . . This sets the stage for the patient's becoming his own therapist.

Mary and Bob Goulding (1979), in their book *Changing Lives Through Redecision Therapy,* highlight the importance of establishing a good change contract at the beginning of treatment (and sessions), often asking: "What are you willing to change today?" Discussing termination, the Gouldings (1979, pp. 280–281) expressed their views as follows:

> Redecision is a beginning rather than an ending. After redecision, the person begins to think, feel and behave in new ways. At this point he may decide to terminate therapy. We applaud this choice. Our philosophy of treatment is that therapy should be as condensed and quick as possible and that termination is a triumph, like graduation. . . . Whatever the treatment format, we believe that the client should be encouraged to terminate when he has made the personal changes he wants to make, and should be welcomed back if he encounters difficulties he doesn't know how to solve on his own. This minimizes dependency and transference problems.

Jay Haley (1977, p. 9), in his book *Problem-Solving Therapy*, came right to the point:

> If therapy is to end properly, it must begin properly—by negotiating a solvable problem and discovering the social situation that makes the problem necessary.

Milton H. Erickson (1980a, volume 4, p. 190) also emphasized the strategic importance of defining achievable goals:

> Long experience in psychotherapy has disclosed the wisdom of avoiding perfectionistic drives and wishes on the part of patients and of motivating

them for the comfortable achievement of lesser goals. This then ensures not only the lesser goal but makes more possible the easy output of effort that can lead to a greater goal. Of even more importance is that the greater accomplishment then becomes more satisfyingly the patient's own rather than a matter of obedience to the therapist.

Richard Fisch, John Weakland, and Lynn Segal (1982, pp. 176–177), chief proponents (along with Paul Watzlawick) of the Mental Research Institute (MRI) strategic-interactional approach, put their termination criteria like this in their book, *The Tactics of Change*:

The therapist wishing to work briefly . . . will be keeping the original complaint and the goal of treatment in mind, and will be looking for the attainment of that goal and for some expression by the client that his complaint has been resolved. The suggestion for terminating will most often be made by the therapist, usually with the expectation that the client will agree. Obviously, the client can also initiate termination for various reasons. Preferably, the client may propose that his problem has been resolved, and, in that case, the therapist is likely to agree to termination. But the converse can occur, the client expressing significant dissatisfaction with treatment and announcing that he is discontinuing the therapy. Or contingencies can arise that prevent the continuation of treatment: the client may have a job change that requires moving from the area, or financial problems may preclude further private therapy. Finally, time-limited treatment will automatically terminate when the agreed-upon number of sessions have run their course, although here the therapist will usually be the one to remind the client that such is the case.

Steve de Shazer (1985, 1988), the prime developer of solution-focused therapy, has also emphasized the importance of establishing clear (relevant, measurable, difficult but achievable) goals at the outset of therapy. In his elegantly minimalistic way, he might ask the client, "How will we know when we can stop meeting like this?"

Insoo Kim Berg, de Shazer's solution-focused collaborator, has elaborated some criteria and methods for termination, including goal achievement, designating a limited number of sessions, no movement in a case, and leaving things open-ended in response to outside restrictions. In her book, *Family Based Services*, Berg wrote (1994b, p. 163):

Life is full of problems to be solved and your clients are no different from anyone else. If you wait until *all* the client's problems are solved, you will never end treatment. . . . What is important to keep in mind is that "empowering" clients means equipping them with the tools to solve their own problems as far as possible. When they can't do it on their own, they need to know when to ask for help and where to go for help. Termination can occur when you are confident that the client will know when and where to go to seek help, and *not* when you are confident that he will never have problems.

Michael White, the coauthor of *Narrative Means to Therapeutic Ends* (White & Epston, 1990; see also Epston & White, 1990/1992a, 1995a), responded like this (1995a, p. 20) when an interviewer asked him, "How do you define the point where therapy is finished?":

> The therapist becomes increasingly decentralised in the whole process, and eventually s/he is discharged from the therapy. The discharge of the therapist generally doesn't take long to happen, and it is rarely much of a surprise when it does happen. Although the therapist has played a very significant part . . . s/he has also worked to ensure that those persons who seek help are the privileged co-authors in this collaboration. So, as persons go some way in the articulation and the experience of other ways of being and thinking that are available to them, as they experience some of the purposes, values, beliefs, commitments, and so on, that are associated with these alternative accounts of life, they approach a point at which the therapist's contribution is unnecessary. It makes perfect sense to discharge the therapist at this point, and this can be celebrated.

☐ But Not Too Fast

While time is of the essence in brief therapy, we have to be mindful—especially with managed care providing a strong push for rapid turnover—that the quest for efficient goal attainment does not become a juggernaut toward termination. "Making the most of each session" may involve a pleasant urgency, but should not feel frantic or pell-mell. Too fast is too fast. Clients need adequate time to get involved, to get their bearings and set their direction. As James Broughton (1990, p. 212) wrote at the beginning of his poem, "Ways of Getting There":

> What makes you think
> you know your way around?
> You add the mileage
> but subtract the scenery.

There is a vital dialectic, a tension between opening and closing, between discovery and direction. While it is true, as they say in golf, that "If you don't know where the hole is, it's a long day on the course" (see Chapter 2, this volume), it is also true that too narrow a focus cuts us off from creativity and flexibility, from the unpredictable and fortuitous, from the serendipitous events that often occur within the therapeutic relationship. As narrative therapist Michael White has said (quoted in Hoyt & Combs, 1996, p. 41):

> There is a certain pleasure or joy available to us in the knowledge that we can't know where we'll be at the end; in the sense that we can't know

beforehand what we will be thinking at the end; in the idea that we can't know what new possibilities for action in the world might be available to us at that time. . . . If I knew where we would be at the end of the session, I don't think I would do this work.

Brief therapists want to "get right to it" and expect to "terminate" as soon as they do, but they should not be in such a rush as to miss the point of Broughton's closing poetic admonition:

> Why not for once
> wander off a path
> without caring how
> long it takes?
> You might bump into
> Time's older brother
> the one who never needs
> to go anywhere.

☐ The Structure of Brief Therapy: With a Focus on Ending Phases

In other publications (e.g., Hoyt, 1990/1995g; Chapter 14, this volume), I have suggested that therapy (and sessions) can be conceptualized to have a structure of sequenced (epigenetic or pyramidal) phases, involving different tasks and skills, as shown schematically in Figure 15.1. (The structure of therapy and session are selfsame when treatment comprises a single meeting.) Change may begin before the first meeting and, especially with skillful facilitation during the termination phases, may continue past the formal ending of treatment.

Let's take a closer look, as seen in Figure 15.2, at some of the activities that may be involved in the ending phases of treatment (and sessions).

In the *Late* phase of a course of therapy (and at the close of each session) there are a number of activities of which to attend:

- *initiation of ending,* shifting the discussion toward finishing, often with an explicit question such as "Is there anything else that we should discuss today before talking about ending?"

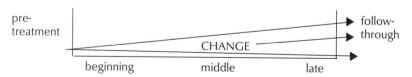

FIGURE 15.1. The structure of brief therapy (and each session).

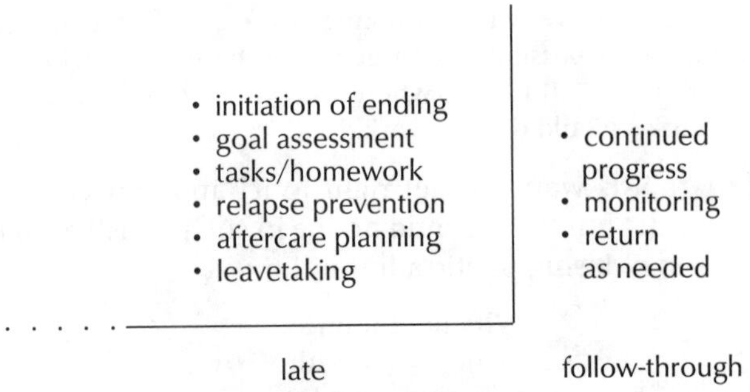

```
              • initiation of ending
              • goal assessment          • continued
              • tasks/homework             progress
              • relapse prevention       • monitoring
              • aftercare planning       • return
              • leavetaking                as needed

 . . . . .  ─────────────────────────┘

                   late                follow-through
```

FIGURE 15.2. The ending (termination) phases of treatment (and sessions): Subtracting the therapist from the successful equation.

- *goal assessment,* the determination with the client of how well the purposes of therapy have been achieved, what may remain to be accomplished during therapist-client meetings, and what does not appear to be achievable within the treatment context.[9] Attention should be directed to helping clients develop an understanding ("empowerment") that emphasizes their role in the attainment of treatment goals (see Eron & Lund, 1998, p. 394). Metadiscussion, reviewing and talking about it, may further enhance the egalitarian therapeutic relationship, "demystifying" treatment and depotentiating therapist-client transference dynamics (see Connell, Mitten, & Bumberry, 1999, pp. 141–153; Coleman et al., 1998; Quintana, 1993; Whitaker & Malone, 1953, pp. 212–214);
- *tasks/homework,* the frequent direction, recommendation or suggestion of activities for the client to carry out after the session (or therapy)—a hallmark of most forms of brief therapy (see Budman et al., 1992);
- *goal maintenance and relapse prevention,* the construction of mnemonics ("anchors") that will help clients recall and "encore" (see Goulding, in Hoyt, 1995b) therapeutic gains; as well as contingency planning to avoid possible return of the presenting problem, sometimes including discussions about the temptations of "self-sabotage" and inoculating predictions of difficult challenges, with the framing of possible "slips" as opportunities to apply therapeutic lessons;
- *aftercare planning,* including discussions of life posttherapy and indications for possible return to treatment;
- *leavetaking,* well-wishing and saying "goodbye," including acknowledgment and validation of feelings (client's and clinician's) about ending. As Karl Lewin (1970, pp. 224–226) wrote: "Before the interviews can be discontinued, the relationship which the patient has made with the

doctor must be resolved. . . . If the patient wants to keep anything of the doctor, he must learn to introject him, to take him inside, to convert him from an external object into a part of himself." This also is what Milton Erickson (quoted in Zeig, 1980, frontispiece) seems to have had in mind when he said, "And my voice goes everywhere with you, and changes into the voice of your parents, your teachers, your playmates and the voices of the wind and of the rain."

In the *Follow-Through* phase of a course of therapy (and after the close of each session), there are a number of activities of which to attend:

- *continued progress*, realization of the encouraging message (and possible "seeding"—see Haley, 1973, p. 34; Zeig, 1990) that growth will continue past the formal ending date—indeed, that application of some of the lessons of therapy can occur only after the end of therapist-client meetings;
- *monitoring*, continued evaluation by the client regarding the status of success, coping, and possible setbacks. The therapist (or agency or case manager) may also elicit feedback via client satisfaction and outcomes assessment questionnaires or phone calls—contacts that ethically should be prearranged with the client's consent;
- *return as needed*, the door being open if the client desires to return for the same or another problem—sometimes knowing that help will be available if truly needed helps clients weather some challenges without additional therapy and thus further appreciate their own strengths and coping abilities.

As Poynter (1998, pp. 132-133) nicely summarized it:

Both the clinical and the procedural tasks involved in the termination phase are critical. Procedurally, this is the major milestone for measurement of effectiveness (though measurements are taken at different points), initiation of aftercare plans, composition of data for statistical analysis, and coordination of care arrangements if the client will be continuing in medication management. Clinically, the closure process involves elucidating integration of the changes, framing unfinished issues, and clarifying relapse prevention. The part of the clinical closure process that involves integrating intrapsychic changes that have occurred in treatment is the overriding task of the termination phase, and therefore it should be pursued as a simultaneous consideration during the process of accomplishing all of the other tasks. Termination can sometimes also produce other benefits.

Again, as Poytner (1998, p. 132–133) observed:

[Although focused] on remediation to previous levels of functioning, the process of accomplishing this invariably generates many other—usually desirable—changes as well. During the change process new understand-

ings are often developed, new and enhanced coping mechanisms are usually generated, interpersonal roles and boundaries may be reorganized,
dysfunctional patterns are frequently broken, and better defenses and coping mechanisms emerge. Especially when therapy is brief, this leaves many
loose ends. My experience is that clients usually continue to undergo intrapsychic reorganization after formal counseling has concluded, and that
reorganization can produce substantial additional growth.[10]

It is important to distinguish life goals from therapy goals (see Ticho,
1972), and to recognize that often we simply need to meet with clients
until they are "unstuck" and back "on track" (O'Hanlon & Wilk, 1987,
pp. 178–179; Walter & Peller, 1994) rather than waiting for everything to
be settled. Sometimes a process will be set in motion or amplified, but not
completely resolved, during a session or course of treatment—both the
therapist and the patient may need to live with a certain amount of sus-
pense.[11] The Milan Family Therapy Group (Selvini Palazzoli, 1980; Selvini
Palazzoli, Boscolo, Cecchin, & Prata, 1978) make a similar point. As Boscolo
and Bertrando wrote in their book, *The Times of Time* (1993, p. 195):

> We often terminate therapy or consultation when the therapist or team see
> highly significant change in clients: more fluent communication and infor-
> mation flow, greater ability to "see" different solutions to the same prob-
> lem, an improvement in emotional atmosphere, and above all, a new abil-
> ity to resolve conflicts. The problems and symptoms that were brought in
> for therapy may still partly be present, but the assumptions that would
> ensure their continuation are beginning to crumble. In short, when we see
> what we, in our jargon, call an "about-turn in the system," we tell our
> clients that our work is done.

It is especially important to leave the door open for possible return. As
my Kaiser colleague, Bob Rosenbaum, wrote (in Rosenbaum, Hoyt, &
Talmon, 1990/1995, pp. 184–185):

> In terminating the session, the . . . therapist may help a client remember to
> remember, forget to remember, remember to forget, or forget to
> remember. . . . The degree of closure appropriate to a termination covers a
> wide range and is influenced by the extent to which the therapy was seek-
> ing resolution of some issue or attempting to open up new possibilities. . . .
> Some clients will need to put the therapist behind them and get on with
> their lives; others will need to recall the therapist or some words of the
> therapist with a high degree of vividness. Because some . . . clients will in
> the future seek further therapy, it is important to structure the termination
> in such a way that a decision for more treatment will be seen by the patient
> as an opportunity for further growth, rather than an indicator of failure.
> Whether the termination turns out to be for just a few weeks or forever,
> though, it still involves saying goodbye to the client, and all goodbyes have
> some degree of both grief and healing, sorrow and hope.

☐ Termination: Tips, Tales, and Twists

Parting is such sweet sorrow.
—William Shakespeare, *Romeo and Juliet* (Act II, Scene 2, line 185)

Termination is not always a big issue—at least not for clients! Oftentimes, the ending goes well and smoothly. We and the client co-create achievable goals; techniques are specific, integrated, and as eclectic as needed; treatment is focused, the therapist appropriately active, and the client responsible for making changes; each session is valuable; therapy ends as soon as possible; and the client carries on, and can return to treatment as needed.

I often find it helpful at the end of sessions:

- to stop a bit earlier than the allotted 50 minutes if we have reached a good point—a "solution" or "victory"—rather than trying to fill the time and risking getting back into "problem talk" without sufficient opportunity to achieve success and finish on a positive note (see Friedman, 1997, p. 228; Goulding & Goulding, 1979);
- to signal that the session is coming to a close by a change in my posture, by ritualistically fiddling with my computer or appointment book, and by future-paced phrases such as "Before we stop in a couple of minutes, when I'll walk you back to the waiting room, let's discuss what's next . . . "
- to ask "Would you like to make another appointment now, or wait and see how things go and call me as needed?"
- to make only one appointment at a time, the implication being that each session is valuable in itself and that we may not need more than one (see Ecker & Hulley, 1996, p. 136);[12]
- to ask clients when they would like to have their next appointment, framing the question within a range that seems appropriate (e.g., "Would you like to make our next appointment for about 3 weeks, or 6 weeks, or wait a bit longer?")[13]
- alternatively, to suggest to clients that they practice whatever activities or tasks we have discussed, and that they wait until they have completed their "homework" before calling me for the next appointment (leaving the door open, of course, that they also can call if some problem or emergency arises);
- to taper the frequency of sessions (see Boegner & Zielenbach-Coenen, 1984), emphasize the idea of intermittent treatment and an "open door," and consider continuous but not intensive meetings as some possible "termination" strategies for efficiently working with clients who may require on-going or extended contact. Getting the job done, appropriate care, is paramount. Remember: *brief* does not always mean quick;

• to keep in mind, as we walk to the door and down the hallway, that every word counts—one patient (see Hoyt & Farrell, 1983–1984) reported that my casual farewell "Hey, man, take care of yourself" had enormous positive meaning to him.

We can expect the termination phase to carry more significance and to be potentially more complicated when there has been an extended therapeutic relationship ("The bigger the Hello, the bigger the Goodbye"), when an impasse has been reached in which significant problems continue without resolution, and when the ending stirs up other issues of loss—for client, therapist, or both. Numerous voices—from the Buddha's "Discourse on the Four Noble Truths" to Freud's (1916) essay, "On Transience," to Cat Stevens' (1973) sweet song, "Oh Very Young"—have given eloquent expression to the human desire for attachment and our reluctance to let go and say goodbye.

Even if we know it will someday end, the work together may make the goodbye harder still. There may be an arousal of dependency and underlying separation-individuation issues, with possible recrudesence of presenting symptomatology.[14] There may be countertransference pulls to avoid ending, to "rescue" the client, to cram "extra" work into the last session or two; alternatively, the last session may be particularly "flat" as participants prematurely detach to avoid a genuine ending. Do client and therapist seek "timelessness" (open-ended or long-term treatment) to avoid change and maintain dependency? Do client and therapist seek an "instant cure" to avoid contact and vulnerability? Is time "squeezed" or "squandered"? Does change occur? How does the client respond to the impending termination of treatment? How does the therapist respond?

Please allow me to relate a few brief clinical vignettes to enliven some of the preceding, to provide some nuance and implication, and to prepare for us to terminate. Some are instances when things went fairly straightforward; others are termination tales with a twist. My structure here is thematically architectonic; my purpose illustrative and pragmatic.

Case 1

A couple sought assistance because of some waning of affection as well as "communication problems" and some specific conflicts regarding housework. In three sessions, we identified their preferences, largely through use of the well-known "Miracle Question" (de Shazer, 1985, 1988) and detailed inquiry into times ("exceptions") when their "presenting problems" had not been present; practiced some more agreeable means of communicating and resolving conflicts; and secured a commitment from both partners to engage in several preferred activities over the next month.

We then scheduled a brief telephone follow-up contact—at which time the couple reported they were doing better, their affection had "rekindled," and that they did not feel they needed to make another appointment. They agreed to call back on an as-needed basis.

Case 2

I met Mr. DeSoto with his adult daughter, and then met with him every 6–8 weeks for almost 2 years. He grieved and mourned the death of his wife, relocated his residence, and maintained and eventually extended various social connections, including some recreational and service associations as well as a new romance. Things were going quite well and I was looking forward to our next appointment. That day, I found a receptionist's phone message in my box that read simply: "Mr. DeSoto cancelled. No need for future appointment." My first thought was, *"How can he do this to me?"* I was quite hurt—he hadn't seemed at all like an "ingrate"—and he wasn't. I phoned him and we had a pleasant chat. As he thanked me for my help, I realized that our meetings perhaps had become more important for me than for him—my theory-driven idea that he had ducked "termination" to avoid reminders of losing his wife gave way to my realization that I had been "in denial" about my impending "obsolescence."

Case 3

Sam was a 67-year-old man when I first met him as he was sitting in a wheelchair next to his wife in the waiting room of the HMO Psychiatry Department. As I described in my 1995 book, *Brief Therapy and Managed Care* (1995a, pp. 320–323), we had an intensive single-session encounter that resulted in his using his abilities to overcome his fear of falling and to get on with living in a manner he found more satisfying.

This was not the end of the story, of course. Consistent with the HMO therapy principle of intermittent treatment throughout the life cycle (M. J. Bennett, 1983, 1984; N. A. Cummings, 1990; N. A. Cummings & Sayama, 1995; Hoyt, 1990/1995g), I met with Sam on several subsequent occasions—when he felt discouraged, when health problems put him in the medical hospital, when his physical condition required him to make the adjustment to life in a nursing home. I also had various encounters with his wife, who would leave me long, rambling phone messages to keep me in the loop. She let me know when Sam's illnesses reached end-stage and he was getting ready to die, and she put Sam's son on the phone for us to have a talk—I was able to answer some questions, make sure the wife and son were okay, convey something of my appreciation for Sam and let the son know how warmly his father had spoken of him. I also requested that they remember me to Sam, and let them know to call if I could be of assistance. The other day, I received a message from Sam's wife that Sam was dead. I called her and wrote a condolence letter. I expect that our brief (family) therapy will continue.

Case 4

Mary was a bright, attractive young woman who had been deeply wounded by her parents' divorce. A person of strong religious conviction and herself a committed partner and parent, her father's affair, some conflicts with her own husband, and a series of panic attacks had torn the fabric of her worldview.

Our meetings sometimes were like intense *dharma* discussions, a mutually respectful struggle to construct a meaningful and workable worldview. I liked her considerably. Her intelligence and spunk, her incisive verbal manner, and her Scriptural knowledge and spiritual passion all were challenges that required me to stretch and learn a great deal. In leavetaking, she told me that she had been dubious about coming to therapy, expecting to be judged rather than accepted, and that she felt that she had been both "blessed" and "lucky" that Fortune and the Lord had brought us together. I told her genuinely that I had felt "lucky" and "blessed," too.

A few months later, her husband called and requested an appointment to see me. He was late for the session, which he claimed was to get help for his own "Type A" compulsiveness. He scheduled a second appointment, but left the waiting room before being seen. When I called him, he reported that he had been feeling ill with the flu, and that he would recontact me when his schedule permitted. I haven't heard from him yet.

Many more months went by, almost a year, and then Mary called. We met, mostly as a "follow-up." She reported that things were going okay, told me about her kids and job at the church, and that she and her husband were working out their problems with some counsel from an older couple they knew. She made a second appointment for 2 weeks later, and kept it—but said that she did not really know why she had made the appointment, that "I guess I just wanted to see you and touch bases." We chatted, and wished each other well—and I left the door open.[15]

Case 5

When you have done what you can do, it is time to stop. It can be a bit awkward, especially if you are heavily invested in being helpful and the client does not seem to be satisfied. In such instances, most clients won't want to stick around anyway. In this situation, however, despite a lack of continuing therapeutic movement, the woman would not take "No" for an answer. She continued to request appointments, during which she "Yes, butted" and "No, butted" and I tried harder and harder (using "Go slow" injunctions, looking for new goals, reframing, externalizing, seeking her theory of change, confronting and interpreting, making a "one down" declaration of my impotence, and so forth), all to no avail. Finally, I decided to heed Grove and Haley's (1993, pp. 64–65; see also Goffman, 1952) strategic advice:

> **Haley:** *He could tell her something that isn't appropriate, or that won't help her.*
> **Grove:** *So that he doesn't have to feel like he's rejecting her. She'll reject him, instead of him rejecting her.*
> **Haley:** *Right. Tell him it's important that she disengage from him, rather than having him disengage from her.*

I also was fortified by rereading the recommendation made by Whitaker and Malone long ago (1953, pp. 215–216):

> Where termination of the relationship has resisted all other technical approaches, the therapy may be administratively ended by the therapist with the flat statement to the patient that he will not see the patient after a specific number of further interviews have ensued. Since the administrative ending occurs thus only after the process of therapy has been completed . . . [such an] ending is a declaration of faith in the patient and a statement of the limitations of the therapist's capacity.[16]

I stopped trying so damn hard. After a couple more sessions, I was about to announce that I would meet with her only another time or two, when she beat me to it. She said therapy had been of some help in relieving her sense of torpor and unhappiness, but she was ready to move on and did not wish to make another appointment.

Case 6

It usually is best when therapy meetings stop by mutual agreement. Sometimes, however, a client leaves abruptly or does not keep an appointment. While we should not immediately assume there has been a "treatment failure," such an unplanned termination at least suggests that we have missed a clue or that something has changed in the client's status since we met last and scheduled the (not-kept) appointment.[17] In such instances, we may call or send a letter, for reasons of clinical treatment, to fill our schedule, and for medical-legal coverage if the client may be at serious adverse risk.

An interesting method of writing a post-scriptum letter to repair a badly ended therapy was described by Omer (1991, pp. 484–486):[18]

> The therapist's significance for clients does not stop when sessions cease. The therapist stays in their memory, fueling anger, disappointment, and feelings of rejection. Changing their perception of the therapist's attitude and behavior, even after therapy has been formally discontinued, is therefore bound to have repercussions. The post-therapy letter . . . aims at changing the client's perception of the therapist so as to counter the ill effects of the negative ending, to provide an opening for renewed contact (by client or therapist), and, hopefully, to serve as a therapeutic intervention in itself. . . . The letter gives the therapist a good reason for calling the client or family some weeks or months later and asking them how they feel about it and how they are doing in general.

In one instance, attending to the many specific guidelines and cautions that Omer provides, I wrote the following to a client whom I had offended by suggesting that his workplace difficulties were due to his being "overly rigid" in his responses to his supervisor and coworkers:

> Dear Fred,
>
> I have been giving a lot of thought to what we discussed at our last meeting and I have reached the conclusion that I misunderstood what you said and your motivations. I now see things differently, appreciating how important honesty is to you. Being true to yourself is vital, and my mistake was to suggest that you should do anything that would compromise your integrity. It will be interesting to learn how you maintain this vital interest while dealing with such an imperfect world. I would be glad to have an honest discussion about these challenges with you.
>
> —Dr. H.

I waited a month, then telephoned the client. He was surprised that I had reached out, and agreed to another appointment. We met several more times. He later thanked me for seeing things from his side and for being helpful, and remarked that he had decided to reconsider his ideas when I had been willing to reconsider mine.

Case 7

A woman, now 92 years of age, became my patient because of what her internist described as "mild depression." A long-retired schoolteacher, she maintained various cultural and family interests and an extraordinary ability to experience the joy of life despite some flagging energies and nagging forgetfulness. An avid reader and music lover, her memory lapses increasingly frustrated her. During one meeting, she lamented how much she had lost, how "dumb" she felt not to have names and ideas easily at her fingertips. As she gently berated herself as "mixed up" and "getting an empty head," I fished around on my desk, found a page I had copied, and read to her:

> This is thy hour O Soul,
> Thy free flight into the wordless,
> Away from books, away from art,
> The day erased, the lesson done,
> Thee fully forth emerging, silent, gazing,
> Pondering the themes thou lovest best:
> Night, sleep, death and the stars.
> —Walt Whitman ("A Clear Midnight," 1891–1992/1940b, p. 596)

She looked at me, paused, and then recited from memory:

> Grow old along with me!
> The best is yet to be,
> The last of life, for which the first was made:
> Our times are in His hand
> Who saith "A whole I planned,
> Youth shows but half; trust God: see all nor be afraid!"
> —Robert Browning ("Rabbi Ben Ezra," first stanza,
>   1864/1997, p. 304)[19]

We continue to meet periodically.

Case 8

A 42-year-old woman, a physician's assistant with a personal and family history of depression, came to the Psychiatry Department. A one-session intake interview determined that, on two previous occasions, she had responded well to treatment with antidepressant medications. Three years prior she had taken the medicine for about a year, and a year prior she had resumed it for about a month. In both instances, she had unilaterally discontinued it, however, despite marked benefit and an absence of side effects, because she felt that, as a strong woman, she "should" be able to handle problems without pills. She again was depressed, irritable, and sleeping poorly.

Discussion revealed that she was highly competent and that she had achieved a great deal of success (career, family, friends, travel, and so forth) even though she had come from a very rough beginning. I asked how she had done so well—she identified a grandmother who had cared for her and taught her to set goals and assume responsibility, plus her own intelligence and an academic flair, and good fortune. She quickly figured out that her otherwise useful drive toward self-sufficiency kept her, inappropriately, from allowing herself to benefit from medication.

"Meds" did not obviate her responsibility nor take away from her success; indeed, they could support her achievements. This "reframing" helped her accept and continue to benefit from referral to a prescribing psychiatrist. It was all the psychotherapy she needed.[20]

Case 9

Were it not for the twinkle in his eye, one might mistake Mr. Burton for an unreconstructed cantankerous curmudgeon. Himself now elderly, irritable, and in pain, he was the no-nonsense son of a Texas sherriff. Failing health (emphysema, congestive heart failure, some small strokes) had landed him in a nursing facility, where he suffered not lightly the stupidities and incompetencies of the semiattentive staff. We joined through some salty "man-to-man" banter, certain shared intolerances, plus my appreciation of his stylish hats and many fascinating life experiences and his appreciation of my practical suggestions regarding how to better manage the nursing staff. His long-time companion, Judy (who he had met and courted 25 years earlier in San Francisco) was his partner in life. She was considerably younger than Mr. Burton. Every night after work she went to the nursing home, where they had dinner together and visited. She brought him to our sessions and joined us.

Mr. Burton's condition progressively weakened over time. His pain became worse, his boredom increased, his breathing became more difficult, and he and Judy were enjoying their nightly visits less and less. He was hesitant to attend another therapy session. We did some work on pain reduction, including both hypnotherapy and a call to his physician to adjust medications. Utilizing his interest in the Old West, I suggested they get a VCR so that they could watch movies together in his room. We discussed his favorite actors and films. Mr. Burton made an allusion to the great film *Shane*—when I caught the reference and answered in kind, he decided to come back to see me again.

Finally, he declared that he did not think he was coming back, saying "There's nothing more you can do for me, Doc." Judy did not look pleased—she knew they were in the ebb tide and that the end was not too far. "Well, you're right, Mr. Burton, I'm not sure what else I may be able to do. And, of course, you're the Boss—you do have the right to fire me whenever you want. But instead of getting rid of me, why not just put me on 'pause' and keep me handy?" Judy brought up that they had been enjoying watching videos together. We talked westerns for a bit, and then she mentioned that they had gone to the theater to see *Titanic*. Mr. Burton had been sleeping more lately, but he had managed to stay awake pretty much throughout the long film. We talked about it. When Judy asked what I had liked, I went on about the scene near the beginning, when the young man so cleverly talks the depressed woman off the ship rail. "How about you?" I finally asked. She liked that scene, and others, but she said what had really moved her was the ending, when the woman (now much older) climbed back on to the rail and threw the long-treasured jewel overboard. But, Judy added, she did not like seeing it sink.

"Yeah," I replied, "but the movie didn't end there. Remember what the woman did then?"

"She went back to bed."

"Right. And do you remember her room?"

Judy thought a minute. "She had all those photos around her bed, the pictures of all the things she had done, things that she and Jack [the movie's protagonist] *had planned to do together."*

"Right. There were pictures of her good memories, of her in different countries, in front of a ferris wheel, in front of a small plane—"

"—and there was a picture of her riding a horse," Judy interrupted. She paused, her eyes brimming with tears, and looked at Mr. Burton . . . and he looked at me and nodded approvingly.

☐ Enough (for Now): Until We Meet Again

> The temple bell stops.
> But the sound keeps coming
> out of the flowers.
> —Matsuo Basho, 1644–1694
> (quoted in Dodge, 1983)

When it is done well, the therapy may be brief, but the benefit may be long term. Getting the job done, finishing successfully, is what counts. In golf they say, "You drive for show, but you putt for dough" (Chapter 2, this volume). In therapy, we call it "termination," knowing *how* and *why* to say *"when."* To make treatment no longer than necessary, we have to *pay attention to ending.*

At the August 1998 "Brief Therapy: Lasting Impressions" conference where this chapter was first presented, I recalled that Milton Erickson (see S. Rosen, 1982) sometimes would say, "My voice will go with you." I also recalled that Ishi (Kroeber, 1961, p. 238), the last aboriginal survivor of California's First Nation Yana people, would say, instead of goodbye, "You stay, I'll go." In leavetaking, dear reader, allow me to thank you for your continuing attention. I leave you with this poem from Charles Bukowski (1996, p. 131), called "Defining the Magic":

a good poem is like a cold beer
when you need it,
a good poem is a hot turkey
sandwich when you're
hungry,
a good poem is a gun when
the mob corners you,
a good poem is something that
allows you to walk through the streets of
death,
a good poem can make death melt like
hot butter,
a good poem can frame agony and
hang it on a wall,
a good poem can let your feet touch
China,
a good poem can make a broken mind
fly,
a good poem can let you shake hands
with Mozart,
a good poem can let you shoot craps
with the devil
and win,
a good poem can do almost anything,
and most important
a good poem knows when to
stop.

☐ Notes

[1]As Strupp and Binder (1984, p. 259) have noted, young therapists in particular may be insufficiently aware of the critical importance of termination due to a number of reasons: it receives inadequate attention in many training programs; young therapists entering the profession may have been spared the personal experiences of separation and loss; and many therapies conducted by graduate students or residents often are not ended for clinical reasons, but because of service rotations or the end of a semester or academic year. It is not only beginning therapists, however, who may underestimate the importance of finishing well.

[2]Failure to accept endings can have far-reaching effects, as writers of various theoretical persuasions have noted (e.g., Mann, 1973; Tobin, 1976; Vorkoper, 1997). One can be left like the character eloquently described in Robert Hellenga's novel, *The Sixteen Pleasures* (1995, p. 267):

He is in the same boat, drifting down the same river, but he has turned around.
The boat is still travelling in the same direction, but instead of standing on the
bow, looking straight ahead to see where he is going, he is standing in the stern,
looking back at where he's been, and this is where he will remain for the rest of
the journey.

[3]Making explicit that therapy will end allows clients and therapists to establish realistic expectations and to pace themselves (see R. T. Sherman & Anderson, 1987), including making an informal decision about what to discuss:

> Endings do not occur just at the moment when we cease to be in an intimate partnership with someone else. . . . Obviously, the course of events may change our predictions, and thus how the story evolves. But our anticipation of the ending can shape the relationship as much as the relationship can shape the actual ending. The anticipated ending can determine in advance what kinds of plots and themes we will allow our story to develop. (Sternberg, 1998, p. 22)

[4]Writing within the context of possible single-session therapies, Rosenbaum (in Hoyt, Rosenbaum, & Talmon, 1992, p. 80) emphasizes present-centeredness: "My desire is not to see everyone for one session; my desire is to see everyone for one full moment, as long as that takes." Gary Snyder (1980, p. 109) also reminds us not to hurry past the moment:

> During the first year or two that I was at Daitoku-ji Sodo, out back working in the garden, helping put in a little firewood, or firing up the bath, I noticed a number of times little improvements that could be made. Ultimately I ventured to suggest to the head monks some labor- and time-saving techniques. They were tolerant of me for a while. Finally, one day one of them took me aside and said, "We don't want to do things any better or any faster, because that's not the point—the point is that you live the whole life. If we speed up the work in the garden, you'll just have to spend that much more time sitting in the zendo, and your legs will hurt more." It's all one meditation. The importance is in the right balance, and not how to save time in one place or another. I've turned that insight over and over ever since.

[5] Following Epston and White (1990/1992a, pp. 14–16), we can extend this deconstructive thrust to see the "termination as loss" metaphor as situated within a certain modern Western tradition that expects us to engage in "therapies of isolation" that encourage "relinquishing" and "letting go" as hallmarks of "individualism" and "mature separation." A different, "Hullo, again" approach, emphasizing a "reincorporation" metaphor and "therapies of inclusion" may be more useful and more natural in the resolution of grief (see Hoyt, 1983; White, 1988/1989c).

[6]"Managed care" is still largely a code word for "cost containment" (sometimes with attendant practices of "invisible rationing" requiring premature or inappropriate termination resulting in systematic undertreatment and possible client abandonment—I. J. Miller, 1996a, 1996b; see Chapter 4, this volume). de Shazer (quoted in Short, 1997, p. 18) has made his position clear: "We are *not* a response to managed care. We've been doing brief therapy for 30 years. We developed this a long time before managed care was even somebody's bad idea."

[7]For a report of a time that did not seem "right," see Hoyt and Farrell (1983–1984). A number of brief therapy advocates (e.g., Lipchik, 1994; Nylund & Corsiglia, 1994; O'Hanlon, 1991) have all written against the use of rigid time limits as a method of "forcing" or curtailing treatment. Others, especially those attempting to adapt psychodynamic methods to briefer time frames (e.g., Appelbaum, 1975; Hoyt, 1979/1995d, 1980; Levenson, 1995; Malan, 1976; Mann, 1973) have found such methods useful—with carefully selected patients. In this regard, Strupp and Binder (1984, pp. 265–266) wisely cautioned "that the time limits be set *after* a therapeutic focus has at least begun to be outlined by the participants, because the introduction of a focus is more likely to provide the patient with a belief that there are circumscribed goals that can be achieved in the available time."

[8]Thirty years later, the well-known psychoanalyst Michael Franz Basch (1995, p. xi) echoed this view in his last book, *Doing Brief Psychotherapy*:

During the training of the dynamic psychotherapist, the idea becomes firmly imprinted that longer is better. Experience has taught me, however, that shorter is anything but second-best. In a majority of cases, short-term treatment [which Basch defined as "concluded in no more than 20 sessions"], effectively applied, enables the patient to reach the same therapeutic goals as long-term psychotherapy, while offering the added advantage of relieving the patient's psychic stress that much sooner. Moreover, I believe that one cannot decide arbitrarily, on the basis of either symptoms or character structure, that a patient will not benefit from brief therapy. Indeed, it is my position that all patients who are not psychotic or suicidal should be thought of as candidates for brief psychotherapy until proven otherwise.

[9]When (and how) to best assess the results of a therapy is a multifaceted question that goes beyond the scope of the present discussion. It should be noted, however, that while the most common time for such assessment is at the end of the last session, brief therapists recognize that change often continues and extends beyond the last meeting and thus we will need to see what happens after the session before assessing its impact (outcome: change and durability) (Hoyt, 1995a, p. 331).

[10]The importance of highlighting for the client the possibilities for continued growth and integration after the formal end of brief treatment were well delineated by Wolberg (1965, pp. 189–191):

> The termination of short-term therapy is predicated on the principle that while immediate accomplishments may be modest (symptom relief, for example) the constant application by the patient of the lessons he has learned will probably bring further substantial changes. Deep personality alterations may require years of reconditioning which may go on outside of a formal treatment situation. . . . Where treatment is to be terminated, I find it helpful to warn the patient that, while he may feel better, there will be required of him a consistent application of what he has learned in therapy to insure a more permanent resolution of his deeper problems.

[11]As Wittgenstein said (1980, p. 77e; quoted by de Shazer in Hoyt, 1996a, p. 8l): "Anything your reader can do for himself, leave to him."

[12]As a variant (learned from observing Carl Whitaker), one also can cultivate the client's initiative and involvement by asking, at the end of a session, "Do you want to keep the appointment next week? We could cancel it if you don't want to work."

[13]See Hoyt (1990/1995g) for an extended discussion of the timing of sessions and related issues. Additional leads may be found in Kramer (1990), Pinkerton and Rockwell (1990), Quintana (1993), Shectman (1986), and Wright and Leahey (1994).

[14]According to Mann (1973), termination often will stimulate four underlying themes, which he conceptualizes as *unresolved mourning, activity versus passivity, independence versus dependence,* and *adequate versus diminished self-esteem.*

[15]I am reminded of Rosenbaum's observation (in Hoyt, Rosenbaum, & Talmon, 1992, pp. 75–76): "Perhaps we meet once, and the client thinks about it for the rest of her life. Perhaps we meet once, the client forgets me, and I think about her the rest of my life."

[16]We might also recall Kenny Rogers's (Schlitz, 1978) words in "The Gambler":

> You've got to know when to hold them
> And know when to fold them
> Know when to walk away
> And know when to run.

[17]In studying the possibilities of single-session therapy, my colleagues and I (Hoyt, 1994/ 1995k; Hoyt et al., 1992; Rosenbaum, Hoyt, & Talmon, 1990; Talmon, 1990) found by doing follow-up interviews that many times when patients cancelled, "no showed," or seemed to "disappear" after an initial session, they did so because they had gotten what they had come for in the first meeting. Their not returning for a second session was not a "premature termination" nor indication of a"treatment failure," but rather that the therapy had been useful and sufficient. It should be noted that termination after one session is the most common length of treatment, occurring in 20% to 50% of cases.

[18]This is different than the end-of-session letters used by the Milan Family Therapy Group (e.g., Selvini Palazzoli, et al., 1980) or by narrative therapists (e.g., Bracero, 1996; Epston, 1989, 1994; Nylund & Thomas, 1994; White & Epston, 1990).

[19]Thus wrote C.P. Cavafy (1911/1975, p. 32) in "The God Abandons Antony":

> When suddenly, at midnight, you hear
> an invisible procession going by
> with exquisite music, voices
>
> . . . .
>
> go firmly to the window
> and listen with deep emotion,
> but not with the whining, the pleas of a coward;
> listen—your final pleasure—to the voices,
> to the exquisite music of that strange procession,
> and say goodbye to her, to the Alexandria you are losing.

[20]From the perspective of a narrative constructivist, I think of the appropriate use of psychopharmacology to support clients' self-empowerment as *restoring restorying*. Medication may allow thinking to focus and mood to abate enough for clients to get on with the "reauthoring" and living of their lives. Respectful collaboration and informed consent ("invitation, not imposition") are paramount, of course.

REFERENCES

Abram, D. (1996). *The spell of the sensuous: Perception and language in a more-than-human world.* New York: Vintage.

Abrams, H. S. (1993). Harvard Community Health Plan's mental health redesign project: A management and clinical partnership. *Psychiatric Quarterly, 84,* 13–31.

Adams, J. F., Piercy, F. P., & Jurich, J. A. (1991). Effects of solution-focused therapy's "formula first session task" on compliance and outcome in family therapy. *Journal of Marital and Family Therapy, 17,* 277–290.

Ackley, D. (1997). *Breaking free of managed care: A step-by-step guide to regaining control of your practice.* New York: Guilford Press.

Acuff, C., Bennett, B. E., Bricklin, P. M., Canter, M. B., Knapp, S. J., Moldawsky, S., & Phelps, R. (1999). Considerations for ethical practice in managed care. *Professional Psychology: Research and Practice, 30*(6), 563–575.

Adler, A. (1958). *What life should mean to you.* New York: Capricorn Books. (Original work published 1931)

Akeret, R.V. (1995). *Tales from a traveling couch.* New York: Norton.

Albee, G. W. (1997). Speak no evil? *American Psychologist, 52,* 1143–1144.

Albom, M. (1997). *Tuesdays with Morrie: An old man, a young man, and life's greatest lesson.* New York: Doubleday.

Alexander, F. (1965). Psychoanalytic contributions to short-term psychotherapy. In L. R. Wolberg (Ed.), *Short-term psychotherapy* (pp. 84–126). New York: Grune & Stratton.

Alexander, F., & French, T. M. (1946). *Psychoanalytic therapy: Theory and applications.* New York: Ronald Press.

Allen, J. R., & Allen, B. A. (1998). Redecision therapy: Through a narrative lens. In M. F. Hoyt (Ed.), *The handbook of constructive therapies* (pp. 31–45). San Francisco: Jossey-Bass.

Allende, I. (1993). *The infinite plan.* New York: HarperCollins.

American Psychiatric Association (1994). *Diagnostic and statistical manual of mental disorders* (4th ed.). Washington, DC: Author.

American Psychological Association. (1996, March 29). *Checklist of common managed care provider contract provisions.* Washington, DC: American Psychological Association, Practice Directorate.

America's top HMOs: Surviving managed care. (1997, October 13). *U. S. News & World Report,* 60–78.

Amundson, J. (1996). Why pragmatics is probably enough for now. *Family Process, 35,* 473–486.

Amundson, J., Stewart, K., & Valentine, L. (1993). Temptations of power and certainty. *Journal of Marital and Family Therapy, 19,* 111–123.

263

Alperin, R. M., & Phillips, D. G. (Eds.). (1997). *The impact of managed care on the practice of psychotherapy: Innovation, implementation, and controversy.* New York: Brunner/Mazel.

Andersen, T. (Ed.). (1991). *The reflecting team: Dialogues and dialogues about the dialogues.* New York: Norton.

Andersen, T. (1992). Reflections on reflecting with families. In S. McNamee & K. J. Gergen (Eds.), *Therapy as social construction* (pp. 54–68). Newbury Park, CA: Sage.

Andersen, T. (1996). Language is not innocent. In F. W. Kaslow (Ed.), *Handbook of relational diagnosis and dysfunctional family patterns* (pp. 119–125). New York: Wiley.

Anderson, C. M., & Stewart, S. (1983). *Mastering resistance: A practical guide to family therapy.* New York: Guilford Press.

Anderson, H. (1997). *Conversation, language, and possibilities: A postmodern approach to therapy.* New York: Basic Books.

Anderson, H., & Goolishian, H. (1988). Human systems as linguistic systems: Preliminary and evolving ideas about the implications for clinical practice. *Family Process, 27,* 371–393.

Anderson, H., & Goolishian, H. A. (1992). The client is the expert: A not-knowing approach to therapy. In S. McNamee & K. J. Gergen (Eds.), *Therapy as social construction* (pp. 25–39). Newbury Park, CA: Sage.

Anderson, W. T. (1990). *Reality isn't what it used to be: Theatrical politics, ready-to-wear religion, global myths, primitive chic, and other wonders of the postmodern world.* San Francisco: HarperCollins.

Angelou, M. (1993). *Wouldn't take nothing for my journey now.* New York: Random House.

Anonymous. (1995). Hidden benefits of managed care. *Professional Psychology: Research and Practice, 26,* 235–237.

Appelbaum, S. A. (1975). Parkinson's law in psychotherapy. *International Journal of Psychoanalytic Psychotherapy, 4,* 426–436.

Aristotle (1976). *Nichomachaen ethics.* (Trans. J. A. K. Thomson, intro., J. Barnes). New York: Penguin.

Atwood, J. D. (1993). Social constructionist couple therapy. *The Family Journal: Counseling and Therapy for Couples and Families, 1,* 116–130.

Auden, W. H. (1989). In memory of Sigmund Freud. In E. Mendelsohn (Ed.), *Selected poems* (pp. 91–95). New York: Vintage. (Original work published 1939)

Aurelius, M. (1964). *Meditations.* (M. Staniforth, Trans.) London: Penguin Books. (Original work written in A.D.167)

Austad, C. S. (1996a). Can psychotherapy be conducted effectively in managed care settings? In A. Lazarus (Ed.), *Controversies in managed mental health care* (p. 229–249). Washington, DC: American Psychiatric Press.

Austad, C. S. (1996b). *Is long-term psychotherapy unethical? Toward a social ethic in an era of managed care.* San Francisco: Jossey-Bass.

Austad, C. S., & Berman, W. H. (Eds.). (1991). *Psychotherapy in managed health care: The optimal use of time and resources.* Washington, DC: American Psychological Association.

Austad, C. S., & Hoyt, M. F. (1992). The managed care movement and the future of psychotherapy. *Psychotherapy, 29,* 109–118.

Austad, C. S., Hunter, R. D. A., & Morgan, T. C. (1998). Managed health care, ethics, and psychotherapy. *Clinical Psychology: Science and Practice, 5,* 67–76.

Avedon, R. (1994). *Evidence 1944–1994.* New York: Random House/Eastman Kodak.

Bailey, R. A. (1999). Care of chronically mentally ill patients in a managed care environment. *American Journal of Psychiatry, 156*(11), 1801–1805.

Baker, W. (1983). *Backward: An essay on Indians, time, and photography.* Berkeley, CA: North Atlantic Press.

Bakhtin, M. M. (1981). *The dialogic imagination: Four essays by M.M. Bakhtin.* Austin: University of Texas Press.

Bandler, R., & Grinder, J. (1975). *The structure of magic.* (Vol.1). Palo Alto, CA: Science & Behavior Books.

Bandler, R., & Grinder, J. (1982). *Reframing.* Moab, UT: Real People Press.

Barks, C., & Green, M. (1997). *The illuminated Rumi.* New York: Broadway Books.

Barron, J. W., & Sands, H. (Eds.). (1996). *Impact of managed care on psychodynamic treatment.* Madison, CT: International Universities Press.

Barth, J. (1995, March). Stories of our lives. *Atlantic Monthly, 275*(3), 96–110.

Bartlett, F. C. (1932). *Remembering.* Cambridge, England: Cambridge University Press.

Barzun, J. (1986). *A word or two before you go. . . .* Middletown, CT: Wesleyan University Press.

Basch, M. F. (1995). *Doing brief therapy.* New York: Basic Books.

Bateson, G. (1972a). *Steps to an ecology of mind.* New York: Ballantine.

Bateson, G. (1972b). The cybernetics of "self": A theory of alcoholism. In *Steps to an ecology of mind* (pp. 309–337). New York: Ballantine.

Bateson, G. (1980). *Mind and nature: A necessary unity.* New York: Dutton.

Bateson, G., Jackson, D. D., Haley, J., & Weakland, J. H. (1956). Toward a theory of schizophrenia. *Behavioral Science, 1,* 251–264.

Bateson, M. C. (1994). *Peripheral visions: Learning along the way.* New York: HarperCollins.

Baucom, D. H., & Epstein, N. (1990). *Cognitive-behavioral marital therapy.* New York: Brunner/Mazel.

Beck, A. T. (1988). *Love is never enough.* New York: Harper & Row.

Beck, A. T., Rush, A. J., Shaw, B. F., & Emery, G. (1979). *Cognitive therapy of depression.* New York: Guilford.

Beitman, B. D., Beck, N. C., Deuser, W., Carter, C., Davidson, J., & Maddock, R. (1994). Patient stages of change predicts outcome in a panic disorder medication trial. *Anxiety, 1,* 64–69.

Benedict, J. G., & Phelps, R. (1998). Introduction: Psychology's view of managed care. *Professional Psychology: Research and Practice, 29,* 29–30.

Bennett, A., & Adams, O. (1993). *Looking north for health: What we can learn from Canada's health care system.* San Francisco: Jossey-Bass.

Bennett, M. J. (1983). Focal psychotherapy—terminable and interminable. *American Journal of Psychotherapy, 37,* 365–375.

Bennett, M. J. (1984). Brief psychotherapy and adult development. *Psychotherapy, 21,* 171–177.

Bennett, M. J. (1988). The greening of the HMO: Implications for prepaid psychiatry. *American Journal of Psychiatry, 145,* 1544–1549.

Bennett, M. J. (1994). The importance of teaching the principles of managed care. *Behavioral Healthcare Tomorrow, 2(3),* 28–32.

Bennington, G. (1989). Deconstruction is not what you think. In A. Papadakis, C. Cooke, & A. Benjamin (Eds.), *Deconstruction: Omnibus volume* (p. 84). New York: Rizzoli.

Bensen, D. R. (1983). *Fore! The best of Wodehouse on golf.* New York: Tickor & Fields.

Berendt, J. (1994). *Midnight in the garden of good and evil.* New York: Random House.

Berg, I. K. (1989). Of visitors, complainants and customers. *Family Therapy Networker, 13*(1), 27.

Berg, I. K. (1994a). *Irreconcilable differences: A solution-focused approach to marital therapy.* [Videotape]. New York: Norton.

Berg, I. K. (1994b). *Family-based services: A solution-focused approach.* New York: Norton.

Berg, I. K. (1995, July). *Beginning with the end: A new therapeutic conversation.* Paper presented at the First Pan-Pacific Brief Psychotherapy Conference, Fukukoa, Japan.

Berg, I. K., & de Shazer, S. (1993). Making numbers talk: Language in therapy. In S. Friedman (Ed.), *The new language of change: Constructive collaboration in psychotherapy* (pp. 5–24). New York: Guilford Press.

Berg, I. K., & Miller, S. D. (1992). *Working with the problem drinker: A solution-focused approach.* New York: Norton.

Berg, I. K., & Reuss, N. H. (1997). *Solutions step by step: A substance abuse treatment manual.* New York: Norton.

Berger, P. L., & Kellner, H. (1979). Marriage and the social construction of reality. In H. Bobboy, S. Greenblatt, & C. Clark (Eds.), *Social interaction: Introductory readings in sociology* (pp. 308–322). New York: St. Martin's Press.

Bergin, A. E., & Strupp, H. H. (1970). New directions in psychotherapy research. *Journal of Abnormal Psychology, 76,* 13–26.

Berne, E. (1972). *What do you say after you say hello?* New York: Grove Press.

Bernstein, A. (1990). Ethical postures that orient one's clinical decision making. *AFTA Newsletter, 41,* 13–15.

Bernstein, M. A. (1998). *Foregone conclusions: Against apocalyptic history.* Berkeley: University of California Press.

Berrin, K. (1978). *Art of the Huichol Indians.* New York: Abrams.

Berry, W. (1982). Rising. In *Collected poems, 1957–1982* (pp. 241–244). San Francisco: North Point Press.

Best HMOs: America's most complete guide. (1998, October 5). *U.S. News & World Report,* 64–91.

Bertolino, B., & O'Hanlon, W. H. (1999). *Welcome to possibility-land: An intensive teaching seminar with Bill O'Hanlon.* Philadelphia: Brunner/Mazel.

Berwick, D. M. (1989). Continuous improvement as an ideal in health care. *New England Journal of Medicine, 320,* 53–56.

Berwick, D. M. (1996). Quality of health care. Part 5: Payment by capitation and the quality of care. *New England Journal of Medicine, 335,* 1227–1231.

Berwick, D. M., Baker, M. W, & Kramer, E. (1992). The state of quality management in HMOs. *HMO Practice, 6,* 26–32.

Beyebach, M., & Morejon, A. R. (1999). Some thoughts on integration in solution-focused therapy. *Journal of Systemic Therapies, 18*(1), 24–42.

Bierce, A. (1957). *The devil's dictionary.* New York: Sagamore Press. (Original work published 1906)

Bilbrey, J., & Bilbrey, P. (1995, July/August). Judging, trusting, and utilizing outcomes data: A survey of behavioral health care payers. *Behavioral Health Care Tomorrow, 4*(4), 62–65.

Bilynsky, N. S., & Vernaglia, E. R. (1998). The ethical practice of psychology in a managed-care framework. *Psychotherapy, 35,* 54–68.

Blake, W. (1965). *Song,* from *Poetical sketches.* In D. V. Erdman (Ed.), *The poetry and prose of William Blake* (pp. 404–405), Garden City, NY: Doubleday. (Original work published 1769–1778)

Blake, W. (1966) *Jerusalem.* In D. V. Erdman (Ed.), *The Poetry and Prose of William Blake* (pp. 143–256). Garden City, NY: Doubleday. (Original work published 1804)

Bloom, B. L. (1992). *Planned short-term psychotherapy: A clinical handbook.* Boston: Allyn & Bacon.

Blount, A. (Ed.). (1998). *Integrated primary care: The future of medical and mental health care.* New York: Norton.

Blum, J. D. (1978). On changes in psychiatric diagnosis over time. *American Psychologist, 33,* 1017–1031.

Blum, S. (1992). Ethical issue in managed mental health. In S. Feldman (Ed.), *Managed mental health services* (pp. 245–265). Springfield, IL: Charles C. Thomas.

Bly, R. (1991). *Iron John.* San Francisco: HarperCollins.

Bly, R. (1996). *The sibling society.* Reading, MA: Addison-Wesley.

Bly, R., & Woodman, M. (1998). *The maiden king: The reunion of masculine and feminine.* New York: Henry Holt.

Bobbitt, B. L., Marques, C. C., & Trout, D. L. (1998). Managed behavioral health care: Current status, recent trends, and the role of psychology. *Clinical Psychology: Science and Practice, 5,* 53–66.

Boegner, I., & Zielenbach-Coenen, H. (1984). On maintaining change in behavioral marital therapy. In K. Hahlweg & N. S. Jacobson (Eds.), *Marital interaction: Analysis and modification* (pp. 27–35). New York: Guilford Press.

Bohart, A. C. (1999). On Suinn's vision. (Letter to the Editor) *APA Monitor,* 30(10), 3.

Bohart, A. C., & Tallman, K. (1999). *How clients make therapy work: The process of active self-healing.* Washington, DC: American Psychological Association.

Bohm, D. (1980). *Wholeness and the implicate order.* New York: Routledge & Kegan Paul.

Bolen, J. S. (1984). *Goddesses in everywoman.* New York: Harper & Row.

Bolen, J. S. (1989). *Gods in everyman.* New York: Harper & Row.

Bologna, N. C., Barlow, D. H., Hollon, S. D., Mitchell, J. E., & Huppert, J. D. (1998). Behavioral health treatment redesign in managed care settings. *Clinical Psychology: Science and Practice, 5,* 94–114.

Bonstedt, T. (1992). Managing psychiatric exclusions. In J. L. Feldman & R. J. Fitzpatrick (Eds.), *Managed mental health care: Administrative and clinical issues* (pp. 69–82). Washington, DC: American Psychiatric Press.

Borges, J. L. (1964). A new refutation of time. In *Labyrinths: Selected stories & other writings* (pp. 217–234). New York: New Directions.

Boscolo, L., & Bertrando, P. (1993). *The times of time.* New York: Norton.

Boswell, J. (1980). *The life of Samuel Johnson, LL.D.* Oxford, England: Oxford University Press/World's Classics. (Original work published 1791)

Boyd, D. (1974). *Rolling thunder.* New York: Delta.

Bracero, W. (1996). The story hour: Narrative and multicultural perspectives on managed care and time-limited psychotherapy. *Psychotherapy Bulletin, 31*(1), 59–65.

Brassai, G. (1995). *Henry Miller. The Paris years.* New York: Arcade.

Bredesen, A. C. (1999). Do as the best PSHPs do. *Emphasis, 2,* 10–13.

Breggin, P. (1994). *Talking back to Prozac.* New York: St. Martin's Press.

Breuer, J., & Freud, S. (1955). Studies in hysteria. In *The standard edition of the complete psychological works of Sigmund Freud* (Vol. 2, pp. vii–305). (J. Strachey, Trans.) London: Hogarth Press, 1955. (Original work published 1893–1895)

Brogan, M. M., Prochaska, J. O., & Prochaska, J. M. (1999). Predicting termination and continuation status in psychotherapy using the transtheoretical model. *Psychotherapy, 36,* 105–113.

Broskowski, A. (1991). Current mental health care environments: Why managed care is necessary. *Professional Psychology: Research and Practice, 22,* 6–14.

Broughton, J. (1990). Ways of getting there. In *Special deliveries: New and selected poems* (p. 212). Seattle, WA: Broken Moon Press.

Brown, F. (1994). Resisting the pull of the healthcare tarbaby: An organizational model for surviving managed care. *Clinical Social Work Journal, 22,* 59–71.

Brown, J., Dreis, S., & Nace, D. (1999). What makes a difference in psychotherapy outcome? And why does managed care want to know? In M. A. Hubble, B. L. Duncan, & S. D. Miller (Eds.), *The heart and soul of change: What works in therapy.* Washington, DC: American Psychological Association.

Brown, L. (1997). The private practice of subversion: Psychotherapy as Tikkun Olam. *American Psychologist,* 52(4), 449–462.

Browning, C. H., & Browning, B. J. (1993). *How to partner with managed care: A "do-it-yourself-kit" for building working relationships and getting steady referrals.* Los Alamitos, CA: Duncliff's International.

Browning, R. (1989). The ring and the book (R. D. Altick, Ed.). New York: Penguine. (Original work published 1868)

Browning, R. (1997). Rabbi Ben Ezra. In *Robert Browning* (pp. 304–310). (A. Roberts, Ed.) New York: Oxford University Press. (Original work published 1864)

Bruner, J. (1986). *Actual minds, possible worlds.* Cambridge, MA: Harvard University Press.

Bruner, J. (1987). Life as narrative. *Social Research, 54,* 11–32.

Buber, M. (1958). *I and thou.* New York: Schribner's Sons.

Budman, S. H. (1990). The myth of termination in brief therapy: Or, it ain't over until it's over. In J. K. Zeig & S .G. Gilligan (Eds.), *Brief therapy: Myths, methods, and metaphors* (pp. 206–218). New York: Brunner/Mazel.

Budman, S. H., & Armstrong, E. (1992). Training for managed-care settings: How to make it happen. *Psychotherapy, 29,* 416–421.

Budman, S. H., & Gurman, A. S. (1988). *Theory and practice of brief therapy.* New York: Guilford Press.

Budman, S. H., Hoyt, M. F., & Friedman, S. (Eds.). (1992). *The first session in brief therapy.* New York: Guilford Press.

Budman, S. H., Simeone, P. G., Reilly, R., & Demby, A. (1994). Progress in short-term and time-limited group psychotherapy: Evidence and implications. In A. Fuhriman & G. M. Burlingame (Eds.), *Handbook of group psychotherapy: An empirical and clinical synthesis* (pp. 319–339). New York: Wiley.

Budman, S. H., & Steenbarger, B. N. (1997). *The essential guide to group practice in mental health.* New York: Guilford Press.

Bukowski, C. (1996). Defining the magic. In *Betting on the muse: Poems and stories* (p. 131). Santa Barbara, CA: Black Sparrow Press.

Cade, B. (1986). The reality of "reality" (or the "reality" of reality). *American Journal of Family Therapy, 14,* 49–56.

Cade, B., & O'Hanlon, W. H. (1993). *A brief guide to brief therapy.* New York: Norton.

Campbell, J. (1968). *The hero with a thousand faces.* Princeton, NJ: Princeton University Press.

Campbell, J. (1972). *Myths to live by.* New York: Viking.

Cantor, D. W. (1999). Ensuring the future of professional psychology. *American Psychologist, 54,* 922–930.

Cantwell, P., & Holmes, S. (1994). Social construction: A paradigm shift for systemic therapy and training. *Australian and New Zealand Journal of Family Therapy, 15,* 17–26.

Carleton, E. K. (1998). An examination of doctoral-level psychotherapy training in light of the proliferation of managed care. *Professional Psychology: Research and Practice, 29,* 304–306.

Carlson, J., Hinkle, J. S., & Sperry, L. (1993). Using diagnosis and DSM-III and IV in marriage and family counseling: Increasing treatment outcomes without losing heart and soul. *The Family Journal: Counseling and Therapy for Couples and Families, 1,* 308–312.

Carlson, J., & Sperry, L. (1998). Adlerian psychotherapy as a constructivist psychotherapy. In M. F. Hoyt (Ed.), *The handbook of constructive psychotherapies* (pp. 68–82). San Francisco: Jossey-Bass.

Carnegie, D. (1964) *How to win friends and influence people.* New York: Simon & Schuster. (Original work published 1936)

Carroll, L. (1997). *Alice's adventures in wonderland and through the looking glass.* London: Penguin/Puffin. (Original work published 1865)

Castaneda, C. (1971). *A separate reality: Further conversations with Don Juan.* New York: Simon & Schuster.

Cavafy, C. P. (1975). The god abandons Antony. In G. Savidis (Ed.), & E. Keeley & P. Sherrard (Trans.), *C. P. Cavafy: Selected poems* (p. 32). Princeton, NJ: Princeton University Press.

Cecchin, G. (1987). Hypothesizing, circularity, and neutrality revisited: An invitation to curiosity. *Family Process, 26,* 405–413.

Cecchin, G., Lane, G., & Ray, W. A. (1992). *Irreverence: A strategy for therapists' survival.* London: Karnac Books.

Chakravarty, A. (Ed.). (1961). Note on the nature of reality. In *A Tagore reader* (pp.110–113). Boston: Beacon Press.

Chang, J., & Phillips, M. (1993). Michael White and Steve de Shazer: New directions in family therapy. In S. G. Gilligan & R. Price (Eds.), *Therapeutic conversations* (pp. 95–111). New York: Norton.

Chinen, A. B. (1992). *Once upon a midlife: Classic stories and mythic tales to illuminate the middle years.* New York: Tarcher/Perigee.

Church, G. J. (1997). Backlash patients, unions, legislators are fed up and say they won't take it anymore. *Time, 149,* 32–36.

Clay, R. A. (1998a, August). Undercapitalization undermines managed care. *APA Monitor, 29,* 30.

Clay, R. A. (1998b, August). Outcries over managed care spur action. *APA Monitor, 29,* 28.

Coale, H. W. (1992). The constructivist emphasis on language: A critical conversation. *Journal of Strategic and Systemic Therapies, 11,* 12–26.

Cohen, R. (1998). *Tough Jews: Fathers, sons, and gangster dreams.* New York: Vintage.

Coleman, S. M., Combs, G., DeLaurenti, B., DeLaurenti, P., Freedman, J., Larimer, D., & Shulman, D. (1998). Minimizing hierarchy in therapeutic relationships: A reflecting team approach. In M. F. Hoyt (Ed.), *The handbook of constructive therapies* (pp. 276–292). San Francisco: Jossey-Bass.

Collins, B. E., & Hoyt, M. F. (1972). Magnitude of inducement, consequences, and responsibility-choice: An integration and extension of the "forced compliance" literature. *Journal of Experimental Social Psychology, 8,* 558–593.

Combs, G., & Freedman, J. (1994). Narrative intentions. In M. F. Hoyt (Ed.), *Constructive therapies* (pp. 67–91). New York: Guilford Press.

Connell, G. Mitten, T., & Bumberry, W. (1999). *Reshaping family relationships: The symbolic therapy of Carl Whitaker.* Philadelphia: Brunner/Mazel.

Coop, R. H. (with Fields, B.). (1993). *Mind over golf.* New York: Macmillan.

Corcoran, K., & Vandiver, V. (1996). *Maneuvering the maze of managed care: Skills for mental health practitioners.* New York: Free Press.

Cowley, G., & Springen, K. (1995, April 17). Rewriting life stories. *Newsweek, 125*(16), 70–74.

Coyne, J. C. (1985). Toward a theory of frames and reframing. *Journal of Marital and Family Therapy, 11,* 337–344.

Crispin, C. (1999). The risk involved with managed care contracts: What providers don't know can kill them. *Group Practice Journal, 48*(10), 36–39.

Cummings, E. E. (1972). Humanity I love you. In G. J. Firmage (Ed.), *E. E. Cummings, Complete poems 1904–1962* (pp. 203–204). Orlando, FL: Harcourt Brace Jovanovich. (Original work published 1925)

Cummings, N. A. (1977). Prolonged (ideal) versus short-term (realistic) psychotherapy. *Professional Psychology: Research and Practice, 4,* 491–501.

Cummings, N. A. (1986). The dismantling of our health care system: Strategies for the survival of psychological practice. *American Psychologist, 41,* 426–431.

Cummings, N. A. (1988). Emergence of the mental health complex: Adaptive and maladaptive responses. *Professional Psychology: Research and Practice, 19,* 308–315.

Cummings, N. A. (1990). Brief intermittent psychotherapy throughout the life cycle. In J. K. Zeig & S. G. Gilligan (Eds.), *Brief therapy: Myths, methods, and metaphors* (pp. 169–184). New York: Brunner/Mazel.

Cummings, N. A. (1991a). The somatizing patient. In C. S. Austad & W. H. Berman (Eds.), *Psychotherapy in managed health care: The optimal use of time and resources* (pp. 234–247). Washington, DC: American Psychological Association.

Cummings, N. A. (1991b). Ten ways to spot mismanaged mental health care. *Psychotherapy in Private Practice, 9*(3), 79–83.

Cummings, N. A. (1995). Impact of managed care on employment and training: A primer for survival. *Professional Psychology: Research and Practice, 26,* 10–15.

Cummings, N. A. (1999). Comment on L'Abate: Psychotherapist future shock. *The Family Journal: Counseling and Therapy for Couples and Families, 7,* 221–223.

Cummings, N. A. (2000). *The collected papers of Nicholas A. Cummings. Vol. 1: The value of psychological treatment* (J. L. Thomas &J. L. Cummings, Eds.). Phoenix, AZ: Zeig, Tucker, & Company.

Cummings, N. A., Budman, S. H., & Thomas, J. L. (1998). Efficient psychotherapy as a viable response to scarce resources and rationing of treatment. *Professional Psychology: Research and Practice, 29,* 460–469.

Cummings, N. A., Cummings, J. L., & Johnson, J. N. (Eds.). (1997). *Behavioral health in primary care: A guide for clinical integration.* Madison, CT: Psychosocial Press.

Cummings, N. A., & Follette, W. T. (1976). Brief psychotherapy and medical utilization. In H. Dorken et al. (Eds.), *The professional psychologist today.* San Francisco: Jossey-Bass.

Cummings, N. A., Pallak, M. S., & Cummings, J. L. (Eds.). (1996). *Surviving the demise of solo practice: Mental health practitioners prospering in the era of managed care.* Madison, CT: Psychosocial Press.

Cummings, N. A., & Sayama, M. (1995). *Focused psychotherapy: A casebook of brief, intermittent psychotherapy throughout the life cycle.* New York: Brunner/Mazel.

Cushman, P. (1995). *Constructing the self, constructing America: A cultural history of psychotherapy.* Reading, MA: Addison-Wesley.

Dalai Lama. (1999). *Ethics for a new millennium.* New York: Riverhead Books/Penguin Putnam.

Dattilio, F. M., & Padesky, C. A. (1990). *Cognitive therapy with couples.* Sarasota, FL: Professional Resource Press.

Davenport, D. S. (1998). Behind closed doors: Pithy management in-service for case managers. *Professional Psychology: Research and Practice, 29,* 200–203.

Davenport, D. S., & Woolley, K. K. (1997). Innovative brief pithy psychotherapy: A contribution from corporate managed mental health care. *Professional Psychology: Research and Practice, 28,*197–200.

Davidson, T., & Davidson, J. (1995). Cost-containment, computers, and confidentiality. *Clinical Social Work Journal, 23,* 453–464.

Davis, M. (Ed.). (1994). *The Hogan mystique.* Greenwich, CT: American Golfer.

DeJong, P., & Berg, I. K. (1997). *Interviewing for solutions.* Pacific Grove, CA: Brooks Cole.

Deming, W. E. (1986). *Out of the crisis.* Cambridge, MA: M.I.T. Press.

Dennett, D. C. (1991). *Consciousness explained.* Boston: Little, Brown.

Derrida, J. (1972). *Limited, Inc.* Evanston, IL: Northwestern University Press.

Derrida, J. (1976). *Grammatology.* Baltimore: Johns Hopkins University Press.

Derrida, J. (1982). Differance. In J. Derrida (Ed.), *Margins of philosophy* (pp. 309–330). Chicago: University of Chicago Press.

de Shazer, S. (1982). *Patterns of brief family therapy.* New York: Guilford Press.

de Shazer, S. (1984). The death of resistance. *Family Process, 23,* 79–93.

de Shazer, S. (1985). *Keys to solution in brief therapy.* New York: Norton.

de Shazer, S. (1986). A requiem for power. *Contemporary Family Therapy, 10*(2), 69–76.

de Shazer, S. (1988). *Clues: Investigating solutions in brief therapy.* New York: Norton.

de Shazer, S. (1991a). *Putting difference to work.* New York: Norton.

de Shazer, S. (1991b). Foreword. In Y. M. Dolan, *Resolving sexual abuse: Solution-focused therapy and Ericksonian hypnosis for adult survivors* (pp. ix–x). New York: Norton.

de Shazer, S. (1993a). Creative misunderstanding: There is no escape from language. In S. G. Gilligan & R. Price (Eds.), *Therapeutic conversations* (pp. 81–90). New York: Norton.

de Shazer, S. (1993b). Commentary: de Shazer and White: Vive la difference. In S. G. Gilligan & R. Price (Eds.), *Therapeutic conversations* (pp. 112–120). New York: Norton.

de Shazer, S. (1994). *Words were originally magic.* New York: Norton.

de Shazer, S., & Berg, I. K. (1985). A part is not apart: Working with only one of the partners present. In A. S. Gurman (Ed.), *Casebook of marital therapy* (pp. 97–110). New York: Guilford Press.

de Shazer, S., & Berg, I. K. (1992). Doing therapy: A post-structural re-vision. *Journal of Marital and Family Therapy, 18,* 71–81.

de Shazer, S., & Berg, I. K. (1997). "What works?" Remarks on research aspects of Solution-Focused Brief Therapy. *Journal of Family Therapy, 19,* 121–124.

de Shazer, S., & White, M. (1994, July). Dialogue held at Therapeutic Conversations 2 Conference, Washington, DC.

Dickerson, V. C., & Zimmerman, J. L. (1995). A constructionist exercise in anti-pathologizing. *Journal of Systemic Therapies, 14*(1), 33–45.

DiClemente, C. C., & Prochaska, J. O. (1982). Self-change and therapy change of smoking: A comparison of processes of change in cessation and maintenance. *Addictive Behaviors, 7,* 133–142.

Dodge, J. (1983). *Fup*. Berkeley, CA: City Miner Books.

Dodson, J. (1996). *Final rounds: A father, a son, the golf journey of a lifetime*. New York: Bantam Books.

Doherty, W. J. (1991). Family therapy goes postmodern. *Family Therapy Networker, 15*(5), 36–42.

Dolan, Y. M. (1991). *Resolving sexual abuse: Solution-focused therapy and Ericksonian hypnosis for adult survivors*. New York: Norton.

Dolan, Y. D. (1998). *One small step*. Watsonville, CA: Papier Mache Press.

Dollard, J., & Miller, N. E. (1950). *Personality and psychotherapy: An analysis in terms of learning, thinking, and culture*. New York: McGraw-Hill.

Donald, K. M., & Wampold, B. E. (1986). Thanatotherapy: A one-session approach to brief psychotherapy. *Journal of Polymorphous Perversity, 3*(2), 3–6.

Donne, J. (1952). Love's progress. In C. M. Coffin (Ed.), *The complete poetry and selected prose of John Donne* (Elegy 18). New York: Modern Library/Random House (Original work published 1633)

Dorfman, H. A., & Kuehl, K. (1989). *The mental game of baseball: A guide to peak performance*. South Bend, IN: Diamond Communications.

Dozier, R., Hicks, M., Cornille, T. A., & Peterson, G. W. (1998). The effect of Tomm's therapeutic questionning styles on therapeutic alliance: A clinical analogue study. *Family Process, 37,* 189–200.

Drengenberg, C. (1996). Cyber-Cyber!!! *Journal of Systemic Therapies, 15*(3), 52.

Drozd, J. F., & Goldfield, M. R. (1996). A critical evaluation of the state of the art in psychotherapy outcome research. *Psychotherapy, 33,* 171–180.

Duncan, B. L., Hubble, M. A., & Miller, S. D. (1997a). Stepping off the throne. *Family Therapy Networker, 21*(4), 22–31, 33.

Duncan, B. L., Hubble, M. A., & Miller, S. D. (1997b). *Psychotherapy with "impossible" cases: The efficient treatment of therapy veterans*. New York: Norton.

Duncan, B. L., Hubble, M. A., & Miller, S. D. (1998, May). *Recasting the client as the star of the drama called therapy*. Keynote presentation at the Therapeutic Conversations 4 Conference, Toronto, Canada.

Duncan, B. L., Hubble, M. A., Miller, S. D., & Coleman, S. T. (1998). Escaping from the lost world of impossibility: Honoring clients' language, motivation, and theories of change. In M. F. Hoyt (Ed.), *The handbook of constructive therapies* (pp. 293–313). San Francisco: Jossey-Bass.

Duncan, B. L., Hubble, M. A., & Rusk, G. (1994). To intervene or not to intervene? That is not the question. *Journal of Systemic Therapies, 13*(4), 22–30.

Duncan, B. L., Solovey, A. D., & Rusk, G. S. (1992). *Changing the rules: A client-directed approach to therapy*. New York: Guilford Press.

272   References

Dunne, J. S. (1975). *Time and myth*. South Bend, IN: University of Notre Dame Press.

Duvall, J. D., & Beier, J. M. (1995). Passion, commitment, and common sense: A unique discussion with Insoo Kim Berg and Michael White. *Journal of Systemic Therapies, 14*(3), 57–80.

Dyckman, J. (1997). The impatient therapist: Managed care and countertransference. *American Journal of Psychotherapy, 51*, 329–342.

Dylan, B. (1974). If you see her, say hello. Song on record album, *Blood on the tracks*. New York: Columbia Records/Ram's Horn Music.

Ecker, B., & Hulley, L. (1996). *Depth-oriented brief therapy*. San Francisco: Jossey-Bass.

Edbril, S. D. (1994). Gender bias in short-term therapy: Toward a new model for working with women patients in managed care settings. *Psychotherapy, 31*, 601–609.

Efran, J. S. (1994). Mystery, abstraction, and narrative psychotherapy. *Journal of Constructivist Psychology, 7*, 219–227.

Efran, J. S., Lukens, M. D., & Lukens, R. J. (1990). *Language, structure, and change: Frameworks of meaning in psychotherapy*. New York: Norton.

Efran, J. S., Lukens, M. D., & Lukens, R. J. (1988). Constructivism: What's in it for you? *Family Therapy Networker, 12*(5), 26–36.

Efron, D. (1995). Conference review. *Journal of Systemic Therapies, 14*(3), 1–3.

Eiseley, L. (1978). *The star thrower*. New York: Harcourt Brace.

Eisler, R. (1987). *The chalice and the blade: Our history, our future*. New York: HarperCollins.

Eist, H. I. (1998). Treatment of major depression in managed care and fee-for-service systems. *American Journal of Psychiatry, 155*, 859–860.

Elder, W. G., Jr. (1997). Who has the "relationship" in managed care? *Professional Psychology: Research and Practice, 28*, 405–406.

Eliot, T. S. (1943a). Burnt Norton. In *Four quartets*, (pp. 3–8). New York: Harcourt, Brace, & World.

Eliot, T. S. (1943b). Little Gidding. In *Four quartets*, (pp. 31–39). New York: Harcourt, Brace, & World.

Ellis, A. (1990). Is rational-emotive therapy (RET) "rationalist" or "constructivist"? In W. Dryden (Ed.), *The essential Albert Ellis* (pp. 114–141). New York: Springer.

Ellis, A. (1998). How rational emotive behavior therapy belongs in the constructivist camp. In M. F. Hoyt (Ed.), *The handbook of constructive therapies* (pp. 83–99). San Francisco: Jossey-Bass.

Ellis, A., Fisch, R., Hoyt, M. F., & Lankton, S. (1998, August). *Topical panel— Psychotherapy: art or science?* Panel conducted at Brief Therapy: Lasting Impressions Conference sponsored by the Milton H. Erickson Foundation, New York.

Engel, S. (1995). *The stories children tell: Making sense of the narratives of childhood*. New York: Freeman.

Epston, D. (1989). *Collected papers*. Adelaide, Australia: Dulwich Centre Publications.

Epston, D. (1993). Internalized other questioning with couples: The New Zealand version. In S. G. Gilligan & R. Price (Eds.), *Therapeutic conversations* (pp. 189–189). New York: Norton.

Epston, D. (1994). Extending the conversation. *Family therapy networker, 18*(6), 30–37, 62–63.

Epston, D. (1995, February). *Towards a child-focused family therapy: Narrative, play, and imagination*. Workshop sponsored by Kaiser Permanente and held in San Rafael, CA.

Epston, D., & White, M. (1992a). Consulting your consultants: The documentation of alternative knowledges. In *Experience, contradiction, narrative and imagination: Selected papers of David Epston and Michael White, 1989–1991* (pp. 11–26). Adelaide, Australia: Dulwich Centre Publications. (Reprinted from *Dulwich Centre Newsletter*, 1990, Number 4)

Epston, D., & White, M. (1992b). *Experience, contradiction, narrative and imagination: Selected papers of David Epston and Michael White, 1989–1991*. Adelaide, Australia: Dulwich Centre Publications.

Erickson, M. H. (1954). Pseudo-orientation in time as a hypnotic procedure. *Journal of Clinical and Experimental Hypnosis, 6,* 183–207.

Erickson, M. H. (1965). Hypnotherapy: The patient's right to both success and failure. *American Journal of Clinical Hypnosis, 7,* 254–257.

Erickson, M. H. (1966). Successful hypnotherapy that failed. *American Journal of Clinical Hypnosis, 9,* 62–65.

Erickson, M. H. (1980a). *Collected papers* (Vol. 1–4). E. L. Rossi (Ed.) New York: Irvington.

Erickson, M. H. (1980b). Hypnosis in medicine. In E. L. Rossi (Ed.), *Collected Papers,* (Vol. 4). New York: Irvington. (Original work published 1944)

Erickson, M. H. (1985). *Life reframing in hypnosis.* In E. L. Rossi & M. O. Ryan (Eds.) New York: Irvington.

Erickson, M. H., & Rossi, E. L. (1979). *Hypnotherapy: An exploratory casebook.* New York: Irvington.

Erickson, M. H., & Rossi, E. L. (1980). Varieties of double bind. In E. L. Rossi (Ed.), *The collected papers of Milton H. Erickson* (Vol. 1, pp. 412–429). New York: Irvington. (Original work published 1975)

Erickson, M. H., & Rossi, E. L. (1981). *Experiencing hypnosis: Therapeutic approaches to altered states.* New York: Irvington.

Erickson, M. H., & Rossi, E. L. (1989). *The February man: Evolving consciousness and identity in hypnotherapy.* New York: Brunner/Mazel.

Erickson, M. H., Rossi, E. L., & Rossi, S. I. (1976). *Hypnotic realities: The induction of clinical hypnosis and forms of indirect suggestion.* New York: Irvington

Eron, J. B., & Lund, T. M. (1989). From magic to method: Principles of effective reframing. *Family Therapy Networker, 13*(1), 64–68, 81–83.

Eron, J. B., & Lund, T. W. (1996). *Narrative solutions in brief therapy.* New York: Guilford Press.

Eron, J. B., & Lund, T. W. (1998). Narrative solutions couple therapy. In F. M. Dattilio (Ed.), *Case studies in couple and family therapy: Systemic and cognitive perspectives* (pp. 371–400). New York: Guilford Press.

Estes, C. P. (1993). *The gift of story.* New York: Ballantine.

Evans, A. (1966). *The Jerusalem Bible: Reader's edition.* Garden City, NY: Doubleday.

Evans, P. (1996). *The verbally abusive relationship: How to recognize it and how to respond* (2nd ed.). Holbrook, MA: Adams Media Corporation.

Fancher, R. T. (1995). *Cultures of healing: Correcting the image of American health care.* New York: Freeman.

Faulkner, W. (1956). *The sound and the fury.* New York: Random House.

Feinstein, J. (1985). *A good walk spoiled: Days and nights on the PGA tour.* Boston: Little, Brown.

Feldman, J. L. (1992). The managed care setting and the patient-therapist relationship. In J. L. Feldman & R. J. Fitzpatrick (Eds.), *Managed mental health care: Administrative and clinical issues* (pp. 219–229). Washington, DC: American Psychiatric Press.

Feldman, S. (Ed.). (1997). Managed behavioral healthcare and academia: Is there a "fit" between services and training? [Special issue]. *Administration and Policy in Mental Health, 25*(1).

Feldstein, B. D. (1998a). Succeeding in managed care—A managed ethics and design approach: Part I. Foundation. *Group Practice Journal, 47*(6), 12–23.

Feldstein, B. D. (1998b). Succeeding in managed care—a managed ethics and design approach. Part II. Case studies. *Group Practice Journal, 47*(7), 21–27.

Fine, M., & Turner, J. (1995). Hypotheses and hypothesizing: Following a thread through the weave. *Journal of Systemic Therapies, 14*(1), 61–68.

Fisch, R. (1982). Erickson's impact on brief psychotherapy. In J. K. Zeig (Ed.), *Ericksonian approaches to hypnosis and psychotherapy* (pp. 155–162). New York: Brunner/Mazel.

Fisch, R. (1990). The broader implications of Milton H. Erickson's work. *Ericksonian Monographs, 7,* 1–5.

Fisch, R., Weakland, J. H., & Segal, L. (1982). *The tactics of change: Doing therapy briefly*. San Francisco: Jossey-Bass.

Fish, J. M. (1995). Does problem behavior just happen? Does it matter? *Behavior and Social Issues, 5,* 3–12.

Fish, V. (1993). Poststructuralism in family therapy: Interrogating the narrative/conversational mode. *Journal of Marital and Family Therapy, 19,* 221–232.

Flinders, C. L. (1998). *At the root of this longing: Reconciling a spiritual hunger and a feminist thirst.* San Francisco: HaperCollins.

Foerster, H. von. (1984). On constructing a reality. In P. Watzlawick (Ed.), *The invented reality* (pp. 41–61). New York: Norton.

Foerster, H. von. (1985). Apropos epistemologies. *Family Process, 24,* 517–524.

Follette, W. T., & Cummings, N. A. (1967). Psychiatric services and medical utilization in a prepaid health plan setting. *Medical Care, 5,* 25–35.

Foucault, M. (1973). *The birth of the clinic: An archeology of medical perception.* London: Tavistock.

Foucault, M. (1977). *Discipline and punish: The birth of the prison.* New York: Pantheon.

Foucault, M. (1980). *Power/knowledge: Selected interviews and other writings, 1972–1977.* New York: Pantheon.

Foucault, M. (1988). On power. In L. Kritzman (Ed.), *Michel Foucault: Politics, philosophy: Interviews and other writings, 1977–1984* (pp. 96–109). New York: Routledge.

Fow, N. R. (1998). Partner-focused reversal in couple therapy. *Psychotherapy, 35,* 231–237.

Fox, P. D., & Wasserman, J. (1993, Spring). Academic medical centers and managed care: Uneasy partners. *Health Affairs,* 85–93.

Fox, R. E. (1995). The rape of psychotherapy. *Professional Psychology: Research and Practice, 26,* 147–155.

Frank, J. D. (1981). *Persuasion and healing.* Baltimore: Johns Hopkins University Press.

Frank, J. D. (1987). Psychotherapy, rhetoric, and hermeneutics: Implications for practice and research. *Psychotherapy, 24,* 293–302.

Frankl, V. E. (1963). *Man's search for meaning: An introduction to logotherapy.* New York: Washington Square Press.

Franko, D. L., & Erb, J. (1998). Managed care or mangled care? Treating eating disorders in the current healthcare climate. *Psychotherapy, 35,* 43–53.

Fraser, J. S. (1996). All that glitters in not always gold: Medical offset effects and managed behavioral health care. *Professional Psychology: Research and Practice, 27,* 335–344.

Fraser, J. S. (1998). People who live in glass houses...: A response to the critique of the article "All that glitters is not always gold." *Professional Psychology: Research and Practice, 29,* 624–627.

Freedman, J., & Combs, G. (1993). Invitations to new stories: Using questions to explore alternative possibilities. In S. G. Gilligan & R. Price (Eds.), *Therapeutic conversations* (pp. 291–303). New York: Norton.

Freedman, J., & Combs, G. (1996). *Narrative therapy: The social construction of preferred realities.* New York: Norton.

Freeman, J., Epston, D., & Lobovits, D. (1997). *Playful approaches to serious problems: Narrative therapy with children and their families.* New York: Norton.

Freeman, M. (1993). *Rewriting the self: History, memory, narrative.* New York: Routledge.

Freeny, M. (1995). Do the walls have ears? *Family Therapy Networker, 19*(5), 36–43, 65.

Freeny, M. (1998). *Terminal consent.* Orlando, FL: William Austin Press.

Freud, S. (1953a). On psychotherapy. In *The standard edition of the complete psychological works of Sigmund Freud* (Vol. 7, pp. 257–268) (J. Strachey, Trans.). London: Hogarth Press. (Original work published 1904)

Freud, S. (1953b). From the history of an infantile neurosis. In *The standard edition of the complete psychological works of Sigmund Freud* (Vol. 17, pp. 1–122) (J. Strachey, Trans.). London: Hogarth Press. (Original work published 1918)

Freud, S. (1957). The future prospects of psycho-analytic therapy. In *The standard edition of the complete psychological works of Sigmund Freud* (Vol. 11, pp. 139–151) (J. Strachey, Trans.). London: Hogarth Press. (Original work published 1910)

Freud, S. (1958). On beginning the treatment. In *The standard edition of the complete psychological works of Sigmund Freud.* (Vol. 12, pp. 121–144) (J. Strachey, Trans.). London: Hogarth Press. (Original work published 1913)

Freud, S. (1959). Some general remarks on the nature of hysterical attacks. In *The standard edition of the complete psychological works of Sigmund Freud* (Vol. 9, pp. 229–234) (J. Strachey, Trans). London: Hogarth Press. (Original work published 1909)

Freud, S. (1961a). Introductory lectures on psycho-analysis. In *The standard edition of the complete psychological works of Sigmund Freud.* (Vols. 15–16, pp. 3–463) (J. Strachey, Trans.) London: Hogarth Press. (Original work published 1915–1917)

Freud, S. (1961b). Lines of advance in psycho-analytic therapy. In *The standard edition of the complete psychological works of Sigmund Freud.* (Vol. 17, pp. 157–168). London: Hogarth Press. (Original work published in 1919)

Freud, S. (1964a). Constructions in analysis. In *The standard edition of the complete psychological works of Sigmund Freud* (Vol. 23, pp. 256–269). London: Hogarth Press. (Original work published in 1937)

Freud, S. (1964b). Analysis terminable and interminable. In *The standard edition of the complete psychological works of Sigmund Freud* (Vol. 23, pp. 211–253). London: Hogarth Press. (Original work published in 1937)

Freud, S. (1964c). Moses and monotheism: Three essays. In *The standard edition of the complete psychological works of Sigmund Freud* (Vol. 23, pp. 1–137). London: Hogarth Press. (Original work published in 1939)

Friedman, S. (1991). Toward a wellness model of time-effective family psychotherapy. *The Family Psychologist, 7*(2), 23–24.

Friedman, S. (Ed.). (1993). *The new language of change: Constructive collaboration in psychotherapy.* New York: Guilford Press.

Friedman, S. (Ed.). (1995). *The reflecting team in action: Collaborative practice in family therapy.* New York: Guilford Press.

Friedman, S. (1996). Couples therapy: Changing conversations. In H. Rosen & K. T. Kuehlwein (Eds.), *Constructing realities: Meaning-making perspectives for psychotherapists* (pp. 413–453). San Francisco: Jossey-Bass.

Friedman, S. (1997). *Time-Effective psychotherapy: Maximizing outcomes in an era of minimized resources.* Needham Heights, MA: Allyn & Bacon.

Friedman, S., & Fanger, M. T. (1991). *Expanding therapeutic possibilities: Getting results in brief therapy.* New York: Lexington Books/Macmillan.

Friedman, S., & Lipchik, E. (1999). A time-effective, solution-focused approach to couple therapy. In J. M. Donovan (Ed.), *Short-term couple therapy* (pp. 325–359). New York: Guilford Press.

Frost, R. (1979). An equalizer. In E. C. Lathem (Ed.), *The poetry of Robert Frost: The collected poems, complete and unabridged* (p. 363). New York: Holt, Rinehart, & Winston. (Original work published 1942)

Fuchs, S., & Ward, S. (1994). What is deconstruction, and where and when does it take place? Making facts in science, building cases in law. *American Sociological Review, 59,* 481–500.

Fuller, B. (1970). *I seem to be a verb.* New York: Bantam Books.

Furman, B., & Ahola, T. (1992a). Adverse effects of psychotherapeutic beliefs. In *Pickpockets on a nudist camp: The systemic revolution in psychotherapy* (pp. 69–86). Adelaide, Australia: Dulwich Centre Publications. (Reprinted from *Family Systems Medicine, 7,* pp. 183–195, 1989)

Furman, B., & Ahola, T. (1992b) *Solution talk: Hosting therapeutic conversations.* New York: Norton.

Gabbard, G. O., Takahashi, T., Davidson, J., Eauman-Bork, M., & Ensroth, K. (1991). A psychodynamic perspective on the clinical impact of insurance review. *American Journal of Psychiatry, 148,* 318–326.

Gabler, N. (1998). *Life the movie: How entertainment conquered reality.* New York: Knopf.

Gale, J. (1999). A response to Barbara Held's "How brief therapy got postmodern": A response in four parts, or How postmodern got Jerry. In W. J. Matthews & J. H. Edgette (Eds.), *Current thinking and research in brief therapy: Solutions, strategies, narratives* (Vol. 3, pp. 164–174). Philadelphia: Brunner/Mazel.

Gale, J., & Newfield, N. (1992). A conversation analysis of a solution-focused marital therapy session. *Journal of Marital and Family Therapy, 18,* 153–165.

Gallway, W. T. (1981). *The inner game of golf.* New York: Random House.

Geertz, C. (1973). Thick description: Toward an interpretive theory of culture. In *The interpretation of cultures.* New York: Basic Books.

Geertz, C. (1983). *Local knowledge: Further essays in interpretive anthropology.* New York: Basic Books.

George, E., Iveson, C., & Ratner, H. (1990). *Problem to solution: Brief therapy with individuals and families.* London: Brief Therapy Press.

Georgoulakis, J. M. (1998). Integrating physical and mental health services: What the United States can learn from Canada. In P. E. Hartman-Stein (Ed.), *Innovative behavioral healthcare for older adults* (pp. 41–56). San Francisco; Jossey-Bass.

Geraty, R., Hendren, R., & Flaa, C. (1992). Ethical perspectives on managed care as it relates to child and adolescent psychiatry. *Journal of the American Academy of Child and Adolescent Psychiatry, 31,* 398–402.

Gergen, K. J. (1985). The social constructionist movement in modern psychology. *American Psychologist, 40,* 266–275.

Gergen, K. J. (1991). *The saturated self: Dilemmas of identity in contemporary life.* New York: Basic Books.

Gergen, K. J. (1993). Foreword. In S. Friedman (Ed.), *The new language of change* (pp. ix–xi). New York: Guilford Press.

Gergen, K. J. (1994a). *Realities and relationships: Soundings in social construction.* Cambridge, MA: Harvard University Press.

Gergen, K. J. (1994b). Therapeutic professions and the diffusion of deficit. In *Realities and relationships: Soundings in social construction.* Cambridge, MA: Harvard University Press.

Gergen, K. J. (1994c). Exploring the postmodern: Perils or potentials? *American Psychologist, 49,* 412–416.

Gergen, K. J. (1998). Foreword. In M. F. Hoyt (Ed.), *The handbook of constructive therapies* (pp. xi–xv). San Francisco: Jossey-Bass.

Gergen, K. J., & Gergen, M. M. (1983). Narratives of the self. In T. R. Sabin & K. E. Scheibe (Eds.), *Studies in social identity.* New York: Praeger.

Gergen, K. J., & Gergen, M. M. (1986). Narrative form and the construction of psychological science. In T. R. Sabin (Ed.), *Narrative psychology: The storied nature of human conduct* (pp. 22–44). New York: Praeger.

Gergen, K. J., Hoffman, L., & Anderson, H. (1996). Is diagnosis a disaster? A constructionist trialogue. In F. W. Kaslow (Ed.), *Handbook of relational diagnosis and dysfunctional family patterns* (pp. 102–118). New York: Wiley.

Gergen, K. J., & Kaye, J. (1992). Beyond narrative in the negotiation of therapeutic meaning. In S. McNamee & K. J. Gergen (Eds.), *Therapy as social construction* (pp.166–185). Newbury Park, CA: Sage.

German, M. (1994). Effective case management in managed mental health care: Conditions, methods and outcomes. *HMO Practice, 8*(1), 34–40.

Gerson, S. N. (1994). When should managed care firms terminate private benefits for chronically mentally ill patients? *Behavioral Healthcare Tomorrow, 3*(2), 31–35.

Giles, T. R. (1993). *Managed mental health care: A guide for practitioners, employers, and hospital administrators*. Needham Heights, MA: Allyn & Bacon.

Giles, T. R., & Marafiote, R. A. (1998). Managed care and the practitioner: A call for unity. *Clinical Psychology: Science and Practice, 5*, 41–50.

Gillieron, E. (1981). Psychoanalysis and brief psychotherapy: Some new considerations on the psychotherapeutic process. *Psychotherapy and Psychosomatics, 35*, 244–256.

Gilligan, S. G. (1987). *Therapeutic trances: The cooperation principle in Ericksonian hypnotherapy*. New York: Brunner/Mazel.

Gilligan S. G. (1996). The relational self: The expanding of love beyond desire. In M. F. Hoyt (Ed.), *Constructive therapies*, (Vol. 2, pp. 211–237). New York: Guilford Press.

Gilligan, S. G., & Price, R. (Eds.). (1993). *Therapeutic conversations*. New York: Norton.

Gimbutas, M. (1989). *The language of the goddess*. San Francisco: HarperCollins.

Glaserfeld, E. von. (1984). An introduction to radical constructivism. In P. Watzlawick (Ed.), *The invented reality* (pp. 17–40). New York: Norton.

Goffman, E. (1952). On cooling the mark out: Some aspects of adaptation to failure. *Psychiatry, 15*, 451–463.

Goldberg, C. (1975). Termination—A meaningful pseudodilemma in psychotherapy. *Psychotherapy: Theory, research & practice, 12*, 341–343.

Goldensohn, S. S., & Haar, E. (1974). Transference and countertransference in a third-party payment system (HMO). *American Journal of Psychiatry, 131*, 256–260.

Goldfield, J. (1994, December). *A utilization approach for working with adolescents and their families*. Workshop held at the Sixth International Congress on Ericksonian Approaches to Hypnosis and Psychotherapy, Los Angeles.

Goldfield, J. (1998). "Master of faster" and "The problem talks back." In M. F. Hoyt (Ed.), *The handbook of constructive therapies* (pp. 241–248). San Francisco: Jossey-Bass.

Goldner, V. (1993). Power and hierarchy: Let's talk about it! *Family Process, 32*(2), 157–162.

Goodman, M., Brown, J., & Deitz, P. (1992). *Managing managed care: A mental health practitioner's survival guide*. Washington, DC: American Psychiatric Press.

Goolishian, H. A., & Anderson, H. (1992). Strategy and intervention versus nonintervention: A matter of theory? *Journal of Marital and Family Therapy* (18), 5–15.

Gottlieb, M. C. (1992). Practicing ethically with managed care patients. In *Innovations in clinical practice: A sourcebook* (Vol. 11, pp. 481–493). Sarasota, FL: Professional Resource Press.

Gould, S. J. (1987). The power of narrative. In *An urchin in the storm: Essays about books and ideas* (pp. 75–92). New York: Norton.

Goulding, M. M. (1985). *Who's been living in your head?* (2nd ed.) Watsonville, CA: Western Institute for Group and Family Therapy Press.

Goulding, M. M., & Goulding, R. L. (1979). *Changing lives through redecision therapy*. New York: Grove Press.

Goulding, M. M., & Hillman, J. (1995, December). *Growth and development of the therapist*. Dialogue held at the Evolution of Psychotherapy Conference sponsored by the Milton H. Erickson Foundation, Las Vegas.

Greenleaf, E. (1994). Solving the unknown problem. In M. F. Hoyt (Ed.), *Constructive therapies* (pp. 251–275). New York: Guilford Press.

Griffith, M. E. (1997). Foreword. In C. Smith & D. Nylund (Eds.), *Narrative therapies with children and adolescents* (pp. xvii–xix). New York: Guilford Press.

Gross, P. R., & Levitt, N. (1994). *Higher superstition: The academic left and its quarrels with science*. Baltimore: Johns Hopkins University Press.

Grove, D. R., & Haley, J. (1993). *Conversations on therapy: Popular problems and uncommon solutions*. New York: Norton.

Gunn, H. E. (1976). *How to play golf with your wife—and survive*. Matteson, IL: Greatlakes Living Press.

Gustafson, J. P. (1986). *The complex secret of brief psychotherapy*. New York: Norton.

Gustafson, J. P. (1992). *Self-delight in a harsh world: The main stories of individual, marital and family psychotherapy*. New York: Norton.

Gustafson, J. P. (1995a). *The dilemmas of brief psychotherapy, and taking care of the patient*. New York: Plenum Press.

Gustafson, J. P. (1995b). *Brief versus long psychotherapy: When, why, and how*. Northvale, NJ: Aronson.

Haas, L. J., & Cummings, N. A. (1991). Managed outpatient mental health plans: Clinical, ethical, and practical guidelines for participation. *Professional Psychology: Research and Practice, 22*, 45–51.

Hale, N. C. (1968). *Embrace of life: The sculpture of Gustav Vigeland*. New York: Abrams.

Haley, J. (1963). *Strategies of psychotherapy*. New York: Grune & Stratton.

Haley, J. (1969). The art of psychoanalysis. In *The power tactics of Jesus Christ and other essays* (pp. 9–26). New York: Avon.

Haley, J. (1973). *Uncommon therapy: The psychiatric techniques of Milton H. Erickson, M.D.* New York: Norton.

Haley, J. (1977). *Problem-solving therapy: New strategies for effective family therapy*. San Francisco: Jossey-Bass.

Haley, J. (Ed.). (1985). *Conversations with Milton H. Erickson, M.D.,* (Vols. 1–3). New York: Triangle Press.

Haley, J. (1990). Why not long-term therapy? In J. K. Zeig & S. G. Gilligan (Eds.), *Brief therapy: Myths, methods, and metaphors* (pp. 3–17). New York: Brunner/Mazel.

Haley, J., & Richeport, M. (1993). *Milton H. Erickson, M.D.: Explorer in hypnosis and therapy* [Videotape]. New York: Brunner/Mazel.

Halifax, J. (1993). *The fruitful darkness: Reconnecting with the body of the earth*. San Francisco: HarperCollins.

Hall, R. C. W. (1994a). Legal precedents affecting managed care: The physician's responsibilities to patients. *Psychosomatics, 35*, 105–117.

Hall, R. C. W. (1994b). Social and legal implications of managed care in psychiatry. *Psychosomatics, 35*, 150–158.

Hallberg, W. (1988). *The rub of the green*. New York: Bantam.

Hare-Mustin, R. T. (1992). Meanings in the mirrored room: On cats and dogs. *Journal of Marital and Family Therapy, 18*, 309–310.

Hare-Mustin, R. T. (1994). Discourses in the mirrored room: A postmodern analysis of therapy. *Family Process, 33*, 19–35.

Hart, B. (1995). Re-authoring the stories we work by: Situating the narrative approach in the presence of the family of therapists. *Australian and New Zealand Journal of Family Therapy, 16*, 181–189.

Havens, L. L. (1986). *Making contact: Uses of language in psychotherapy*. Cambridge, MA: Harvard University Press.

Havens, R. A. (Ed.). (1989a). *The wisdom of Milton H. Erickson: Vol. 1. Hypnosis and Hypnotherapy*. New York: Irvington.

Havens, R. A. (Ed.). (1989b). *The wisdom of Milton H. Erickson: Vol. 2. Human behavior and psychotherapy*. New York: Irvington.

Hays, K. F. (1999). Book review of *The handbook of constructive therapies*. *Psychotherapy, 36*, 199–200.

Health security: The president's report to the American people. (1993). New York: Touchstone/Simon & Schuster.

Healy, D. (1997). *The anti-depressant era*. Cambridge, MA: Harvard University Press.

Heidegger, M. (1962). *Being and time*. New York: Harper & Row.

Heidegger, M. (1971). *On the way to language*. San Francisco: Harper & Row.

Held, B. S. (1992). The problem of strategy within the systemic therapies. *Journal of Marital and Family Therapy, 18,* 25–34.

Held, B. S. (1995). *Back to reality: A critique of postmodern theory in psychotherapy.* New York: Norton.

Held, B. S. (1999). How brief therapy got postmodern, or where's the brief? In W. J. Matthews & J. H. Edgette (Eds.), *Current thinking and research in brief therapy: Solutions, strategies, narratives* (Vol. 3, pp. 135–164 and 174–178). Philadelphia: Brunner/Mazel.

Hellenga, R. (1995). *The sixteen pleasures.* New York: Delta.

Henricks, R. (1993). *A model for national health care: The history of Kaiser Permanente.* New Brunswick, NJ: Rutgers University Press.

Hernandez, K. (1994). *Pure baseball: Pitch by pitch for the advanced fan.* New York: HarperCollins.

Herron, W. G., Eisenstadt, E. N., Javier, R. A., Primavera, L. H., & Schultz, C. L. (1994). Session effects, comparability, and managed care in the psychotherapies. *Psychotherapy, 31,* 279–285.

Hersch, L. (1995). Adapting to health care reform and managed care: Three strategies for survival and growth. *Professional Psychology: Research and Practice, 26,* 16–26.

Hillman, J. (1975). *Re-visioning psychology.* New York: Harper & Row. (Excerpted in T. Moore, Ed., 1989, *A blue fire: Selected writings of James Hillman.* New York: HarperCollins)

Hillman, J. (1983). The fiction of case history. In *Healing fiction* (pp. 3–49). Woodstock, CT: Spring Publications.

Hillman, J. (1995). *Kinds of power: A guide to its intelligent uses.* New York: Doubleday.

Hillman, J. (1996). *The soul's code: In search of character and calling.* New York: Random House.

Himmelstein, D. U., Woolhandler, S., Hellander, I., & Wolfe, S. M. (1999). Quality of care in investor-owned vs. not-for-profit HMOs. *Journal of the American Medical Association, 282,* 159–163.

Hoffman, L. (1981). *Foundations of family therapy.* New York: Basic Books.

Hoffman, L. (1993a). Definitions for simple folk. In *Exchanging voices: A collaborative approach to family therapy* (pp. 103–109). London: Karnac Books.

Hoffman, L. (1993b). *Exchanging voices: A collaborative approach to family therapy.* London: Karnac Books.

Hoffman, L. (1993c). Constructing realities: An art of lenses. In *Exchanging voices: A collaborative approach to family therapy* (pp. 86–102). London: Karnac Books. (Reprinted from *Family Process,* 1990, *29,* pp. 1–12)

Hoffman, L. (1997). Postmodernism and family therapy. In J. K. Zeig (Ed.), *The evolution of psychotherapy: The third conference* (pp. 337–348). New York: Brunner/Mazel.

Hoffman, L. (1998). Setting aside the model in family therapy. In M. F. Hoyt (Ed.), *The handbook of constructive therapies* (pp. 100–115). San Francisco: Jossey-Bass.

Holleman, W., Holleman, M., & Graves, M. (1997). Are ethics and managed care strange bedfellows or a marriage made in heaven? *Lancet, 349,* 350–351.

Horgan, J. (1996). *The end of science: Facing the limits of knowledge in the twilight of the scientific age.* Reading, MA: Addison-Wesley.

Horn, R. (1994, August 8). Tee ceremony. *Sports Illustrated.* 81(5), n.p.

Horowitz, M. J. (1976). *Stress response syndromes.* Northvale, NJ: Aronson.

Horvoth, A. O., & Greenberg, L. S. (Eds.). (1994). *The working alliance: Theory, research, and practice.* New York: Wiley.

Howard, G. S. (1991). Culture tales: A narrative approach to thinking, cross-cultural psychology, and psychotherapy. *American Psychologist, 46,* 187–197.

Howard, R. C. (1998). The sentinel effect in an outpatient managed care setting. *Professional psychology: Research and practice, 29,* 262–269.

How good is your health plan? (1996, August). *Consumer Reports, 61*(8), 28–42.

How HMOs decide your fate. (1998, March 9). *U.S. News & World Report,* 40–50.

Hoyt, M. F. (1977). Primal scene and self creation. *Voices, 13*, 24–28.

Hoyt, M. F. (1980). Therapist and patient actions in "good" psychotherapy sessions. *Archives of General Psychiatry, 37*, 159–161.

Hoyt, M. F. (1983). Concerning remorse: With special attention to its defensive function. *Journal of the American Academy of Psychoanalysis, 11*, 435–444.

Hoyt, M. F. (1986). Mental-imagery methods in short-term dynamic psychotherapy. In M. Wolpin, J. Shorr, & L. Krueger (Eds.), *Imagery 4*. New York: Plenum.

Hoyt, M. F. (1987). Resistances to brief therapy. *American Psychologist, 42*, 408–409.

Hoyt, M. F. (1989). Letter to the editor. *The Milton H. Erickson Foundation Newsletter, 9*(1), 5.

Hoyt, M. F. (1992a). Psychotherapy in HMOs: Some information for private practitioners. *Psychotherapy in Private Practice, 11*(2), 47–54.

Hoyt, M. F. (1992b). Discussion of the effects of managed care on psychotherapy. *Psychotherapy in Private Practice, 11*(2), 79–84.

Hoyt, M. F. (1992c). Personal and powerful. In C. L. Pelton & I. Myers-Pelton (Eds.), *Reflections of Robert L. Goulding* (pp. 179–182). Aberdeen, SD: Family Health Media.

Hoyt, M. F. (1993). Termination in the case of Gary: Overdue, not premature. *Psychotherapy, 30*, 536–537.

Hoyt, M. F. (Ed.). (1994a). *Constructive therapies* (Vol. 1). New York: Guilford Press.

Hoyt, M. F. (1994b). On the importance of keeping it simple and taking the patient seriously: A conversation with Steve de Shazer and John Weakland. In M. F. Hoyt (Ed.), *Constructive therapies* (pp. 11–40). New York: Guilford Press.

Hoyt, M. F. (1994c). Therapeutic flexibility in the case of Gary: Too little, too late. *Psychotherapy, 31*, 545–546.

Hoyt, M. F. (1995a). *Brief therapy and managed care: Readings for contemporary practice*. San Francisco: Jossey-Bass.

Hoyt, M. F. (1995b). Contact, contract, change, encore: A conversation with Bob Goulding. *Transactional Analysis Journal, 25*, 300–311.

Hoyt, M. F. (1995c). "Patient" or "client": What's in a name? In *Brief therapy and managed care: Readings for contemporary practice* (pp. 205–207). San Francisco: Jossey-Bass. (Reprinted from *Psychotherapy: Theory, Research and Practice*, 1979, *16*, 46–47)

Hoyt, M. F. (1995d). Aspects of termination in a brief time-limited psychotherapy. In *Brief therapy and managed care: Readings for contemporary practice* (pp.183–204). San Francisco: Jossey-Bass. (Reprinted from *Psychiatry*, 1979, *42*, 208–219)

Hoyt, M. F. (1995e). "Shrink" or "expander": An issue in forming a therapeutic alliance. In *Brief therapy and managed care: Readings for contemporary practice* (pp. 209–211). San Francisco: Jossey-Bass. (Reprinted from *Psychotherapy*, 1985, *22*, 813–814)

Hoyt, M. F. (1995f). Therapist resistances to short-term dynamic psychotherapy. In *Brief therapy and managed care: Readings for contemporary practice* (pp. 219–235). San Francisco: Jossey-Bass. (Reprinted from *Journal of the American Academy of Psychoanalysis*, 1985, *13*, 93–112)

Hoyt, M. F. (1995g). On time in brief therapy. In *Brief therapy and managed care: Readings for contemporary practice* (pp. 69–104). San Francisco: Jossey-Bass. (Reprinted from *Handbook of the Brief Psychotherapies*, pp. 115–143, by R. A. Wells & V. J. Giannetti, Eds., 1990, New York: Plenum)

Hoyt, M. F. (1995h). Group practice in an HMO. In *Brief therapy and managed care: Readings for contemporary practice* (pp. 51–62). San Francisco: Jossey-Bass. (Reprinted from *HMO Practice*, 1993, *7*, 129–132)

Hoyt, M. F. (1995i). The four questions of brief therapy. Reprinted in *Brief therapy and managed care: Readings for contemporary practice* (pp. 217–218). San Francisco: Jossey-Bass. (Reprinted from *Journal of Systemic Therapies*, 1994, *13*, 77–78)

Hoyt, M. F. (1995j). Is being "in recovery" self-limiting? In *Brief therapy and managed care: Readings for contemporary practice* (pp. 213–215). San Francisco: Jossey-Bass. (Reprinted from *Transactional Analysis Journal*, 1994, *24*, 222–223)

Hoyt, M. F. (1995k). Single session solutions. In *Brief therapy and managed care: Readings for contemporary practice* (pp. 141–162). San Francisco: Jossey-Bass. (Reprinted from *Constructive therapies*, pp. 140–159, by M. F. Hoyt, Ed., 1994, New York: Guilford Press)

Hoyt, M. F. (1995l). Promoting HMO values and a culture of quality: Doing the right thing in a staff-model HMO mental-health department. In *Brief therapy and managed care: Readings for contemporary practice* (pp. 41–50). San Francisco: Jossey-Bass. (Reprinted from *HMO Practice*, 1994, *8*, 37–41)

Hoyt, M. F. (1995m). Characteristics of psychotherapy under managed health care. In M. F. Hoyt, *Brief therapy and managed care: Readings for contemporary practice* (pp. 1–8). San Francisco: Jossey-Bass. (Reprinted from *Behavioral Healthcare Tomorrow*, 1994, *3*(5), 59–62)

Hoyt, M. F. (1996a). Postmodernism, the relational self, constructive therapies, and beyond: A conversation with Kenneth Gergen. In M. F. Hoyt (Ed.), *Constructive therapies* (Vol. 2, pp. 347–368). New York: Guilford Press.

Hoyt, M. F. (Ed.). (1996b). *Constructive therapies* (Vol. 2). New York: Guilford Press.

Hoyt, M. F. (1996c). Solution building and language games: A conversation with Steve de Shazer. In M. F. Hoyt (Ed.), *Constructive therapies* (Vol. 2, pp. 60–86). New York: Guilford Press.

Hoyt, M. F. (1996d). Cognitive-behavioral treatment of posttraumatic stress disorder from a narrative constructivist perspective: A conversation with Donald Meichenbaum. In M. F. Hoyt (Ed.), *Constructive therapies* (Vol. 2, pp. 124–147). New York: Guilford Press.

Hoyt, M. F. (1996e). Welcome to Possibilityland: A conversation with Bill O'Hanlon. In M. F. Hoyt (Ed.), *Constructive therapies* (Vol. 2, pp. 87–123). New York: Guilford Press.

Hoyt, M. F. (1997). Foreword. In C. Lennox (Ed.), *Redecision therapy: A brief, action-oriented approach* (pp. xii–xix). Northvale, NJ: Aronson.

Hoyt, M. F. (Ed.). (1998). *The handbook of constructive therapies*. San Francisco: Jossey-Bass.

Hoyt, M. F. (1999). Comment on L'Abate. *The Family Journal: Counseling and Therapy for Couples and Families, 7*, 224–226.

Hoyt, M. F. (2000). Solution-focused couple therapy. In A. S. Gurman & N. S. Jacobson (Eds.), *Clinical handbook of couple therapy* (3rd ed.). New York: Guilford Press, in preparation.

Hoyt, M. F., & Austad, C. S. (1995). Psychotherapy in a staff-model HMO: Providing and assuring quality care in the future. In M. F. Hoyt, *Brief therapy and managed care: Readings for contemporary practice* (pp. 23–40). San Francisco: Jossey-Bass. (Reprinted from *Psychotherapy*, 1992, *29*, 119–129)

Hoyt, M. F., & Berg, I. K. (1998). Solution-focused couple therapy: Helping clients construct self-fulfilling realities. In M. F. Hoyt (Ed.), *The handbook of constructive therapies* (pp. 314–340). San Francisco: Jossey-Bass. (Reprinted from *Case studies in couple and family therapy: Systemic and cognitive perspectives*, pp. 203–232, by F. M. Dattilio, Ed., 1998, New York: Guilford Press)

Hoyt, M. F., & Budman, S. H. (1996). Fear and loathing on the managed-care trail: A response to Pipal (1995). *Psychotherapy, 33*, 121–123.

Hoyt, M. F., & Combs, G. (1996). On ethics and the spiritualities of the surface: A conversation with Michael White. In M. F. Hoyt (Ed.), *Constructive therapies* (Vol. 2, pp. 33–59). New York: Guilford Press

Hoyt, M. F., & Farrell, D. (1983–1984). Countertransference difficulties in a time-limited psychotherapy. *International Journal of Psychoanalytic Psychotherapy, 10*, 191–203.

Hoyt, M. F., & Goulding, R. L. (1995). Resolution of a transference-countertransference impasse using Gestalt techniques in supervision. In *Brief therapy and managed care: Readings for contemporary practice* (pp. 237–256). San Francisco: Jossey-Bass. (Reprinted from *Transactional Analysis Journal*, 1989, *19*, 201–211)

Hoyt, M. F., Miller, S. D., Held, B. S., & Matthews, W. J., Jr. (in press). A conversation about constructivism: Or, if four colleagues talked in New York, would anyone hear it? *Journal of Systemic Therapies*.

Hoyt, M. F., & Ordover, J. (1988). Book review of J. K. Zeig (Ed.), *The evolution of psychotherapy. Imagination, Cognition, and Personality, 8,* 181–186.

Hoyt, M. F., Rosenbaum, R., & Talmon, M. (1992). Planned single-session psychotherapy. In S. H. Budman, M. F. Hoyt, & S. Friedman (Eds.), *The first session in brief therapy* (pp. 59–86). New York: Guilford Press.

Hoyt, M. F., & Talmon, M. (1990). Single-session therapy in action: A case example. In M. Talmon, *Single session therapy* (pp. 78–96). San Francisco: Jossey-Bass.

Hubble, M. A., Duncan, B. L., & Miller, S. D. (Eds.). (1999). *The heart and soul of change: What works in therapy.* Washington, DC: American Psychological Association.

Hubble, M. A., & O'Hanlon, W. H. (1992). Theory countertransference. *Dulwich Centre Newsletter, 1,* 25–30.

Hudson, P. O., & O'Hanlon, W. H. (1991). *Rewriting love stories: Brief marital therapy.* New York: Norton.

Hunter, R. D. A., & Austad, C. S. (1997). Mental health care benefits and perceptions of health insurance agents and clinical psychologists. *Professional Psychology: Research and Practice, 28,* 365–367.

Hyde, L. (1998). *Trickster makes this world: Mischief, myth and art.* New York: Farrar, Straus and Giroux.

Illich, I. (1976). *Medical nemesis: The expropriation of health.* New York: Pantheon Books/Random House.

Illich, I., & Sanders, B. (1988). *ABC: The alphabetization of the popular mind.* San Francisco: North Point Press.

Iveson, C. (1990). *Whose life? Community care of older people and their families.* London: Brief Therapy Press.

Jackson, D., & Weakland, J. H. (1961). Conjoint family therapy: Some considerations on theory, technique, and results. *Psychiatry, 24*(2), 30–45.

Jacobson, N. S. (1995). The overselling of therapy. *Family Therapy Networker, 19*(2), 40–47.

Jacobson, N. S., & Margolin, G. (1979). *Marital therapy: Strategies based on social learning and behavior exchange principles.* New York: Brunner/Mazel.

Jaynes, J. (1990). *The origins of consciousness in the breakdown of the bicameral mind.* New York: Houghton Mifflin.

Johnson, C. E., & Goldman, J. (1996). Taking safety home: A solution-focused approach with domestic violence. In M. F. Hoyt (Ed.), *Constructive therapies* (Volume 2) (pp.184–196). New York: Guilford Press.

Johnson, E. L., & Sandage, S. J. (1999). A postmodern reconstruction of psychotherapy: Orienteering, religion, and the healing of the soul. *Psychotherapy, 36,* 1–15.

Johnson, L. D. (1995). *Psychotherapy in the age of accountability.* New York: Norton.

Johnson, L. D., & Shaha, S. (1996). Improving quality in psychotherapy. *Psychotherapy, 33,* 225–236.

Johnson, V. E. (1973). *I'll quit tomorrow.* New York: Harper & Row.

Johnson, V. E. (1986). *Intervention: How to help someone who doesn't want help.* Minneapolis, MN: Johnson Institute Books.

Jones, E. E., Kanouse, D. E., Kelley, H. H., Nisbett, R. E., Valins, S., & Weiner, B. (Eds.). (1972). *Attribution: Perceiving the causes of behavior.* New York: General Learning Press.

Jones, R. T. (1960). *Golf is my game.* Garden City, NY: Doubleday.

Jongsma, A. E., Jr., & Peterson, L. M. (1995). *The complete psychotherapy treatment planner.* New York: Wiley.

Jongsma, A. E., Jr., Peterson, L. M., & McInnis, W. P. (1996). *The child and adolescent psychotherapy treatment planner.* New York: Wiley.

Jung, C. G. (1966). Problems of modern psychotherapy. In *The collected works of C. G. Jung.* (2nd ed., Vol. 16, pp. 53–75) Princeton, NJ: Bollingen/Princeton University Press. (Original work published 1929)

Jung, C. G. (1977). Foreword. In R. Wilhelm (Trans.), *The I Ching, or book of changes* (pp. xxi–xxxix). Princeton, NJ: Bollingen/Princeton University Press. (Original work published 1949)

Kabat-Zinn, J. (1994). *Wherever you go, there you are: Mindfulness meditation in everyday life.* New York: Hyperion.

Kahn, E. (1996). The intersubjective perspective and the client-centered approach: Are they one at their core? *Psychotherapy, 33,* 30–42.

Karon, B. P. (1995). Provision of psychotherapy under managed health care: A growing crisis and national nightmare. *Professional Psychology: Research and Practice, 26,* 5–9.

Karrass, C. L. (1992). *The negotiating game.* (Rev. ed.) New York: HarperCollins.

Kaslow, F. W. (Ed.). (1996). *Handbook of relational diagnosis and dysfunctional family patterns.* New York: Wiley.

Kazantzakis, N. (1971). *Report to Greco.* New York: Bantam Books. (Original work published 1961)

Kazantzis, N., & Deane, F. P. (1999). Psychologists' use of homework assignments in clinical practice. *Professional Psychology: Research and Practice, 30*(6), 581–585.

Keeney, B. P. (1982). What is an epistemology of family therapy? *Family Process, 21,* 153–168.

Keeney, B. P. (1983). *The aesthetics of change.* New York: Guilford Press.

Keeney, B. P. (1991). *Improvisational therapy: A practice guide to creative clinical strategies.* New York: Guilford Press.

Kelly, G. A. (1955). *The psychology of personal constructs.* New York: Norton.

Kelly, T. A. (1997). A wake-up call: The experience of a mental health commissioner in times of change. *Professional Psychology: Research and Practice, 28,* 317–322.

Kerfoot, E. M. (1997). Using redecision therapy in groups. In C. E. Lennox (Ed.), *Redecision therapy: A brief, action-oriented approach* (pp. 127–142). Northvale, NJ: Jason Aronson.

Kierkegaard, S. (1959). *Journals.* A. Dru (Ed.). New York: Harper. (Original work published 1843)

Kirk, S. A., & Kutchins, H. (1992). *The selling of DSM: The rhetoric of science in psychiatry.* Hawthorne, NY: Aldine de Gruyter.

Kirsch, I., & Lynn, S. J. (1999). Automaticity in clinical psychology. *American Psychologist, 54,* 504–515.

Koop, C. E. (1996). Manage with care. *Time, 148,* 69, Special Issue.

Korzybski, A. (1933). *Science and sanity.* New York: Non-Aristotelian Library.

Kotelchuck, D. (Ed.). (1976). *Prognosis negative: Crisis in the health care system.* New York: Vintage/Random House.

Kotre, J. (1996). *White gloves: How we create ourselves through memory.* New York: Norton.

Kovacs, A. L. (1998). Thoughts on achievable health care reform. *Professional Psychology: Research and Practice, 29,* 100–101.

Kowalski, K., & Kral, R. (1989). The geometry of solution: Using the scaling technique. *Family Therapy Case Studies, 4,* 59–66.

Kramer, S. A. (1990). *Positive endings in psychotherapy: Bringing meaningful closure to therapeutic relationships.* San Francisco: Jossey-Bass.

Kramer, P. (1993). *Listening to Prozac.* New York: Viking.

Kreider, J. W. (1998). Solution-focused ideas for briefer therapy with longer-term clients. In M. F. Hoyt (Ed.), *The handbook of constructive therapies* (pp. 341–357). San Francisco: Jossey-Bass.

Kremer, T. G., & Gesten, E. L. (1998). Confidentiality limits of managed care and clients' willingness to self-disclose. *Professional Psychology: Research and Practice, 29,* 553–558.

Kroeber, T. (1961). *Ishi in two worlds: A biography of the last wild Indian in North America.* Berkeley: University of California Press.

Kushner, T. (1995). American things. In *Thinking about the longstanding problems of virtue and happiness* (pp. 3–11). New York: Theatre Communications Group.

L'Abate, L. (1997). The paradox of change: Better them than us! In S. R. Sauber (Ed.), *Managed mental health care: Major diagnostic and treatment approaches* (pp. 40–66). Philadelphia: Brunner/Mazel.

L'Abate, L. (1999). Taking the bull by the horns: Beyond talk in psychological interventions. *The Family Journal: Counseling and Therapy for Couples and Families, 7,* 206–220.

Lacan, J. (1977). The function and field of speech and language in psychoanalysis. In J. Lacan (Ed.), *Ecrits* (pp. 30–113). New York: Norton.

Lahr, J. (1996, December 9). The imperfectionist [Woody Allen profile]. *The New Yorker,* 68–82.

Laing, R. D. (1967). *The politics of experience.* New York: Pantheon.

Laing, R. D. (1970). *Knots.* New York: Pantheon.

Lakoff, G. (1995). Body, brain, and communication (I.A. Boal, Int.) In J. Brook & I. A. Boal (Eds.), *Resisting the virtual life: The culture and politics of information* (pp.115–129). San Francisco: City Lights Books.

Lakoff, G., & Johnson, M. (1980). *Metaphors we live by.* Chicago: University of Chicago Press.

Lambert, M. J. (1992). Implications of outcome research for psychotherapy integration. In J. C. Norcross & M. R. Goldfried (Eds.), *Handbook of psychotherapy integration.* New York: Basic Books.

Lambert, M. J., & Bergin, A. E. (1994). The effectiveness of psychotherapy. In A. E. Bergin & S. L. Garfield (Eds.), *Handbook of psychotherapy and behavior change* (4th ed.). New York: Wiley.

Lambert, W., Saltzer, M. S., & Bickman, L. (1998). Clinical outcome, consumer satisfaction, and ad hoc ratings of improvement in children's mental health. *Journal of Consulting and Clinical Psychology, 66,* 270–279.

Lamott, A. (1994). *Bird by bird: Some instructions on writing and life.* New York: Anchor/Doubleday.

Lankton, S., & Lankton, C. (1998). Ericksonian emergent epistemologies: Embracing a new paradigm. In M. F. Hoyt (Ed.), *The handbook of constructive therapies* (pp. 116–136). San Francisco: Jossey-Bass.

Lardner, R. (1960). *Out of the bunker and into the trees: Or, the secret of high-tension golf.* Indianapolis, IN: Bobbs-Merrill.

Larsen, S., & Larsen, R. (1991). *A fire in the mind: The life of Joseph Campbell.* New York: Doubleday.

Lavizzo-Mourey, R., & Mackenzie, E. R. (1996). Cultural competence: Essential measurements of quality for managed care organizations. *Annals of Internal Medicine, 124,* 919–920.

Lax, W. D. (1992). Postmodern thinking as a clinical practice. In S. McNamee & K. J. Gergen (Eds.), *Therapy as social construction* (pp. 69–85). Newbury Park, CA: Sage.

Lazarus, A. A. (1997a). Disenchantment and hope: Will we ever occupy center stage? A personal odyssey. *Behavior Therapy, 28,* 363–370.

Lazarus, A. A. (1997b). *Brief but comprehensive psychotherapy: The multimodal way.* New York: Springer.

Leary, K. (1994). Psychoanalytic "problems" and postmodern "solutions." *Psychoanalytic Quarterly, 68,* 433–465.

Lennon, J. (1971). Imagine, Song on a record album *Imagine.* New York: Apple Records.

Lerner, M. (1995). The assault on psychotherapy. *Family Therapy Networker, 19*(5), 44–52.

Lethem, J. (1994). *Moved to tears, moved to action: Solution-focused brief therapy with women and children.* London: BT Press.

Levenson, H. (1995). *Time-limited dynamic psychotherapy: A guide to clinical practice.* New York: Basic Books.

Levenson, H., & Burg, J. (in press). Training psychologists in the era of managed care. In A. Kent & M. Hersen (Eds.), *A psychologist's proactive guide to managed mental health care.* Hillsdale, NJ: Erlbaum.

Levin, D. M. (1987). *Mudra* as thinking: Developing our wisdom-of-being in gesture and movement. In G. Parkes (Ed.), *Heidegger and Asian thought* (pp. 245–269). Honolulu: University of Hawaii Press.

Levine, L. B., & Stone Fish, L. (1999). The integration of constructivism and social constructionist theory in family therapy: A Delphi study. *Journal of Systemic Therapies, 18*(1), 58–84.

Levy, R. L., & Shelton, J. L. (1990). Tasks in brief therapy. In R. A. Wells & V. J. Giannetti (Eds.), *Handbook of the brief psychotherapies* (pp. 145–163). New York: Plenum Press.

Lewin, K. K. (1970). *Brief psychotherapy: Brief encounters.* St. Louis, MO: Warren H. Green.

Lewis, C. S. (1956). *Surprised by joy.* San Diego, CA: Harcourt Brace Jovanovich.

Lewis, C. S. (1982). *The screwtape letters.* New York: Bantam Books. (Original work published 1942)

Lincoln, Y. S. (1990). The making of a constructivist. In E. G. Guba (Ed.), *The paradigm dialogue.* Newbury Park, CA: Sage.

Lincoln, Y. S., & Guba, E. G. (1985). *Naturalistic inquiry.* Newbury Park, CA: Sage.

Lipchik, E. (Ed.) (1987). *Interviewing.* Rockville, MD: Aspen.

Lipchik, E. (1994). The rush to be brief. *Family Therapy Networker, 18*(2), 34–39.

Lipchik, E. (1999). Book review of *The Handbook of Constructive Therapies. Journal of Systemic Therapies, 5,* 88–89.

Lipchik, E., & de Shazar, S. (1986). The purposeful interview. *Journal of Strategic and Systemic Therapies, 5,* 88–89.

Lipchik, E., & Kubicki, A.D. (1996). Solution-focused domestic violence views: Bridges toward a new reality in couples therapy. In S. D. Miller, M. A. Hubble, & B. L. Duncan (Eds.), *Handbook of solution-focused brief therapy* (pp. 65–98). San Francisco: Jossey-Bass.

Lipp, M. R. (1980). *The bitter pill: Doctors, patients, and failed expectations.* New York: Harper & Row.

London, P. (1964). *The modes and morals of psychotherapy.* New York: Holt, Rinehart & Winston.

Lopez, B. (1990). *Crow and weasel.* San Francisco: North Point Press.

Lopez, N. (with Schwed, P.). (1979). *The education of a woman golfer.* New York: Simon & Schuster.

Lown, B. (1983). Introduction. In N. Cousins, *The healing heart* (pp. 11–25). New York: Avon.

Luepnitz, D. A. (1988). Bateson's heritage: Bitter fruit. *Family Therapy Networker, 2*(5), 48–50, 52–53, 73.

Lyddon, W. J. (1990). First- and second-order change: Implications for rationalist and constructivist cognitive therapies. *Journal of Counseling and Development, 69,* 122–127.

Lyddon, W. J., & Bradford, E. (1995). Philosophical commitments and therapy approach preferences among psychotherapy trainees. *Journal of Theoretical and Philosophical Psychology, 15,* 1–15.

Lyons, A. S., & Petrucelli, R. J. (1987). *Medicine: An illustrated history.* New York: Abrams.

Lyotard, J. F. (1984). *The postmodern condition: A report on knowledge.* Minneapolis: University of Minnesota Press.

MacCormack, T., & Tomm, K. (1998) Social constructionist/narrative couple therapy. In F. M. Dattilio (Ed.), *Case studies in couple and family therapy: Systemic and cognitive perspectives* (pp. 303–330). New York: Guilford Press.

MacKenzie, K. R. (1994). Where is here and when is now? The adaptational challenge of mental health reform for group psychotherapy. *International Journal of Group Psychotherapy, 44,* 407–428.

Mackenzie, M. M. (with Denlinger, K.). (1990). *Golf: The mind game.* New York: Dell.

Madanes, C. (1981). *Strategic family therapy.* San Francisco: Jossey-Bass.

Madanes, C. (1999). Rebels with a cause: Honoring the subversive power of psychotherapy. *Family Therapy Networker, 23*(4), 44–49, 57.

Madanes, C., Keim, I., Lentine, G., & Keim, J. P. (1990). No more John Wayne: Strategies for changing the past. In C. Madanes (Ed.), *Sex, love, and violence: Strategies for transformation* (pp. 218–247). New York: Norton.

Madigan, R., Johnson, S., & Linton, P. (1995). The language of psychology: APA style as epistemology. *American Psychologist, 50*(6), 428–436.

Madigan, S. P. (1992). The application of Michel Foucault's philosophy in the problem externalizing discourse of Michael White. *Journal of Family Therapy, 14,* 265–279.

Madigan, S. P. (1993). Questions about questions: Situating the therapist's curiosity in front of the family. In S. Gilligan & R. Price (Eds.), *Therapeutic conversations* (pp. 219–230; with commentary by D. Epston, pp. 231–236). New York: Norton.

Madigan, S. P. (1997). Re-considering memory: Re-remembering lost identities back toward re-membered selves (with commentary by L. Grieves). In C. Smith & D. Nylund (Eds.), *Narrative therapies with children and adolescents* (pp. 338–355). New York: Guilford.

Madigan, S. P., & Epston, D. (1995). From "spy-chiatric gaze" to communities of concern: From professional monologue to dialogue. In S. Friedman (Ed.), *The reflecting team in action: Collaborative practice in family therapy* (pp. 257–276). New York: Guilford Press.

Madigan, S. P., & Goldner, E. M. (1998). A narrative approach to anorexia: Discourse, reflexivity, and questions. In M. F. Hoyt (Ed.), *The handbook of constructive therapies* (pp. 380–400). San Francisco: Jossey-Bass.

Mahoney, M. J. (1991). *Human change processes: The scientific foundations of psychotherapy.* New York: Basic Books.

Mahoney, M. J. (1995). The psychological demands of being a constructive psychotherapist. In R. A. Neimeyer & M. J. Mahoney (Eds.), *Constructivism in Psychotherapy* (pp. 385–399). Washington, DC: American Psychological Association.

Mahoney, M. J. (1999). Are there constructive alternatives to pathology-focused treatments? Yes! [Review of *The handbook of constructive therapies*]. *Contemporary Psychology: APA Review of Books, 44,* 423–424.

Mahoney, M. J. (in press). *Constructive psychotherapy.* New York: Guilford Press.

Mahrer, A. R., Nordin, S., & Miller, L. S. (1995). If a client has this kind of problem, prescribe that kind of post-session behavior. *Psychotherapy, 32,* 194–203.

Malamud, B. (1993). *The natural.* New York: Avon. (Original work published 1952)

Malan, D. H. (1976). *The frontier of brief psychotherapy.* New York: Plenum Press.

Managed or mangled? *60 Minutes.* (1997, January 5). New York: CBS.

Mann, J. (1973). *Time-limited psychotherapy.* Cambridge, MA: Harvard University Press.

Markowitz, L. (1997). The cultural context of intimacy. *Family Therapy Networker, 21*(5), 51–58.

Marrow, A. J. (1977). *The practical theorist: The life and work of Kurt Lewin.* New York: Teachers' College Press.

Matthews, W. J. (1985). A cybernetic model of Ericksonian hypnotherapy: One hand draws the other. *Ericksonian Monographs, 1,* 42–60.

Matthews, W. J. (1990). More than a doorway, a shift in epistemology. *Ericksonian Monographs, 7,* 15–21.

Matthews, W. J. (1997). Constructing meaning and action in therapy: Confessions of an early pragmatist. *Journal of Systemic Therapies, 16,* 134–144.

Maturana, H. R. (1988). Reality: The search for objectivity or the quest for a compelling argument. *Irish Journal of Psychology, 9,* 46–48.

Maturana, H. R., & Varela, F. J. (1980). *Autopoiesis and cognition.* Dordrecht, the Netherlands: Reidel.

May, R., Angel, E., & Ellenberger, H. F. (Eds.). (1958). *Existence: A new dimension in psychiatry and psychology.* New York: Basic Books.

McAdams, D. P. (1993). *The stories we live by: Personal myths and the making of the self.* New York: Guilford Press.

McBride, J. (1996). *The color of water: A Black man's tribute to his White mother.* New York: Riverhead Books.

McCarthy, I. C., & Byrne, N. O. (1988). Mis-taken love: Conversations on the problem of incest in an Irish context. *Family Process, 27,* 181–199.

McCarthy, I. C., & Byrne, N. O. (1995). A spell in the fifth province: It's between meself, herself, yerself, and yer two imaginary friends. In S. Friedman (Ed.), *The reflecting team in action: Collaborative practice in family therapy* (pp. 119–142). New York: Guilford Press.

McClosky, K. A., & Fraser, J. S. (1997). Using feminist MRI brief therapy during initial contact with victims of domestic violence. *Psychotherapy, 34*(4), 433–446.

McCormick, M. H. (1984). *What they don't teach you at Harvard Business School.* New York: Bantam Books.

McGoldrick, M. (1995). *You can go home again.* New York: Norton.

McKibben, B. (1992). *The age of missing information.* New York: Plume.

McLean, C. (1994). A conversation about accountability with Michael White. In M. White, *Re-authoring lives: Interviews and essays* (pp. 155–171). Adelaide, Australia: Dulwich Centre Publications. (Reprinted from *Dulwich Centre Newsletter,* 1994, *3,* 68–79)

McNally, D. (1991). *Even eagles need a push.* New York: Delacorte.

McNamee, S., & Gergen, K. J. (Eds.). (1992). *Therapy as social construction.* Newbury Park, CA: Sage.

McNeel, J. (1976). The Parent interview. *Transactional Analysis Journal, 6,* 61–68.

Meichenbaum, D. (1977). *Cognitive-behavior modification: An integrative approach.* New York: Plenum Press.

Meichenbaum, D. (1985). *Stress inoculation training: A clinical guidebook.* Elmsford, NY: Pergamon.

Meichenbaum, D. (1994). *A clinical handbook/practical therapist manual for treating PTSD.* Waterloo, Canada: Institute Press.

Meichenbaum, D., & Fitzpatrick, D. (1993). A constructive narrative perspective on stress and coping: Stress inoculation implications. In L. Goldberger & S. Breznitz (Eds.), *Handbook of stress* (pp. 695–710). New York: Free Press.

Meichenbaum, D., & Turk, D. (1987), *Facilitating treatment adherence: A practitioner's guidebook.* New York: Plenum Press.

Melges, F. T. (1982), *Time and the inner future: A temporal approach to psychiatric disorders.* New York: Wiley.

Melville, H. (1979). *Moby Dick: Or, the whale.* Berkeley: The Arion Press/University of California Press. (Original work published 1851)

Menninger, K. (1958). *Theory and practice of psychoanalytic technique.* New York: Basic Books.

Mental Health: Does therapy help? (1995, November). *Consumer Reports, 61*(8), 28–42.

Miller, B., & Farber, L. (1996). Delivery of mental health services in the changing health care system. *Professional Psychology: Research and Practice, 27,* 527–529.

Miller, E. E. (1992). Birds. In M. Decosta-Willis, R. Martin, & R. P. Bell (Eds.), *Erotique noire/ Black erotica* (p. 160). New York: Anchor Books.

Miller, G. (1997). *Becoming miracle workers: Language and meaning in brief therapy.* Hawthorne, NY: Aldine de Gruyter.

Miller, G., & de Shazer, S. (1998). Have you heard the latest about . . . ? Solution-focused therapy as a rumor. *Family Process, 37,* 363–378.

Miller, G., & de Shazer, S. (in press). Emotions in solution-focused therapy: A re-examination. *Family Process.*

Miller, I. J. (1996a). Managed care is harmful to outpatient mental health services: A call for accountability. *Professional Psychology: Research and Practice, 27,* 349–363.

Miller, I. J. (1996b). Time-limited brief therapy has gone too far: The result is invisible rationing. *Professional Psychology: Research and Practice, 27,* 567–576.

Miller, I. J. (1996c). Some "short-term therapy values" are a formula for invisible rationing. *Professional Psychology: Research and Practice, 27,* 577–582.

Miller, I. J. (1996d). Ethical and liability issues concerning invisible rationing. *Professional Psychology: Research and Practice, 27,* 583–587.

Miller, I. J. (1998). Response to "All that glitters is not always gold: Medical offset effects and managed behavioral health care." *Professional Psychology: Research and Practice, 29,* 622–624.

Miller, S. D. (1992). The symptoms of solution. *Journal of Strategic and Systemic Therapies, 11,* 1–11.

Miller, S. D. (1994). Some questions (not answers) for the brief treatment of people with drug and alcohol problems. In M. F. Hoyt (Ed.), *Constructive therapies* (pp. 91–110). New York: Guilford Press.

Miller, S. D., & Berg, I. K. (1991). Working with the problem drinker: A solution-focused approach. *Arizona Counseling Journal, 16,* 3–12.

Miller, S. D., & Berg, I. K. (1995). *The miracle method: A radically new approach to problem drinking.* New York: Norton.

Miller, S. D., Duncan, B. L., & Hubble, M. A. (1997). *Escape from Babel: toward a unifying language for psychotherapy practice.* New York: Norton.

Miller, S. D., Duncan, B. L., Hubble, M. A., & Johnson, L. D. (1999). Jurassic practice: Why the field is on the verge of extinction and what we can do to save it. In M. A. Hubble, B. L. Duncan, & S. D. Miller (Eds.), *The heart and soul of change: What works in therapy.* Washington, DC: American Psychological Association.

Miller, S. D., Duncan, B. L., & Johnson, L. D. (1999). Their verdict is the key. *Family Therapy Networker, 23*(2), 46–51, 54–55.

Miller, S. D., Hubble, M. A., & Duncan, B. L. (Eds.). (1996). *Handbook of solution-focused brief therapy.* San Francisco: Jossey-Bass.

Miller, W. R. (1986). Increasing motivation for change. In W. R. Miller & N. H. Heather (Eds.), *Addictive behaviors: Processes of change.* New York: Plenum Press.

Milne, A. A. (1999). *The complete tales of Winnie-the-Pooh.* (Illust. by F. H. Shephard). New York: Dutton. (Original work published 1926)

Minsky, T. (1987). Prisoners of psychotherapy. *New York Magazine, 20,* 34–40.

Minuchin, S. (1982). Foreword. In J. R. Neill & D. P. Kniskern (Eds.), *From psyche to system: The evolving therapy of Carl Whitaker* (pp. vii–ix). New York: Guilford Press.

Minuchin, S. (1987). My many voices. In J. K. Zeig (Ed.), *The evolution of psychotherapy* (pp. 5–14) New York: Brunner/Mazel.

Minuchin, S. (1991). The seductions of constructivism. *Family Therapy Networker, 9*(5), 47–50.

Minuchin, S. (1992). The restoried history of family therapy. In J. K. Zeig (Ed.), *The evolution of psychotherapy: The second conference* (pp. 3–12). New York: Brunner/Mazel.

Minuchin, S., & Nichols, M. P. (1993). *Family healing: Strategies for hope and understanding.* New York: Simon & Schuster.

Mirowsky, J., & Ross, C. E. (1987). *Social causes of psychological distress.* Hawthorne, NY: Aldine de Gruyter.

Moffic, H. S. (1997). *The ethical way: Challenges and solutions for managed behavioral healthcare.* San Francisco: Jossey-Bass.

Mohr, D. C. (1995). The role of proscription in psychotherapy. *Psychotherapy, 32,* 187–193.

Moldawsky, S. (1990). Is solo practice really dead? *American Psychologist, 45,* 544–546.

Monk, G., Winslade, J., Crocket, K., & Epston, D. (Eds.). (1997). *Narrative therapy in practice: The archaeology of hope.* San Francisco: Jossey-Bass.

Moore, R. L. (1994). Series foreword. In M. P. Somé, *Ritual: Power, healing and community* (pp. 9–10). Portland, OR: Swan/Raven.

Morrison, A. (Ed.). (1994). *The impossible art of golf.* New York: Oxford University Press.

Mumford, E., & Schlesinger, H. J. (1987). Assessing consumer benefit: Cost offset as an incidental effect of psychotherapy. *General Hospital Psychiatry, 9,* 360–363.

Mumford, E., Schlesinger, H. J., Glass, G., Parick, C., & Cuerdon, T. (1984). A new look at evidence about reduced cost of medical utilization following mental-health treatment. *American Journal of Psychiatry, 141,* 1145–1158.

Murphy, J. J. (1997). *Solution-focused counseling in middle and high schools.* Alexandria, VA: American Counseling Association.

Murphy, M. (1972). *Golf in the kingdom.* New York: Viking.

Murphy, M. (1997). *The kingdom of Shivas Irons.* New York: Broadway Books.

Murphy, M., & White, R. A. (1978). *The psychic side of sports.* Reading, MA: Addison-Wesley.

Nahmias, V. R. (1992). Training for a managed care setting. *Psychotherapy in Private Practice, 11,* 15–19.

Nathan, P. E. (1998). Practice guidelines: Not yet ideal. *American Psychologist, 53,* 290–299.

Neal, J. H. (1996). Narrative training therapy and supervision. *Journal of Systemic Therapies, 15,* 63–78.

Neill, J. R., & Kniskern, D. P. (Eds.). (1982). *From psyche to system: The evolving therapy of Carl Whitaker.* New York: Guilford Press.

Neimeyer, R. A. (1993a). Constructivism and the cognitive therapies: Some conceptual and strategic contrasts. *Journal of Cognitive Psychotherapy, 7,* 159–171.

Neimeyer, R. A. (1993b). Constructivism and the problem of psychotherapy integration. *Journal of Psychotherapy Integration, 3,* 133–157.

Neimeyer, R. A. (1993c). An appraisal of constructivist psychotherapies. *Journal of Consulting and Clinical Psychology, 61,* 221–234.

Neimeyer, R.A. (1995). Constructivist psychotherapies: Features, foundations, and future directions. In R. A. Neimeyer & M. J. Mahoney (Eds.), *Constructivism in psychotherapy* (pp. 11–38). Washington, DC: American Psychological Association.

Neimeyer, R. A. (1998a). Cognitive therapy and the narrative trend: A bridge too far? *Journal of Cognitive Psychotherapy, 12,* 57–65.

Neimeyer, R. A. (1998b). Social constructionism in the counselling context. *Counselling Psychology Quarterly, 11,* 135–149.

Neimeyer, R. A., & Freixas, G. (1990). Constructivist contributions to psychotherapy integration. *Journal of Integrative and Eclectic Psychotherapy, 9,* 4–20.

Neimeyer, R. A., & Mahoney, M. J. (Eds.) (1995). *Constructivism in psychotherapy.* Washington, DC: American Psychological Association.

Neimeyer, R. A., & Neimeyer, G. J. (1987). *Personal construct therapy casebook.* New York: Springer.

Nelson, K. (1992). *The greatest golf shot ever, and other lively and entertaining tales from the lore and history of golf.* New York: Fireside/Simon & Schuster.

Nelson, W. (1998, December). What I've learned. *Esquire, 130,* 110.

Newman, R., & Bricklin, P. M. (1991). Parameters of managed mental health care: Legal, ethical, and professional guidelines. *Professional Psychology: Research and Practice, 22,* 26–35.

Newsweek (1999, November 8). How HMOs measure up. *134*(18), pp. 69–72.

Nickelson, D. W. (1998). Telehealth and the evolving health care system: Strategic opportunities for professional psychology. *Professional Psychology: Research and Practice, 29,* 527–535.

Nicklaus, J. (1994, May). Arnie and Jack: Golf's two leading legends go head to head as never before. *Golf Magazine, 36*(5), 58–68, 136–140.

Nicklaus, J. (with Bowden, K). (1974). *Golf my way.* New York: Fireside/Simon & Schuster.

Nichols, M. P. (1993). The therapist as authority figure. *Family Process, 32,* 163–165.

Nightline. (1996, November 8). New York: ABC.

Norcross, J. C., Alford, B. A., & DeMichele, J. (1992). The future of psychotherapy: Delphi data and concluding observations. *Psychotherapy, 29,* 150–158.

Norcross, J. C., & Beutler, L. E. (1997). Determining the therapeutic relationship of choice in brief therapy. In J. N. Butcher (Ed.), *Personality assessment in managed health care: A practitioner's guide.* New York: Oxford University Press.

Norris, M. P., Molinari, V., & Rosowsky, E. (1998). Providing mental health care to older adults: Unraveling the maze of Medicare and managed care. *Psychotherapy, 35,* 490–497.

Novack, D., Deterling, B. J., Arnold, R. Forrow, L. Ladinsky, M., & Pezzullo, J. C. (1989). Physicians attitudes towards using deception to resolve difficult ethical problems. *Journal of the American Medical Association, 261,* 2980–2985.

Nunnally, E. (1993). Solution focused therapy. In R. A. Wells & V. J. Giannetti (Eds.), *Casebook of the brief psychotherapies* (pp. 271–286). New York: Plenum Press.

Nylund, D., & Corsiglia, V. (1993). Internalized other questioning with men who are violent (with commentary by A. Jenkins). In M. F. Hoyt (Ed.), *The handbook of constructive therapies* (pp. 401–413). San Francisco: Jossey-Bass. (Reprinted from *Dulwich Centre Newsletter*, 1993, 4, pp. 29–34)

Nylund, D., & Corsiglia, V. (1994). Becoming solution-focused forced in brief therapy: Remembering something important we already knew. *Journal of Systemic Therapies, 13,* 5–12.

Nylund, D., & Corsiglia, V. (1996). From deficits to special abilities: Working narratively with children labeled "ADHD." In M. F. Hoyt (Ed.), *Constructive therapies* (Vol. 2, pp. 163–183). New York: Guilford Press.

Nylund, D., & Thomas, J. (1994). The economics of narrative. *Family Therapy Networker, 18*(6), 38–39.

O'Donohue, W., & Szymanski, J. (1994). How to win friends and not influence clients: Popular but problematic ideas that impair treatment decisions. *The Behavior Therapist, 17*(2), 29–33.

Oh, S. (1985). A Zen way of baseball. In R. S. Heckler (Ed.), *Aikido and the new warrior* (pp. 99–113). Berkeley, CA: North Atlantic Books. (Excerpted from S. Oh, with D. Falkner, 1994, *Sadaharu Oh*. New York: Random House)

O'Hanlon, W. H. (1987). *Taproots: Underlying principles of Milton H. Erickson's therapy and hypnosis.* New York: Norton.

O'Hanlon, W. H. (1990). Debriefing myself: When a brief therapist does long-term work. *Family Therapy Networker, 14*(2), 48–50.

O'Hanlon, W. H. (1991). Not strategic, not systemic: Still clueless after all these years. *Journal of Strategic and Systemic Therapies, 10,* 105, 109.

O'Hanlon, W. H. (1994). The third wave. *Family Therapy Networker, 18*(6), 18–26, 28–29.

O'Hanlon, W. H. (1998). Possibility therapy: An inclusive, collaborative, solution-based model of psychotherapy. In M. F. Hoyt (Ed.), *The handbook of constructive therapies* (pp. 137–158). San Francisco: Jossey-Bass.

O'Hanlon, W. H. (1999). Possibility therapy: From iatrogenic injury to iatrogenic healing. In S. O'Hanlon & B. Bertolino (Eds.), *Evolving possibilities: Selected papers of Bill O'Hanlon* (pp. 143–157). Philadelphia: Brunner/Mazel.

O'Hanlon, W. H., & Beadle, S. (1994). *A field guide to possibility-land: Possibility therapy methods.* Omaha, NE: Center Press.

O'Hanlon, S., & Bertolino, B. (Eds.). (1999). *Evolving possibilities: Selected papers of Bill O'Hanlon.* Philadelphia: Brunner/Mazel.

O'Hanlon, W. H., & Hexum, A. L. (1990). *An uncommon casebook: The complete clinical work of Milton H. Erickson, M.D.* New York: Norton.

O'Hanlon, W. H., & Hudson, P. O. (1994). Coauthoring a love story: Solution-oriented marital therapy. In M. F. Hoyt (Ed.), *Constructive Therapies* (pp. 160–188). New York: Guilford Press.

O'Hanlon, W. H., & Hudson, P. O. (1995). *Love is a verb.* New York: Norton.

O'Hanlon, W. H., & Weiner-Davis, M. (1989). *In search of solutions: A new direction in psychotherapy.* New York: Norton.

O'Hanlon, W. H., & Wilk, J. (1987). *Shifting contexts: The generation of effective psychotherapy.* New York: Guilford Press.

Olson, K. R., Jackson, T. T., & Nelson, J. (1997). Attributional biases in clinical practice. *Journal of Psychological Practice, 3,* 27–33.

Omer, H. (1991). Writing a post-scriptum to a badly-ended therapy. *Psychotherapy, 28,* 484–492.

Omer, H. (1993). Quasi-literary elements in psychotherapy. *Psychotherapy, 30*(1), 59–66.

Omer, H. (1994). *Critical interventions in psychotherapy.* New York: Norton.

Omer, H., & Alon, N. (1997). *Constructing therapeutic narratives.* Northvale, NJ: Aronson.

Omer, H., & Stregner, C. (1992). The pluralist revolution: From the one true meaning to an infinity of constructed ones. *Psychotherapy, 29,* 253–261.

Oremland, J. D. (1972). Transference cure and flight into health. *International Journal of Psychoanalytic Psychotherapy, 1,* 61–75.

O'Toole, F. (1998, December 28–1999, January 4). The many stories of Billy the Kid. *The New Yorker,* 86–97.

Ottens, A. J., & Hanna, F. J. (1998). Cognitive and existential therapies: Toward an integration. *Psychotherapy, 35,* 312–324.

Paglia, C. (1992). *Sex, art, and American culture.* New York: Vintage.

Paige, L. S. (1962). *Maybe I'll pitch forever.* Garden City, NY: Doubleday.

Palmer, A., & Dobereiner, P. (1986). *Arnold Palmer's complete book of putting.* New York: Atheneum.

Papadakis, A., Cooke, C., & Benjamin, A. (Eds.). (1989). *Deconstruction: Omnibus volume.* New York: Rizzoli.

Parry, A. (1991). A universe of stories. *Family Process, 30,* 37–54.

Parry, A., & Doan, R. E. (1994). *Story re-visions: Narrative therapy in the postmodern world.* New York: Guilford Press.

Patterson, T. E. (1993). The ethics of diagnosis in family therapy. *The Family Psychologist, 9.*

Patterson, T. E., & Lusterman, D.-D. (1996). The relational reimbursement dilemma. In F. W. Kaslow (Ed.), *Handbook of relational diagnosis and dysfunctional family patterns* (pp. 46–58). New York: Wiley.

Pekarik, G., & Guidry, L. L. (1999). Relationship of satisfaction to symptom change, follow-up adjustment, and clinical significance in private practice. *Professional Psychology: Research and Practice, 30*(5), 474–478.

Penick, H. (with Shrake, B.). (1992). *Harvey Penick's little red book: Lessons and teachings from a lifetime in golf.* New York: Simon & Schuster.

Penick, H. (with Shrake, B.). (1993). *And if you play golf, you're my friend: Further reflections of a grown caddie.* New York: Simon & Schuster.

Penn, P. (1985). Feed-forward: Future questions, future maps. *Family Process, 24,* 289–310.

Pepe, P. (1988). *The wit and wisdom of Yogi Berra.* Westport, CT: Meekler Books.

Perrott, L. A. (1998). When will it be coming to the large discount chain stores? Psychotherapy as commodity. *Professional Psychology: Research and Practice, 29,* 168–173.

Phelps, R., Eisman, E. J., & Kohout, J. (1998). Psychological practice and managed care: Results of the CAPP practitioner survey. *Professional Psychology: Research and Practice, 29,* 31–36.

Pincus, H. A., Zarin, D. A., & West, J. C. (1996). Peering into the "black box": Measuring outcomes of managed care. *Archives of General Psychiatry, 53,* 870–877.

Pinkerton, R. S., & Rockwell, W. J. K. (1990). Termination in brief psychotherapy: The case for an eclectic approach. *Psychotherapy, 27,* 362–365.

Pipal, J. E. (1995). Managed care: Is it the corpse in the living room? An exposé. *Psychotherapy, 32,* 323–332.

Pipal, J. E. (1996). Without apology or fear: Reflections on Hoyt and Budman (1996) and managed mental health care. *Psychotherapy, 33,* 124–128.

Pirsig, R. M. (1974). *Zen and the art of motorcycle maintenance: An inquiry into values.* New York: Vintage.

Pittman, F. (1992). It's not my fault. *Family Therapy Networker, 16*(1), 56–63.

Pittman, F. (1999). Screening room: Us and them. *Family Therapy Networker, 23*(4), 71–74, 76, 78.

Polkinghorne, D. E. (1988). *Narrative knowing and the human sciences.* Albany, NY: SUNY Press.

Pollan, M. (1991). *Second nature.* New York: Dell.

Polster, E. (1987). *Every person's life is worth a novel.* New York: Norton.

Polster, E. (1992). The self in action: A gestalt outlook. In J. K. Zeig (Ed.), *The Evolution of Psychotherapy: The Second Conference* (pp. 143–151). New York: Brunner/Mazel.

Polster, E., & Polster, M. (1976). Therapy without resistance. In A. Burton (Ed.), *What makes behavior change possible?* New York: Brunner/Mazel.

Postman, N. (1976). *Crazy talk, stupid talk.* New York: Delacorte.

Ponce, M. H. (1993). *Hoyt Street: Memories of a Chicana childhood.* New York: Doubleday/Anchor.

Poynter, W. L. (1994). *The preferred provider's handbook: Building a successful private practice in the managed care marketplace.* New York: Brunner/Mazel.

Poynter, W. L. (1998). *The textbook of behavioral managed care: From concept through management to treatment.* New York: Brunner/Mazel.

Practice Strategies. (Available from P.O. Box 79445, Baltimore, MD 21279-0445).

Pressfield, S. (1995). *The legend of Bagger Vance: Golf and the game of life.* New York: William Morrow.

Prilleltensky, I. (1997). Values, assumptions, and practices: Assessing the moral implications of psychological discourse and action. *American Psychologist, 52,* 517–535.

Prochaska, J. O. (1991). Prescribing to the stage and level of phobia patients. *Psychotherapy, 28,* 463–468.

Prochaska, J. O. (1993). Working in harmony with how people change naturally. *The Weight Control Digest, 3,* 249, 252–255.

Prochaska, J. O. (1995). Common problems: Common solutions. *Clinical Psychology: Science and Practice, 2,* 101–105.

Prochaska, J. O. (1999). How do people change and how can we change to help many more people? In M. A. Hubble, B. L. Duncan, & S. D. Miller (Eds.), *The heart and soul of change: What works in therapy.* Washington, DC: American Psychological Association.

Prochaska, J. O., & DiClemente, C. C. (1982). Transtheoretical therapy: Toward a more integrative model of change. *Psychotherapy, 19,* 276–288.

Prochaska, J. O., & DiClemente, C. C. (1983). Stages and processes of self-change in smoking: Toward an integrative model of change. *Journal of Consulting and Clinical Psychology, 5,* 390–395.

Prochaska, J. O., & DiClemente, C. C. (1984). *The transtheoretical approach: Crossing traditional boundaries of therapy.* Homewood, IL: Dow Jones-Irwin.

Prochaska, J. O., & DiClemente, C. C. (1992). The transtheoretical approach. In J. C. Norcross & M. R. Goldfried (Eds.), *Handbook of psychotherapy integration.* New York: Basic Books.

Prochaska, J. O., DiClemente, C. C., & Norcross, J. C. (1992). In search of how people change. *American Psychologist, 47,* 1102–1114.

Prochaska, J., Norcross, J., & DiClemente, C. (1994) *Changing for good.* New York: William Morrow.

Prochaska, J. O., Velicer, W. F., Fava, J., Ruggiero, L., Laforge, R., & Rossi, K. (1997). *Counselor and stimulus control enhancements of a stage-matched expert system for smokers in a managed-care setting.* Unpublished manuscript.

Proust, M. (1981). *Within a budding grove.* In *Remembrance of things past* (Vol. 1, pp. 463–1018). (C. K. S. Moncrieff & T. Kilmartin, Trans.) New York: Random House. (Original work published 1919)

Psychotherapy Finances. (Available from P.O. Box 8979, Jupiter, FL 33468-8979).

Quick, E. K. (1996). *Doing what works in brief therapy: A strategic solution focused approach.* San Diego, CA: Academic Press.

Quintana, S. M. (1993). Toward an expanded and updated conceptualization of termination: Implications for short-term, individual psychotherapy. *Professional Psychology: Research and Practice, 24*, 426–432.

Rabasca, L. (1998a, November). APA helps prompt suit against California MCOs. *APA Monitor, 29*, 1, 21.

Rabasca, L. (1998b, November). APA pursues "test cases" to set legal precedents. *APA Monitor, 29*, 20.

Rabasca, L. (1998c). Putting the quality back in health care. *APA Monitor, 29*, 34–35.

Rabasca, L. (1999). House gives patients right to sue managed-care plans. *APA Monitor, 30*, 20.

Rabkin, R. (1977). *Strategic psychotherapy.* New York: Basic Books.

Rainer, J. P. (1996). Psychotherapy outcomes [Special issue]. *Psychotherapy, 33*(2).

Ramsay, J. R. (1998). Postmodern cognitive therapy: Cognitions, narratives, and personal meaning-making. *Journal of Cognitive Psychotherapy, 12*.

Reamy-Stephenson, M. (1983). The assumption of non-objective reality: A missing link in the training of strategic family therapists. *Journal of Strategic and Systemic Therapies, 2*, 51–67.

Reddy, M. (1993). The conduit metaphor. In A. Ortony (Ed.), *Metaphor and thought* (2nd ed.). Cambridge, England: Cambridge University Press.

Redekop, F. (1995). The "problem" of Michael White and Michel Foucault. *Journal of Marital and Family Therapy, 21*, 308–318.

Reilly, R. (1995, April 17). For you, Harvey. *Sports Illustrated, 82*, 16–23.

Reis, B. F., & Brown, L. G. (1999). Reducing psychotherapy dropouts: Maximizing perspective convergence in the psychotherapy dyad. *Psychotherapy, 36*, 123–136.

Rennie, D. L. (1994). Storytelling in psychotherapy: The client's subjective experience. *Psychotherapy, 31*, 234–243.

Rice, L. N., & Greenberg, L. S. (1992). Humanistic approaches to psychotherapy. In D. K. Freedheim (Ed.), *History of psychotherapy: A century of change* (pp. 197–224). Washington, DC: American Psychological Association.

Rich, A. (1979). When we dead awaken: Writing as re-vision. In *Lies, secrets, and silence: Selected prose 1966–1978* (pp. 33–49). New York: Norton.

Ricoeur, P. (1983). *Time and narrative.* Chicago: University of Chicago Press.

Rilke, R. M. (1962). *Letters to a young poet.* In M. D. Herter (Trans.), New York: Norton. (Original work published 1904)

Rimler, G. W., & Morrison, R. D. (1993). The ethical impacts of managed care. *Journal of Business Ethics, 12*, 493–501.

Roberts, J. (1994). *Tales and transformations: Stories in families and family therapy.* New York: Norton.

Rogers, C. (1951). *Client-centered therapy.* Boston: Houghton Mifflin.

Rorty, R. (1979). *Philosophy and the mirror of nature.* Princeton, NJ: Princeton University Press.

Rosen, H. (1999). Book review of *The handbook of constructive therapies. Journal of Cognitive Psychotherapy, 13*, 71–74.

Rosen, H., & Kuelhwein, K. (Eds.) (1996). *Constructing realities: Meaning-making perspectives for psychotherapists.* San Francisco: Jossey-Bass.

Rosen, S. (1982). *My voice will go with you: The teaching tales of Milton H. Erickson.* New York: Norton.

Rosenau, P. M. (1992). *Postmodernism and the social sciences.* Princeton, NJ: Princeton University Press.

Rosenbaum, R. (1990). Strategic psychotherapy. In R. A. Wells & V. J. Giannetti (Eds.), *Handbook of the brief psychotherapies* (pp. 351–403). New York: Plenum Press.

Rosenbaum, R. (1993). Heavy ideals: Strategic single-session hypnotherapy. In R. A. Wells & V. J. Giannetti (Eds.), *Casebook of the brief psychotherapies* (pp. 109–128). New York: Plenum Press.

Rosenbaum, R. (1994). Single-session therapy: Intrinsic integration? *Journal of Psychotherapy Integration, 4,* 229–252.

Rosenbaum, R. (1998). *Zen and the heart of psychotherapy.* Philadelphia: Brunner/Mazel.

Rosenbaum, R., & Bohart, A. C. (1994). *Psychotherapy: The art of experience.* Unpublished manuscript.

Rosenbaum, R., & Dyckman, J. (1996). No self? No problem! Actualizing empty self in psychotherapy. In M. F. Hoyt (Ed.), *Constructive therapies* (Vol. 2, pp. 238–274).

Rosenbaum, R., Hoyt, M. F., & Talmon, M. (1995). The challenge of single-session therapies: Creating pivotal moments. In M. F. Hoyt, *Brief therapy and managed care: Readings for contemporary practice* (pp. 105–139). San Francisco: Jossey-Bass. (Reprinted from *Handbook of the brief psychotherapies,* pp. 165–189, by R. A. Wells & V. J. Giannetti, Eds., 1990, New York: Plenum Press)

Rossi, E. L. (1973). Psychological shocks and creative moments in psychotherapy. *American Journal of Clinical Hypnosis, 16,* 9–22.

Roth, S., & Chasin, R. (1994). Entering one another's worlds of meaning and imagination: Dramatic enactment and narrative couple therapy. In M. F. Hoyt (Ed.), *Constructive Therapies* (pp. 189–216). New York: Guilford Press.

Roth, S., & Epston, D. (1996). Consulting the problem about the problematic relationship: An exercise for experiencing a relationship with an externalized problem. In M. F. Hoyt (Ed.), *Constructive therapies* (Vol. 2, pp. 148–162). New York: Guilford Press.

Rowen, T., & O'Hanlon, B. (1999). *Solution-oriented therapy for chronic and severe mental illness.* New York: Wiley.

Rubenstein, L. (1991). *Links: An exploration into the mind, heart, and soul of golf.* Rocklin, CA: Prima.

Ruesch, J., & Bateson, G. (1951). *Communication: The social matrix of psychiatry.* New York: Norton.

Rukeyser, M. (1992). The speed of darkness. In K. Daniels (Ed.), *Out of silence: Selected poems* (pp. 133–136). Evanston, IL: TriQuarterly Books/Northwestern University Press. (Original work published 1968)

Rushdie, S. (1990). *Haroun and the sea of stories.* New York: Holt.

Rushdie, S. (1999). *The ground beneath her feet.* New York: Holt.

Rybczynski, W. (1986). *Home: A short history of an idea.* New York: Penguin.

Sabin, J. E. (1991). Clinical skills for the 1990s: Six lessons from HMO practice. *Hospital and Community Psychiatry, 42,* 601–608.

Sabin, J. E. (1992). The therapeutic alliance in managed care mental health practice. *Journal of Psychotherapy Practice and Research, 1,* 29–36.

Sabin, J. E. (1994a). Caring about patients and caring about money: The American Psychiatric Association code of ethics meets managed care. *Behavioral Sciences and the Law, 12,* 317–330.

Sabin, J. E. (1994b). Ethical issues under managed care. In R. K. Schreter, S. S. Sharfstein, & C. A. Schreter (Eds.), *Allies and adversaries: The impact of managed care on mental health services* (pp. 187–200). Washington, DC: American Psychiatric Press.

Sabin, J. E. (1995). General hospital psychiatry and the ethics of managed care. *General Hospital Psychiatry, 17,* 293–298.

Sacks, O. (1987). *The man who mistook his wife for a hat and other clinical tales.* New York: Harper & Row.

Safran, J. D., & Muran, J. C. (Eds.). (1998). *The therapeutic alliance in brief psychotherapy.* Washington, DC: American Psychological Association.

Sanders, S. R. (1997, September–October). The most human art. (Reprinted from *Utne Reader,* 54–56. *The Georgia Review,* Spring 1997)

Sank, L. I. (1997). Taking on managed care: One reviewer at a time. *Professional Psychology: Research and Practice, 28,* 548–554.

Sapir, E. (1949). The status of linguistics as a science. In D. G. Mandelbaum (Ed.), *Selected writings of Edward Sapir*. Berkeley: University of California Press.

Sarbin, T. R. (Ed.). (1986). *Narrative psychology: The storied nature of human conduct*. New York: Praeger.

Satir, V. (1993). My declaration of self-esteem. In J. Canfield & M. V. Hansen (Compilers), *Chicken soup for the soul: 101 stories to open the heart and rekindle the spirit* (pp. 75–76). Deerfield Beach, FL: Health Communications.

Sauber, S. R. (Ed.). (1997). *Managed mental health care: Major diagnostic and treatment approaches*. Philadelphia: Brunner/Mazel.

Schafer, R. (1992). *Retelling a life: Narration and dialogue in psychoanalysis*. New York: Basic Books.

Schlesinger, M., Dorwart, R. A., & Epstein, S. S. (1996). Managed care constraints on psychiatrists' hospital practices: Bargaining power and professional autonomy. *American Journal of Psychiatry, 153*, 256–260.

Schlitz, D. (1978). The gambler. [Recorded by Kenny Rogers] on *The Gambler* [record album]. Los Angeles: United Artists (ASCAP).

Schloegl, I. (1976). *The wisdom of the Zen masters*. New York: New Directions.

Schmidt, G., & Trenkle, B. (1985). An integration of Ericksonian techniques with concepts of family therapy. In J. K. Zeig (Ed.), *Ericksonian psychotherapy: Vol. 2: Clinical applications* (pp. 132–154). New York: Brunner/Mazel.

Schuster, J. M. (1995). Frustration or opportunity? The impact of managed care on emergency psychiatry. *New Directions for Mental Health Services, 67*, 101–108.

Schuster, J. M., Lovell, M. R., & Trachta, A. M. (Eds.). (1997). *Training behavioral healthcare professionals: Higher learning in the era of managed care*. San Francisco: Jossey-Bass.

Schutz, W. C. (1967). *Joy: Expanding human awareness*. New York: Grove Press.

Schwartz, J. (1997). Meaning vs. medical necessity: Can psychoanalytic treatments exist in a managed care world? *Psychotherapy, 34*, 115–123.

Schwarz, R. A. (1998). From "either-or" to "both-and": Treating dissociative disorders collaboratively. In M. F. Hoyt (Ed.), *The handbook of constructive therapies* (pp. 428–448). San Francisco: Jossey-Bass.

Segal, L. (1986). *The dream of reality: Heinz von Foerster's constructivism*. New York: Norton.

Segal, L., & Watzlawick, P. (1985). On window-shopping or being a non-customer. In S. B. Coleman (Ed.), *Failures in family therapy* (pp. 73–90). New York: Guilford Press.

Seligman, L. (1998). *Selecting effective treatments: A comprehensive, systematic guide to treating mental disorders*. (Rev. ed.). San Francisco: Jossey-Bass.

Seligman, M. E. P. (1995). The effectiveness of psychotherapy: The *Consumer Reports* study. *American Psychologist, 51*, 1072–1079.

Seligman, M. E. P., & Levant, R. F. (1998). Managed care policies rely on inadequate science. *Professional Psychology: Research and Practice, 29*, 211–212.

Selvini Palazzoli, M. (1980). Why a long interval between sessions? In M. Andolfi & I. Zwerling (Eds.), *Dimensions of family therapy*. New York: Guilford Press.

Selvini Palazzoli, M., Boscolo, L., Cecchin, G., & Prata, G. (1978). *Paradox and counterparadox*. New York: Aronson.

Sexton, T. L., & Whiston, S. C. (1994). The status of the counseling relationship: An empirical review, theoretical implications, and research directions. *The Counseling Psychologist, 22*, 6–78.

Shafarman, G. (1996, No. 268, June–July). Thirteen ways of looking at how a poet and a therapist are one. *Poetry Flash*, 25.

Shakespeare, W. (1974). *The riverside Shakespeare*. G. B. Evans (Ed.). Boston: Houghton Mifflin.

Sharry, J. (1998). The ethics of speaking and the politics of listening [interview with Dr. Imelda McCarthy]. *Eisteach: A Quarterly Journal of Counselling and Therapy, 2*, 21–25.

Shaw, G. B. (1967). *Pygmalion and other plays.* New York: Dodd, Mead & Company. (Original work published 1913)

Shawver, L. (1996). What postmodernism can do for psychoanalysis: A guide to the postmodern vision. *American Journal of Psychoanalysis, 56,* 371–394.

Shectman, F. (1986). Time and the practice of psychotherapy. *Psychotherapy, 23,* 521–525.

Sherman, R. T., & Anderson, C. A. (1987). Decreasing premature termination from psychotherapy. *Journal of Personality and Social Psychology, 5,* 298–312.

Sherman, S. J., & Lynn, S. J. (1990). Social psychological principles in Milton Erickson's psychotherapy. *British Journal of Experimental and Clinical Hypnosis, 7,* 37–46.

Shlain, L. (1998). *The alphabet versus the goddess: The conflict between word and image.* New York: Viking.

Shoemaker, F. (with Shoemaker, P.). (1996). *Extraordinary golf: The art of the possible.* New York: Perigee/Berkeley Publishing Group.

Shoham, V., Rohrbaugh, M., & Patterson, J. (1995). Problem- and solution-focused couple therapies: The MRI and Milwaukee models. In N. S. Jacobson & A. S. Gurman (Eds.), *Clinical handbook of couple therapy* (2nd ed., pp. 142–163). New York: Guilford Press.

Shore, K. (1995). Managed care: The subjugation of a profession. *Psychotherapy in Private Practice, 14,* 67–75.

Short, D. (1996). Interview: Viktor Frankl, M.D., Ph.D. *The Milton H. Erickson Foundation Newsletter, 16,* 1, 18–20.

Short, D. (1997). Interview: Steve de Shazer and Insoo Kim Berg. *The Milton H. Erickson Foundation Newsletter, 17,* 1, 18–20.

Shueman, S. A. (1997). Confronting health care realities: A reply to Sank (1997). *Professional Psychology: Research and Practice, 28,* 555–558.

Siegel, S. (with Lowe, E.). (1992). *The patient who cured his therapist, and other stories of unconventional therapy.* New York: Marlowe & Company.

Sifneos, P. E. (1972). *Short-term psychotherapy and emotional crisis.* Cambridge, MA: Harvard University Press.

Sifneos, P. E. (1987). *Short-term dynamic psychotherapy: Evaluation and technique.* (Rev. ed.) New York: Plenum Press.

Sifneos, P. E. (1992). *Short-term anxiety-provoking psychotherapy: A treatment manual.* New York: Plenum Press.

Silverman, W. H. (1996). Cookbooks, manuals, and paint-by-numbers: Psychotherapy in the 90's. *Psychotherapy, 33,* 207–215.

Simon, P. (1975). 50 Ways to Leave Your Lover. Song on record album, *Still crazy after all these years.* New York: Columbia Records (BMI).

Simon, R. (1996). It's more complicated than that: An interview with Salvador Minuchin. *Family Therapy Networker, 20*(6), 50–56.

Simon, R. (1998). Soaring on the edge. *Family Therapy Networker, 22*(2), 58–67.

Singer, A. (1994). Gestalt couples therapy with gay male couples: Enlarging the therapeutic ground of awareness. In G. Wheeler & S. Backman (Eds.), *On intimate ground: A Gestalt approach to working with couples* (pp. 166–187). San Francisco: Jossey-Bass.

Singer, E. (1994). *Key concepts in psychotherapy* (2nd ed.). New York: Aronson.

Singer, J. A., & Salovey, P. (1993). *The remembered self: Emotion and memory in personality.* New York: Free Press.

Singer, M. (1998, September 7). What are you afraid of? [Stephen King profile]. *The New Yorker,* 56–67.

Sleek, S. (1997). The "cherrypicking" of treatment research. *APA Monitor, 29,* 1, 21.

Sluzki, C. (1988). Case commentary II. *Family Therapy Networker, 12*(5), 77–79.

Sluzki, C. E. (1992). Transformations: A blueprint for narrative changes in therapy. *Family Process, 31,* 217–230.

Sluzki, C. E. (1998). Strange attractors and the transformation of narratives in family therapy.

In M. F. Hoyt (Ed.), *The handbook of constructive therapies* (pp. 159–179). San Francisco: Jossey-Bass.

Small, R. F. (1992). Managed care: A guide for psychotherapists. In *Innovations in clinical practice: A sourcebook,* (Vol. 11, 241–250). Sarasota, FL: Professional Resources Press.

Small, R. F., & Barnhill, L. R. (Eds.). (1998). *Practicing in the new mental health marketplace: Ethical, legal, and moral issues.* Washington, DC: American Psychological Association.

Smillie, J. (1991). *Can physicians manage the quality and costs of health care? The story of the Permanente Medical Group.* New York: McGraw-Hill.

Smith, C. (1997). Introduction: Comparing traditional therapies with narrative approaches. In C. Smith & D. Nylund (Eds.), *Narrative therapies with children and adolescents* (pp. 1–52). New York: Guilford Press.

Smith, C., & Nylund, D. (Eds.). (1997). *Narrative therapies with children and adolescents.* New York: Guilford.

Smith, M. B. (1994). Selfhood at risk: Postmodern perils and the perils of postmodernism. *American Psychologist, 49,* 405–411.

Snead, S. (with Wade, D.). (1989). *The lessons I've learned: Better golf the Sam Snead way.* New York: Macmillan.

Snyder, G. (1980). *The real work: Interviews and talks 1964–1979.* New York: New Directions.

Sokal, A., & Bricmont, J. (1998). *Fashionable nonsense: Postmodern intellectuals' abuse of science.* New York: Picador/St. Martin's Press.

Solovey, A. D., & Duncan, B. L. (1992). Ethics and strategic therapy: A proposed ethical direction. *Journal of Marital and Family Therapy, 18,* 53–61.

Solzhenitsyn, A. I. (1973). *The Gulag Archipelago, 1918–1956.* New York: Harper & Row.

Sontag, S. (1964). *Against interpretation.* New York: Delta.

Speed, B. (1984). How really real is real? *Family Process, 23,* 511–520.

Speed, B. (1991). Reality exists, OK? An argument against constructivism and social constructivism. *Family Therapy, 13,* 395–409.

Speer, D. C. (1970). Family systems: Morphostasis and morphogenesis. Or "Is homeostasis enough?" *Family Process, 9,* 259–278.

Spence, D. P. (1982). *Narrative truth and historical truth: Meaning and interpretation in psychoanalysis.* New York: Norton.

Sperry, L., Grissom, G., Brill, P., & Marion, D. (1997). Changing clinicians' practice patterns and managed care culture with outcomes systems. *Psychiatric Annals, 27,* 127–132.

Spitz, H. I. (1996). *Group psychotherapy and managed mental health care: A clinical guide for providers.* New York: Brunner/Mazel.

Stamm, B. H. (1998). Clinical applications of telehealth in mental health care. *Professional psychology: Research and practice, 29,* 536–542.

Steenbarger, B. N., & Budman, S. H. (1996). Group psychotherapy and managed behavioral health care: Current trends and future challenges. *International Journal of Group Psychotherapy, 46*(9), 297–309.

Steenbarger, B. N., & Greenberg, R. P. (1996) Sometimes no heads are better than one: Decapitated programs for mental health services delivery. In G. C. Ellenbogen (Ed.), *More oral sadism and the vegetarian personality* (pp. 167–171). New York: Brunner/Mazel.

Steenbarger, B. N., Smith, H. B., & Budman, S. H. (1996). Integrating science and practice in outcomes assessment: A bolder model for a managed era. *Psychotherapy, 33,* 246–253.

Steiner, C. M. (1974). *Scripts people live.* New York: Bantam Books.

Stern, S. (1993). Managed care, brief therapy, and therapeutic integrity. *Psychotherapy, 30,* 162–175.

Sternberg, R. J. (1998). *Love is a story: A new theory of relationships.* New York: Oxford University Press.

Stevens, C. (1973). Oh very young. Song on record album, *Buddha and the chocolate box.* Beverley Hills, CA: A & M Records (ASCAP).

Stevens, C. (1974). The first cut is the deepest. [recorded by R. Stewart] on record album, *A night on the town*. Burbank, CA: Warner Brothers, (1976).

Stix, G. (1994, July). Managed care, circa 1300. *Scientific American, 271*(1), 20.

Stone, A. A. (1995). Paradigms, pre-emptions, and stages: Understanding the transformation of American psychiatry by managed care. *International Journal of Law and Psychiatry, 18*, 353–387.

Storm, C. L. (Ed.). (1995). Postmodern supervision [whole issue]. *Journal of Systemic Therapies, 14*(2).

Strauss, S. (1991). *Coyote stories for children: Tales from Native America*. Hillsboro, OH: Beyond Words Publishing.

Strong, T. (1997). Can you get it down to one page? *Journal of Systemic Therapies, 16*, 69–72.

Strosahl, K. D. (1994). New dimensions in behavioral health/primary care integration. *HMO Practice, 8*, 176–179.

Strosahl, K. D. (1998). The dissemination of manual-based psychotherapies in managed care: Promises, problems, and prospects. *Clinical Psychology: Science and Practice, 5*, 382–386.

Strosahl, K. D., & Quirk, M. (1994, July). The trouble with carve-outs. *Business and Health*, July, 52.

Strupp, H. H. (1997). Research, practice, and managed care. *Psychotherapy, 34*, 91–94.

Strupp, H. H., & Binder, J. L. (1984). *Psychotherapy in a new key: A guide to time-limited dynamic psychotherapy*. New York: Basic Books.

Sullivan, H. S. (1954). *The psychiatric interview*. New York: Norton.

Szasz, T. S. (1974). *The myth of mental illness*. (rev. ed.) New York: Harper & Row.

Talmon, M. (1990). *Single session therapy: Maximizing the effect of the first (and often only) therapeutic encounter*. San Francisco: Jossey-Bass.

Talmon, M. (1993). *Single session solutions*. Reading, MA: Addison-Wesley.

Talmon, M., Hoyt, M. F., & Rosenbaum, R. (1990). Effective single-session therapy: Step-by-step guidelines. In M. Talmon, *Single session therapy* (pp. 34–56). San Francisco: Jossey-Bass. (Original paper presented, under the title *When the first session may be the last*, at the Brief Therapy Congress sponsored by the Milton H. Erickson Foundation held in San Francisco, December 1988)

Taylor, S. E. (1989). *Positive illusions: Creative self-deception and the healthy mind*. New York: Basic Books.

Thomas, J. (1999). Barriers that have prevented patients from suing HMOs are slowly falling. *The National Psychologist, 8*(6), 10–11.

Thoreau, H. D. (1975). *Walden*. In C. Bode (Ed.), *The portable Thoreau* (pp. 258–572). New York: Penguin. (Original work published 1854)

Ticho, E. A. (1972). Termination of psychoanalysis: Treatment goals, life goals. *Psychoanalytic Quarterly, 41*, 315–333.

Tischler, G. L., & Astrachan, B. M. (1996). A funny thing happened on the way to reform. *Archives of General Psychiatry, 53*, 959–963.

Tobin, S. A. (1976). Saying goodbye in Gestalt therapy. In C. Hatcher & P. Himmelman (Eds.), *The handbook of Gestalt therapy* (pp. 371–383). New York: Aronson.

Todd, T. (1994). *Surviving and prospering in the managed mental healthcare marketplace*. Sarasota, FL: Professional Resource Press.

Tomm, K. (1987). Interventive interviewing: I. Strategizing as a fourth guideline for the therapist. *Family Process, 26*, 3–13.

Tomm, K. (1988). Interventive interviewing: III. Intending to ask lineal, circular, strategic and reflexive questions. *Family Process, 27*, 1–16.

Tomm, K. (1989). Externalizing the problem and internalizing personal agency. *Journal of Strategic and Systemic Therapies, 8*, 54–59.

Tomm, K. (1990). A critique of the *DSM. Dulwich Centre Newsletter, 3*, 5–8.

Tomm, K. (1991a). The ethics of dual relationships. *The Calgary Participator, 1,* 11–15.

Tomm, K. (1991b). Beginnings of a "HIPs and PIPs" approach to psychiatric assessment. *The Calgary Participator, 1,* 25–28.

Tomm, K. (1992). *Interviewing the internalized other: Toward a systemic reconstruction of the self and other.* Workshop sponsored by the California School of Professional Psychology, Alameda.

Tomm, K. (1993). The courage to protest: A commentary on Michael White's work. In S. G. Gilligan & R. Price (Eds.), *Therapeutic conversations* (pp. 62–80). New York: Norton.

Tomm, K., Hoyt, M. F., & Madigan, S. P. (1998). Honoring our internalized others and the ethics of caring: A conversation with Karl Tomm. In M. F. Hoyt (Ed.), *The handbook of constructive therapies* (pp. 198–218). San Francisco: Jossey-Bass.

Tulkin, S. R., & Frank, G. W. (1985). The changing role of psychologists in health maintenance organizations. *American Psychologist, 40,* 1125–1130.

Tutu, D. (1995, January) My first *Ebony. Ebony, 51,* 35.

Updike, J. (1996). Those three- and four-footers. In *Golf dreams: Writings on golf* (pp. 29–34). New York: Knopf. (Reprinted from *Golf Digest,* January 1995, 104–107)

Vaihinger, H. (1924). *The philosophy of "as if."* (C. K. Ogden, Trans.). Orlando, FL: Harcourt Brace.

Vaillant, G. E. (1992). The beginning of wisdom is never calling a patient a borderline: Or, the clinical management of immature defenses in the treatment of individuals with personality disorders. *Journal of Psychotherapy Practice and Research, 1,* 117–134.

Valéry, P. (1958). *The art of poetry.* Princeton, NJ: Bollingen.

VandenBos, G. R. (Ed.). (1996). Outcome assessment of psychotherapy. [Special issue]. *American Psychologist, 51*(10).

VandenBos, G. R., Cummings, N. A., & DeLeon, P. H. (1992). A century of psychotherapy: Economic and environmental influences. In D. K. Freedheim (Ed.), *History of psychotherapy: A century of change* (pp. 65–102). Washington, DC: American Psychological Association.

VanDyck, C., & Schlesinger, H. (1997). Training the trainers. *Administration and Policy in Mental Health, 25,* 47–69.

Vidal, G. (1995). *Palimpsest: A memoir.* New York: Penguin.

Volz, J. (1999). Angered by managed care, practitioners look to unions. *APA Monitor, 30*(8), 1, 24.

Vorkoper, C. F. (1997). The importance of saying goodbye. In C. E. Lennox (Ed.), *Redecision therapy: A brief, action-oriented approach* (pp. 95–108). Northvale, NJ: Aronson.

Waldegrave, C. (1990). Just therapy. *Dulwich Centre Newsletter, 1,* 1–47.

Wallach, J. (1995). *Beyond the fairway: Zen lessons, insights, and inner attitudes of golf.* New York: Bantam Books.

Walter, J., & Peller, J. (1992). *Becoming solution-focused in brief therapy.* New York: Brunner/ Mazel.

Walter, J., & Peller, J. (1994). "On track" in solution-focused brief therapy. In M. F. Hoyt (Ed.), *Constructive Therapies* (pp. 111–125). New York: Guilford Press.

Ward, G. C., & Burns, K. (1994). *Baseball: An illustrated history.* New York: Knopf.

Watson, T. (with Hannigan, F.) (1984). *The new rules of golf.* New York: Random House.

Watzlawick, P. (1976). *How real is real? Communication, disinformation, confusion.* New York: Vintage.

Watzlawick, P. (1978). *The language of change: Elements of therapeutic communication.* New York: Norton.

Watzlawick, P. (Ed.). (1984). *The invented reality: How do we know what we believe we know? (Contributions to constructivism).* New York: Norton.

Watzlawick, P. (1992). The construction of clinical "realities." In J. K. Zeig (Ed.), *The evolution of psychotherapy: The second conference* (pp. 55–62). New York: Brunner/Mazel.

Watzlawick, P. (1994, December). *The construction of therapeutic "realities."* Workshop held at the Sixth International Congress on Ericksonian Approaches to Hypnosis and Psychotherapy, sponsored by the Milton H. Erickson Foundation, Los Angeles.

Watzlawick, P., Beavin, J. B., & Jackson, D. D. (1967). *Pragmatics of human communication: A study of interactional patterns, pathologies, and paradoxes.* New York: Norton.

Watzlawick, P., & Hoyt, M. F. (1998). Constructing therapeutic realities: A conversation with Paul Watzlawick. In M. F. Hoyt (Ed.), *The handbook of constructive therapies* (pp. 183–197). San Francisco: Jossey-Bass.

Watzlawick, P., Weakland, J. H., & Fisch, R. (1974). *Change: Principles of problem formation and problem resolution.* New York: Norton.

Waymack, M. (1992). Health care as a business: The ethic of Hippocrates versus the ethic of managed care. *Business and Professional Ethics Journal, 9,* 69–78.

Weakland, J. H. (1991). Foreword. In S. de Shazer, *Putting difference to work* (pp. vii–ix). New York: Norton.

Weakland, J. H. (1993). Conversation—but what kind? In S. G. Gilligan & R. Price (Eds.), *Therapeutic conversations* (pp. 136–145). New York: Norton.

Weakland, J. H. (1995). Letter. *Family Therapy Networker, 19*(5),16.

Weakland, J. H., & Fisch, R. (1992). Brief therapy—MRI style. In S. H. Budman, M. F. Hoyt, & S. Friedman (Eds.), *The first session in brief therapy* (pp. 306–323). New York: Guilford Press.

Wedding, D., Ritchie, P., Kitchen, A., & Binner, P. (1993). Mental health services in a single-payer system: Lessons from Canada and principles for an American plan. *Professional Psychology: Research and Practice, 24,* 387–393.

Weiner, I. J. (1975). *Principles of psychotherapy.* New York: Wiley.

Weiner-Davis, M. (1992). *Divorce busting.* New York: Simon & Schuster.

Weiner-Davis, M. (1993). Pro-constructed realities. In S. Gilligan & R. Price (Eds.), *Therapeutic conversations* (pp. 149–157). New York: Norton.

Weiner-Davis, M., de Shazer, S., & Gingrich, W. J. (1987). Using pretreatment change to construct a therapeutic solution: An exploratory study. *Journal of Marital and Family Therapy, 13,* 359–363.

Welch, B. L. (1994). Managed care: The "basic fault." *Psychoanalysis and Psychotherapy, 11,* 166–176.

Wells, R. A., & Phelps, P. A. (1990). The brief psychotherapies: A selective review. In R. A. Wells & V. J. Giannetti (Eds.), *Handbook of the brief psychotherapies* (pp. 3–26). New York: Plenum Press.

Werhane, P. (1992). The ethics of healthcare as a business. *Business and Professional Ethics Journal, 9,* 7–20.

West, C. (1993). *Race matters.* New York: Vintage.

Whitaker, C. A. (1975). Psychotherapy of the absurd: With a special emphasis on the psychotherapy of aggression. *Family Process, 4,* 1–16.

Whitaker, C. A. (1982). The hindrance of theory in clinical work. In J. R. Neill & D. P. Kniskern (Eds.), *From psyche to system: The evolving therapy of Carl Whitaker* (pp. 317–329). New York: Guilford Press. (Reprinted from *Family Therapy: Theory and Practice,* pp. 154–164, by P. J. Guerin, Jr., Ed., 1976, New York: Gardner Press)

Whitaker, C. A. (1987). The dynamics of the American family as deduced from 20 years of family therapy: The family unconscious. In J. K. Zeig (Ed.), *The evolution of psychotherapy* (pp. 75–83). New York: Brunner/Mazel.

Whitaker, C. A. (1989a). Tricks of the psychotherapy trade. In M. O. Ryan, (Ed.), *Midnight musings of a family therapist* (pp. 186–196). New York: Norton.

Whitaker, C. A. (1989b). *Midnight musing of a family therapist* (M. O. Ryan, Ed.) New York: Norton.

Whitaker, C. A., & Bumberry, W. M. (1988). *Dancing with the family: A symbolic-experiential approach.* Bristol, PA: Brunner/Mazel.

Whitaker, C. A., & Malone, T. P. (1953) Some techniques in brief psychotherapy. In *The roots of psychotherapy* (pp. 194–230). New York: Blakiston.

Whitaker, C. A., & Napier, A. Y. (1978). *The family crucible.* New York: Harper & Row.

White, M. (1989a). Negative explanation, restraint, and double description: A template for family therapy. In M. White, *Selected papers* (pp. 85–99). Adelaide, Australia: Dulwich Centre Publications. (Reprinted from *Family Process*, 1986, 25)

White, M. (1989b). The process of questioning: A therapy of literary merit? In *Selected papers* (pp. 37–46). Adelaide, Australia: Dulwich Centre Publications. (Reprinted from *Dulwich Centre Newsletter*, 1988, 8-14)

White, M. (1989c). Saying hullo again: The incorporation of the lost relationship in the resolution of grief. In *Selected papers* (pp. 29–36). Adelaide, Australia: Dulwich Centre Publications. (Reprinted from *Dulwich Centre Newsletter*, 1988)

White, M. (1989d). The externalizing of the problem and the re-authoring of lives and relationships. In *Selected papers* (pp. 5–28). Adelaide, Australia: Dulwich Centre Publications, 1989. (Reprinted from *Dulwich Centre Newsletter*, 1989)

White, M. (1989e). *Selected papers.* Adelaide, Australia: Dulwich Centre Publications.

White, M. (1992a). Men's culture, the men's movement, and the constitution of men's lives. *Dulwich Centre Newsletter, 3,* 1–21.

White, M. (1992b). Family therapy training and supervision in a world of experience and narrative. In D. Epston & M. White, *Experience, contradiction, narrative and imagination* (pp. 75–95). Adelaide, Australia: Dulwich Centre Publications.

White, M. (1993a). Commentary: The histories of the present. In S. G. Gilligan & R. Price (Eds.), *Therapeutic conversations* (pp. 121–135). New York: Norton.

White, M. (1993b). Deconstruction and therapy. In S. G. Gilligan & R. Price (Eds.), *Therapeutic conversations* (pp. 22–61). New York: Norton. (Reprinted from *Dulwich Centre Newsletter*, 3, pp. 1–21, 1991)

White, M. (1995a). *Re-authoring lives: Interviews and essays.* Adelaide, Australia: Dulwich Centre Publications.

White, M. (1995b). *Inspiration in narrative therapy: The life of the therapist.* Workshop sponsored by Bay Area Family Therapy Training Associates, Cupertino, CA.

White, M. (1996). *Narrative therapy renewed.* Workshop sponsored by Bay Area Therapy Training Associates, Cupertino, CA.

White, M. (1997). *Narratives of therapists' lives.* Adelaide, Australia: Dulwich Centre Publications.

White, M., Hoyt, M. F., & Zimmerman, J. L. (2000). Direction and discovery: A conversation about power and politics in narrative therapy. In M. White (Ed.), *Reflections on narrative practice: Essays and interviews* (pp. 97–116). Adelaide: Dulwich Centre Publications.

White, M., & de Shazer, S. (1996, October 10–11). *Narrative solutions/Solution narratives.* Conference sponsored by Brief Family Therapy Center, Milwaukee, WI.

White, M., & Epston, D. (1990). *Narrative means to therapeutic ends.* New York: Norton.

Whiting, R. (1990). *You gotta have wa.* New York: Vintage.

Whitman, W. (1940a). Song of myself. In *Leaves of grass* (Rev. ed.). (pp. 29–74). New York: Random House/Modern Library. (Original work published 1891–1892)

Whitman, W. (1940b). A clear midnight. In *Leaves of grass* (Rev. ed.). New York: Random House/Modern Library. (Original work published 1891–1892)

Whitson, S. C., & Sexton, T. L. (1993). An overview of psychotherapy outcome research: Implications for practice. *Professional Psychology: Research and Practice, 24,* 43–51.

Who's reaping the benefits? (1999, July 12). *20/20.* New York: ABC.

Whyte, D. (1994). *The heart aroused: Poetry and the preservation of the soul in corporate America.* New York: Doubleday.

Whyte, D. (1997). Yorkshire. In *The house of belonging* (pp. 41–46). Langley, WA: Many Rivers Press.

Wick, D. T. (1996). Social constructionism: Groping toward this something. *Journal of Systemic Therapies, 15*(3), 65–81.

Wilbur, K. (1996). *A brief history of everything*. Boston: Shambala.

Wilbur, K. (1998). *The marriage of sense and soul*. New York: Random House.

Wile, D. B. (1993). *Couples therapy: A nontraditional approach*. New York: Wiley.

Will, G. F. (1990). *Men at work: The craft of baseball*. New York: Macmillan.

Wilson, G. T. (1998). Manual-based treatment and clinical practice. *Clinical Psychology: Science and Practice, 5*, 363–375.

Wind, H. W. (1985). Nicklaus and Watson at Turnberry. In *Following through* (pp. 168–181). New York: Ticknor & Fields.

Winnicott, D. W. (1971). *Playing and reality*. London: Tavistock.

Wittgenstein, L. (1968). *Philosophical investigations* (3rd ed., G. E. M. Anscombe, Trans.). New York: Macmillan.

Wittgenstein, L. (1980). *Culture and value* (P. Winch, Trans.) Chicago: University of Chicago Press.

Wolberg, L. R. (1965). The technic of short-term psychotherapy. In L. R. Wolberg (Ed.), *Short-term psychotherapy* (pp. 127–200). New York: Grune & Stratton.

Wolberg, L. R. (1985). Foreword. In J. K. Zeig, *Experiencing Erickson: An introduction to the man and his work* (pp. v–ix). New York: Brunner/Mazel.

Wolf, J., & Bistline, J. (1998). The application of solution-focused therapy to care management. *Journal of Systemic Therapies, 17*(3), 34–44.

Wooley, S. C. (1993). Managed care and mental health: The silencing of a profession. *International Journal of Eating Disorders, 14*, 387–401.

Woolgar, S., & Pawluch, D. (1985a). Ontological gerrymandering: The anatomy of social problems explanations. *Social Problems, 32*(3), 214–227.

Woolgar, S., & Pawluch, D. (1985b). How shall we move beyond constructivism? *Social Problems, 33*(2), 159–162.

Woollams, S., & Brown, M. (1978). *Transactional analysis*. Ann Arbor, MI: Huron Valley Institute Press.

Wright, L. M., & Leahey, M. (1994, Spring). *Finishing well: Tips for terminating treatment*. Paper presented at Family Therapy Networker Conference, Washington, DC.

Wright, R. H. (1992). The cons of psychotherapy in managed health care. *Psychotherapy in Private Practice, 11*(2), 71–78.

Wylie, M. S. (1994a). Panning for gold. *Family Therapy Networker, 18*(6), 40–48.

Wylie, M. S. (1994b). Endangered species. *Family Therapy Networker, 18*(2), 20–33.

Wylie, M. S. (1995). Diagnosing for dollars? *Family Therapy Networker, 19*(3), 22–33.

Wynne, L. (1983). Foreword. In C. M. Anderson & S. Stewart, *Mastering resistance: A practical guide to family therapy*. New York: Guilford Press.

Yalom, I. D. (1996). *Lying on the couch*. New York: HarperCollins.

Yapko, M. D. (1990). Brief therapy tactics in longer-term psychotherapies. In J. K. Zeig & S. G. Gilligan (Eds.), *Brief therapy: Myths, methods, and metaphors* (pp. 185–195). New York: Brunner/Mazel.

Yeats W. B. (1989a). Sailing to Byzantium. In R. J. Finneran (Ed.), *The collected poems of W.B. Yeats* (pp.193–194). New York: Collier. (Original work published 1927)

Yeats, W. B. (1989b). Among school children. In R. J. Finneran (Ed.), *The collected poems of W.B. Yeats* (pp. 215–217). New York: Collier.

Yeung, F. K.-C. (1995, July) *Reflections on the use of solution-focused therapy among the Chinese in Hong Kong*. Paper presented at the First Pan-Pacific Brief Psychotherapy Conference, Fukuoka, Japan.

Zeig, J. K. (Ed.). (1980). *A teaching seminar with Milton H. Erickson*. New York: Brunner/Mazel.

Zeig, J. K. (1985). *Experiencing Erickson: An introduction to the man and his work.* New York: Brunner/Mazel.

Zeig, J. K. (Ed.). (1987). *The evolution of psychotherapy.* Philadelphia: Brunner/Mazel.

Zeig, J. K. (1990). Seeding. In J. K. Zeig & S. G. Gilligan (Eds.), *Brief therapy: Myths, methods, and metaphors* (pp. 221–246). New York: Brunner/Mazel.

Zeig, J. K., & Gilligan, S. G. (Eds.). (1990). *Brief therapy: Myths, methods, and metaphors.* New York: Brunner/Mazel.

Zeig, J. K., & Munion, W. M. (1990). What is psychotherapy? In J. K. Zeig & W. M. Munion (Eds.), *What is psychotherapy? Contemporary perspectives* (pp 1–14). San Francisco: Jossey-Bass.

Zieman, G. L. (Ed.). (1995). *The complete capitation handbook: How to design and implement at-risk contracts for behavioral healthcare.* San Francisco: Jossey-Bass.

Zieman, G. L. (1998). *The handbook of managed behavioral healthcare.* San Francisco: Jossey-Bass.

Zimet, C. N. (1989). The mental health care revolution: Will psychology survive? *American Psychologist, 44,* 703–708.

Zimmerman, J. L., & Dickerson, V. C. (1994). Using a narrative metaphor: Implications for theory and clinical practice. *Family Process, 33,* 233–246.

Zimmerman, J. L., & Dickerson, V. C. (1996). *If problems talked: Narrative therapy in action.* New York: Guilford Press.

Zinser, G. R. (1997). Social responsibility among not-for-profit organizations devoted to behavioral health services. *Group Practice Journal, 46*(7), 35–36.

Zinsser, W. (Ed.). (1995). *Inventing the truth: The art and craft of memoir* (2nd ed.) Boston: Houghton Mifflin.

ABOUT THE AUTHOR

Michael F. Hoyt, Ph.D. (Yale '76), is a senior staff psychologist at the Kaiser Permanente Medical Center in Hayward, California, and serves on the clinical faculty of the University of California School of Medicine, San Francisco. An expert clinician and an internationally respected teacher and lecturer, Hoyt is the author of *Brief Therapy and Managed Care* (1995), the editor of *The Handbook of Constructive Therapies* (1998) and *Constructive Therapies, Volumes 1 & 2* (1994, 1996), and co-editor (with Simon Budman and Steven Friedman) of *The First Session in Brief Therapy* (1992). Dr. Hoyt has been honored as a Woodrow Wilson Fellow, as a Continuing Education Distinguished Speaker by the American Psychological Association, and as a Distinguished Presenter by the International Association of Marriage and Family Counselors. With his wife and son, he resides in Mill Valley, California.

ABOUT THE CO-AUTHORS

Insoo Kim Berg, M.S.S.W., is the co-founder (with Steve de Shazer) and director of the Brief Family Therapy Center in Milwaukee, Wisconsin. She is the author of *Family-Based Services: A Solution-Focused Approach* and the co-author of *How to Interview for Client Strengths and Solutions, Working with the Problem Drinker: A Solution-Focused Approach, Solutions Step by Step: A Substance Abuse Treatment Manual, Interviewing for Solutions, Building Solutions in Child Protective Services,* and forthcoming in 2000, *Tales of Solutions.* Her works are translated into nine languages.

Jon Matthew Carlson, M.A., M.Ed., is a doctoral student in counseling psychology at the Pennsylvania State University. He also serves on the editorial board for *The Family Journal: Counseling and Therapy for Couples and Families.*

Steven Friedman, Ph.D., provides consultation and training to human service professionals on the benefits of strength-based, collaborative relationships in promoting change. He serves as a Senior Clinical Consultant at Beacon Health Strategies in Woburn, Massachusetts, and teaches at the University of Massachusetts-Boston and Northeastern University. He is the author of *Time-Effective Psychotherapy: Maximizing Outcomes in an Era of Minimized Resources;* co-author of *Expanding Therapeutic Possibilities: Getting Results in Brief Psychotherapy;* editor of *The New Language of Change: Constructive Collaboration in Psychotherapy* and *The Reflecting Team in Action: Collaborative Practice in Family Therapy;* and co-editor of *The First Session in Brief Therapy.*

Scott D. Miller, Ph.D., is a co-founder (with Barry Duncan and Mark Hubble) of the Institute for the Study of Therapeutic Change, based in Chicago, Illinois. He is the co-author of *Finding the Adult Within: A Solution-Focused Self-Help Guide, Working with the Problem-Drinker: A Solution-Focused Approach, The Miracle Method: A Radically New Approach to Problem*

Drinking, Escape from Babel: Toward a Unifying Language of Psychotherapy Practice and *Psychotherapy with Impossible Cases: Efficient and Effective Treatment of Therapy Veterans;* and the co-editor of *Handbook of Solution-Focused Brief Therapy* and *The Heart and Soul of Change: What Works in Therapy.*

David Nylund, L.C.S.W., is the coordinator of training at the Kaiser Permanente Medical Center, Department of Mental Health, in Stockton, California. He is also affiliated with the Professional School of Psychology in Stockton, California, and La Familia Counseling in Sacramento. He also teaches in the Social Work Department at California State University, Sacramento. He is co-editor of *Narrative Therapy with Children and Adolescents.* His forthcoming book, *Treating Huckleberry Finn,* will be published by Jossey-Bass.

CREDITS

Chapter 1: The article by M. F. Hoyt, "It's Not My Therapy—It's The Client's Therapy," which appeared in *Psychotherapy Bulletin*, 1999, 24(1), 31–33, is used by permission of the American Psychological Association.

Chapter 2: The chapter by M. F. Hoyt, "A Golfer's Guide to Brief Therapy (with Footnotes for Baseball Fans)," which appeared in *Constructive Therapies, Volume 2* (M. F. Hoyt, Editor, 1996), is used by permission of Guilford Press.

Chapter 3: The excerpt from the poem, "Rising," which appeared in *Wendel Berry: Collected Poems 1957–1982*, is used by permission of Farrer, Strauss & Giroux.

The table, "The Process of Collaborative Helping," from the article by Tom Strong, "Can You Get It Down To One Page?" which appeared in the *Journal of Systemic Therapies*, 1997, 16(1), 69–72, is used by permission of Guilford Press.

The excerpt from the poem, "Among School Children," from *The Poems of W. B. Yeats: A New Edition* (R. J. Finneran, Editor), copyright 1928 by Macmillan Publishing Company, renewed 1956 by Georgie Yeats, is used by permission of Simon & Schuster.

The excerpt from the article, "Passion, Commitment and Common Sense: A Unique Discussion with Insoo Kim Berg and Michael White," taken from the *Journal of Systemic Therapies*, 1995, 14(3), 57–80, is used by permission of Guilford Press. In addition, Guilford Press grants permission for the use of the poem "Cyber-Cyber" by C. Drengenberg from the *Journal of Systemic Therapies*, 1995, 15(3), 52.

The chapter by M. F. Hoyt, "Introduction: Competency-Based Future-Oriented Therapy" (including Table 1.2) from *Constructive Therapies* (M. F. Hoyt, Editor, 1994) is used by permission of Guilford Press. Guilford Press also grants permission for use of the chapter by M. F. Hoyt, "Introduction: Some Stories are Better than Others," (including Table 1.1) from *Constructive Therapies, Volume 2* (M. F. Hoyt, Editor, 1996).

The excerpts from "Burnt Norton" and "Little Gidding" from *Four Quartets* by T. S. Eliot, copyright 1943 by T. S. Eliot and renewed 1971 by Esme Valerie Eliot, are used by permission of Harcourt Brace & Company.

The poem "Yorkshire" from *The House of Belonging* by David Whyte is used by permission of the Many Rivers Company.

Excerpts from the E. E. Miller poem, "Birds," which appeared in *Erotique Noire/Black Erotica* (M. Decosta-Willis, R. Martin & R. P. Bell, Editors, 1992) is used by permission of the author.

The excerpt from the W. B. Yeats poem, "Among School Children," which appeared in *The Poems of W. B. Yeats: A New Edition* (R. J. Finneran, Editor), copyright 1928 by Macmillan Company, renewed 1956 by Georgie Yeats, is used by permission of Simon & Schuster.

Chapter 7: The article by M. F. Hoyt, "Autologue: Reflections on Brief Therapy, Social Constructivism and Managed Care," from the *Journal of Psychological Practice*, 1997, (3), 1–6, is used by permission of the *Journal of Psychological Practice*.

The excerpts from William Blake's poem, "Poetical Sketches," from *William Blake: Complete Writings with Variant Readings* (G. Keynes, Editor, 1966), is used by permission of Oxford University Press.

Chapter 8: The chapter by M. F. Hoyt and I. K. Berg, "Solution Focused Couples Therapy: Helping Clients Construct Self-Fulfilling Realities," which appeared in *Case Studies in Couple and Family Therapy* (F. Dattilio, Editor, 1998), is used by permission of I. K. Berg and Guilford Publications. This permission includes the use of transcribed excerpts from a videotape entitled *Irreconcilable Differences* by I. K. Berg, copyright 1994.

Chapter 9: The poem by M. F. Hoyt, "Solution-ku," which appeared in *Constructive Therapies, Volume 2* (M. F. Hoyt, Editor, 1996), is used by permission of Guilford Press.

Chapter 10: Material from M. F. Hoyt and M. Talmon's chapter, "Single Session Therapy: A Case Example," which appeared in M. Talmon *Single Session Therapy*, is used with permission of Jossey-Bass Publishers.

The excerpts from the Cat Steven's song "The First Cut Is The Deepest," 1967, is used by permission of MCA Music Publishing.

Chapter 12: The article by M. F. Hoyt, "Unmuddying the Waters," from the *Journal of Systemic Therapies*, 1997, 16(3), 195–200, is used by permission of Guilford Press.

Excerpts from the W. B. Yeats poem "Sailing to Byzantium," which appeared in *The Poems of W. B. Yeats: A New Edition* (R. J. Finneran, Editor), copyright 1928 by Macmillan Publishing Company, renewed 1956 by Georgie Yeats is used with permission by Simon & Schuster.

Chapter 13: Excerpts from Bob Dylan's song, "If You See Her Say Hello," 1974, is used by permission of Ram's Horn Music.

The article by M. F. Hoyt and David Nylund, "The Joy of Narrative," from *The Journal of Systemic Therapies*, 1997, 16(4), 361–366, is used with permission by Guilford Press and David Nylund.

Chapter 14: The chapter by M. F. Hoyt and S. D. Miller, "Stage Appropriate Change Oriented Brief Therapy Strategies," which appears in *Brief Therapy Strategies with Individuals and Couples* (J. Carlson & L. Sperry, Editors, 2000), is used with permission by Zeig, Tucker & Company and Scott Miller.

Chapter 15: Excerpts from C. P. Cavafy's poem: "The God Abandons Antony," which appeared in *C. P. Cavafy: Collected Poems* (G. Savidis, Editor, 1992) is used with permission by Princeton University Press.

The poem "defining the magic," which appeared in Charles Bukowski's *Betting on the Muse: Poems & Stories*, 1996, is used with permission by Black Sparrow Press.

Excerpts from Robert Browning's poem, "Rabbi Ben Ezra," which appeared in *Robert Browning* (A. Roberts, Editor, 1997), is used with permission by Oxford University Press.

Excerpts from the James Broughton poem, "Ways of Getting There," which appeared in *Special Deliveries: New and Selected Poems* (Broken Moon Press, Seattle, WA, 1990), is used by permission of Joel Singer.

Excerpts from the song "The Gambler" by Don Schlitz, 1977, is used with permission by Sony/ATV Music Publishing.

INDEX